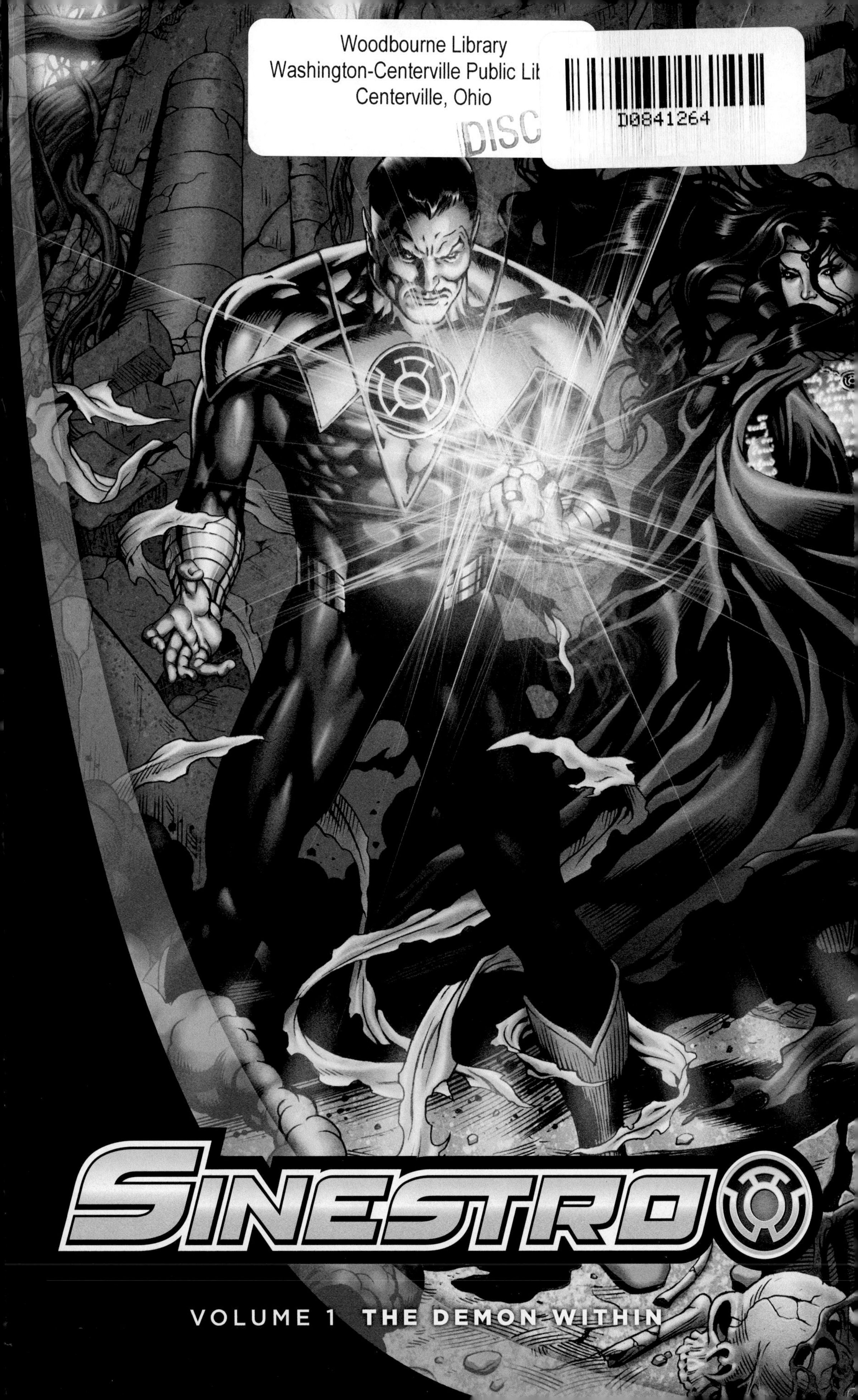

SINESTRO

VOLUME 1 THE DEMON WITHIN

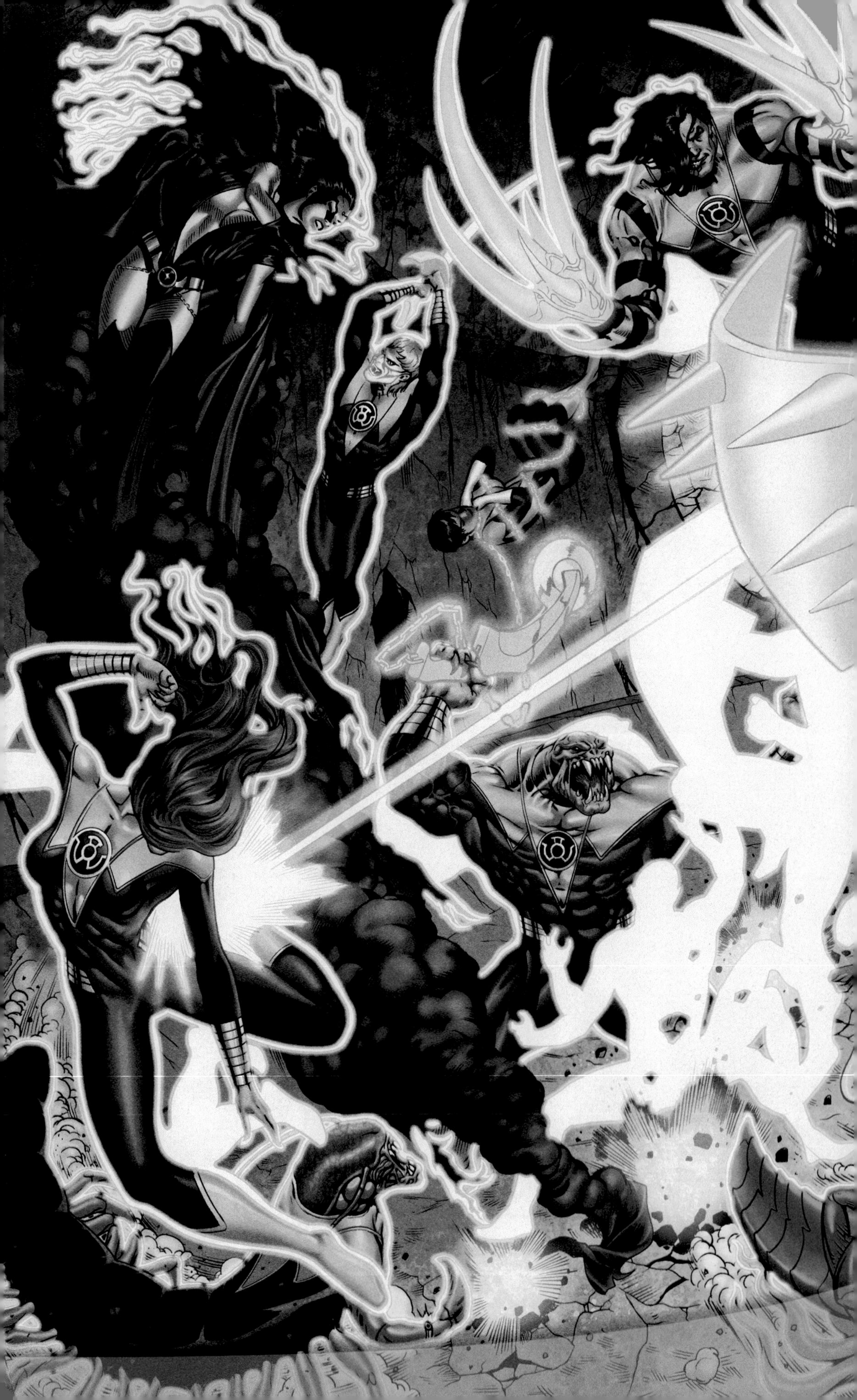

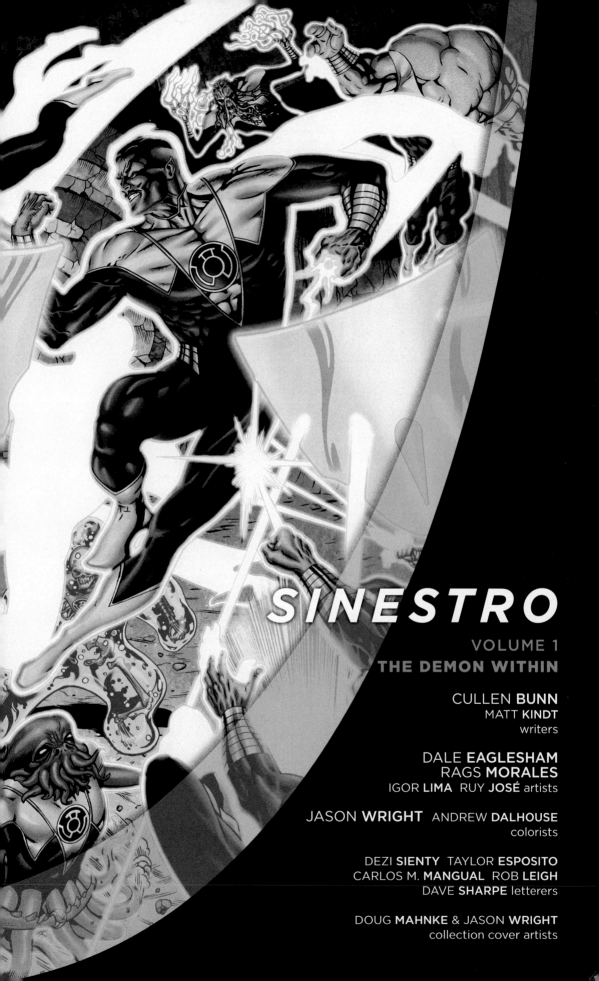

SINESTRO

VOLUME 1
THE DEMON WITHIN

CULLEN **BUNN**
MATT **KINDT**
writers

DALE **EAGLESHAM**
RAGS **MORALES**
IGOR **LIMA** RUY **JOSÉ** artists

JASON **WRIGHT** ANDREW **DALHOUSE**
colorists

DEZI **SIENTY** TAYLOR **ESPOSITO**
CARLOS M. **MANGUAL** ROB **LEIGH**
DAVE **SHARPE** letterers

DOUG **MAHNKE** & JASON **WRIGHT**
collection cover artists

MATT IDELSON Editor – Original Series   CHRIS CONROY   DARREN SHAN Associate Editors – Original Series   JEREMY BENT Editor
ROBBIN BROSTERMAN Design Director – Books   ROBBIE BIEDERMAN Publication Design

BOB HARRAS Senior VP – Editor-in-Chief, DC Comics

DIANE NELSON President   DAN DIDIO and JIM LEE Co-Publishers   GEOFF JOHNS Chief Creative Officer
AMIT DESAI Senior VP – Marketing and Franchise Management
AMY GENKINS Senior VP – Business and Legal Affairs   NAIRI GARDINER Senior VP – Finance
JEFF BOISON VP – Publishing Planning   MARK CHIARELLO VP – Art Direction and Design
JOHN CUNNINGHAM VP – Marketing   TERRI CUNNINGHAM VP – Editorial Administration
LARRY GANEM VP – Talent Relations and Services   ALISON GILL Senior VP – Manufacturing and Operations
HANK KANALZ Senior VP – Vertigo and Integrated Publishing   JAY KOGAN VP – Business and Legal Affairs, Publishing
JACK MAHAN VP – Business Affairs, Talent   NICK NAPOLITANO VP – Manufacturing Administration   SUE POHJA VP – Book Sales
FRED RUIZ VP – Manufacturing Operations   COURTNEY SIMMONS Senior VP – Publicity   BOB WAYNE Senior VP – Sales

SINESTRO VOLUME 1: THE DEMON WITHIN

DC Comics, 1700 Broadway, New York, NY 10019
A Warner Bros. Entertainment Company.
Printed by RR Donnelley, Owensville, MO, USA. 12/5/14. First Printing.

ISBN: 978-1-4012-5050-8

SUSTAINABLE
FORESTRY
INITIATIVE

Certified Chain of Custody
20% Certified Forest Content,
80% Certified Sourcing
www.sfiprogram.org
SFI-01042
APPLIES TO TEXT STOCK ONLY

Library of Congress Cataloging-in-Publication Data

Bunn, Cullen, author.
Sinestro. Volume 1, The Demon Within / Cullen Bunn, writer ; Dale Eaglesham, artist.
pages cm
ISBN 978-1-4012-5050-8 (pbk.)
1. Graphic novels. I. Eaglesham, Dale, illustrator. II. Title. III. Title: Demon Within.

PN6728.S496B86 2015
741.5'973—dc23

2014034200

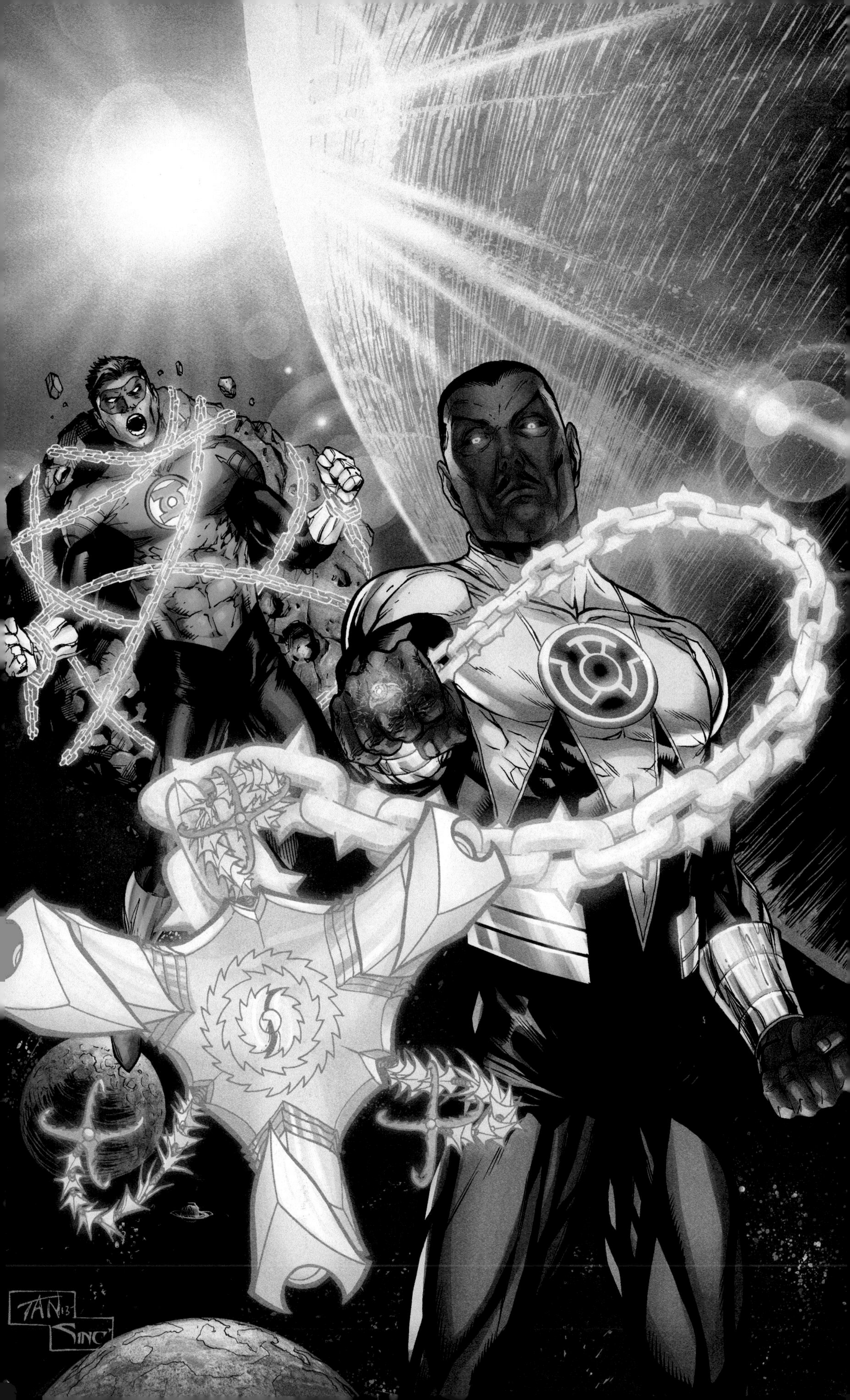

SINESTRO

MATT KINDT writer **DALE EAGLESHAM** writer **ANDREW DALHOUSE** colorist **ROB LEIGH** letterer

cover art by **BILLY TAN** & **ALEX SINCLAIR**

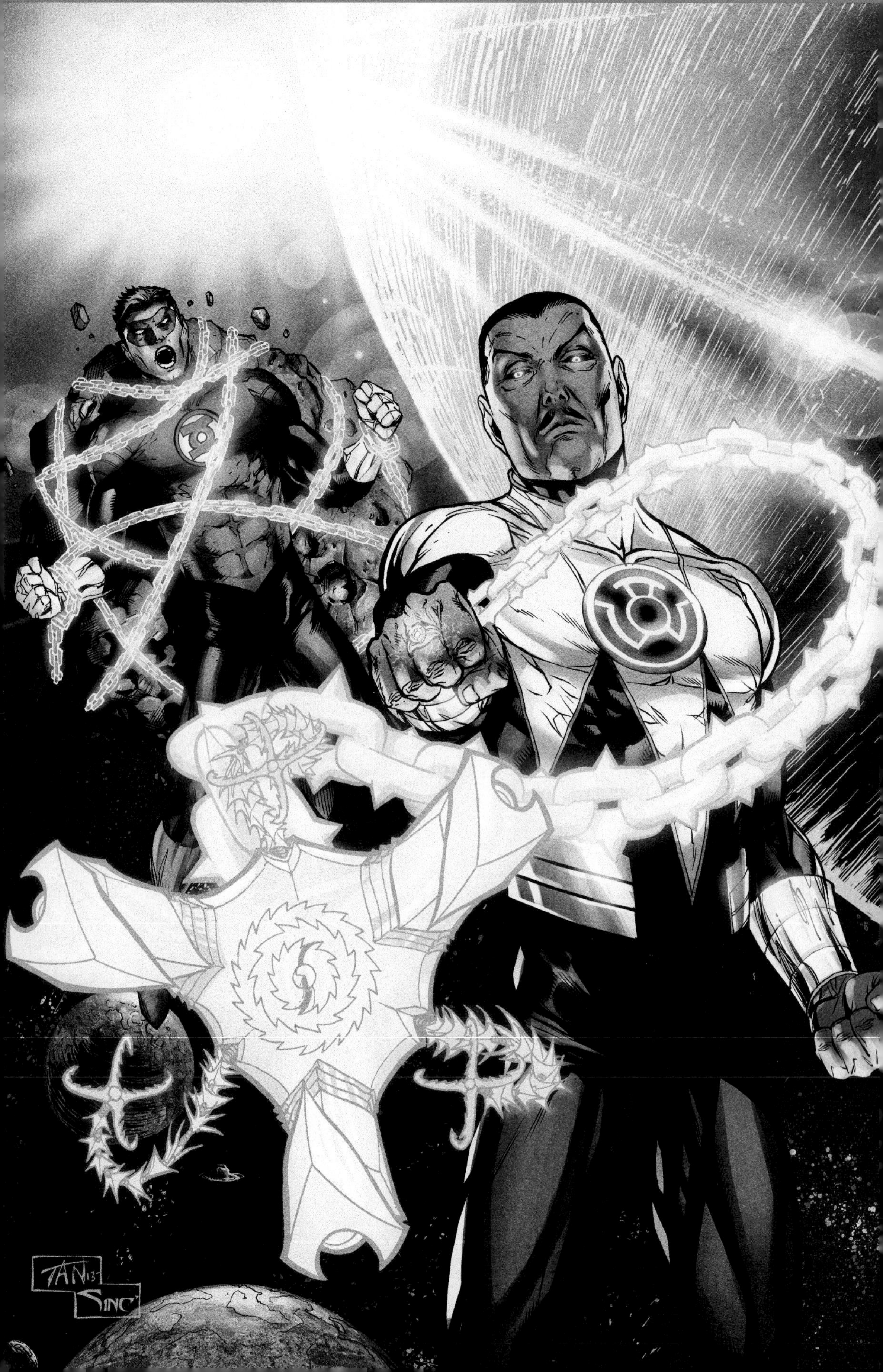
TAN '13
SINC

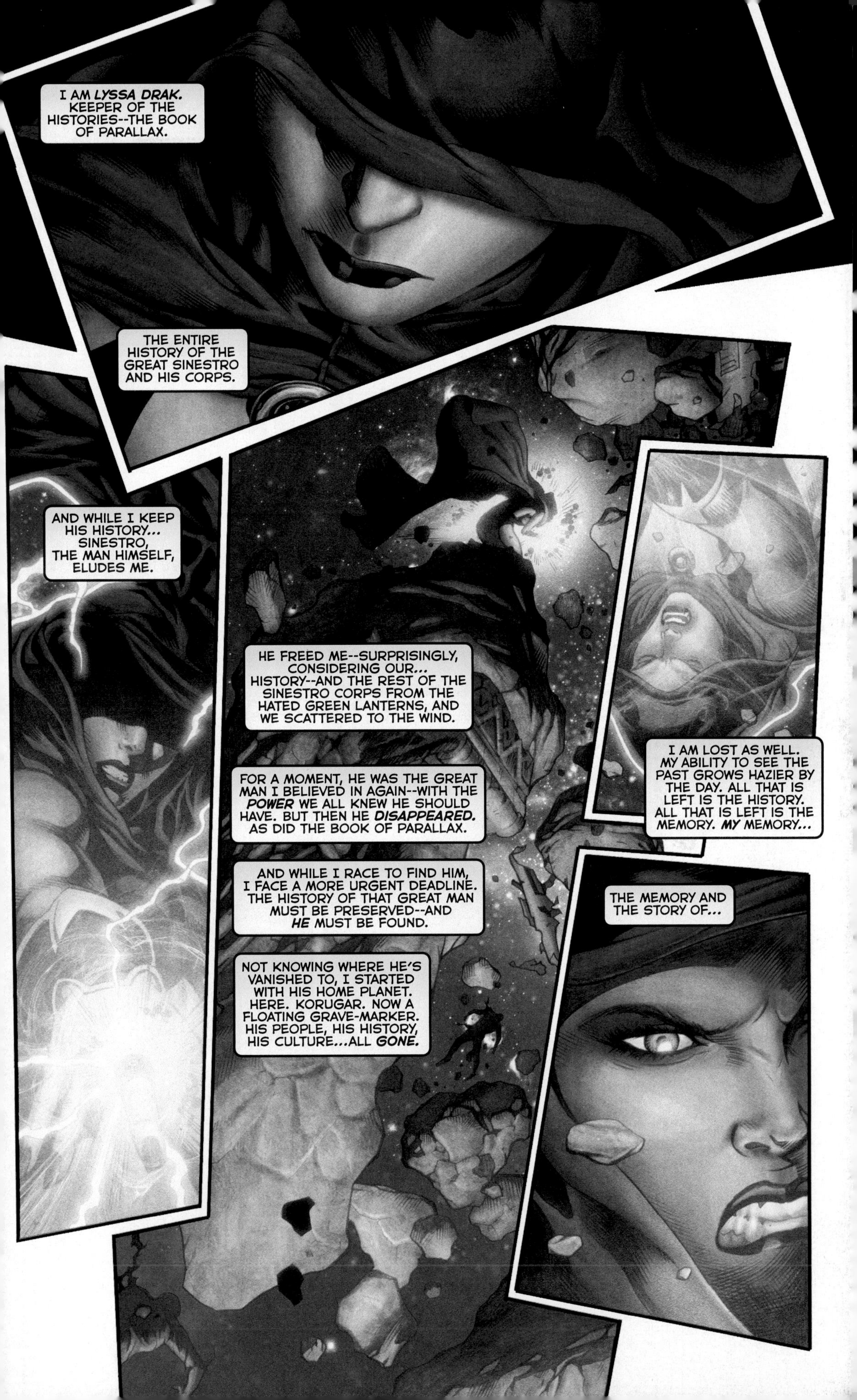
I AM *LYSSA DRAK.* KEEPER OF THE HISTORIES--THE BOOK OF PARALLAX.
THE ENTIRE HISTORY OF THE GREAT SINESTRO AND HIS CORPS.
AND WHILE I KEEP HIS HISTORY... SINESTRO, THE MAN HIMSELF, ELUDES ME.
HE FREED ME--SURPRISINGLY, CONSIDERING OUR... HISTORY--AND THE REST OF THE SINESTRO CORPS FROM THE HATED GREEN LANTERNS, AND WE SCATTERED TO THE WIND.
FOR A MOMENT, HE WAS THE GREAT MAN I BELIEVED IN AGAIN--WITH THE *POWER* WE ALL KNEW HE SHOULD HAVE. BUT THEN HE *DISAPPEARED.* AS DID THE BOOK OF PARALLAX.
AND WHILE I RACE TO FIND HIM, I FACE A MORE URGENT DEADLINE. THE HISTORY OF THAT GREAT MAN MUST BE PRESERVED--AND *HE* MUST BE FOUND.
NOT KNOWING WHERE HE'S VANISHED TO, I STARTED WITH HIS HOME PLANET. HERE. KORUGAR. NOW A FLOATING GRAVE-MARKER. HIS PEOPLE, HIS HISTORY, HIS CULTURE...ALL *GONE.*
I AM LOST AS WELL. MY ABILITY TO SEE THE PAST GROWS HAZIER BY THE DAY. ALL THAT IS LEFT IS THE HISTORY. ALL THAT IS LEFT IS THE MEMORY. *MY* MEMORY...
THE MEMORY AND THE STORY OF...

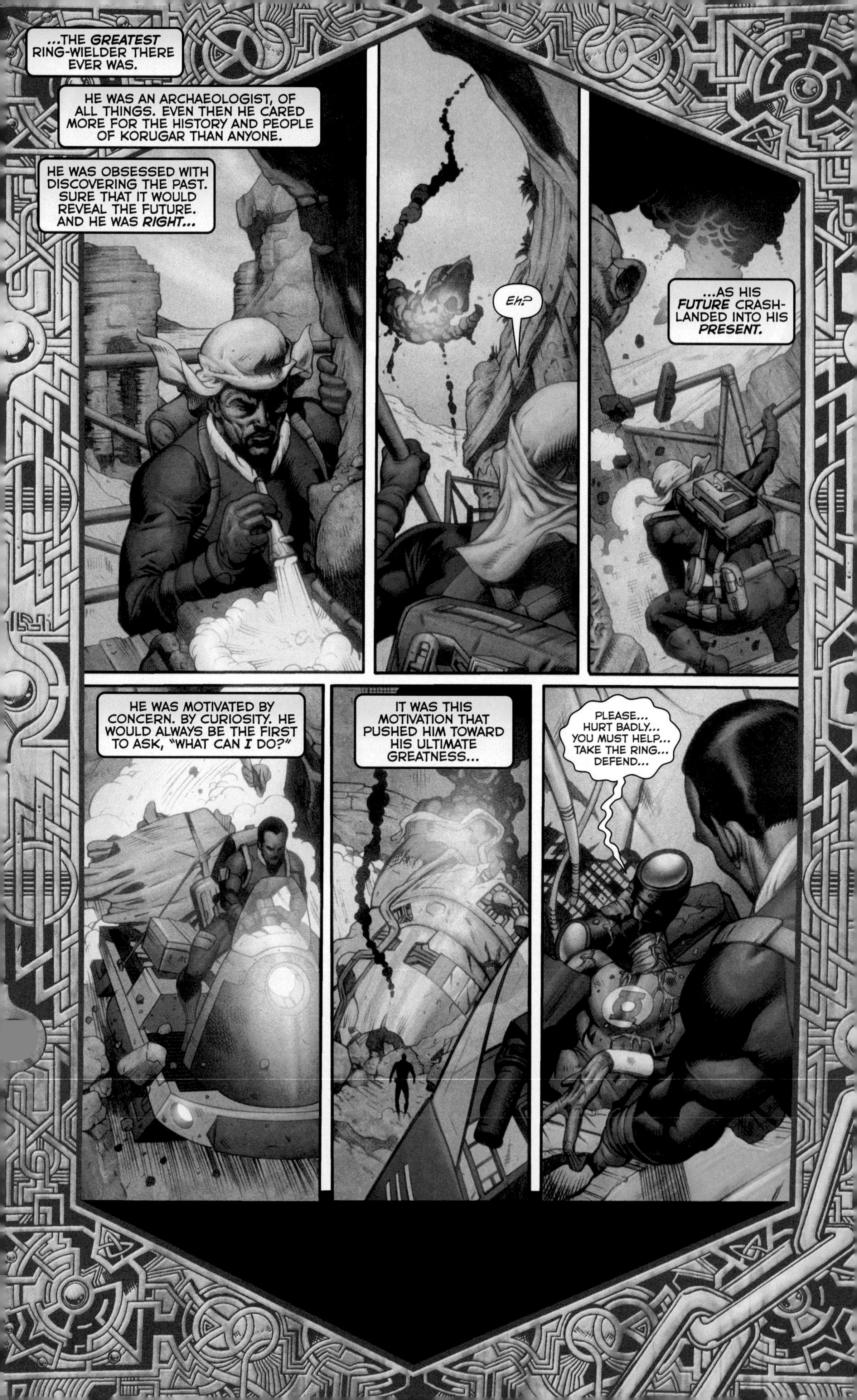
...THE GREATEST RING-WIELDER THERE EVER WAS.
HE WAS AN ARCHAEOLOGIST, OF ALL THINGS. EVEN THEN HE CARED MORE FOR THE HISTORY AND PEOPLE OF KORUGAR THAN ANYONE.
HE WAS OBSESSED WITH DISCOVERING THE PAST. SURE THAT IT WOULD REVEAL THE FUTURE. AND HE WAS RIGHT...
Eh?
...AS HIS FUTURE CRASH-LANDED INTO HIS PRESENT.
HE WAS MOTIVATED BY CONCERN. BY CURIOSITY. HE WOULD ALWAYS BE THE FIRST TO ASK, "WHAT CAN I DO?"
IT WAS THIS MOTIVATION THAT PUSHED HIM TOWARD HIS ULTIMATE GREATNESS...
PLEASE... HURT BADLY... YOU MUST HELP... TAKE THE RING... DEFEND...

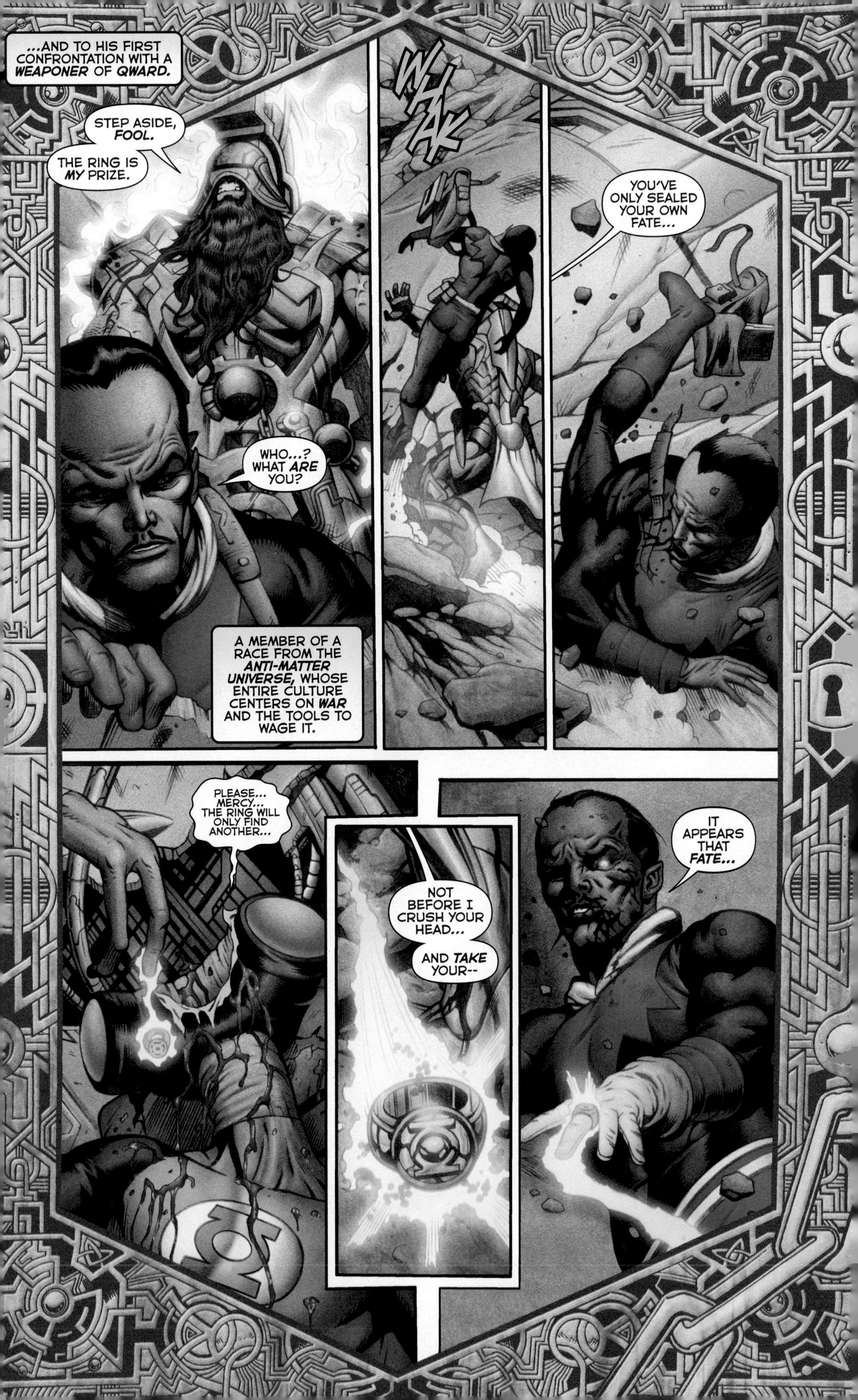
...AND TO HIS FIRST CONFRONTATION WITH A WEAPONER OF QWARD.
STEP ASIDE, FOOL.
THE RING IS MY PRIZE.
WHO...? WHAT ARE YOU?
A MEMBER OF A RACE FROM THE ANTI-MATTER UNIVERSE, WHOSE ENTIRE CULTURE CENTERS ON WAR AND THE TOOLS TO WAGE IT.
WHAK
YOU'VE ONLY SEALED YOUR OWN FATE...
PLEASE... MERCY... THE RING WILL ONLY FIND ANOTHER...
NOT BEFORE I CRUSH YOUR HEAD...
AND TAKE YOUR--
IT APPEARS THAT FATE...

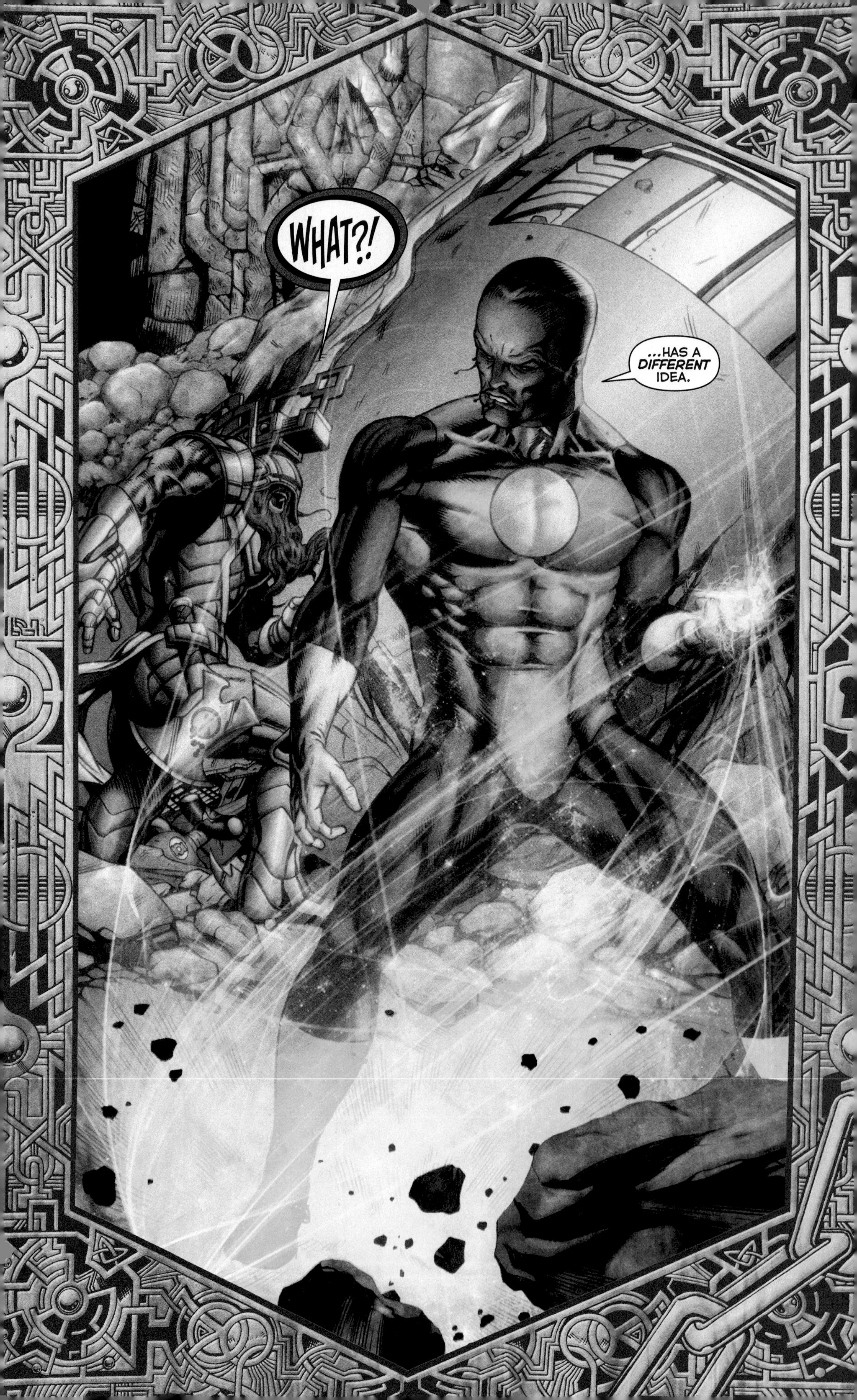
WHAT?!
...HAS A DIFFERENT IDEA.

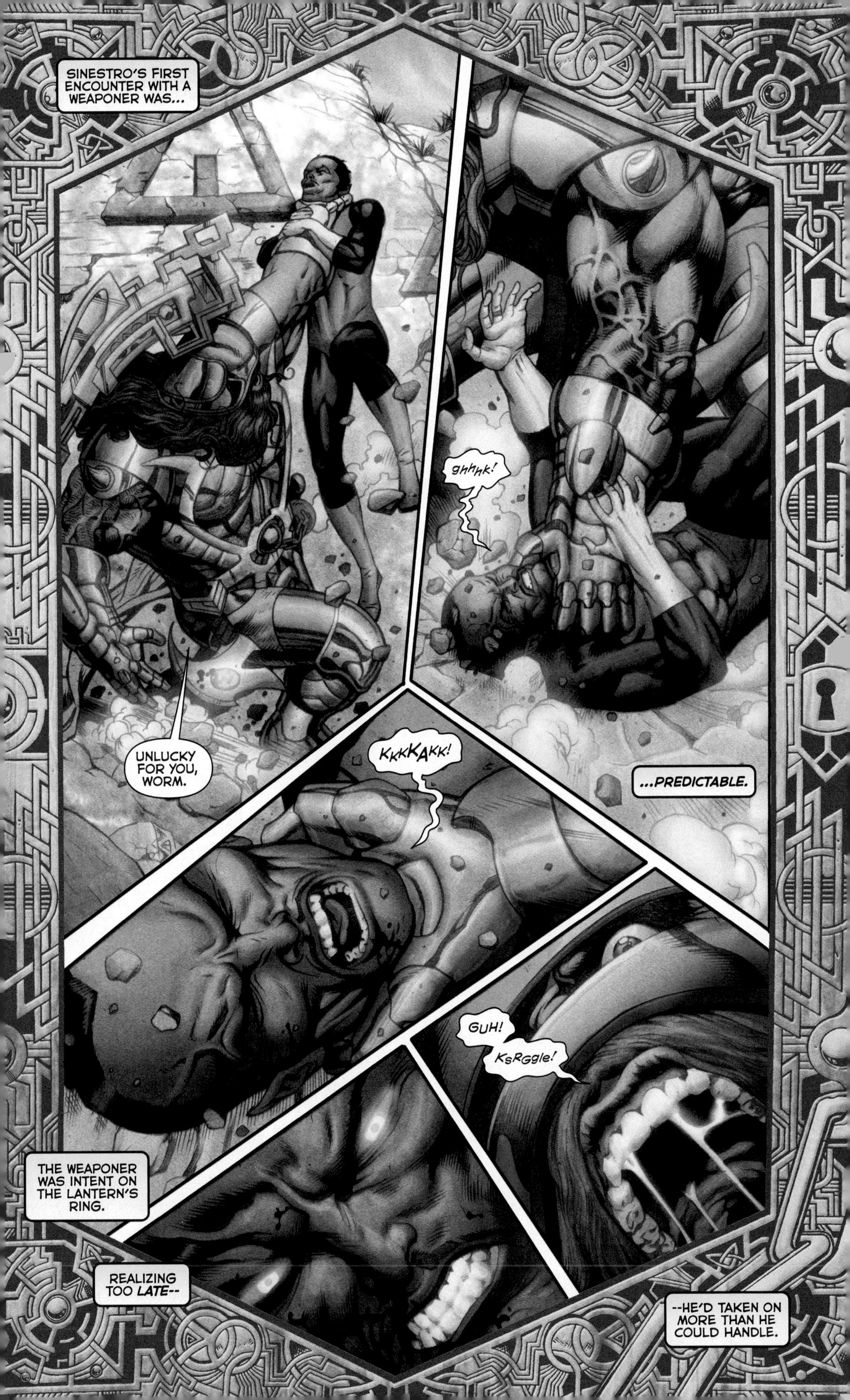
SINESTRO'S FIRST ENCOUNTER WITH A WEAPONER WAS...
UNLUCKY FOR YOU, WORM.
ghhhk!
...PREDICTABLE.
KKKKAKK!
GUH!
KSRGGLE!
THE WEAPONER WAS INTENT ON THE LANTERN'S RING.
REALIZING TOO LATE--
--HE'D TAKEN ON MORE THAN HE COULD HANDLE.

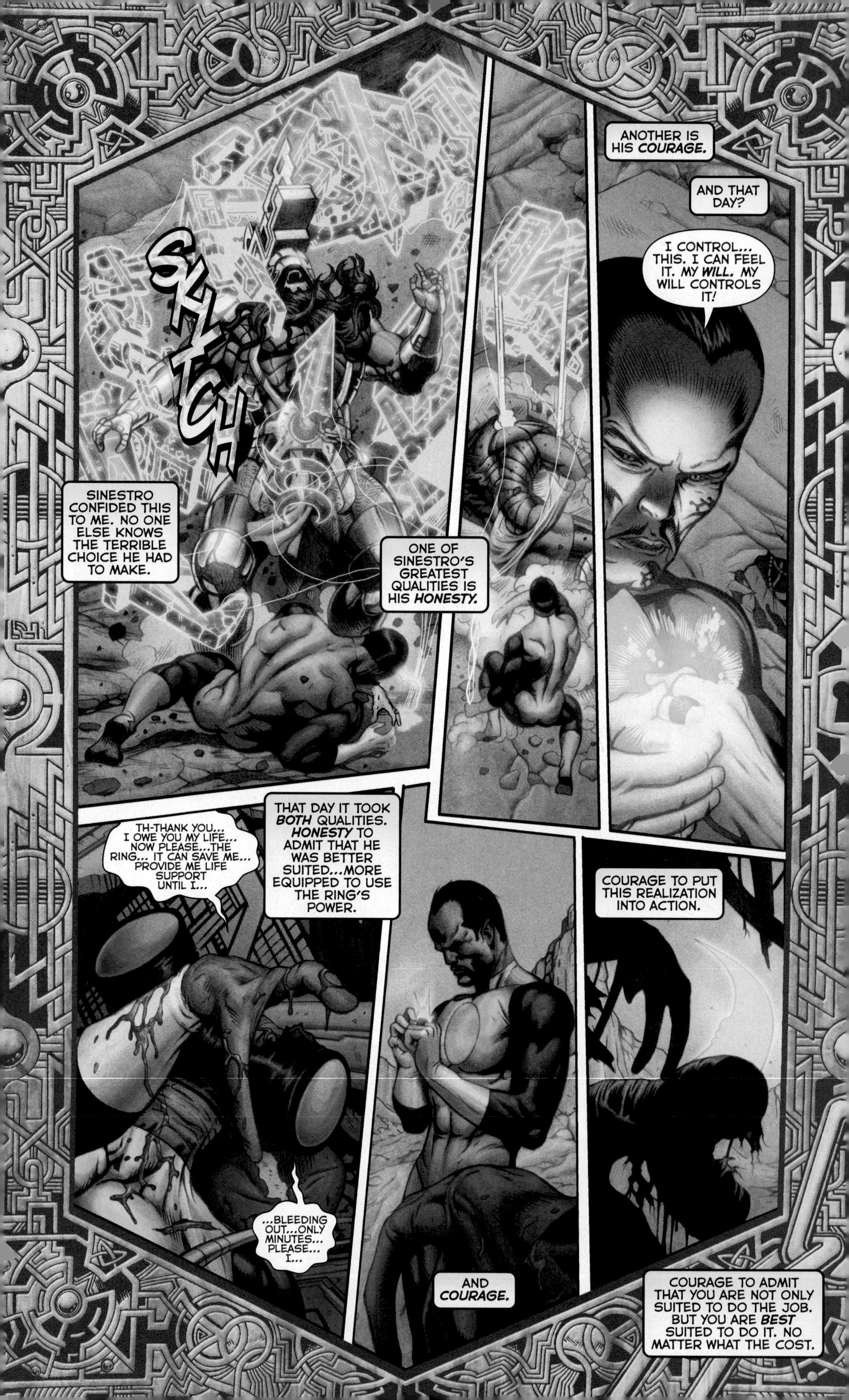
SKLTCH
SINESTRO CONFIDED THIS TO ME. NO ONE ELSE KNOWS THE TERRIBLE CHOICE HE HAD TO MAKE.
ONE OF SINESTRO'S GREATEST QUALITIES IS HIS *HONESTY.*
ANOTHER IS HIS *COURAGE.*
AND THAT DAY?
I CONTROL... THIS. I CAN FEEL IT. MY *WILL.* MY WILL CONTROLS IT!
TH-THANK YOU... I OWE YOU MY LIFE... NOW PLEASE...THE RING... IT CAN SAVE ME... PROVIDE ME LIFE SUPPORT UNTIL I...
...BLEEDING OUT...ONLY MINUTES... PLEASE... I...
THAT DAY IT TOOK *BOTH* QUALITIES. *HONESTY* TO ADMIT THAT HE WAS BETTER SUITED...MORE EQUIPPED TO USE THE RING'S POWER.
AND *COURAGE.*
COURAGE TO PUT THIS REALIZATION INTO ACTION.
COURAGE TO ADMIT THAT YOU ARE NOT ONLY SUITED TO DO THE JOB. BUT YOU ARE *BEST* SUITED TO DO IT. NO MATTER WHAT THE COST.

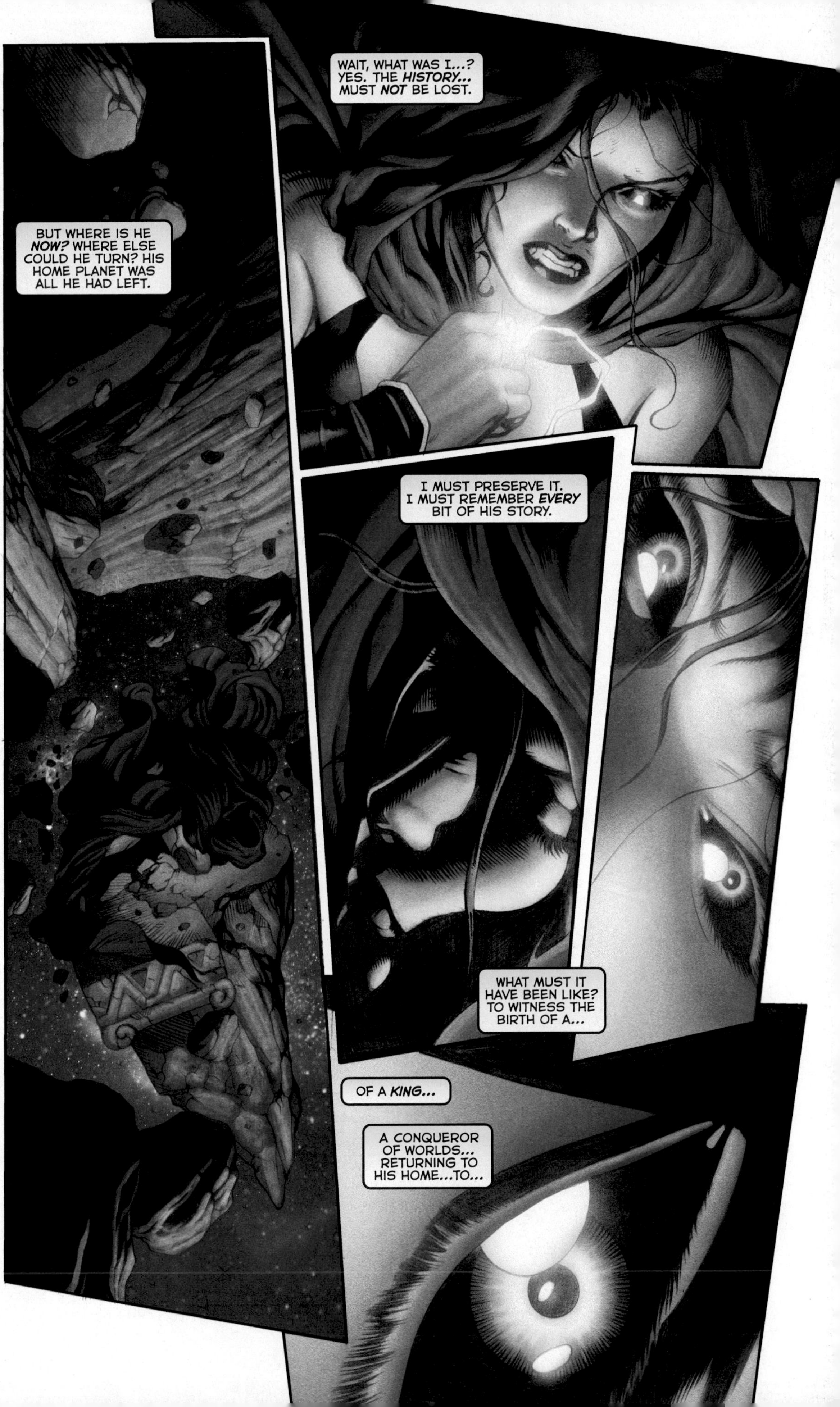
WAIT, WHAT WAS I...? YES. THE *HISTORY...* MUST *NOT* BE LOST.
BUT WHERE IS HE *NOW?* WHERE ELSE COULD HE TURN? HIS HOME PLANET WAS ALL HE HAD LEFT.
I MUST PRESERVE IT. I MUST REMEMBER *EVERY* BIT OF HIS STORY.
WHAT MUST IT HAVE BEEN LIKE? TO WITNESS THE BIRTH OF A...
OF A *KING...*
A CONQUEROR OF WORLDS... RETURNING TO HIS HOME...TO...

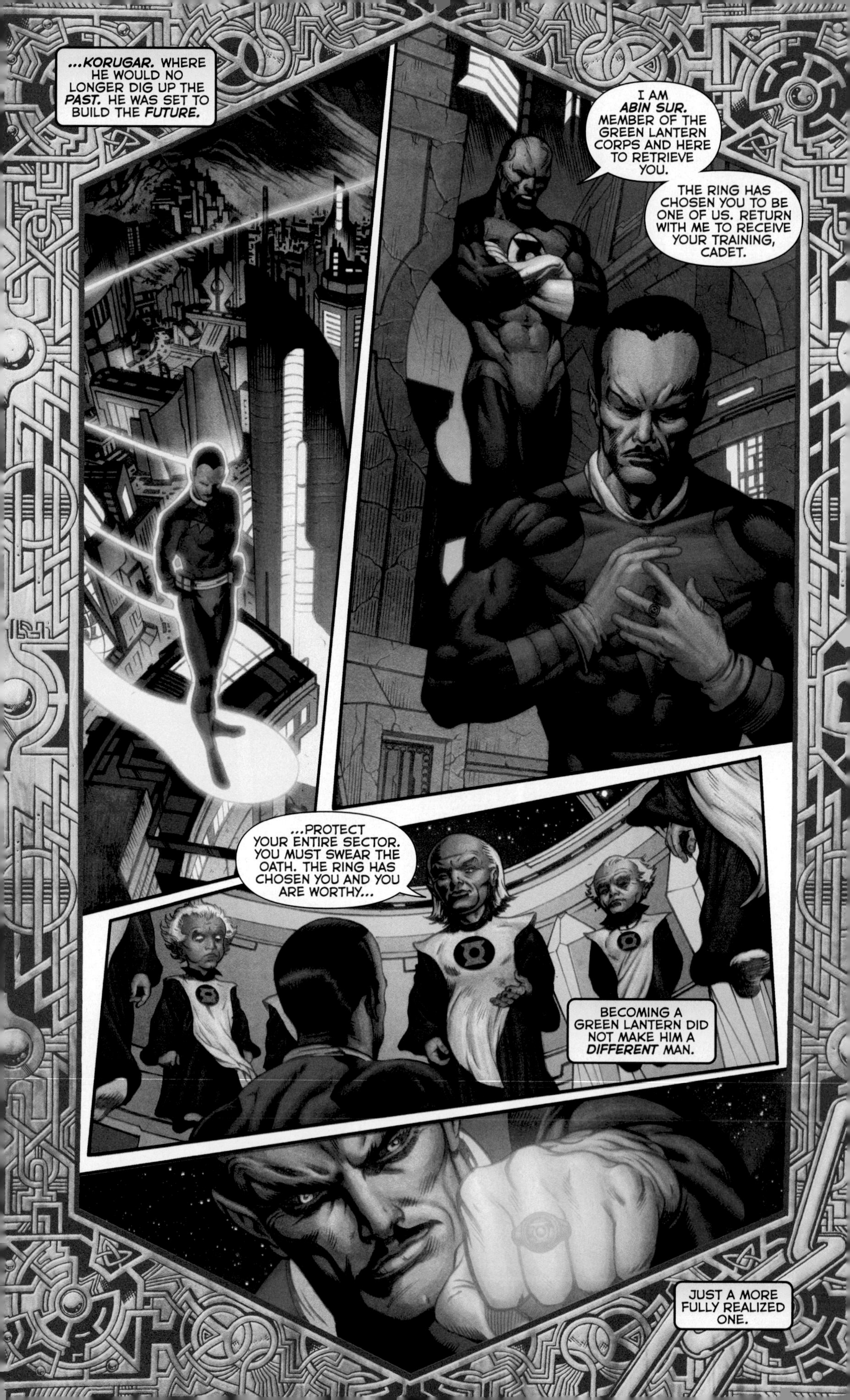
...KORUGAR. WHERE HE WOULD NO LONGER DIG UP THE PAST. HE WAS SET TO BUILD THE FUTURE.
I AM ABIN SUR. MEMBER OF THE GREEN LANTERN CORPS AND HERE TO RETRIEVE YOU.
THE RING HAS CHOSEN YOU TO BE ONE OF US. RETURN WITH ME TO RECEIVE YOUR TRAINING, CADET.
...PROTECT YOUR ENTIRE SECTOR. YOU MUST SWEAR THE OATH. THE RING HAS CHOSEN YOU AND YOU ARE WORTHY...
BECOMING A GREEN LANTERN DID NOT MAKE HIM A DIFFERENT MAN.
JUST A MORE FULLY REALIZED ONE.

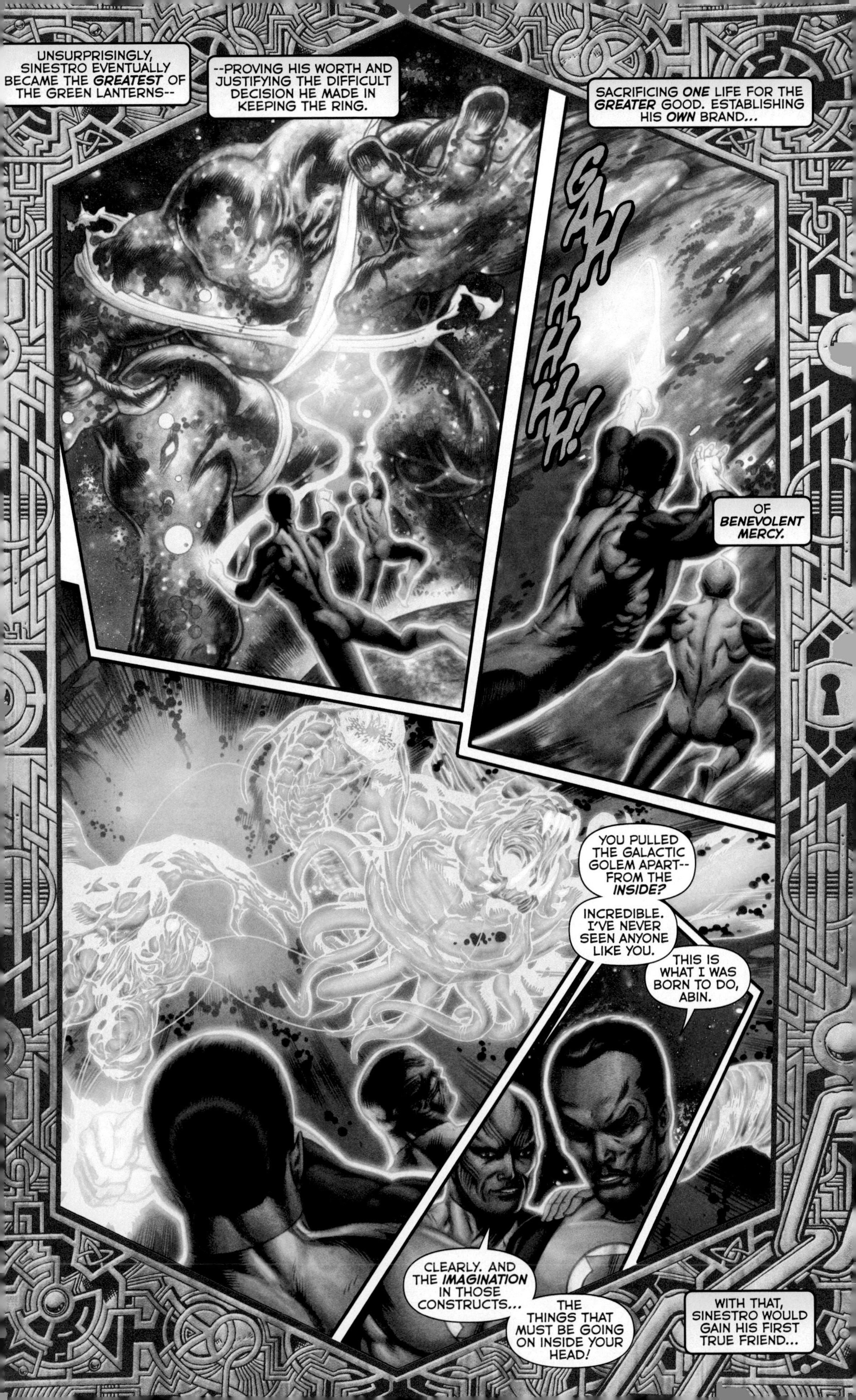
UNSURPRISINGLY, SINESTRO EVENTUALLY BECAME THE *GREATEST* OF THE GREEN LANTERNS--
--PROVING HIS WORTH AND JUSTIFYING THE DIFFICULT DECISION HE MADE IN KEEPING THE RING.
SACRIFICING *ONE* LIFE FOR THE *GREATER* GOOD. ESTABLISHING HIS *OWN* BRAND...
GAAHHHHHHH!
OF *BENEVOLENT MERCY.*
YOU PULLED THE GALACTIC GOLEM APART-- FROM THE *INSIDE?*
INCREDIBLE. I'VE NEVER SEEN ANYONE LIKE YOU.
THIS IS WHAT I WAS BORN TO DO, ABIN.
CLEARLY. AND THE *IMAGINATION* IN THOSE CONSTRUCTS...
THE THINGS THAT MUST BE GOING ON INSIDE YOUR HEAD!
WITH THAT, SINESTRO WOULD GAIN HIS FIRST TRUE FRIEND...

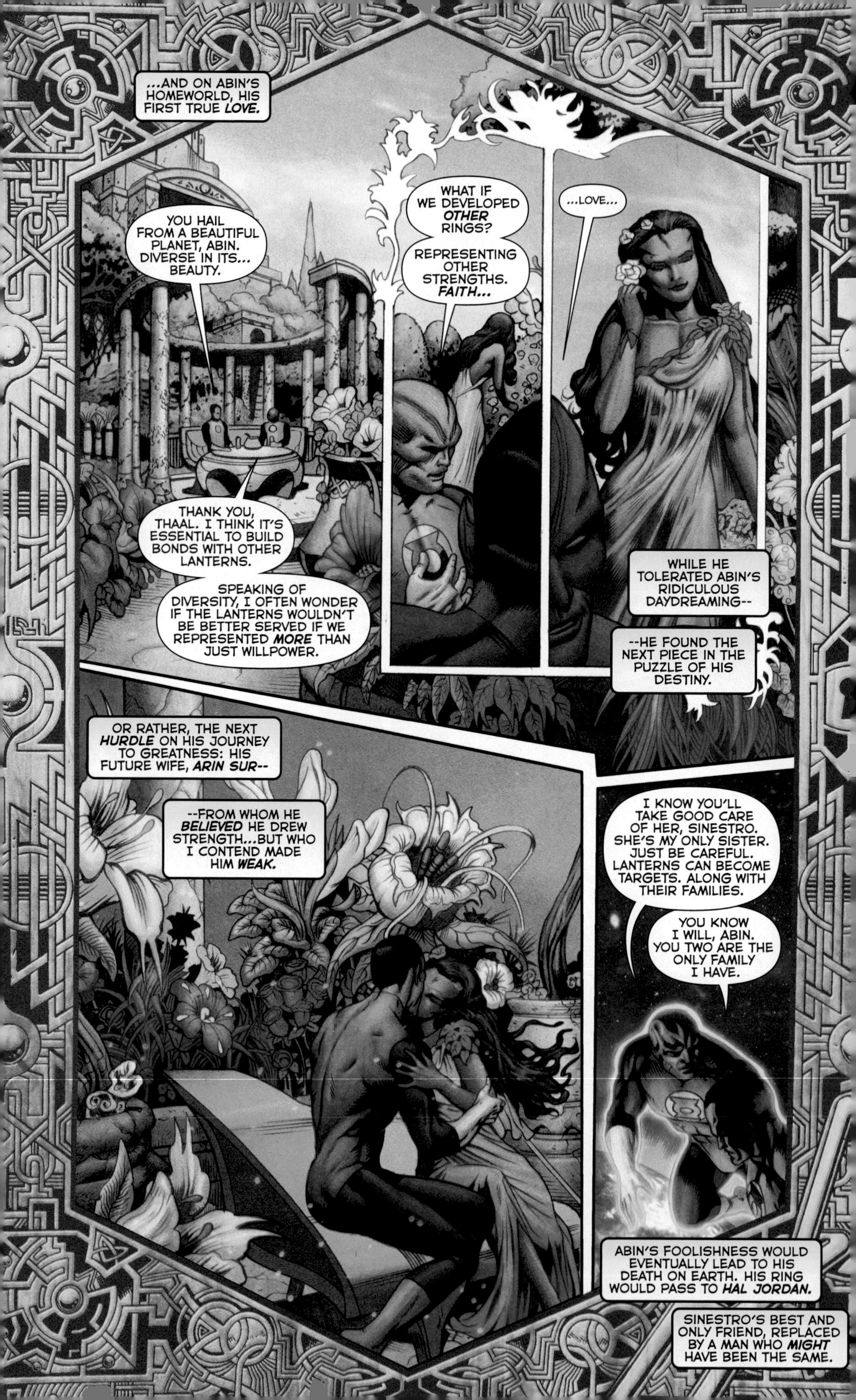
...AND ON ABIN'S HOMEWORLD, HIS FIRST TRUE *LOVE.*
YOU HAIL FROM A BEAUTIFUL PLANET, ABIN. DIVERSE IN ITS... BEAUTY.
THANK YOU, THAAL. I THINK IT'S ESSENTIAL TO BUILD BONDS WITH OTHER LANTERNS.
SPEAKING OF DIVERSITY, I OFTEN WONDER IF THE LANTERNS WOULDN'T BE BETTER SERVED IF WE REPRESENTED *MORE* THAN JUST WILLPOWER.
WHAT IF WE DEVELOPED *OTHER* RINGS?
REPRESENTING OTHER STRENGTHS. *FAITH...*
...LOVE...
WHILE HE TOLERATED ABIN'S RIDICULOUS DAYDREAMING--
--HE FOUND THE NEXT PIECE IN THE PUZZLE OF HIS DESTINY.
OR RATHER, THE NEXT *HURDLE* ON HIS JOURNEY TO GREATNESS: HIS FUTURE WIFE, *ARIN SUR--*
--FROM WHOM HE *BELIEVED* HE DREW STRENGTH...BUT WHO I CONTEND MADE HIM *WEAK.*
I KNOW YOU'LL TAKE GOOD CARE OF HER, SINESTRO. SHE'S MY ONLY SISTER. JUST BE CAREFUL. LANTERNS CAN BECOME TARGETS. ALONG WITH THEIR FAMILIES.
YOU KNOW I WILL, ABIN. YOU TWO ARE THE ONLY FAMILY I HAVE.
ABIN'S FOOLISHNESS WOULD EVENTUALLY LEAD TO HIS DEATH ON EARTH. HIS RING WOULD PASS TO *HAL JORDAN.*
SINESTRO'S BEST AND ONLY FRIEND, REPLACED BY A MAN WHO *MIGHT* HAVE BEEN THE SAME.

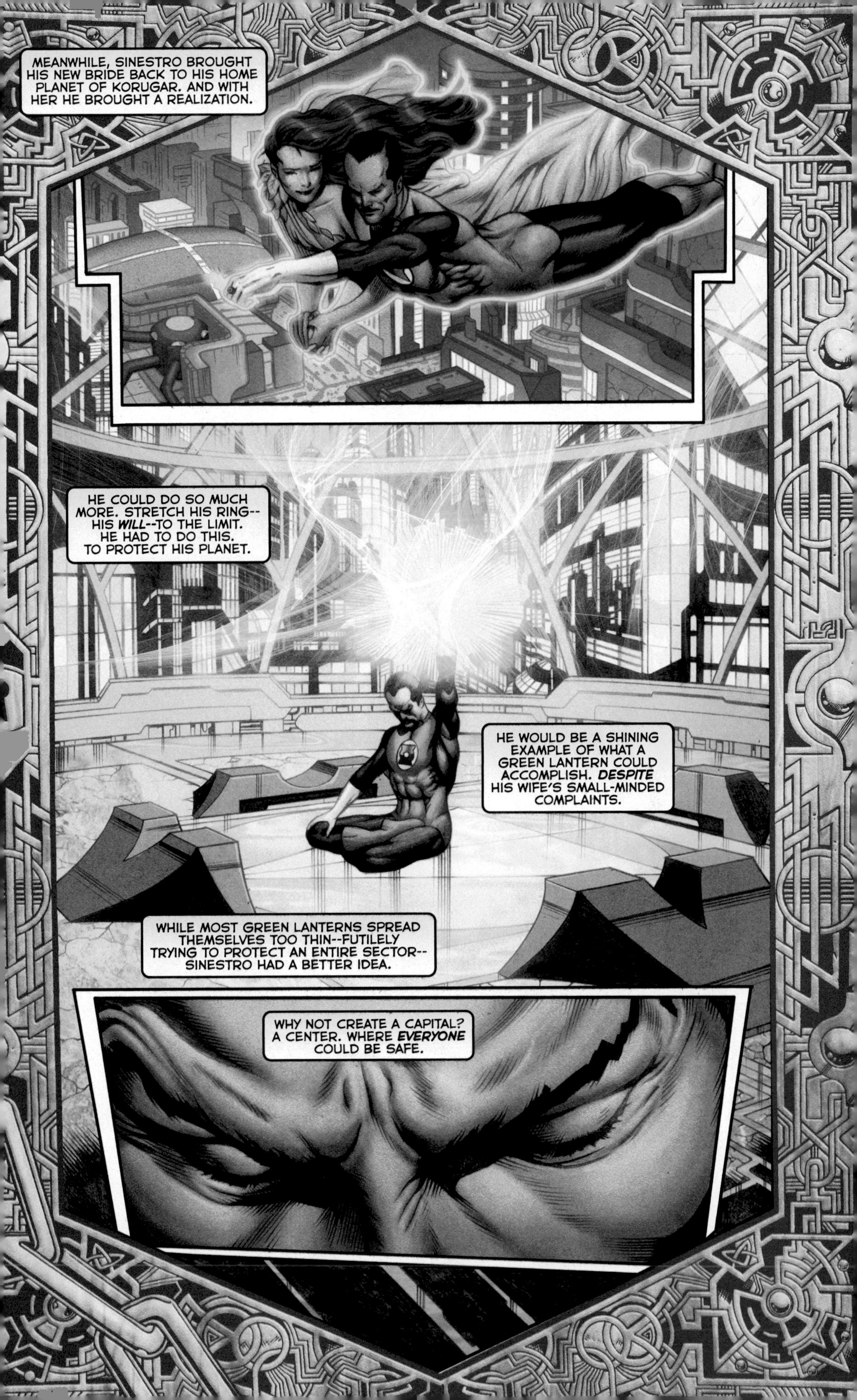
MEANWHILE, SINESTRO BROUGHT HIS NEW BRIDE BACK TO HIS HOME PLANET OF KORUGAR. AND WITH HER HE BROUGHT A REALIZATION.
HE COULD DO SO MUCH MORE. STRETCH HIS RING--HIS *WILL*--TO THE LIMIT. HE HAD TO DO THIS. TO PROTECT HIS PLANET.
HE WOULD BE A SHINING EXAMPLE OF WHAT A GREEN LANTERN COULD ACCOMPLISH. *DESPITE* HIS WIFE'S SMALL-MINDED COMPLAINTS.
WHILE MOST GREEN LANTERNS SPREAD THEMSELVES TOO THIN--FUTILELY TRYING TO PROTECT AN ENTIRE SECTOR--SINESTRO HAD A BETTER IDEA.
WHY NOT CREATE A CAPITAL? A CENTER. WHERE *EVERYONE* COULD BE SAFE.

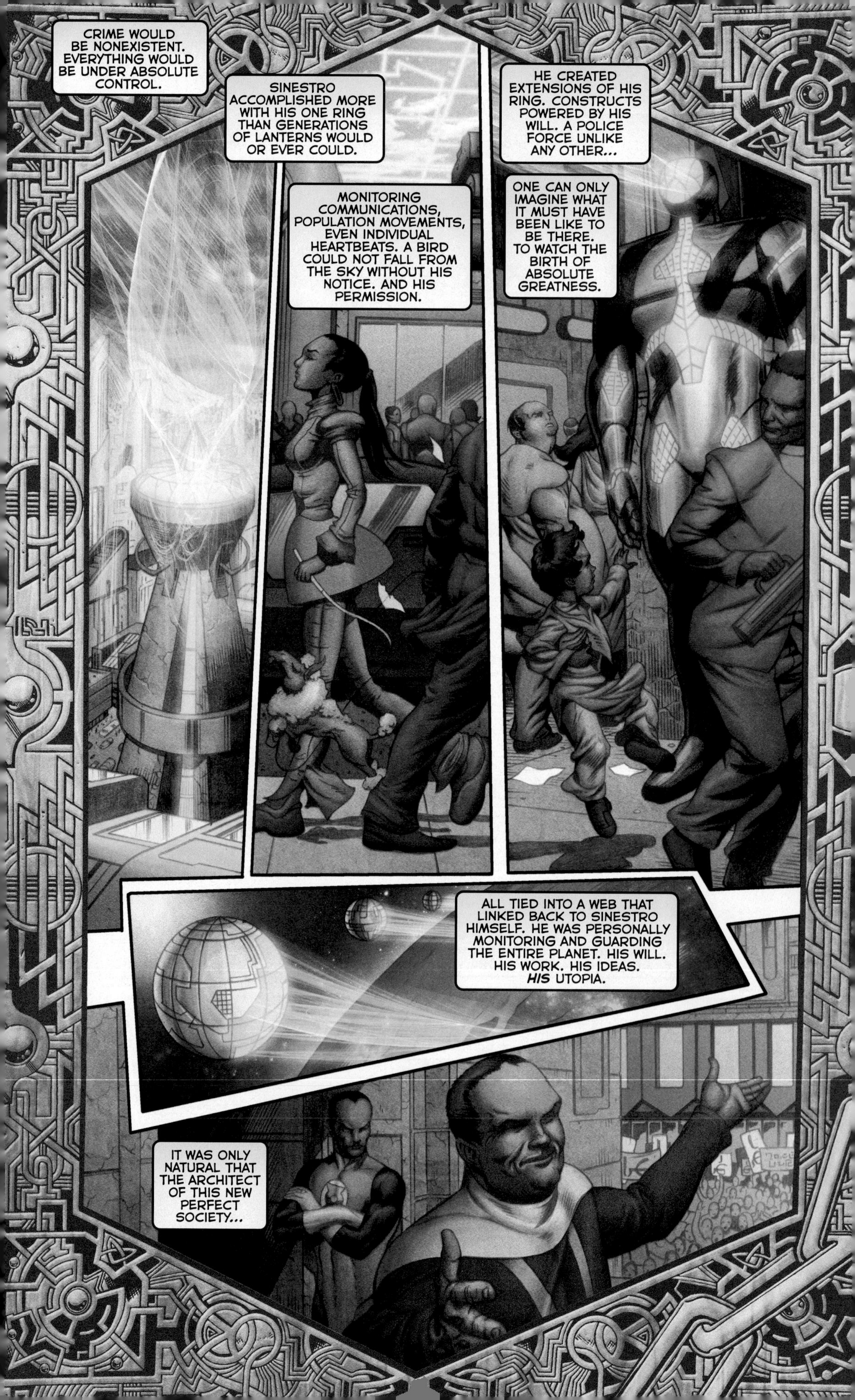
CRIME WOULD BE NONEXISTENT. EVERYTHING WOULD BE UNDER ABSOLUTE CONTROL.
SINESTRO ACCOMPLISHED MORE WITH HIS ONE RING THAN GENERATIONS OF LANTERNS WOULD OR EVER COULD.
MONITORING COMMUNICATIONS, POPULATION MOVEMENTS, EVEN INDIVIDUAL HEARTBEATS. A BIRD COULD NOT FALL FROM THE SKY WITHOUT HIS NOTICE. AND HIS PERMISSION.
HE CREATED EXTENSIONS OF HIS RING. CONSTRUCTS POWERED BY HIS WILL. A POLICE FORCE UNLIKE ANY OTHER...
ONE CAN ONLY IMAGINE WHAT IT MUST HAVE BEEN LIKE TO BE THERE. TO WATCH THE BIRTH OF ABSOLUTE GREATNESS.
ALL TIED INTO A WEB THAT LINKED BACK TO SINESTRO HIMSELF. HE WAS PERSONALLY MONITORING AND GUARDING THE ENTIRE PLANET. HIS WILL. HIS WORK. HIS IDEAS. *HIS* UTOPIA.
IT WAS ONLY NATURAL THAT THE ARCHITECT OF THIS NEW PERFECT SOCIETY...

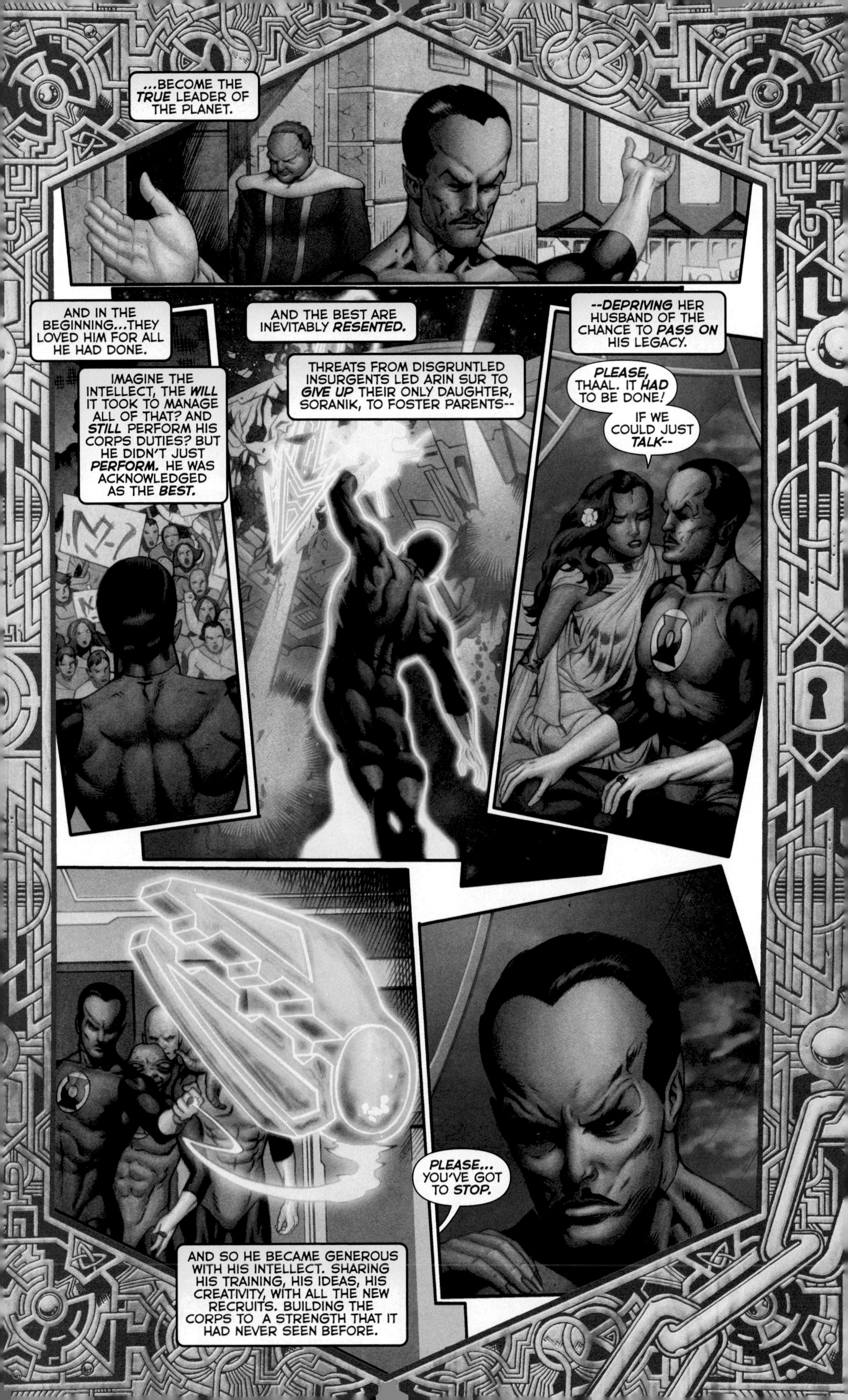
...BECOME THE TRUE LEADER OF THE PLANET.
AND IN THE BEGINNING...THEY LOVED HIM FOR ALL HE HAD DONE.
IMAGINE THE INTELLECT, THE WILL IT TOOK TO MANAGE ALL OF THAT? AND STILL PERFORM HIS CORPS DUTIES? BUT HE DIDN'T JUST PERFORM. HE WAS ACKNOWLEDGED AS THE BEST.
AND THE BEST ARE INEVITABLY RESENTED.
THREATS FROM DISGRUNTLED INSURGENTS LED ARIN SUR TO GIVE UP THEIR ONLY DAUGHTER, SORANIK, TO FOSTER PARENTS--
--DEPRIVING HER HUSBAND OF THE CHANCE TO PASS ON HIS LEGACY.
PLEASE, THAAL. IT HAD TO BE DONE!
IF WE COULD JUST TALK--
AND SO HE BECAME GENEROUS WITH HIS INTELLECT. SHARING HIS TRAINING, HIS IDEAS, HIS CREATIVITY, WITH ALL THE NEW RECRUITS. BUILDING THE CORPS TO A STRENGTH THAT IT HAD NEVER SEEN BEFORE.
PLEASE... YOU'VE GOT TO STOP.

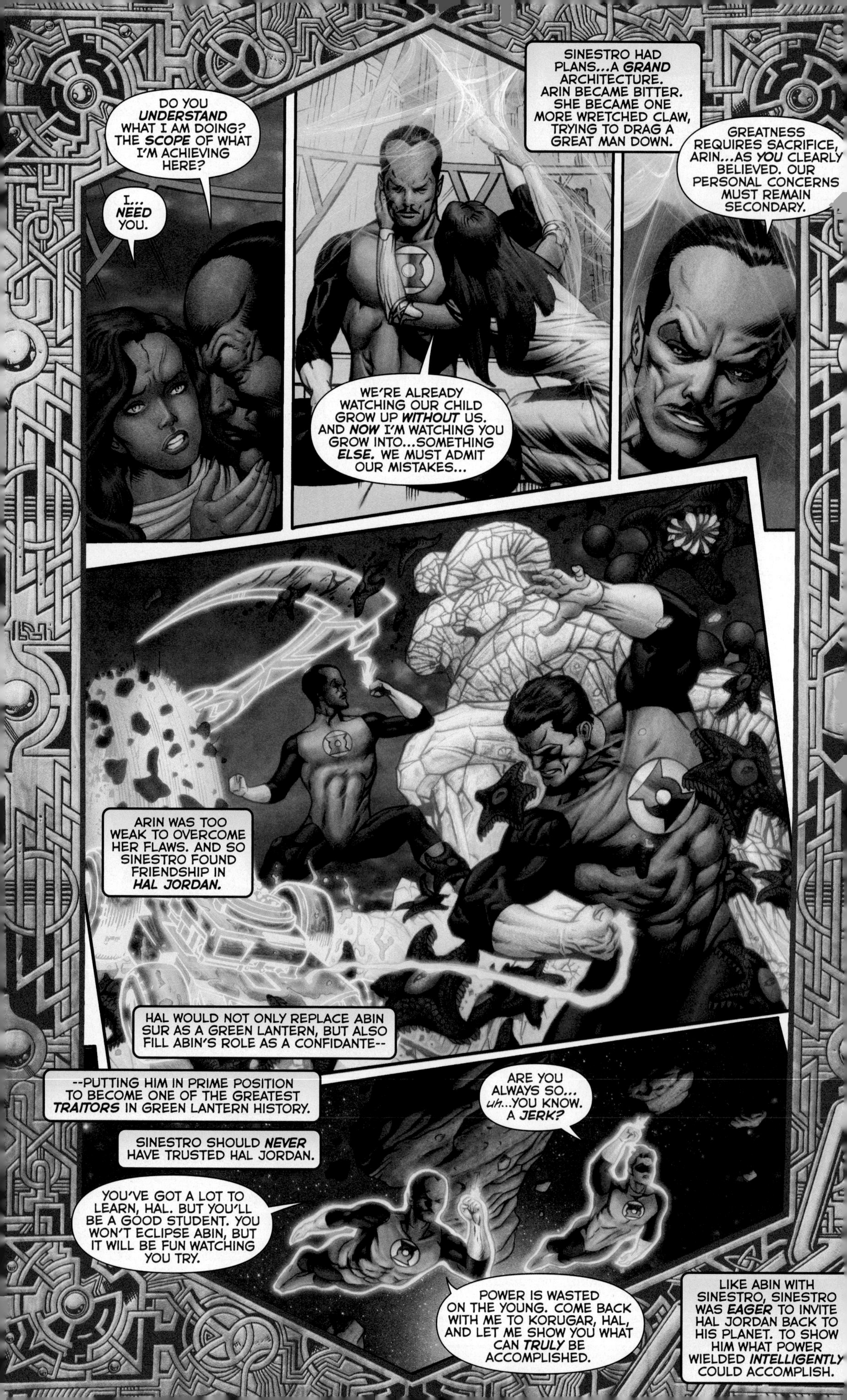
DO YOU UNDERSTAND WHAT I AM DOING? THE SCOPE OF WHAT I'M ACHIEVING HERE?
I... NEED YOU.
SINESTRO HAD PLANS...A GRAND ARCHITECTURE. ARIN BECAME BITTER. SHE BECAME ONE MORE WRETCHED CLAW, TRYING TO DRAG A GREAT MAN DOWN.
WE'RE ALREADY WATCHING OUR CHILD GROW UP WITHOUT US. AND NOW I'M WATCHING YOU GROW INTO...SOMETHING ELSE. WE MUST ADMIT OUR MISTAKES...
GREATNESS REQUIRES SACRIFICE, ARIN...AS YOU CLEARLY BELIEVED. OUR PERSONAL CONCERNS MUST REMAIN SECONDARY.
ARIN WAS TOO WEAK TO OVERCOME HER FLAWS. AND SO SINESTRO FOUND FRIENDSHIP IN HAL JORDAN.
HAL WOULD NOT ONLY REPLACE ABIN SUR AS A GREEN LANTERN, BUT ALSO FILL ABIN'S ROLE AS A CONFIDANTE--
--PUTTING HIM IN PRIME POSITION TO BECOME ONE OF THE GREATEST TRAITORS IN GREEN LANTERN HISTORY.
SINESTRO SHOULD NEVER HAVE TRUSTED HAL JORDAN.
ARE YOU ALWAYS SO... uh...YOU KNOW. A JERK?
YOU'VE GOT A LOT TO LEARN, HAL. BUT YOU'LL BE A GOOD STUDENT. YOU WON'T ECLIPSE ABIN, BUT IT WILL BE FUN WATCHING YOU TRY.
POWER IS WASTED ON THE YOUNG. COME BACK WITH ME TO KORUGAR, HAL, AND LET ME SHOW YOU WHAT CAN TRULY BE ACCOMPLISHED.
LIKE ABIN WITH SINESTRO, SINESTRO WAS EAGER TO INVITE HAL JORDAN BACK TO HIS PLANET. TO SHOW HIM WHAT POWER WIELDED INTELLIGENTLY COULD ACCOMPLISH.

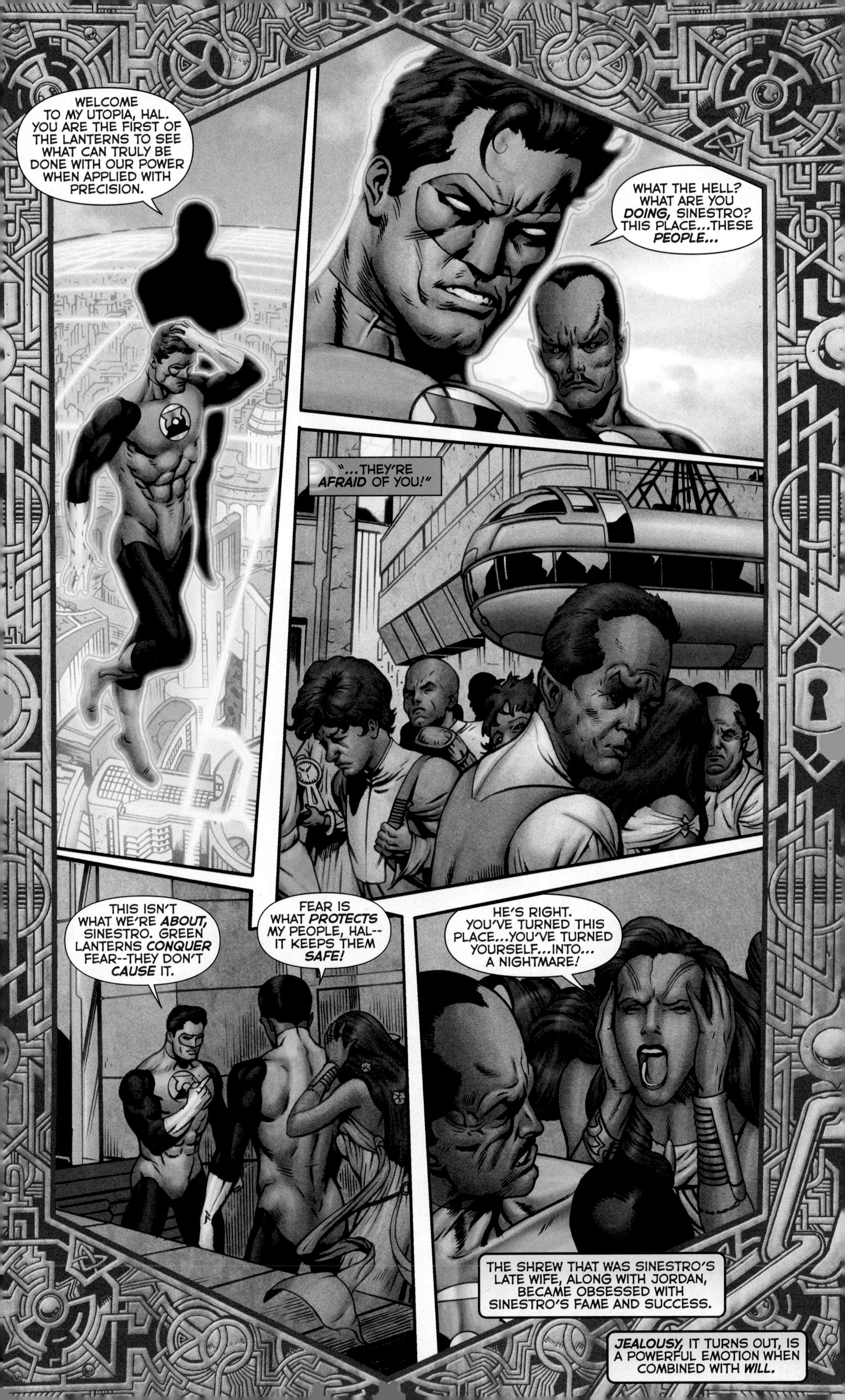

WELCOME TO MY UTOPIA, HAL. YOU ARE THE FIRST OF THE LANTERNS TO SEE WHAT CAN TRULY BE DONE WITH OUR POWER WHEN APPLIED WITH PRECISION.
WHAT THE HELL? WHAT ARE YOU *DOING*, SINESTRO? THIS PLACE...THESE *PEOPLE*...
"...THEY'RE *AFRAID* OF YOU!"
THIS ISN'T WHAT WE'RE *ABOUT*, SINESTRO. GREEN LANTERNS *CONQUER* FEAR--THEY DON'T *CAUSE* IT.
FEAR IS WHAT *PROTECTS* MY PEOPLE, HAL--IT KEEPS THEM *SAFE!*
HE'S RIGHT. YOU'VE TURNED THIS PLACE...YOU'VE TURNED YOURSELF...INTO... A NIGHTMARE!
THE SHREW THAT WAS SINESTRO'S LATE WIFE, ALONG WITH JORDAN, BECAME OBSESSED WITH SINESTRO'S FAME AND SUCCESS.
JEALOUSY, IT TURNS OUT, IS A POWERFUL EMOTION WHEN COMBINED WITH *WILL.*

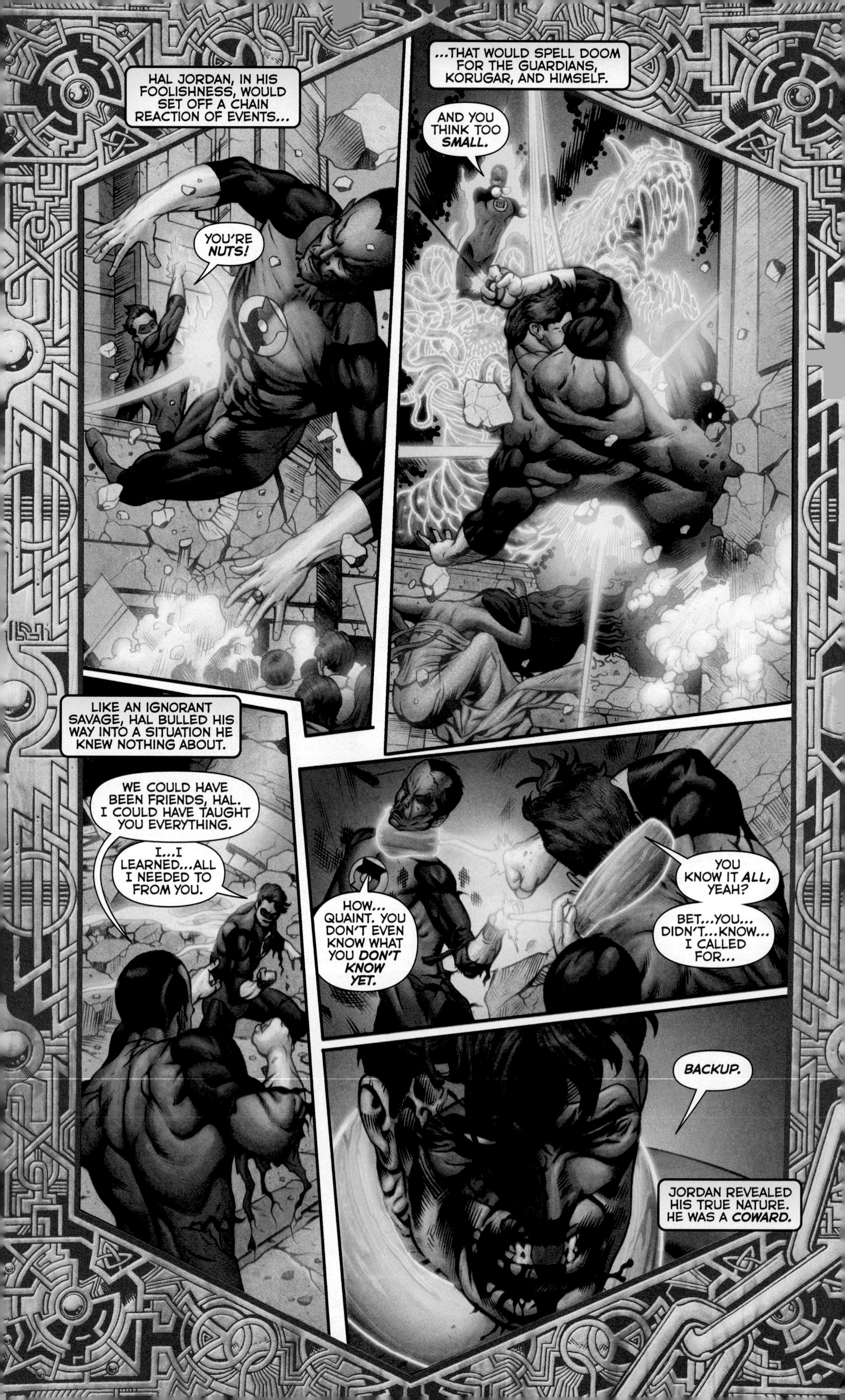
HAL JORDAN, IN HIS FOOLISHNESS, WOULD SET OFF A CHAIN REACTION OF EVENTS...
YOU'RE NUTS!
...THAT WOULD SPELL DOOM FOR THE GUARDIANS, KORUGAR, AND HIMSELF.
AND YOU THINK TOO SMALL.
LIKE AN IGNORANT SAVAGE, HAL BULLED HIS WAY INTO A SITUATION HE KNEW NOTHING ABOUT.
WE COULD HAVE BEEN FRIENDS, HAL. I COULD HAVE TAUGHT YOU EVERYTHING.
I...I LEARNED...ALL I NEEDED TO FROM YOU.
HOW... QUAINT. YOU DON'T EVEN KNOW WHAT YOU DON'T KNOW YET.
YOU KNOW IT ALL, YEAH?
BET...YOU... DIDN'T...KNOW... I CALLED FOR...
BACKUP.
JORDAN REVEALED HIS TRUE NATURE. HE WAS A COWARD.

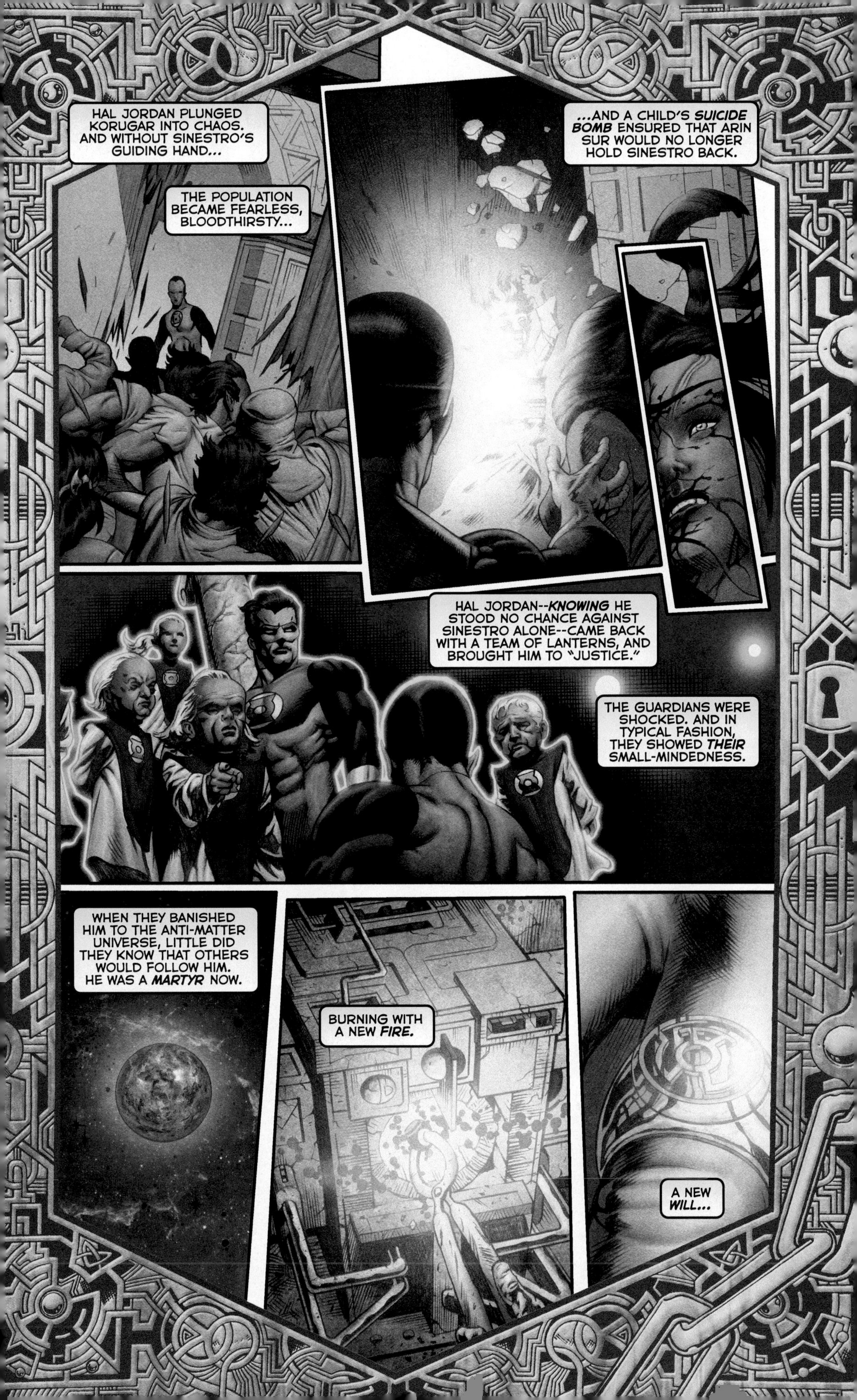
HAL JORDAN PLUNGED KORUGAR INTO CHAOS. AND WITHOUT SINESTRO'S GUIDING HAND...
THE POPULATION BECAME FEARLESS, BLOODTHIRSTY...
...AND A CHILD'S SUICIDE BOMB ENSURED THAT ARIN SUR WOULD NO LONGER HOLD SINESTRO BACK.
HAL JORDAN--KNOWING HE STOOD NO CHANCE AGAINST SINESTRO ALONE--CAME BACK WITH A TEAM OF LANTERNS, AND BROUGHT HIM TO "JUSTICE."
THE GUARDIANS WERE SHOCKED. AND IN TYPICAL FASHION, THEY SHOWED THEIR SMALL-MINDEDNESS.
WHEN THEY BANISHED HIM TO THE ANTI-MATTER UNIVERSE, LITTLE DID THEY KNOW THAT OTHERS WOULD FOLLOW HIM. HE WAS A MARTYR NOW.
BURNING WITH A NEW FIRE.
A NEW WILL...

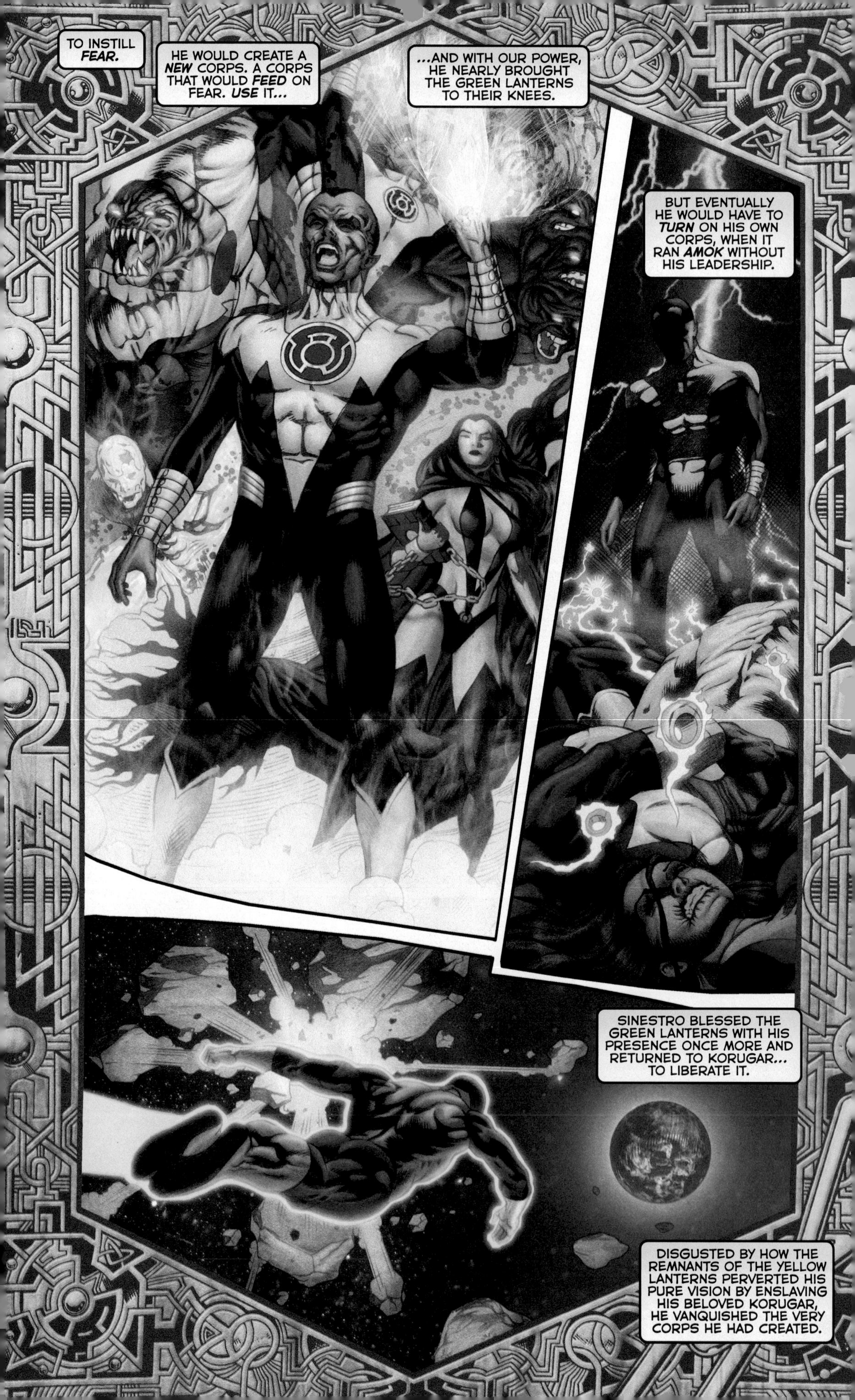

TO INSTILL **FEAR.**
HE WOULD CREATE A ***NEW*** CORPS. A CORPS THAT WOULD ***FEED*** ON FEAR. ***USE*** IT...
...AND WITH OUR POWER, HE NEARLY BROUGHT THE GREEN LANTERNS TO THEIR KNEES.
BUT EVENTUALLY HE WOULD HAVE TO ***TURN*** ON HIS OWN CORPS, WHEN IT RAN ***AMOK*** WITHOUT HIS LEADERSHIP.
SINESTRO BLESSED THE GREEN LANTERNS WITH HIS PRESENCE ONCE MORE AND RETURNED TO KORUGAR... TO LIBERATE IT.
DISGUSTED BY HOW THE REMNANTS OF THE YELLOW LANTERNS PERVERTED HIS PURE VISION BY ENSLAVING HIS BELOVED KORUGAR, HE VANQUISHED THE VERY CORPS HE HAD CREATED.

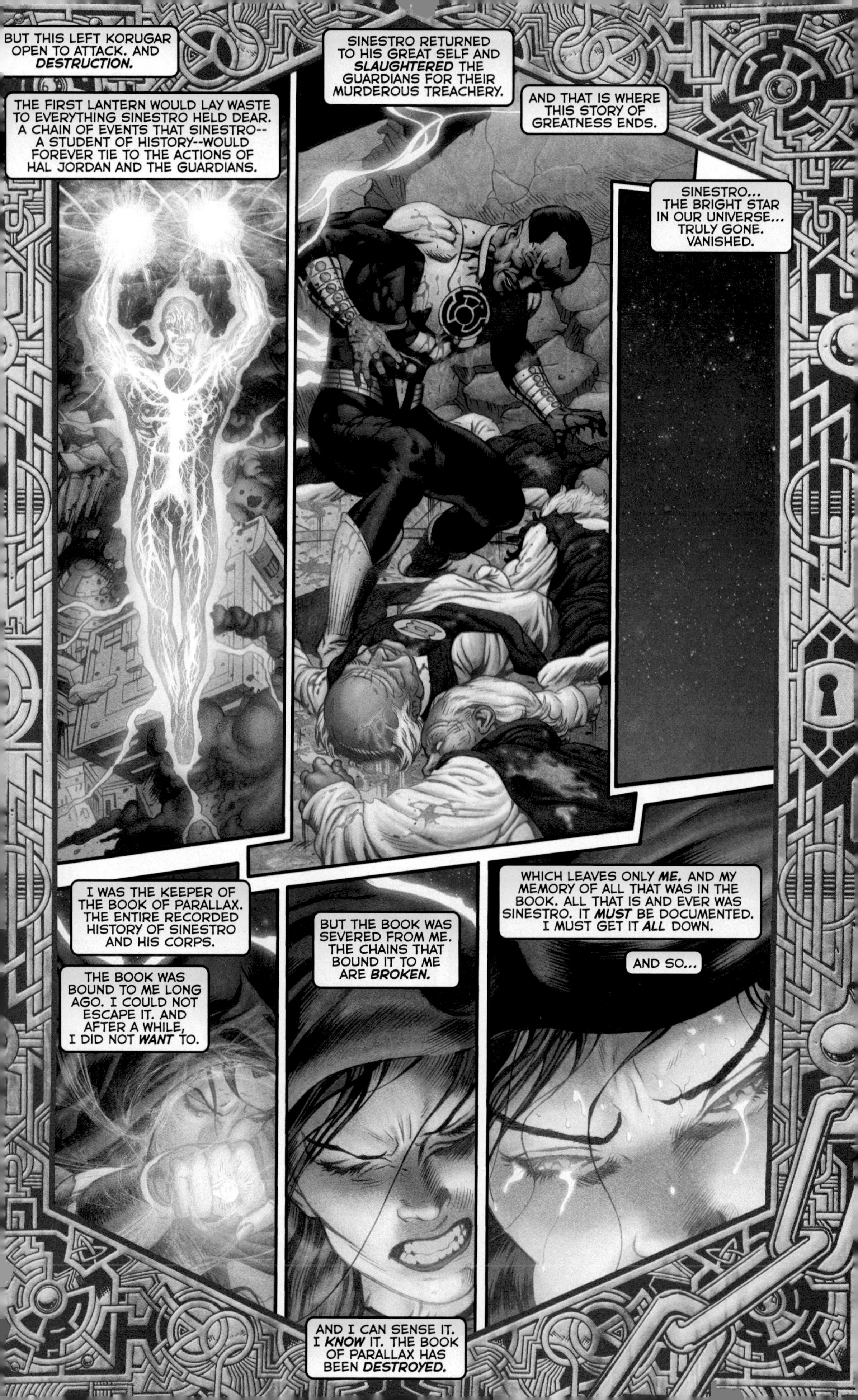
BUT THIS LEFT KORUGAR OPEN TO ATTACK. AND DESTRUCTION.
THE FIRST LANTERN WOULD LAY WASTE TO EVERYTHING SINESTRO HELD DEAR. A CHAIN OF EVENTS THAT SINESTRO-- A STUDENT OF HISTORY--WOULD FOREVER TIE TO THE ACTIONS OF HAL JORDAN AND THE GUARDIANS.
SINESTRO RETURNED TO HIS GREAT SELF AND SLAUGHTERED THE GUARDIANS FOR THEIR MURDEROUS TREACHERY.
AND THAT IS WHERE THIS STORY OF GREATNESS ENDS.
SINESTRO... THE BRIGHT STAR IN OUR UNIVERSE... TRULY GONE. VANISHED.
I WAS THE KEEPER OF THE BOOK OF PARALLAX. THE ENTIRE RECORDED HISTORY OF SINESTRO AND HIS CORPS.
THE BOOK WAS BOUND TO ME LONG AGO. I COULD NOT ESCAPE IT. AND AFTER A WHILE, I DID NOT WANT TO.
BUT THE BOOK WAS SEVERED FROM ME. THE CHAINS THAT BOUND IT TO ME ARE BROKEN.
WHICH LEAVES ONLY ME. AND MY MEMORY OF ALL THAT WAS IN THE BOOK. ALL THAT IS AND EVER WAS SINESTRO. IT MUST BE DOCUMENTED. I MUST GET IT ALL DOWN.
AND SO...
AND I CAN SENSE IT. I KNOW IT. THE BOOK OF PARALLAX HAS BEEN DESTROYED.

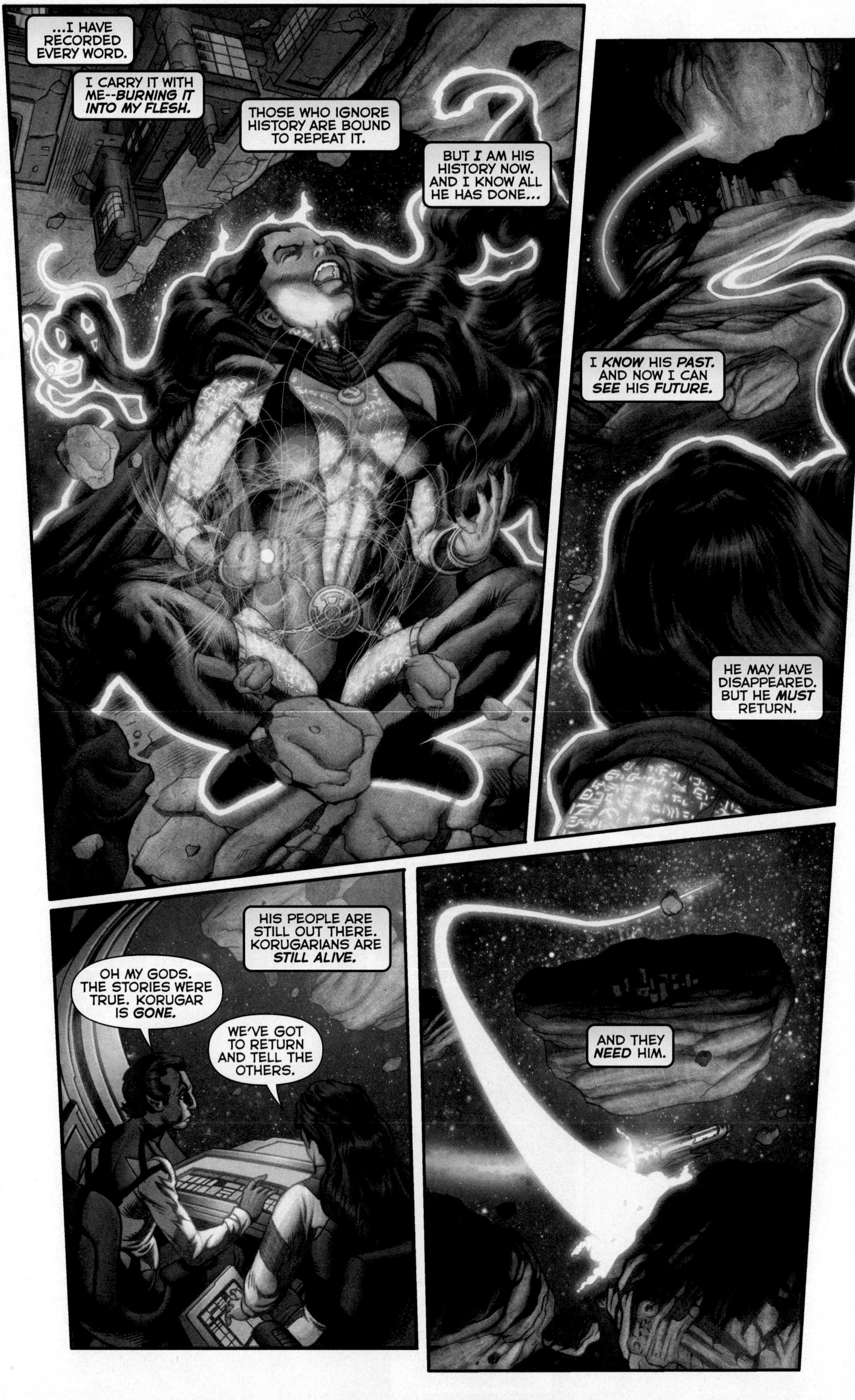
...I HAVE RECORDED EVERY WORD.
I CARRY IT WITH ME--*BURNING IT INTO MY FLESH.*
THOSE WHO IGNORE HISTORY ARE BOUND TO REPEAT IT.
BUT *I* AM HIS HISTORY NOW. AND I KNOW ALL HE HAS DONE...
I *KNOW* HIS *PAST.* AND NOW I CAN *SEE* HIS *FUTURE.*
HE MAY HAVE DISAPPEARED. BUT HE *MUST* RETURN.
HIS PEOPLE ARE STILL OUT THERE. KORUGARIANS ARE *STILL ALIVE.*
OH MY GODS. THE STORIES WERE TRUE. KORUGAR IS *GONE.*
WE'VE GOT TO RETURN AND TELL THE OTHERS.
AND THEY *NEED* HIM.

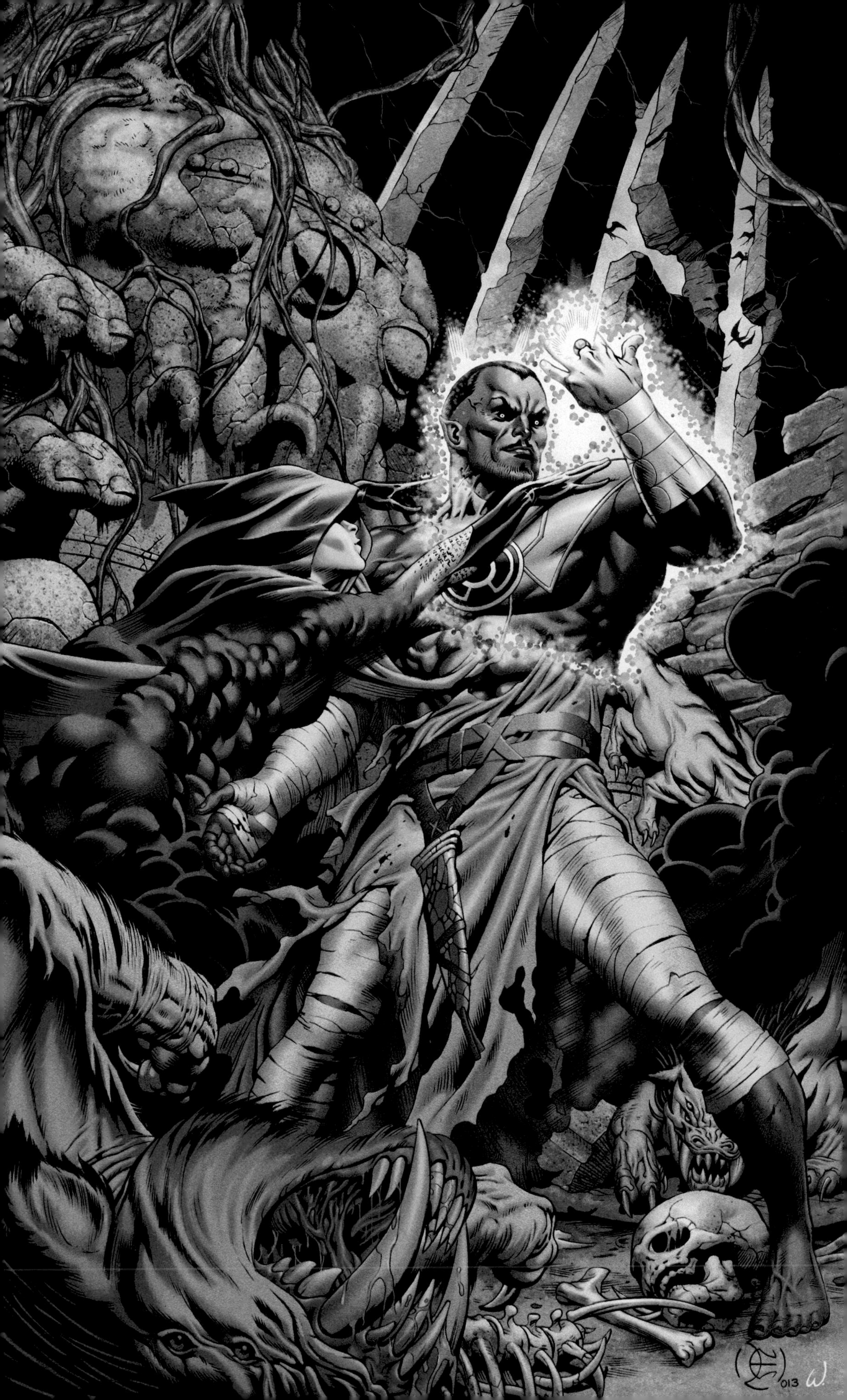

BLACKEST DAY, BRIGHTEST NIGHT

CULLEN BUNN writer **DALE EAGLESHAM** artist **JASON WRIGHT** colorist **DEZI SIENTY** letterer

cover art by **DALE EAGLESHAM** & **JASON WRIGHT**

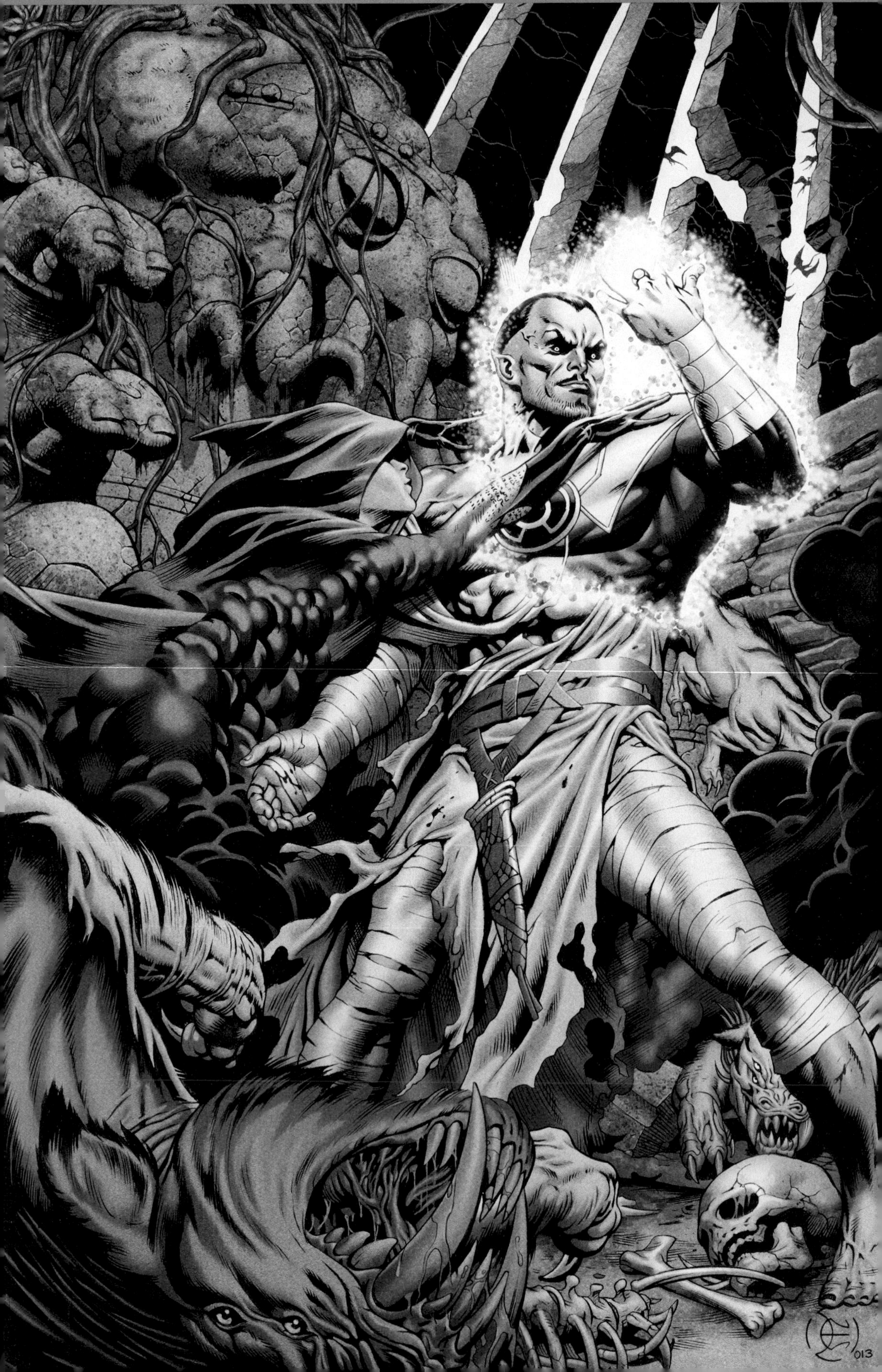

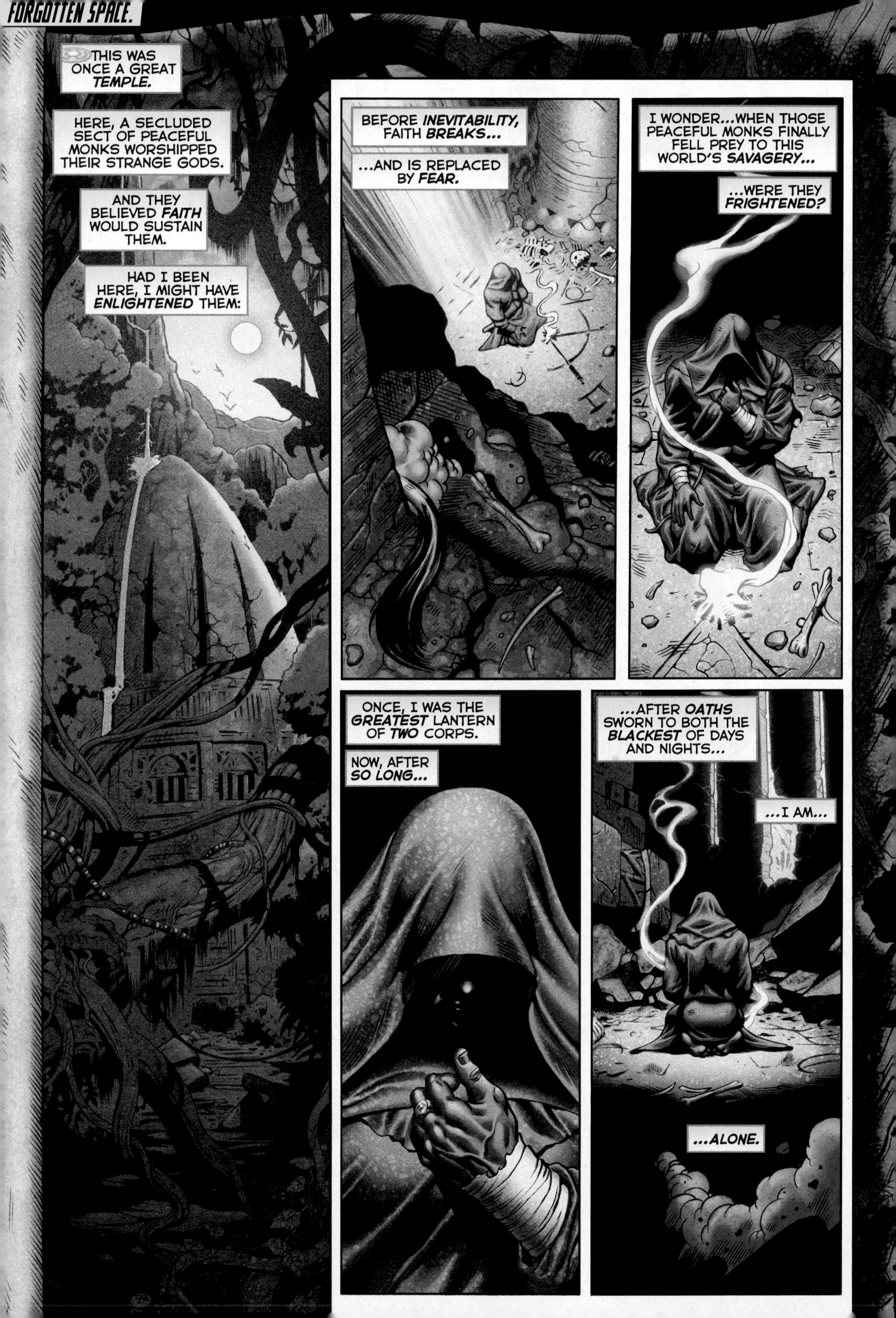
FORGOTTEN SPACE.
THIS WAS ONCE A GREAT TEMPLE.
HERE, A SECLUDED SECT OF PEACEFUL MONKS WORSHIPPED THEIR STRANGE GODS.
AND THEY BELIEVED FAITH WOULD SUSTAIN THEM.
HAD I BEEN HERE, I MIGHT HAVE ENLIGHTENED THEM:
BEFORE INEVITABILITY, FAITH BREAKS...
...AND IS REPLACED BY FEAR.
I WONDER...WHEN THOSE PEACEFUL MONKS FINALLY FELL PREY TO THIS WORLD'S SAVAGERY...
...WERE THEY FRIGHTENED?
ONCE, I WAS THE GREATEST LANTERN OF TWO CORPS.
NOW, AFTER SO LONG...
...AFTER OATHS SWORN TO BOTH THE BLACKEST OF DAYS AND NIGHTS...
...I AM...
...ALONE.

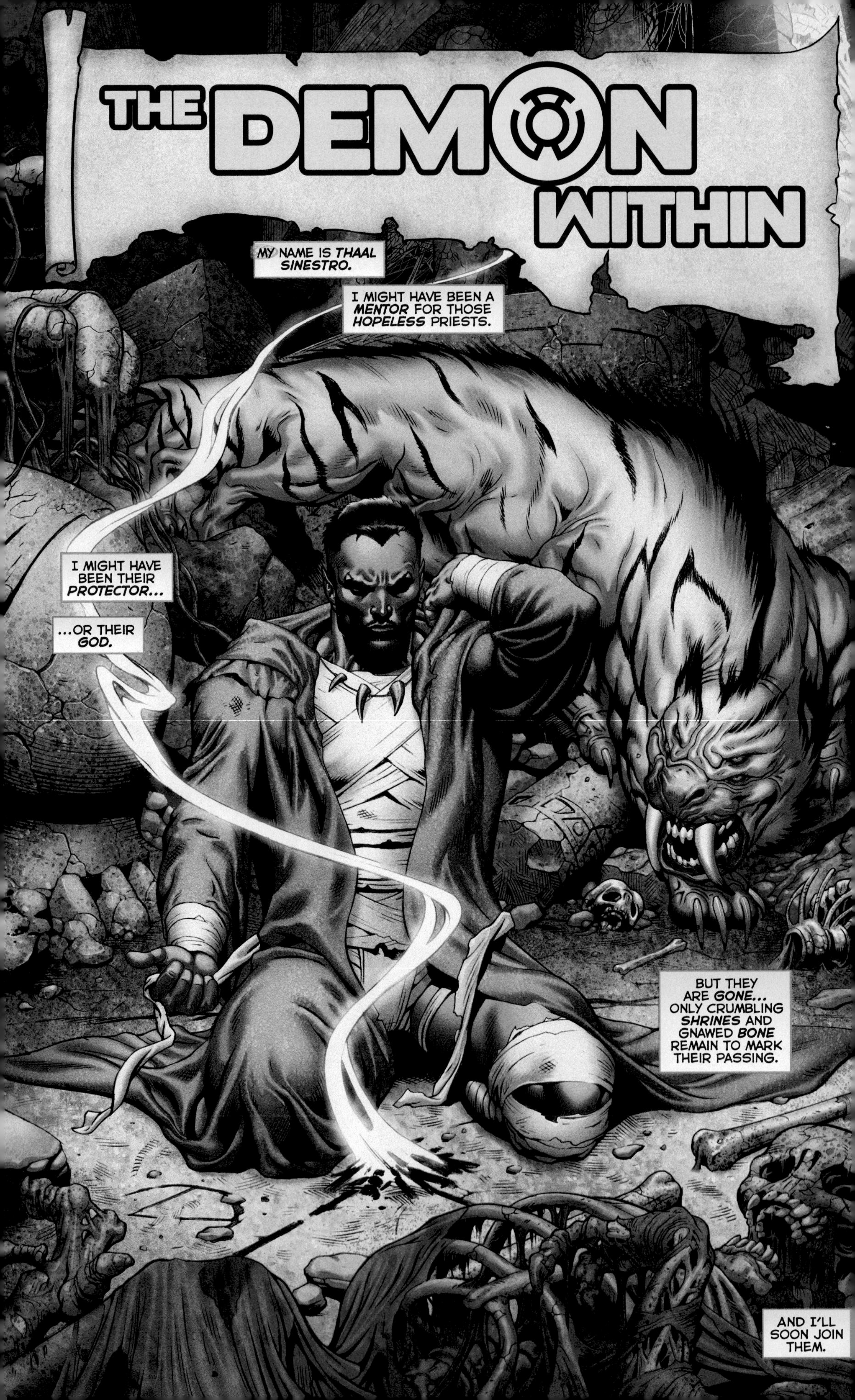
THE DEMON WITHIN
MY NAME IS THAAL SINESTRO.
I MIGHT HAVE BEEN A MENTOR FOR THOSE HOPELESS PRIESTS.
I MIGHT HAVE BEEN THEIR PROTECTOR...
...OR THEIR GOD.
BUT THEY ARE GONE... ONLY CRUMBLING SHRINES AND GNAWED BONE REMAIN TO MARK THEIR PASSING.
AND I'LL SOON JOIN THEM.

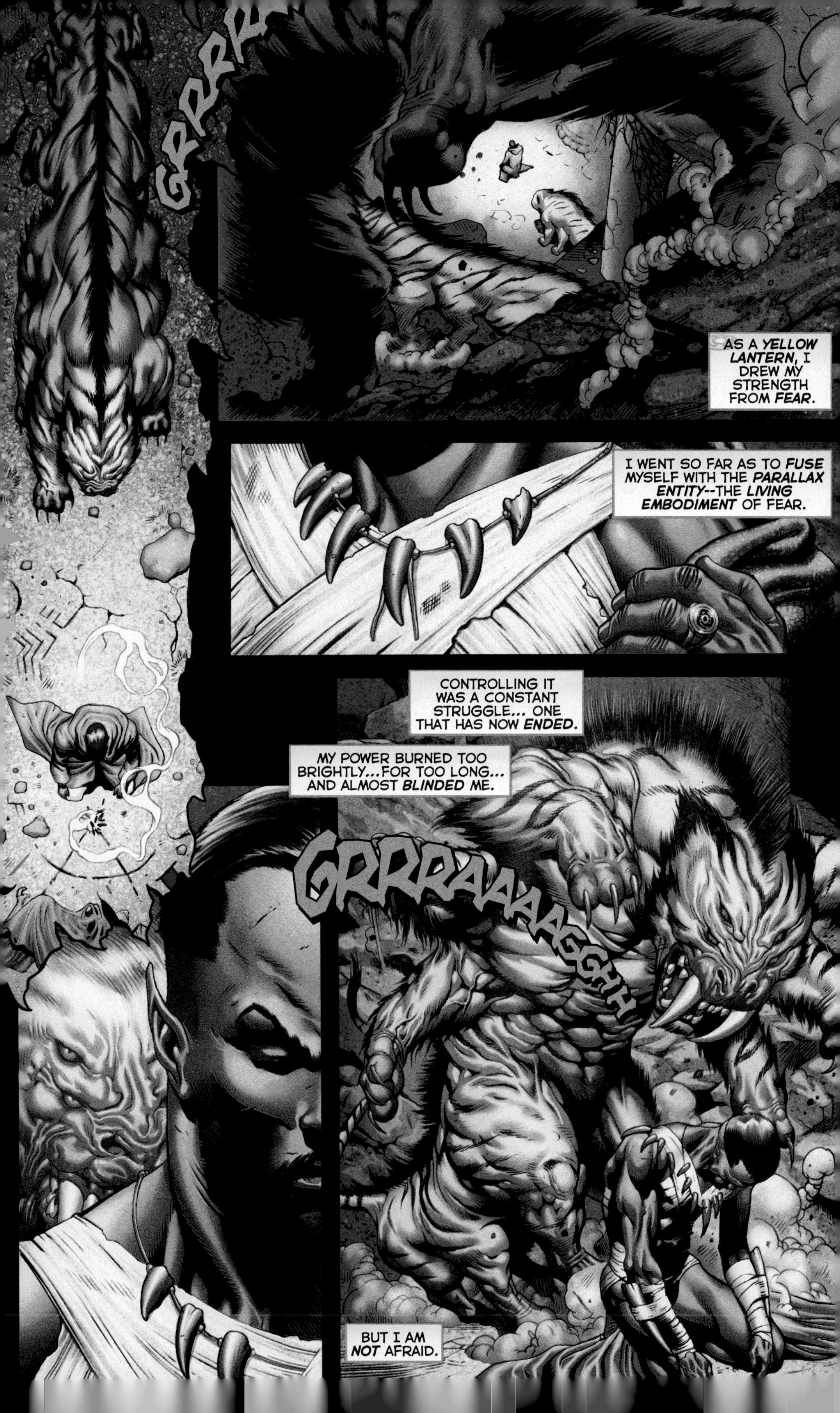
GRRRR
AS A *YELLOW LANTERN*, I DREW MY STRENGTH FROM *FEAR*.
I WENT SO FAR AS TO *FUSE* MYSELF WITH THE *PARALLAX ENTITY*--THE *LIVING EMBODIMENT* OF FEAR.
CONTROLLING IT WAS A CONSTANT STRUGGLE... ONE THAT HAS NOW *ENDED*.
MY POWER BURNED TOO BRIGHTLY...FOR TOO LONG... AND ALMOST *BLINDED* ME.
GRRRAAAAAGGHH
BUT I AM *NOT* AFRAID.

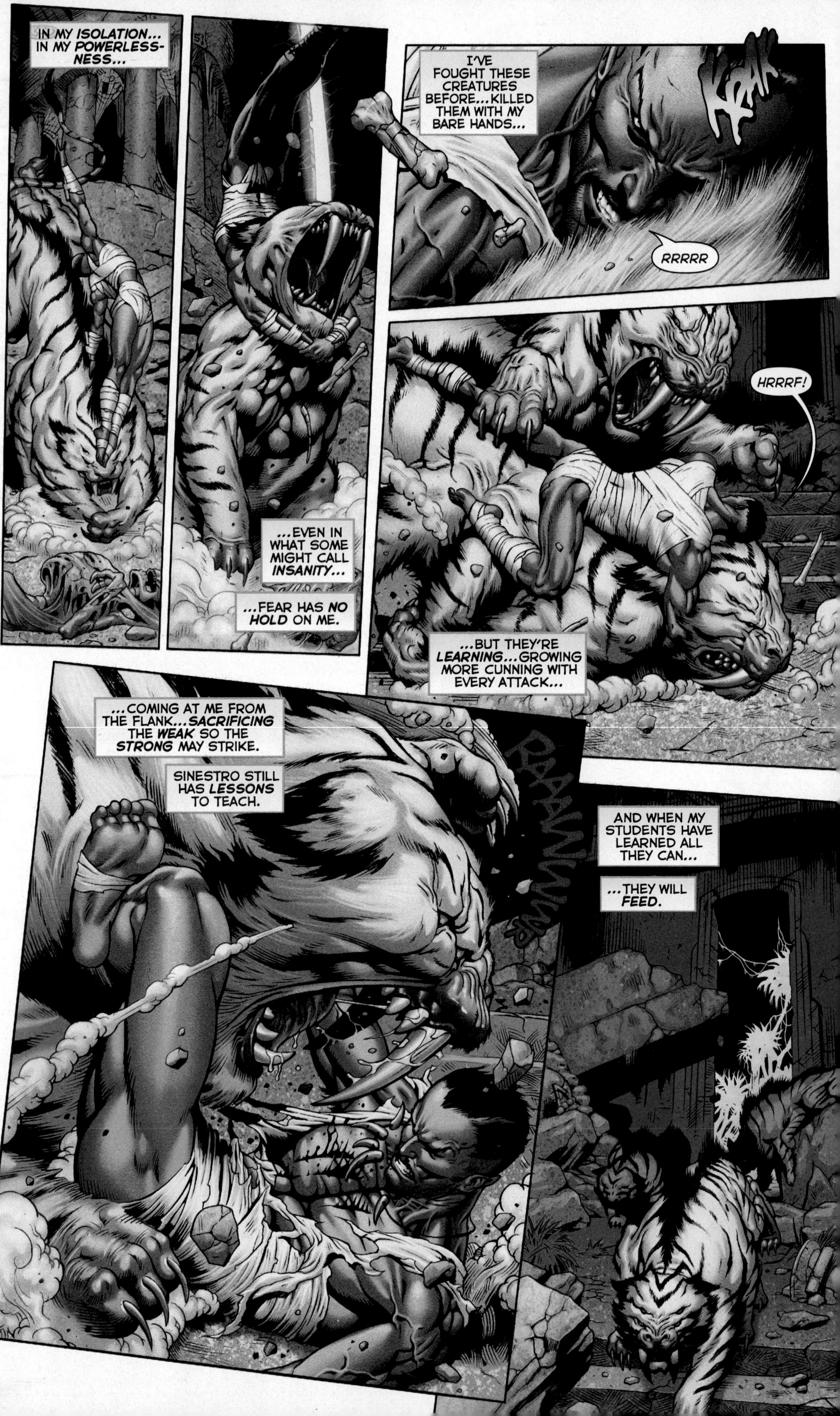

IN MY ISOLATION... IN MY POWERLESS-NESS...
...EVEN IN WHAT SOME MIGHT CALL INSANITY...
...FEAR HAS NO HOLD ON ME.
I'VE FOUGHT THESE CREATURES BEFORE...KILLED THEM WITH MY BARE HANDS...
KRAK
RRRRR
HRRRF!
...BUT THEY'RE LEARNING...GROWING MORE CUNNING WITH EVERY ATTACK...
...COMING AT ME FROM THE FLANK...SACRIFICING THE WEAK SO THE STRONG MAY STRIKE.
SINESTRO STILL HAS LESSONS TO TEACH.
AND WHEN MY STUDENTS HAVE LEARNED ALL THEY CAN...
...THEY WILL FEED.

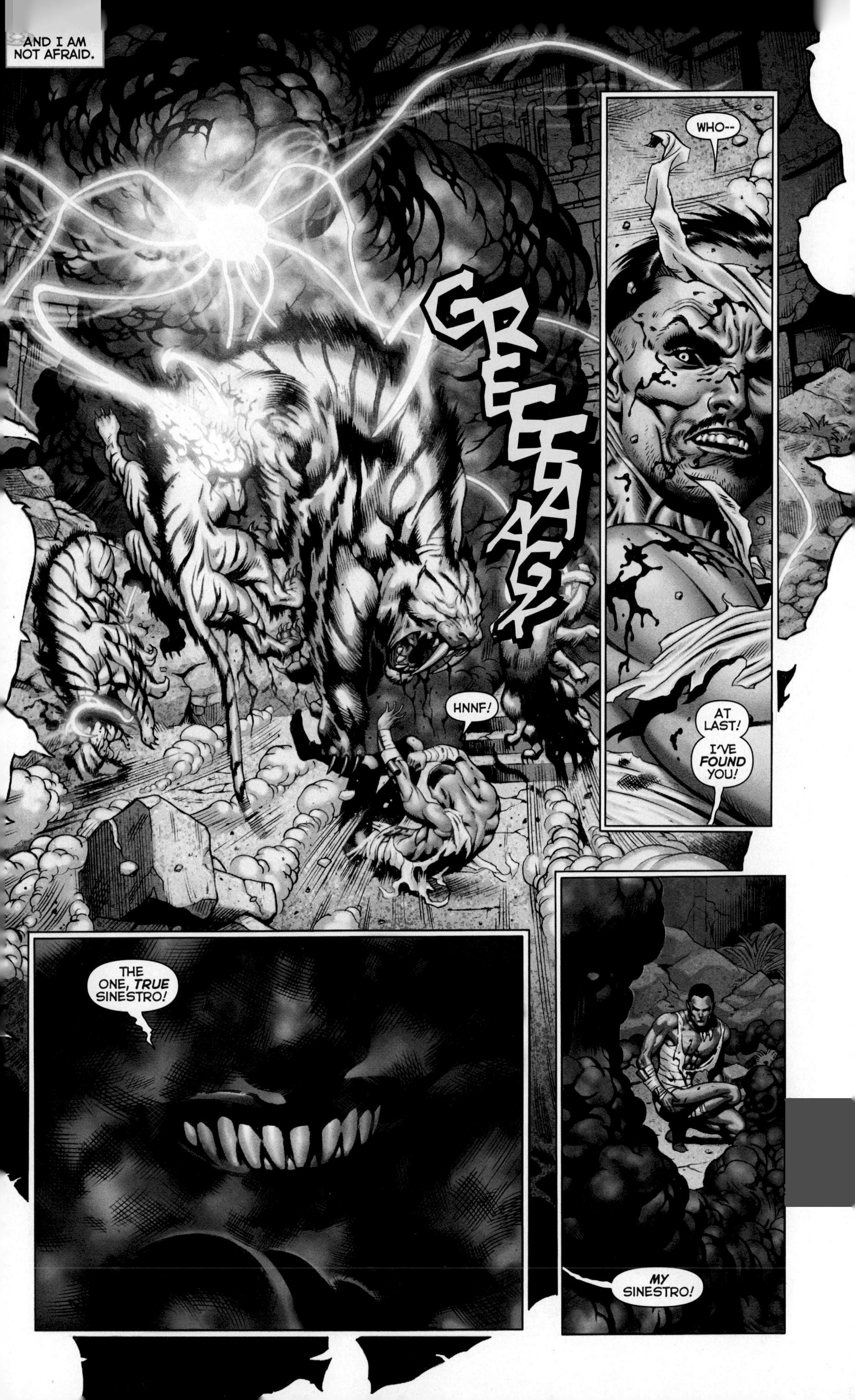
AND I AM NOT AFRAID.
GREEAAAGK
WHO--
HNNF!
AT LAST!
I'VE FOUND YOU!
THE ONE, TRUE SINESTRO!
MY SINESTRO!

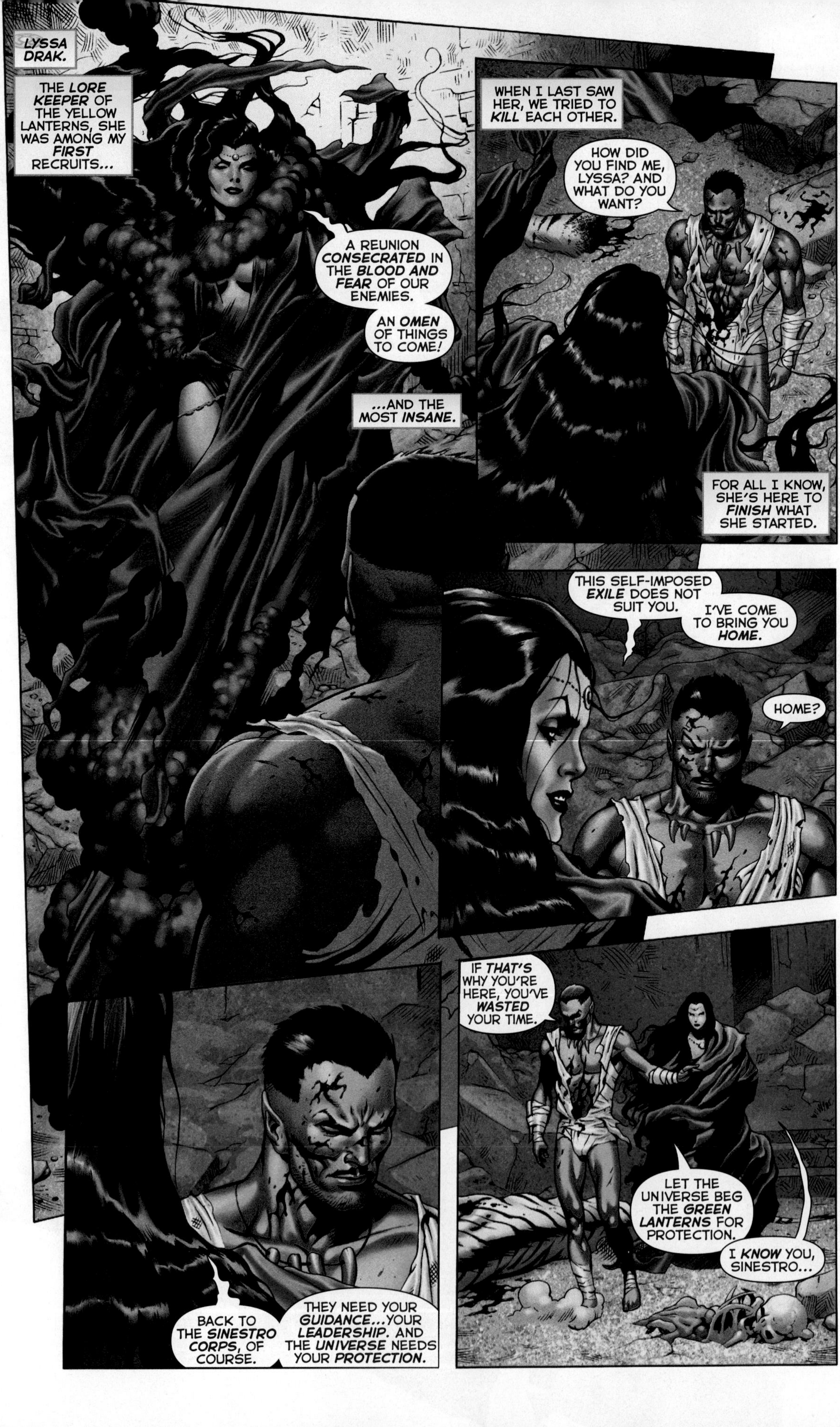
LYSSA DRAK.
THE LORE KEEPER OF THE YELLOW LANTERNS, SHE WAS AMONG MY FIRST RECRUITS...
A REUNION CONSECRATED IN THE BLOOD AND FEAR OF OUR ENEMIES.
AN OMEN OF THINGS TO COME!
...AND THE MOST INSANE.
WHEN I LAST SAW HER, WE TRIED TO KILL EACH OTHER.
HOW DID YOU FIND ME, LYSSA? AND WHAT DO YOU WANT?
FOR ALL I KNOW, SHE'S HERE TO FINISH WHAT SHE STARTED.
THIS SELF-IMPOSED EXILE DOES NOT SUIT YOU.
I'VE COME TO BRING YOU HOME.
HOME?
BACK TO THE SINESTRO CORPS, OF COURSE.
THEY NEED YOUR GUIDANCE...YOUR LEADERSHIP. AND THE UNIVERSE NEEDS YOUR PROTECTION.
IF THAT'S WHY YOU'RE HERE, YOU'VE WASTED YOUR TIME.
LET THE UNIVERSE BEG THE GREEN LANTERNS FOR PROTECTION.
I KNOW YOU, SINESTRO...

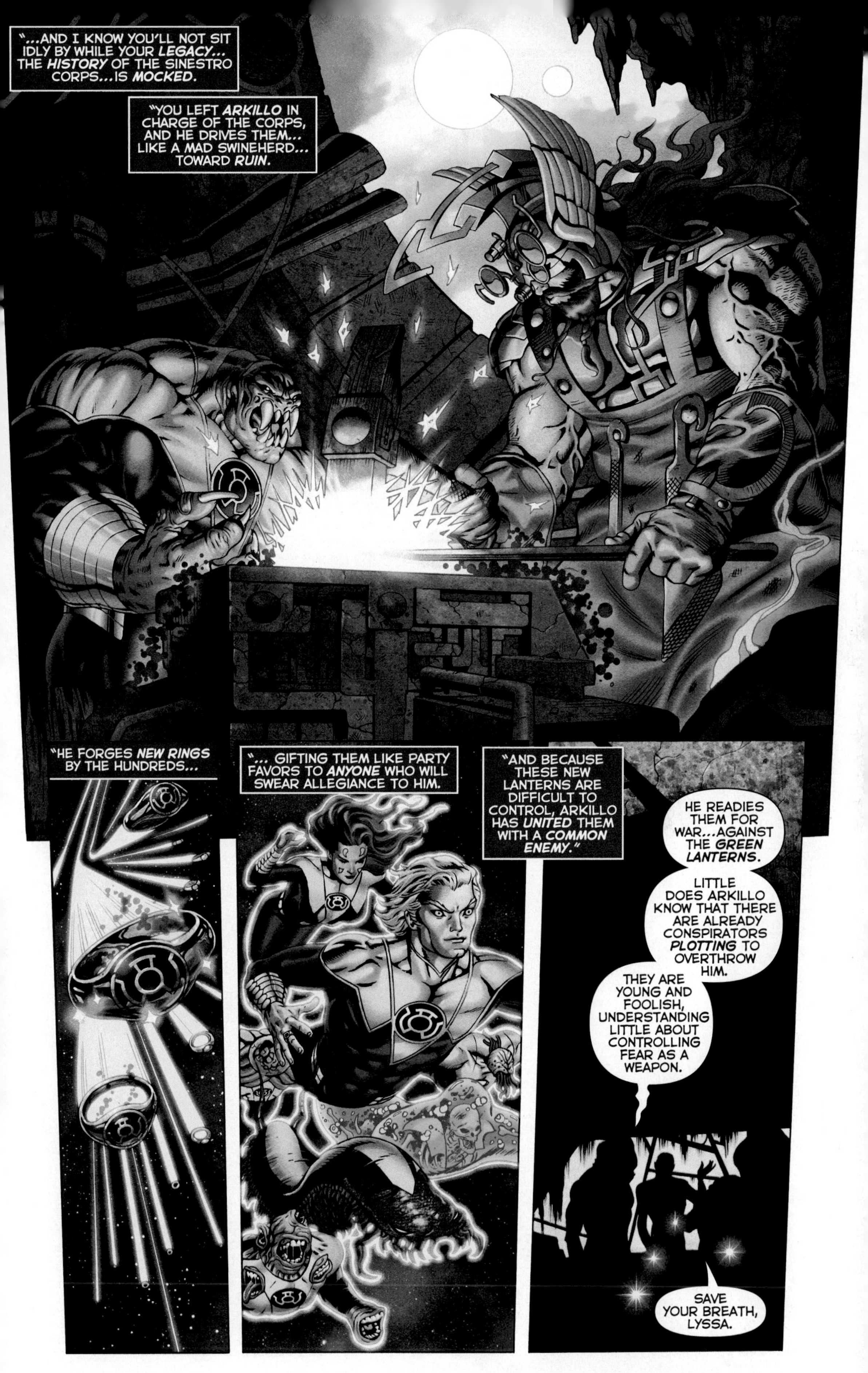
"...AND I KNOW YOU'LL NOT SIT IDLY BY WHILE YOUR LEGACY... THE HISTORY OF THE SINESTRO CORPS...IS MOCKED.
"YOU LEFT ARKILLO IN CHARGE OF THE CORPS, AND HE DRIVES THEM... LIKE A MAD SWINEHERD... TOWARD RUIN.
"HE FORGES NEW RINGS BY THE HUNDREDS...
"... GIFTING THEM LIKE PARTY FAVORS TO ANYONE WHO WILL SWEAR ALLEGIANCE TO HIM.
"AND BECAUSE THESE NEW LANTERNS ARE DIFFICULT TO CONTROL, ARKILLO HAS UNITED THEM WITH A COMMON ENEMY."
HE READIES THEM FOR WAR...AGAINST THE GREEN LANTERNS.
LITTLE DOES ARKILLO KNOW THAT THERE ARE ALREADY CONSPIRATORS PLOTTING TO OVERTHROW HIM.
THEY ARE YOUNG AND FOOLISH, UNDERSTANDING LITTLE ABOUT CONTROLLING FEAR AS A WEAPON.
SAVE YOUR BREATH, LYSSA.

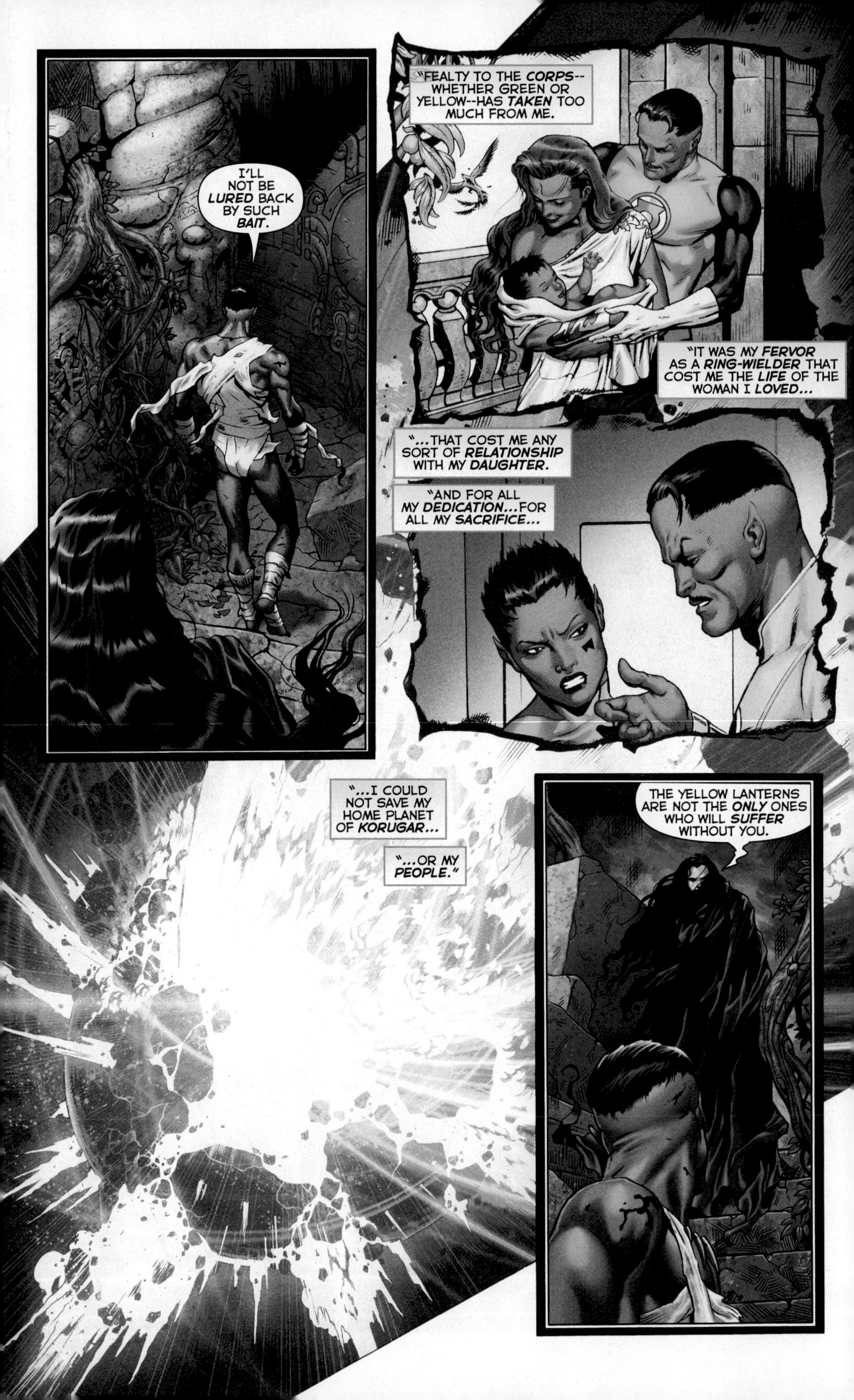
I'LL NOT BE LURED BACK BY SUCH BAIT.
"FEALTY TO THE CORPS--WHETHER GREEN OR YELLOW--HAS TAKEN TOO MUCH FROM ME.
"IT WAS MY FERVOR AS A RING-WIELDER THAT COST ME THE LIFE OF THE WOMAN I LOVED...
"...THAT COST ME ANY SORT OF RELATIONSHIP WITH MY DAUGHTER.
"AND FOR ALL MY DEDICATION...FOR ALL MY SACRIFICE...
"...I COULD NOT SAVE MY HOME PLANET OF KORUGAR...
"...OR MY PEOPLE."
THE YELLOW LANTERNS ARE NOT THE ONLY ONES WHO WILL SUFFER WITHOUT YOU.

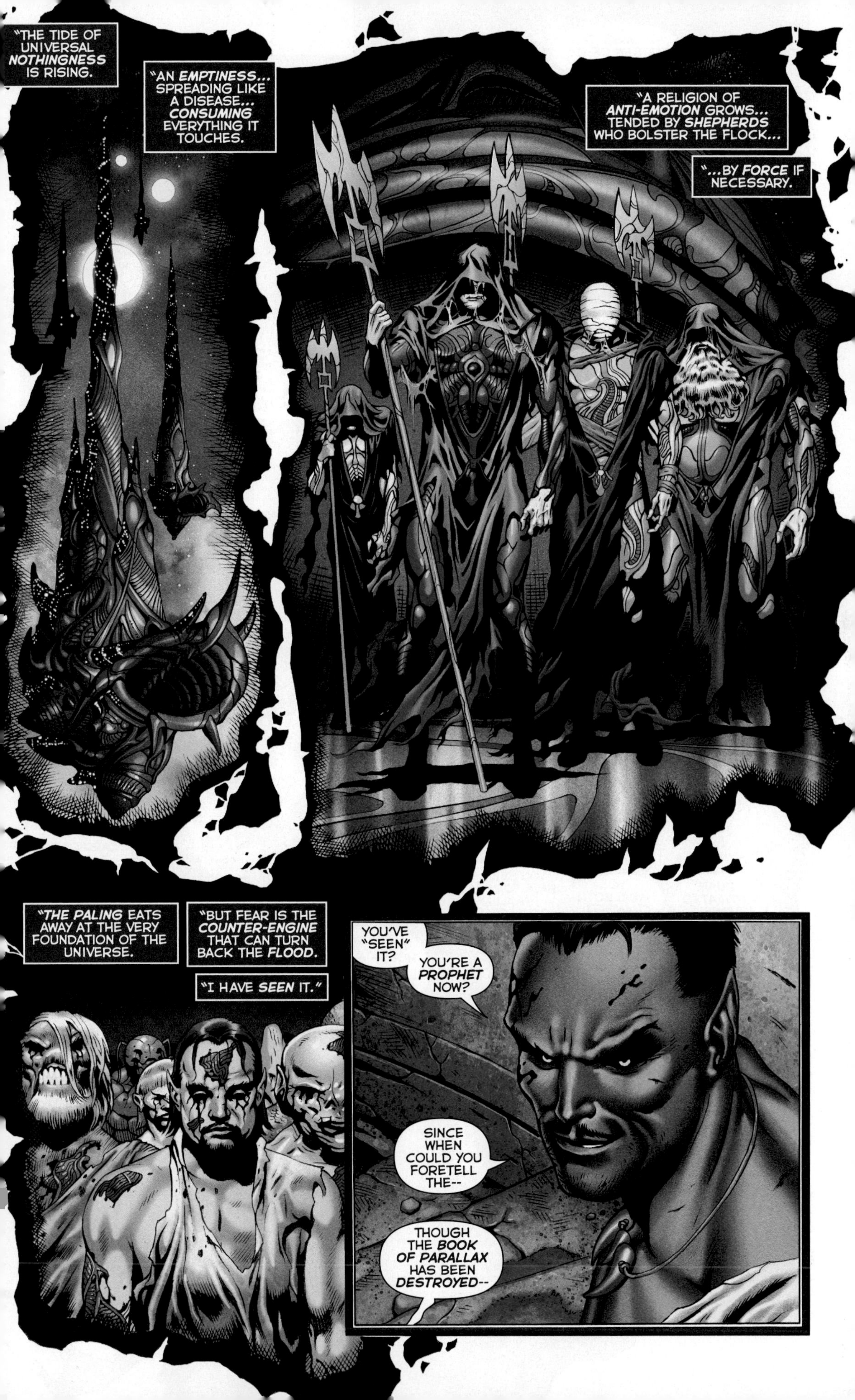
"THE TIDE OF UNIVERSAL NOTHINGNESS IS RISING.
"AN EMPTINESS... SPREADING LIKE A DISEASE... CONSUMING EVERYTHING IT TOUCHES.
"A RELIGION OF ANTI-EMOTION GROWS... TENDED BY SHEPHERDS WHO BOLSTER THE FLOCK...
"...BY FORCE IF NECESSARY.
"THE PALING EATS AWAY AT THE VERY FOUNDATION OF THE UNIVERSE.
"BUT FEAR IS THE COUNTER-ENGINE THAT CAN TURN BACK THE FLOOD.
"I HAVE SEEN IT."
YOU'VE "SEEN" IT?
YOU'RE A PROPHET NOW?
SINCE WHEN COULD YOU FORETELL THE--
THOUGH THE BOOK OF PARALLAX HAS BEEN DESTROYED--

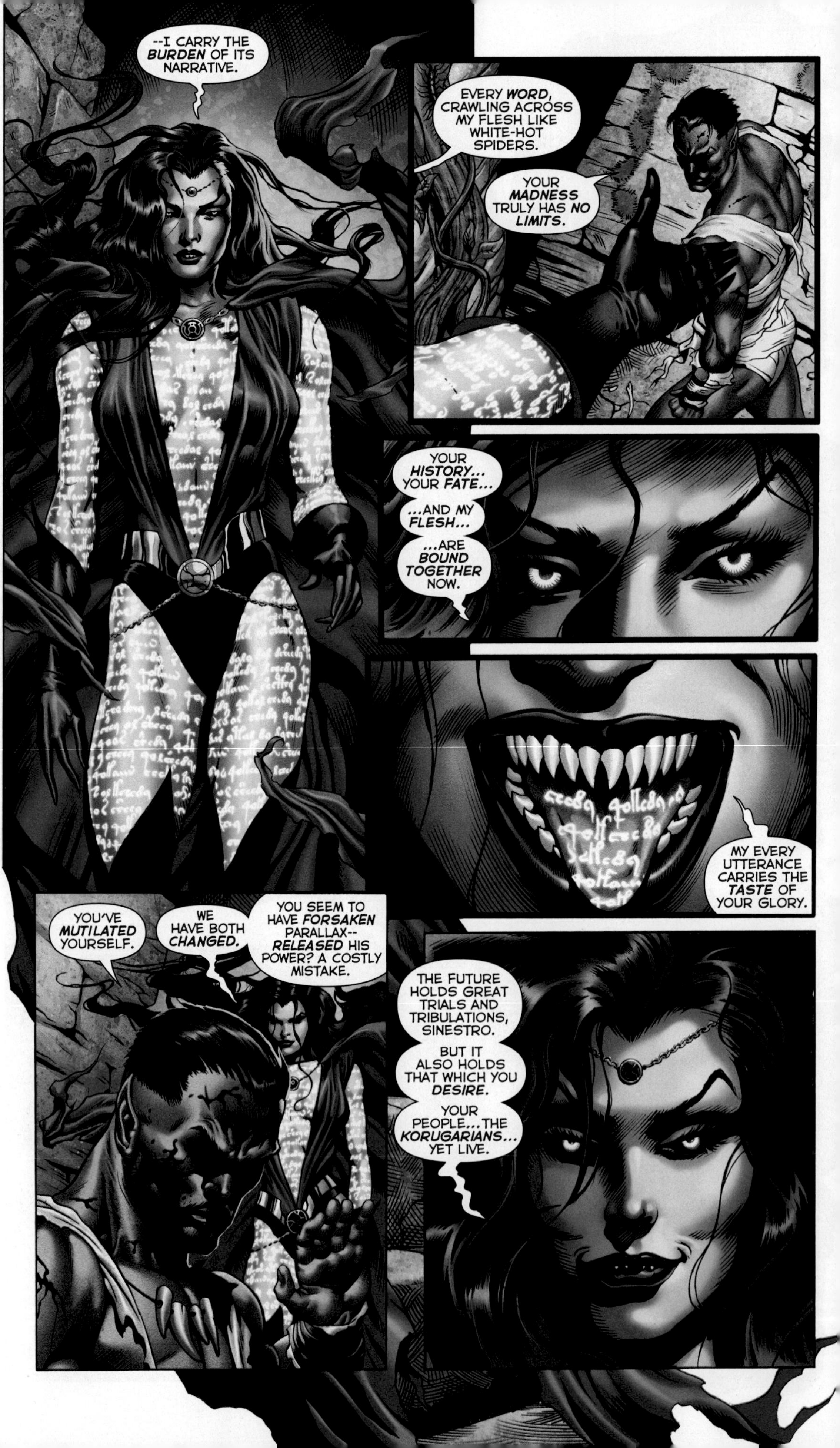
--I CARRY THE BURDEN OF ITS NARRATIVE.
EVERY WORD, CRAWLING ACROSS MY FLESH LIKE WHITE-HOT SPIDERS.
YOUR MADNESS TRULY HAS NO LIMITS.
YOUR HISTORY... YOUR FATE...
...AND MY FLESH...
...ARE BOUND TOGETHER NOW.
MY EVERY UTTERANCE CARRIES THE TASTE OF YOUR GLORY.
YOU'VE MUTILATED YOURSELF.
WE HAVE BOTH CHANGED.
YOU SEEM TO HAVE FORSAKEN PARALLAX-- RELEASED HIS POWER? A COSTLY MISTAKE.
THE FUTURE HOLDS GREAT TRIALS AND TRIBULATIONS, SINESTRO.
BUT IT ALSO HOLDS THAT WHICH YOU DESIRE.
YOUR PEOPLE...THE KORUGARIANS... YET LIVE.

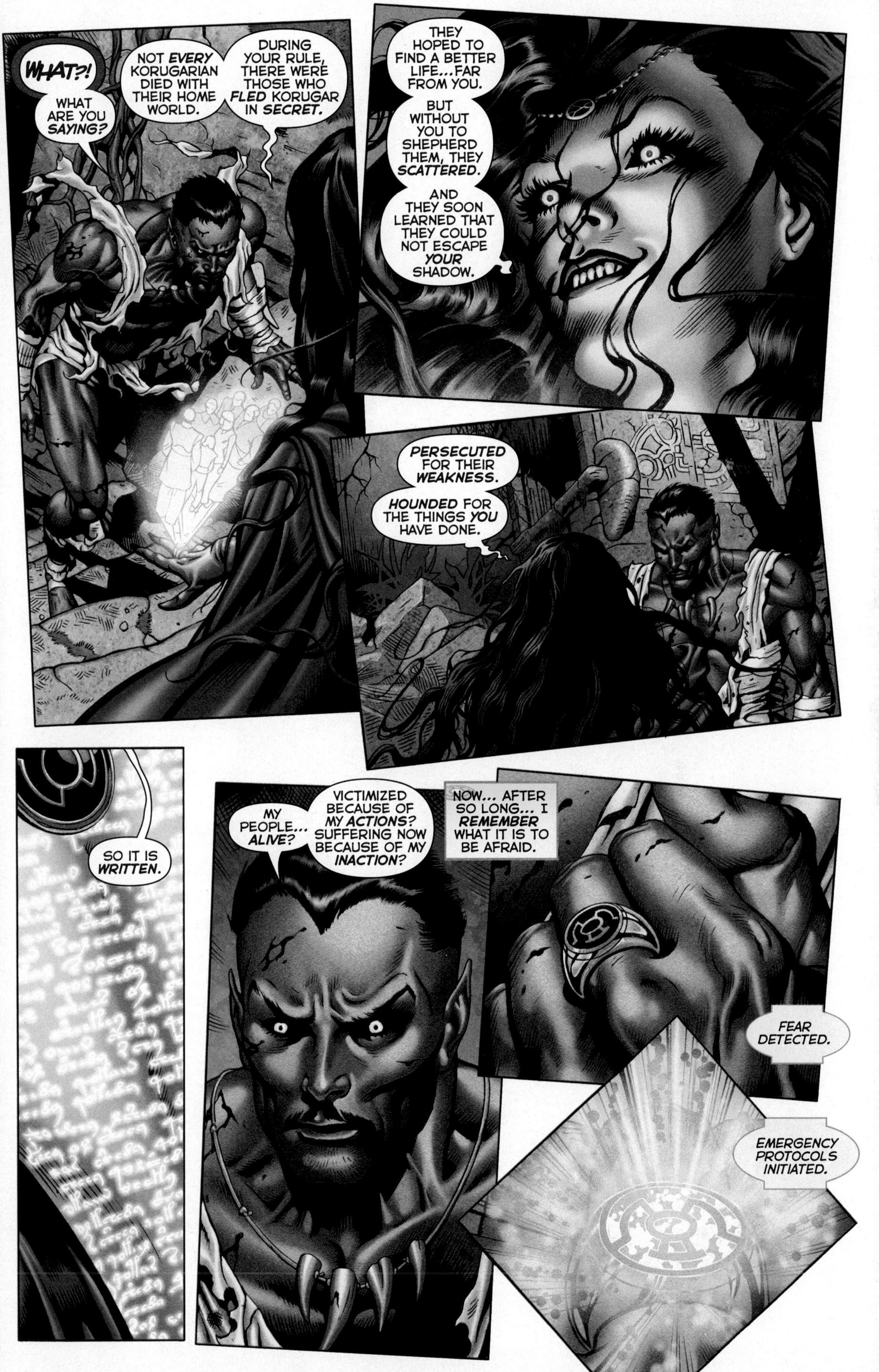
WHAT?!
WHAT ARE YOU SAYING?
NOT EVERY KORUGARIAN DIED WITH THEIR HOME WORLD.
DURING YOUR RULE, THERE WERE THOSE WHO FLED KORUGAR IN SECRET.
THEY HOPED TO FIND A BETTER LIFE...FAR FROM YOU.
BUT WITHOUT YOU TO SHEPHERD THEM, THEY SCATTERED.
AND THEY SOON LEARNED THAT THEY COULD NOT ESCAPE YOUR SHADOW.
PERSECUTED FOR THEIR WEAKNESS.
HOUNDED FOR THE THINGS YOU HAVE DONE.
SO IT IS WRITTEN.
MY PEOPLE... ALIVE?
VICTIMIZED BECAUSE OF MY ACTIONS? SUFFERING NOW BECAUSE OF MY INACTION?
NOW... AFTER SO LONG... I REMEMBER WHAT IT IS TO BE AFRAID.
FEAR DETECTED.
EMERGENCY PROTOCOLS INITIATED.

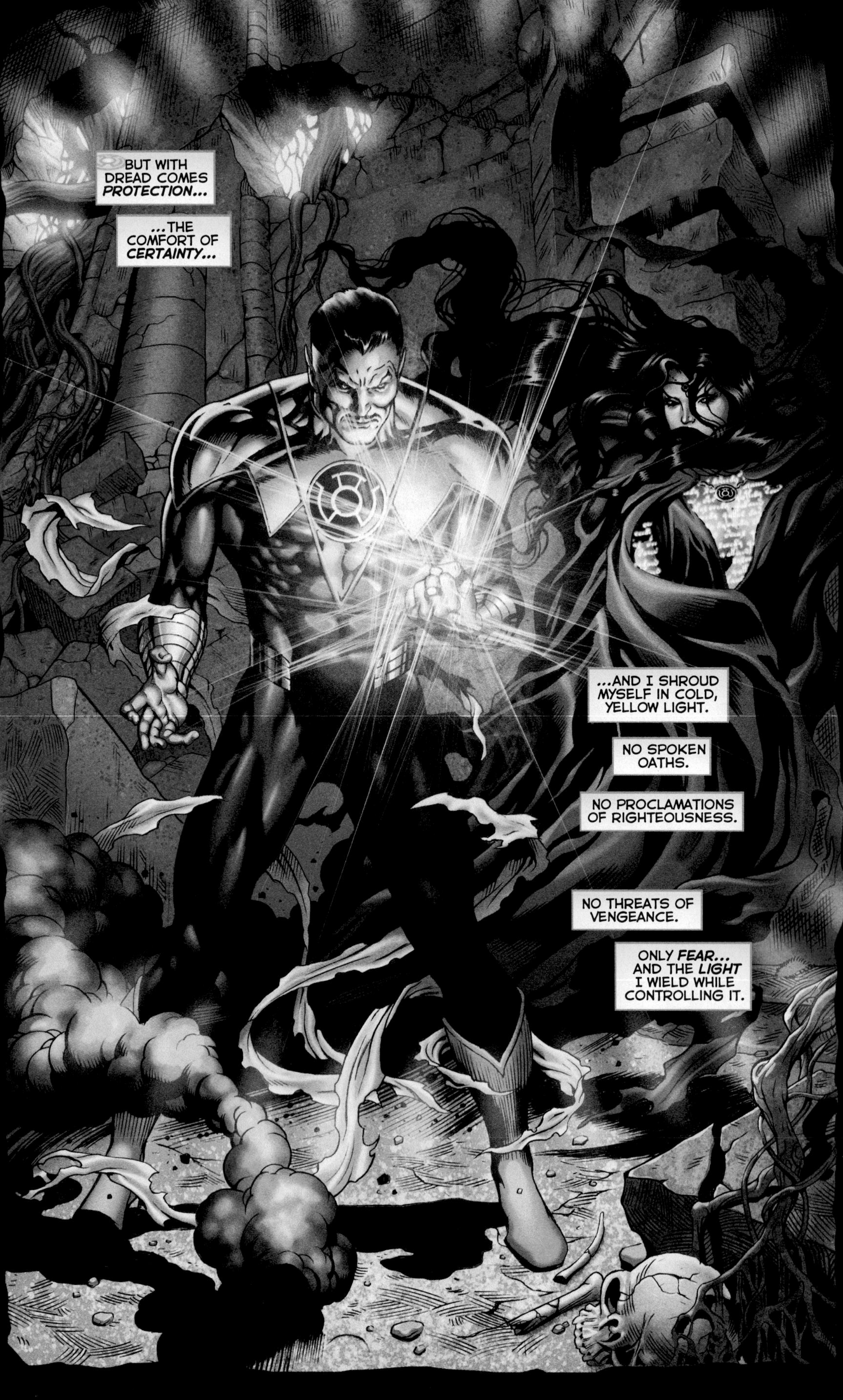

BUT WITH DREAD COMES *PROTECTION*...
...THE COMFORT OF *CERTAINTY*...
...AND I SHROUD MYSELF IN COLD, YELLOW LIGHT.
NO SPOKEN OATHS.
NO PROCLAMATIONS OF RIGHTEOUSNESS.
NO THREATS OF VENGEANCE.
ONLY *FEAR*... AND THE *LIGHT* I WIELD WHILE CONTROLLING IT.

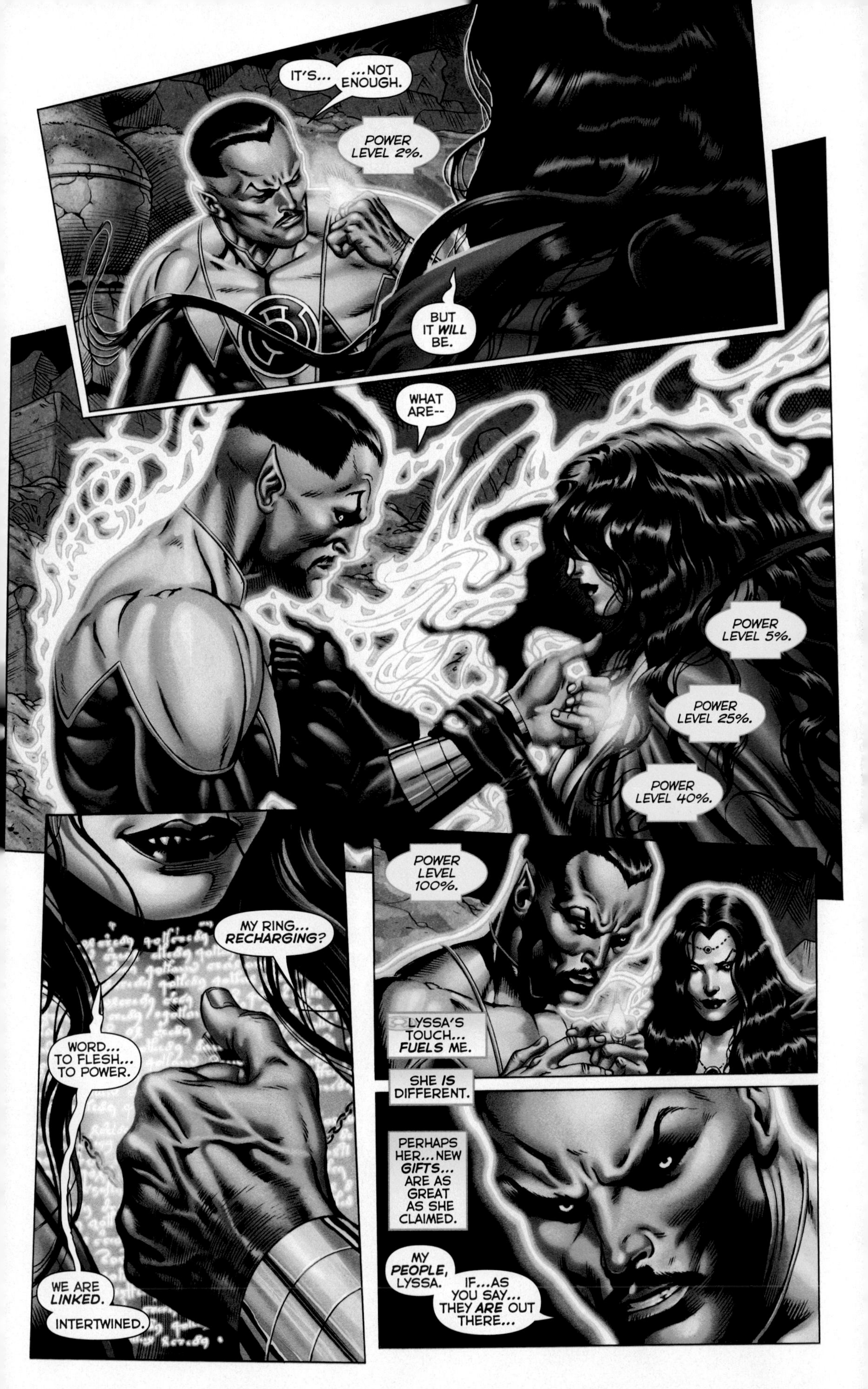
IT'S...
...NOT ENOUGH.
POWER LEVEL 2%.
BUT IT WILL BE.
WHAT ARE--
POWER LEVEL 5%.
POWER LEVEL 25%.
POWER LEVEL 40%.
MY RING... RECHARGING?
WORD... TO FLESH... TO POWER.
WE ARE LINKED.
INTERTWINED.
POWER LEVEL 100%.
LYSSA'S TOUCH... FUELS ME.
SHE IS DIFFERENT.
PERHAPS HER... NEW GIFTS... ARE AS GREAT AS SHE CLAIMED.
MY PEOPLE, LYSSA.
IF... AS YOU SAY... THEY ARE OUT THERE...

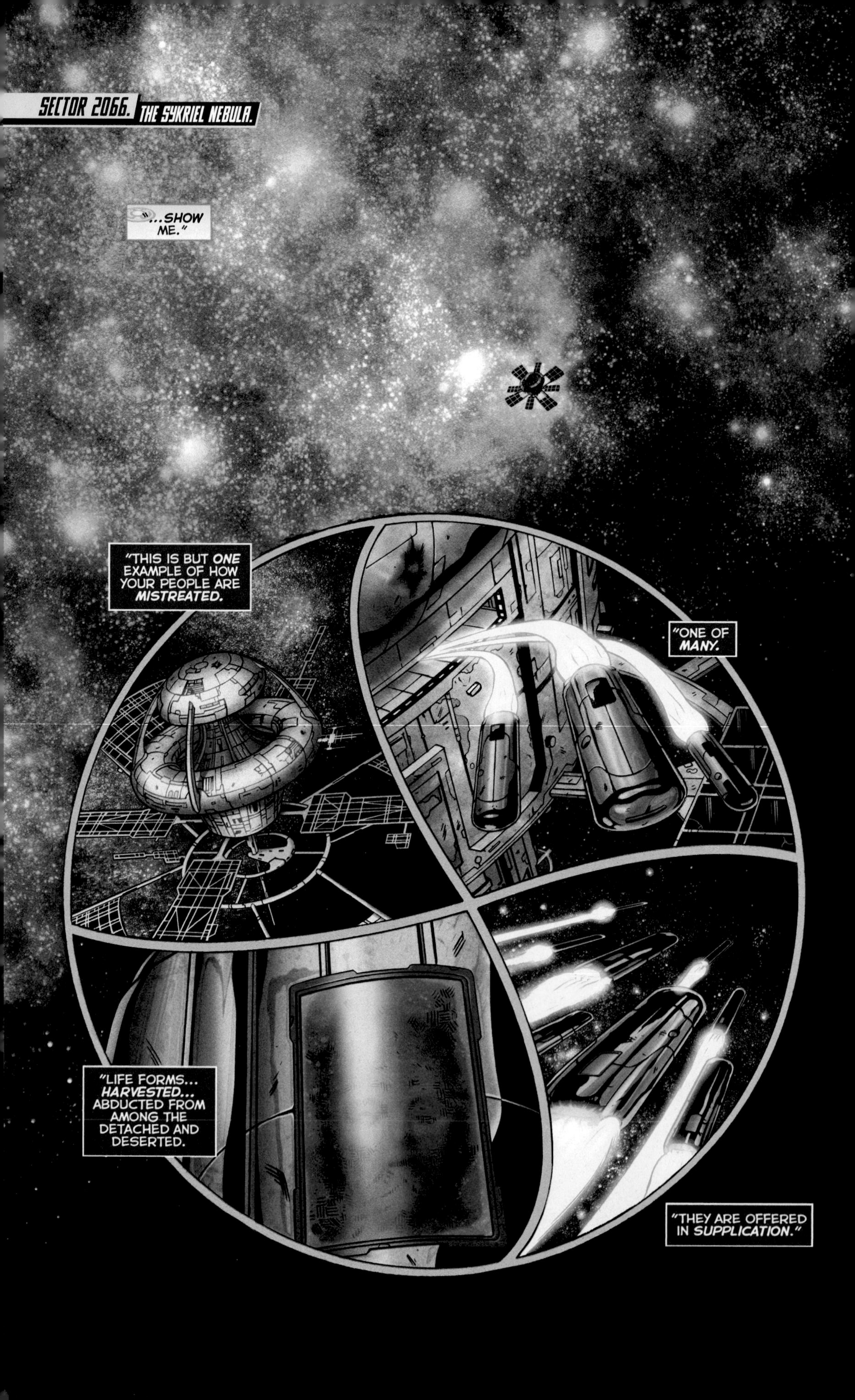
SECTOR 2066. THE SYKRIEL NEBULA.
"...SHOW ME."
"THIS IS BUT ONE EXAMPLE OF HOW YOUR PEOPLE ARE MISTREATED.
"ONE OF MANY.
"LIFE FORMS... HARVESTED... ABDUCTED FROM AMONG THE DETACHED AND DESERTED.
"THEY ARE OFFERED IN SUPPLICATION."

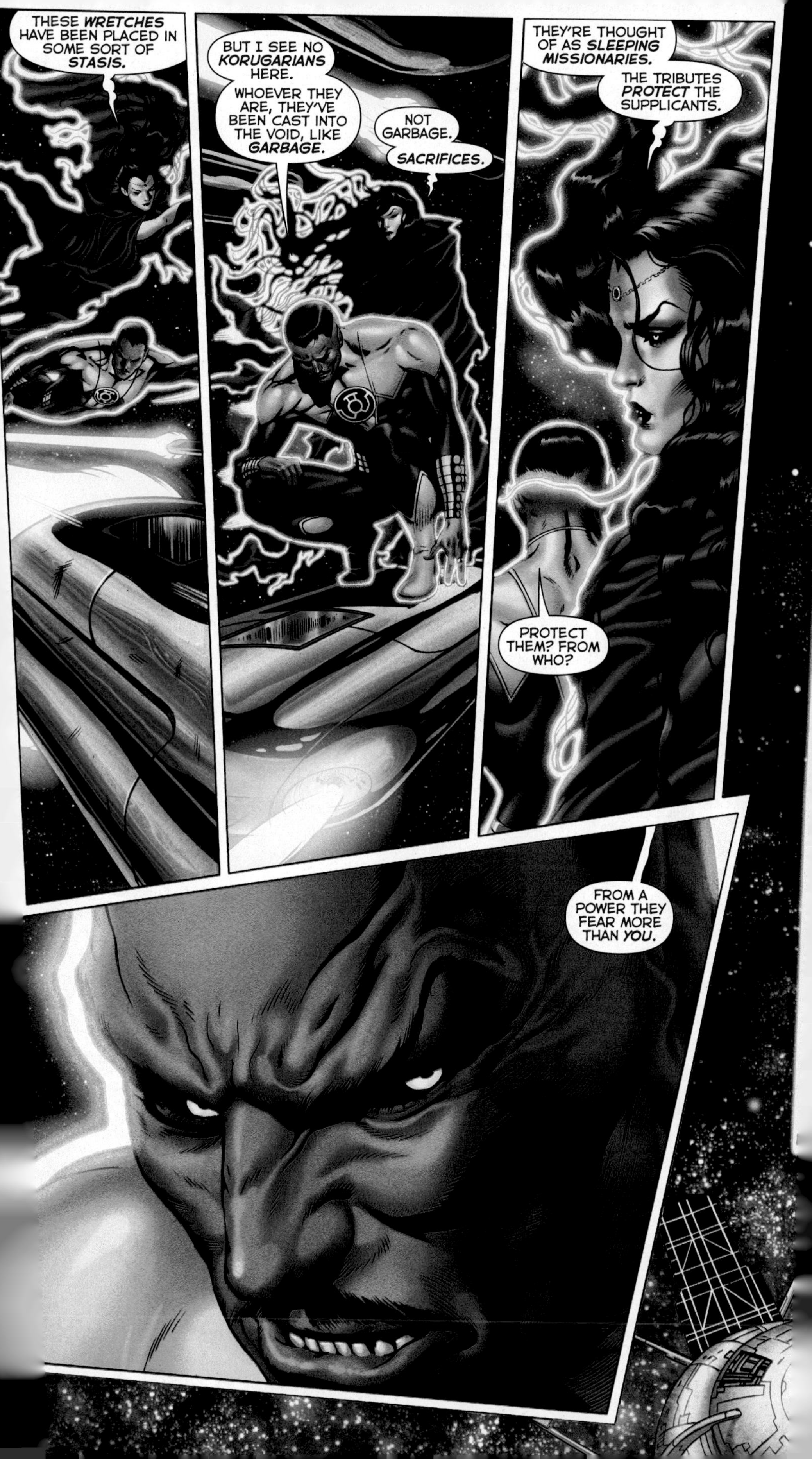
THESE *WRETCHES* HAVE BEEN PLACED IN SOME SORT OF *STASIS.*
BUT I SEE NO *KORUGARIANS* HERE.
WHOEVER THEY ARE, THEY'VE BEEN CAST INTO THE VOID, LIKE *GARBAGE.*
NOT GARBAGE.
SACRIFICES.
THEY'RE THOUGHT OF AS *SLEEPING MISSIONARIES.*
THE TRIBUTES *PROTECT* THE SUPPLICANTS.
PROTECT THEM? FROM WHO?
FROM A POWER THEY FEAR MORE THAN *YOU.*

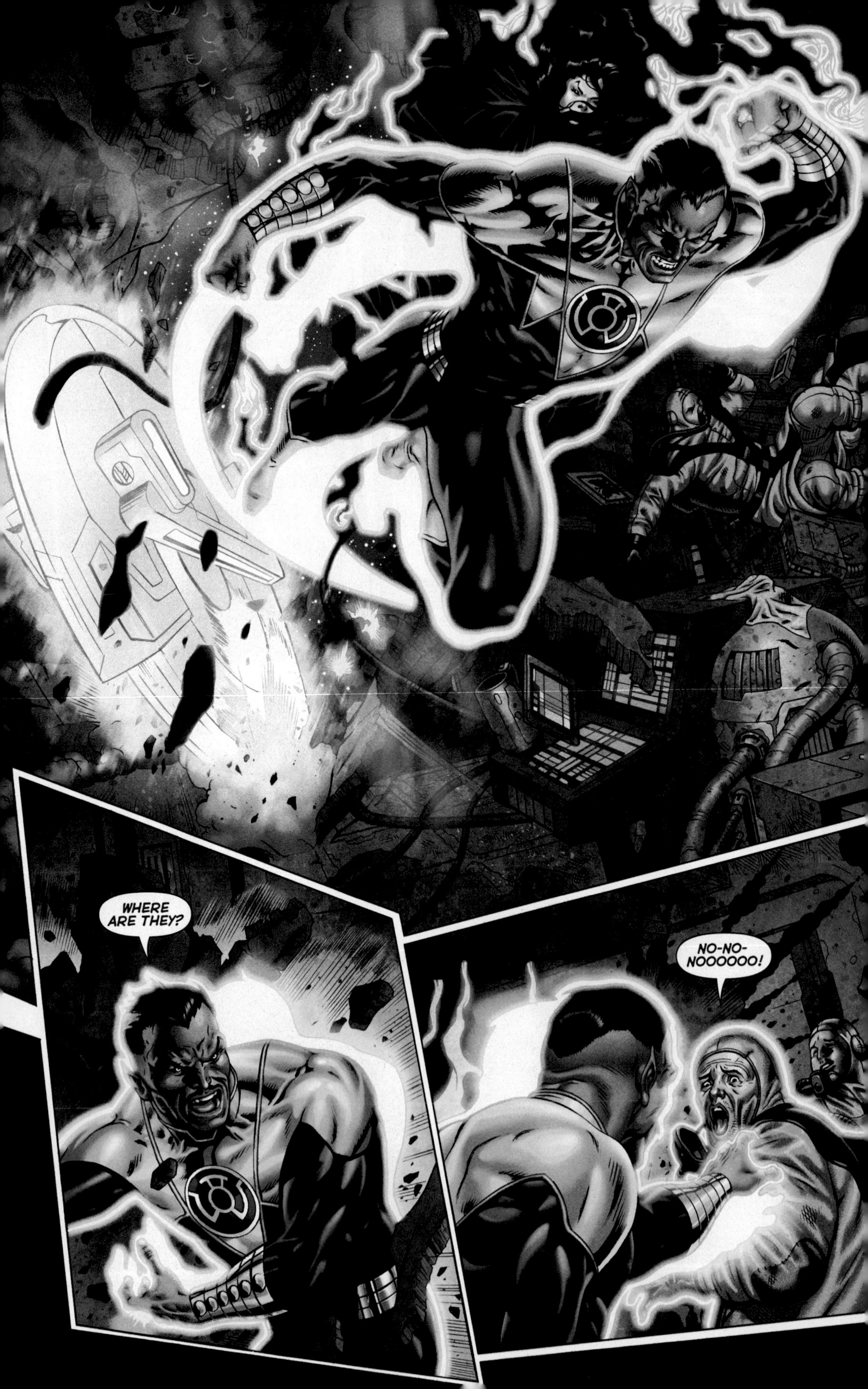
WHERE ARE THEY?
NO-NO-NOOOOOO!

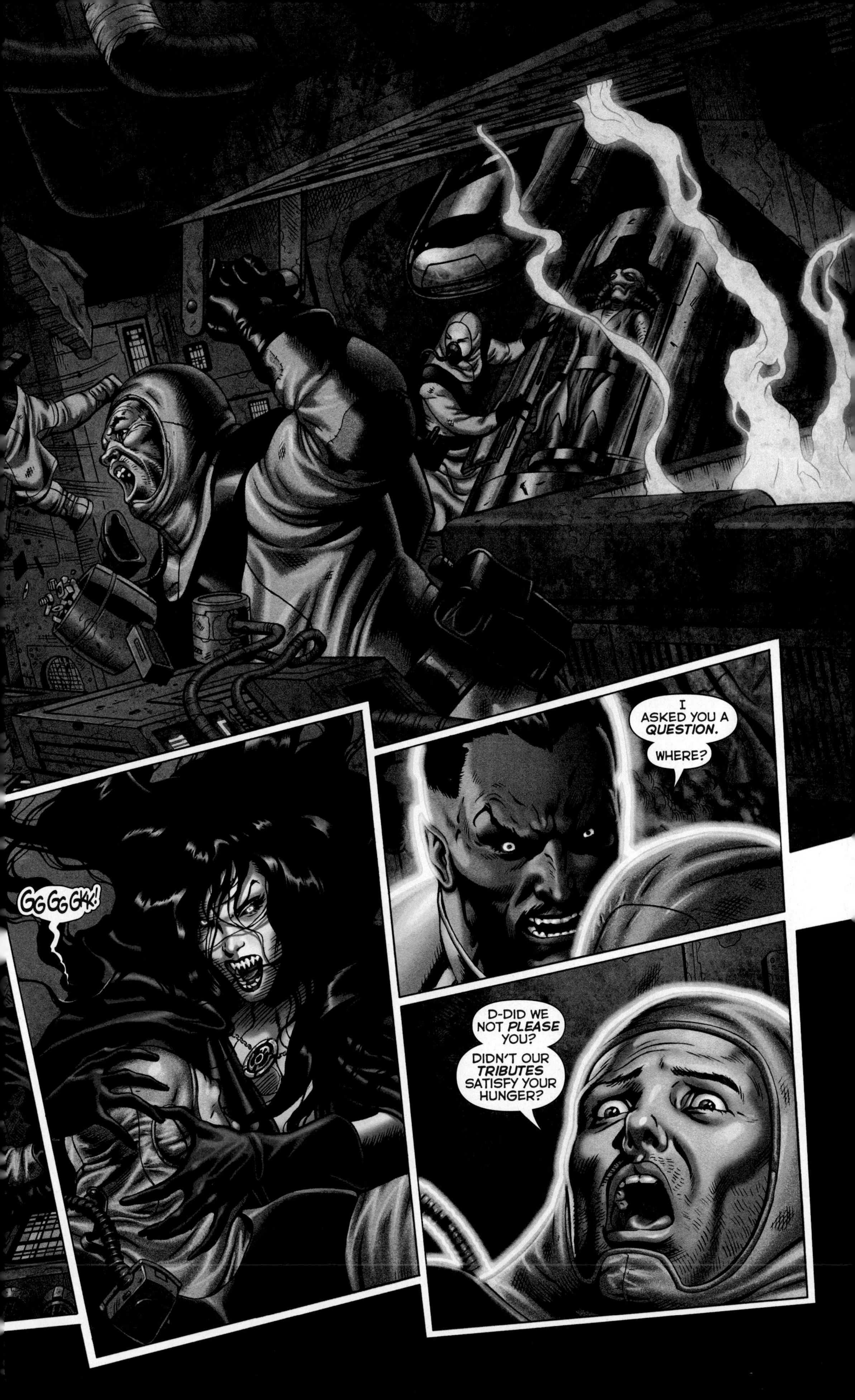
I ASKED YOU A QUESTION.
WHERE?
GGGGKK!
D-DID WE NOT PLEASE YOU?
DIDN'T OUR TRIBUTES SATISFY YOUR HUNGER?

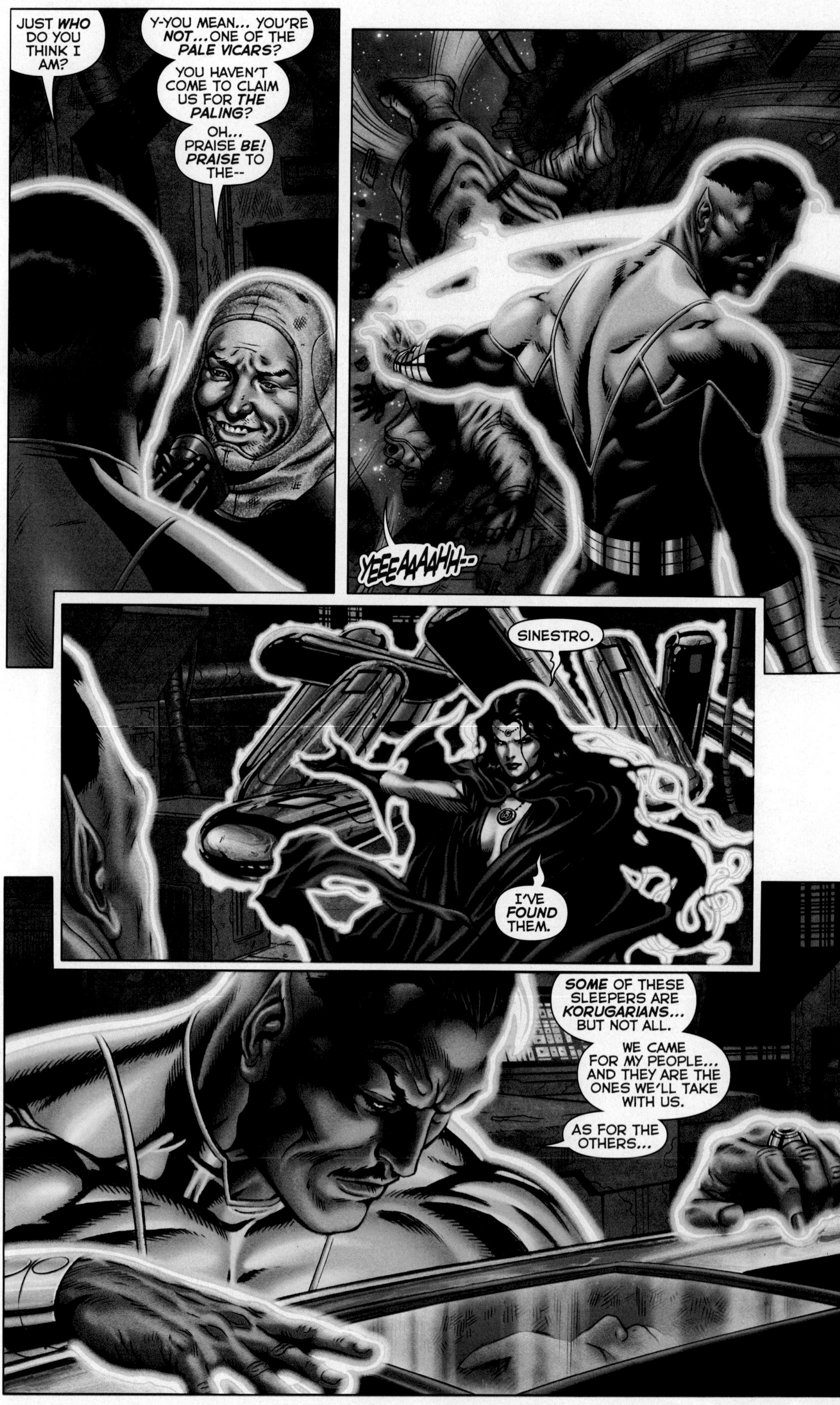
JUST WHO DO YOU THINK I AM?
Y-YOU MEAN... YOU'RE NOT...ONE OF THE PALE VICARS?
YOU HAVEN'T COME TO CLAIM US FOR THE PALING?
OH... PRAISE BE! PRAISE TO THE--
YEEEAAAAHH--
SINESTRO.
I'VE FOUND THEM.
SOME OF THESE SLEEPERS ARE KORUGARIANS... BUT NOT ALL.
WE CAME FOR MY PEOPLE... AND THEY ARE THE ONES WE'LL TAKE WITH US.
AS FOR THE OTHERS...

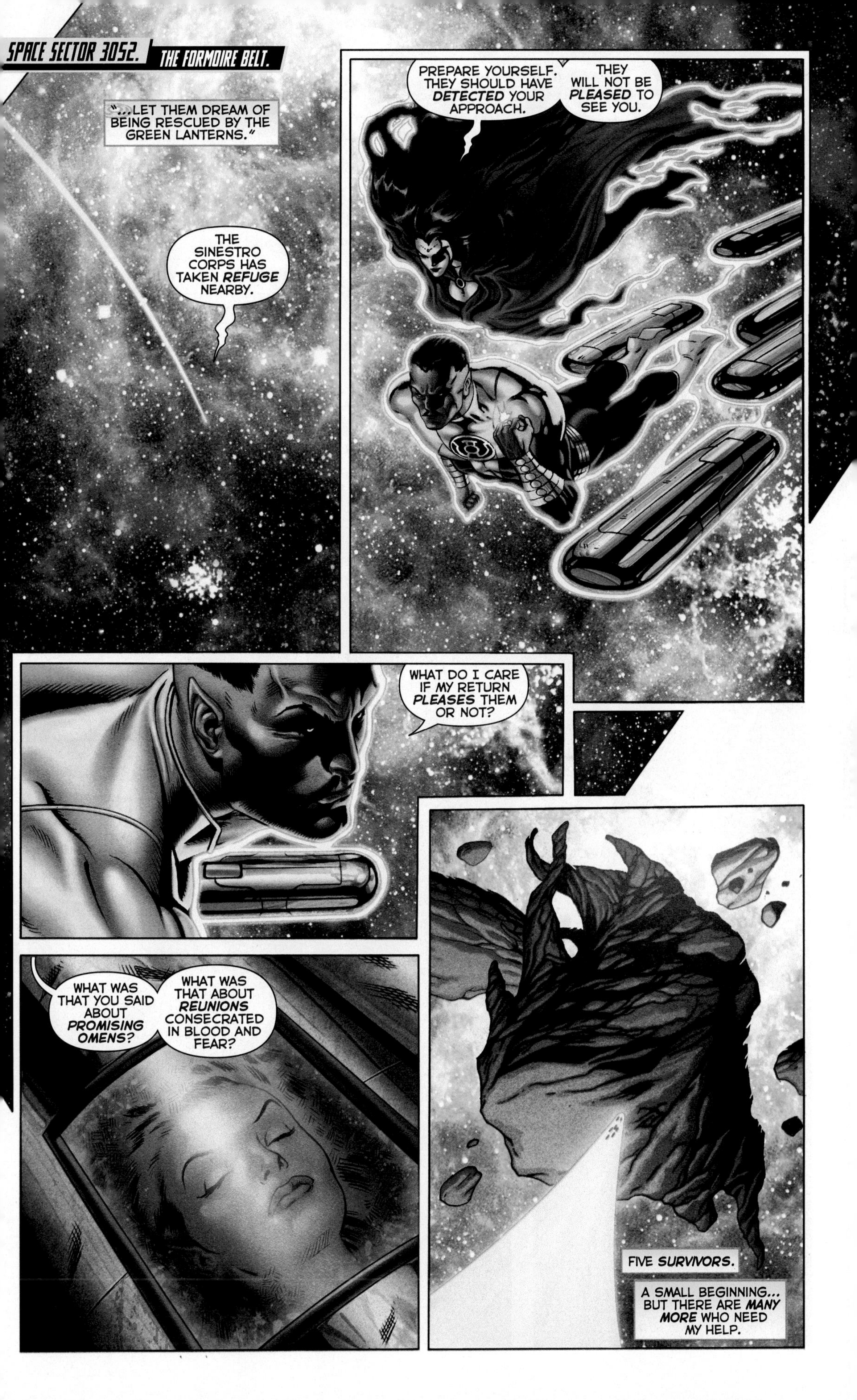
SPACE SECTOR 3052.
THE FORMOIRE BELT.
"...LET THEM DREAM OF BEING RESCUED BY THE GREEN LANTERNS."
THE SINESTRO CORPS HAS TAKEN REFUGE NEARBY.
PREPARE YOURSELF. THEY SHOULD HAVE DETECTED YOUR APPROACH.
THEY WILL NOT BE PLEASED TO SEE YOU.
WHAT DO I CARE IF MY RETURN PLEASES THEM OR NOT?
WHAT WAS THAT YOU SAID ABOUT PROMISING OMENS?
WHAT WAS THAT ABOUT REUNIONS CONSECRATED IN BLOOD AND FEAR?
FIVE SURVIVORS.
A SMALL BEGINNING... BUT THERE ARE MANY MORE WHO NEED MY HELP.

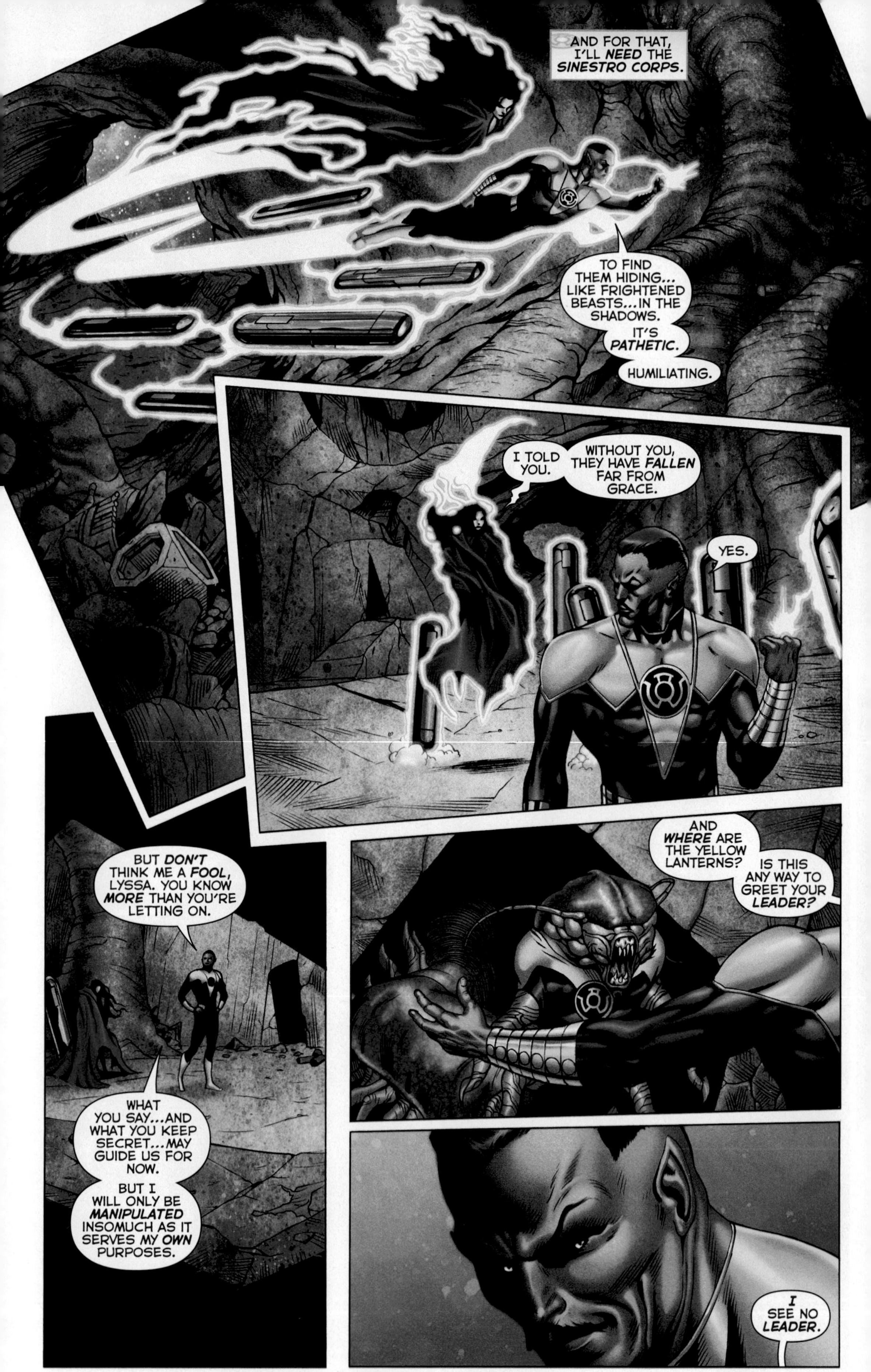
AND FOR THAT, I'LL NEED THE SINESTRO CORPS.
TO FIND THEM HIDING... LIKE FRIGHTENED BEASTS...IN THE SHADOWS.
IT'S PATHETIC.
HUMILIATING.
I TOLD YOU.
WITHOUT YOU, THEY HAVE FALLEN FAR FROM GRACE.
YES.
BUT DON'T THINK ME A FOOL, LYSSA. YOU KNOW MORE THAN YOU'RE LETTING ON.
WHAT YOU SAY...AND WHAT YOU KEEP SECRET...MAY GUIDE US FOR NOW.
BUT I WILL ONLY BE MANIPULATED INSOMUCH AS IT SERVES MY OWN PURPOSES.
AND WHERE ARE THE YELLOW LANTERNS?
IS THIS ANY WAY TO GREET YOUR LEADER?
I SEE NO LEADER.

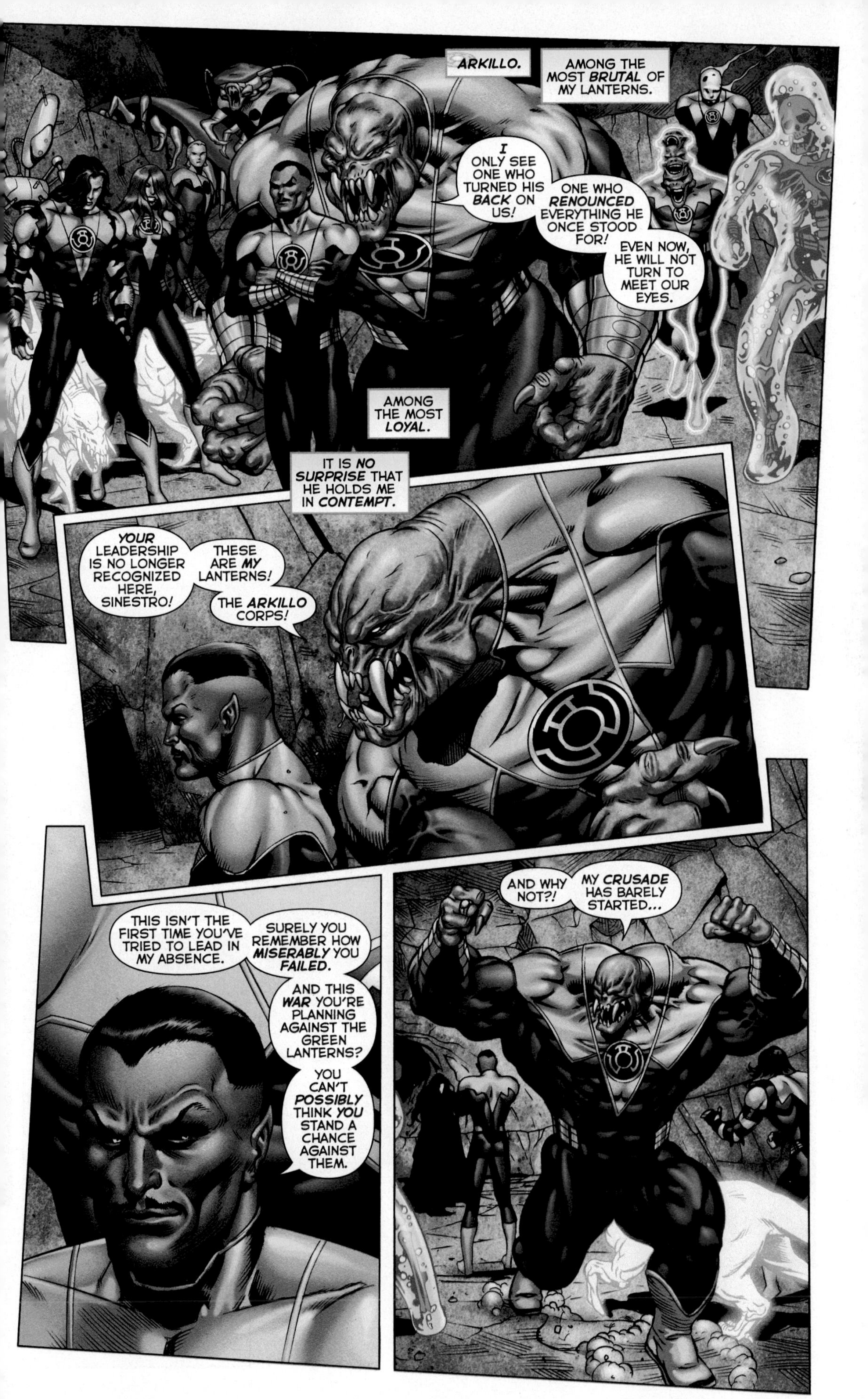
ARKILLO.
AMONG THE MOST BRUTAL OF MY LANTERNS.
I ONLY SEE ONE WHO TURNED HIS BACK ON US!
ONE WHO RENOUNCED EVERYTHING HE ONCE STOOD FOR!
EVEN NOW, HE WILL NOT TURN TO MEET OUR EYES.
AMONG THE MOST LOYAL.
IT IS NO SURPRISE THAT HE HOLDS ME IN CONTEMPT.
YOUR LEADERSHIP IS NO LONGER RECOGNIZED HERE, SINESTRO!
THESE ARE MY LANTERNS!
THE ARKILLO CORPS!
THIS ISN'T THE FIRST TIME YOU'VE TRIED TO LEAD IN MY ABSENCE.
SURELY YOU REMEMBER HOW MISERABLY YOU FAILED.
AND THIS WAR YOU'RE PLANNING AGAINST THE GREEN LANTERNS?
YOU CAN'T POSSIBLY THINK YOU STAND A CHANCE AGAINST THEM.
AND WHY NOT?!
MY CRUSADE HAS BARELY STARTED...

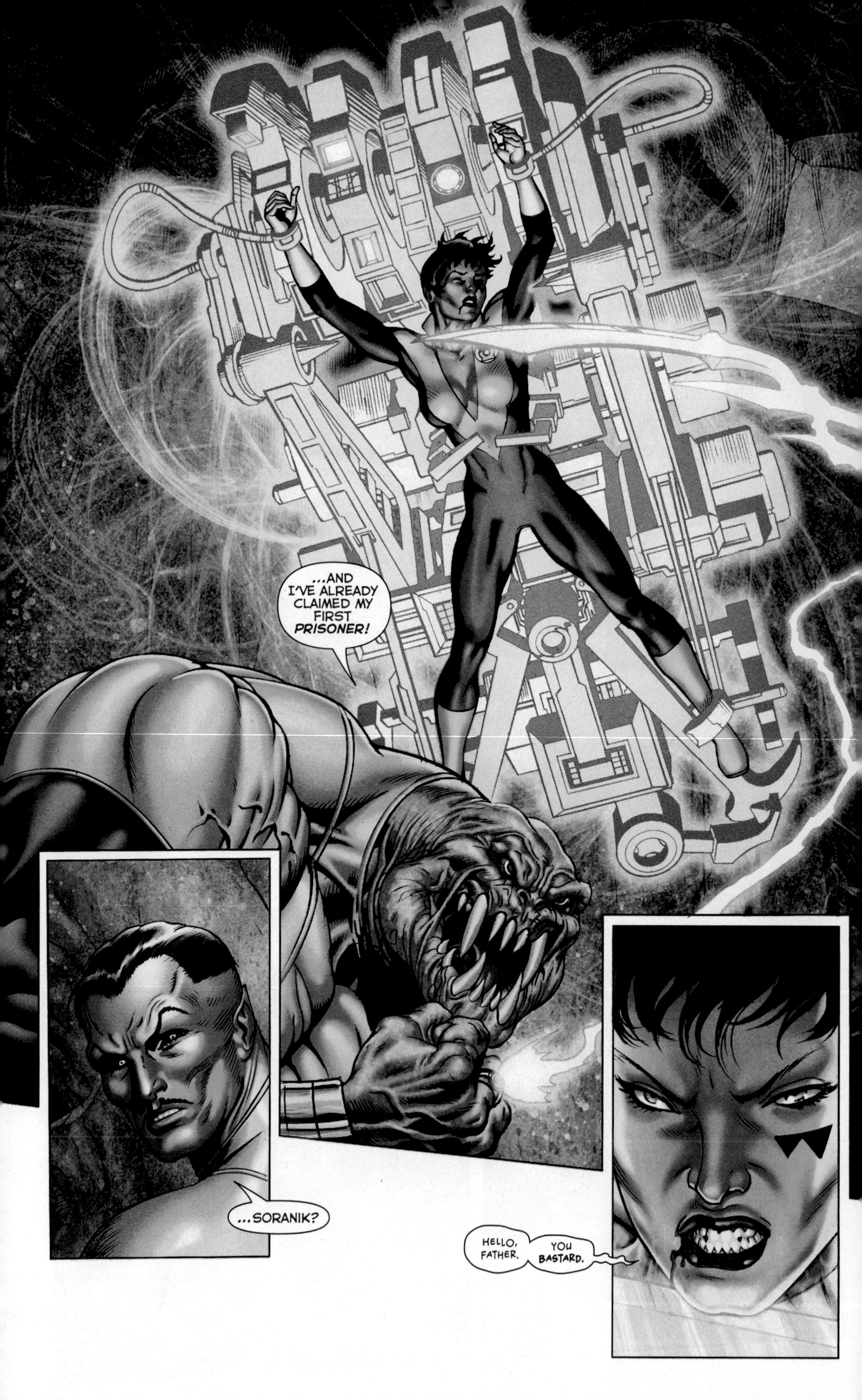
...AND I'VE ALREADY CLAIMED MY FIRST PRISONER!
...SORANIK?
HELLO, FATHER.
YOU BASTARD.

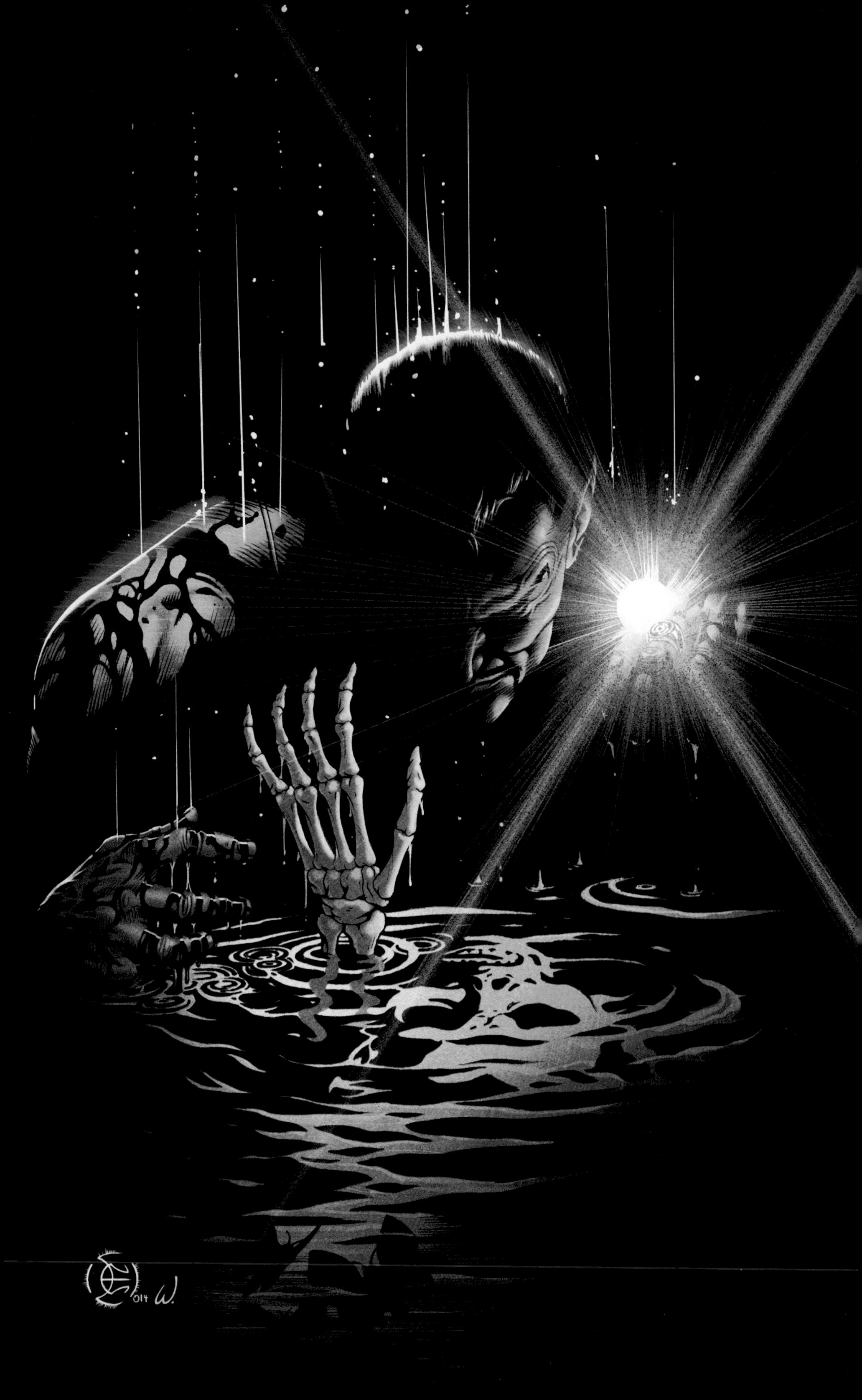

NECROPOLIS

CULLEN BUNN writer DALE EAGLESHAM artist JASON WRIGHT colorist TAYLOR ESPOSITO letterer
cover art by DALE EAGLESHAM & JASON WRIGHT

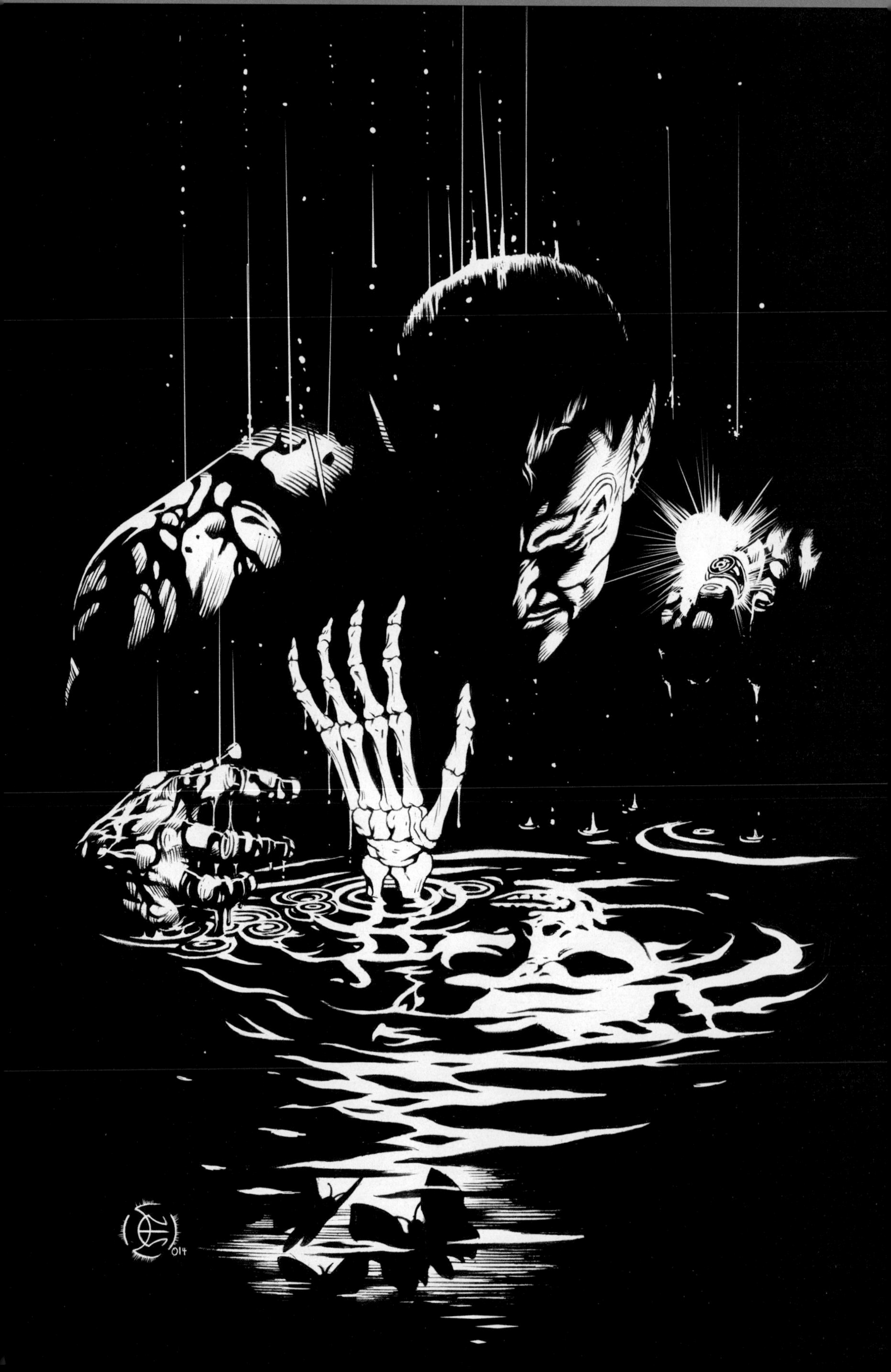

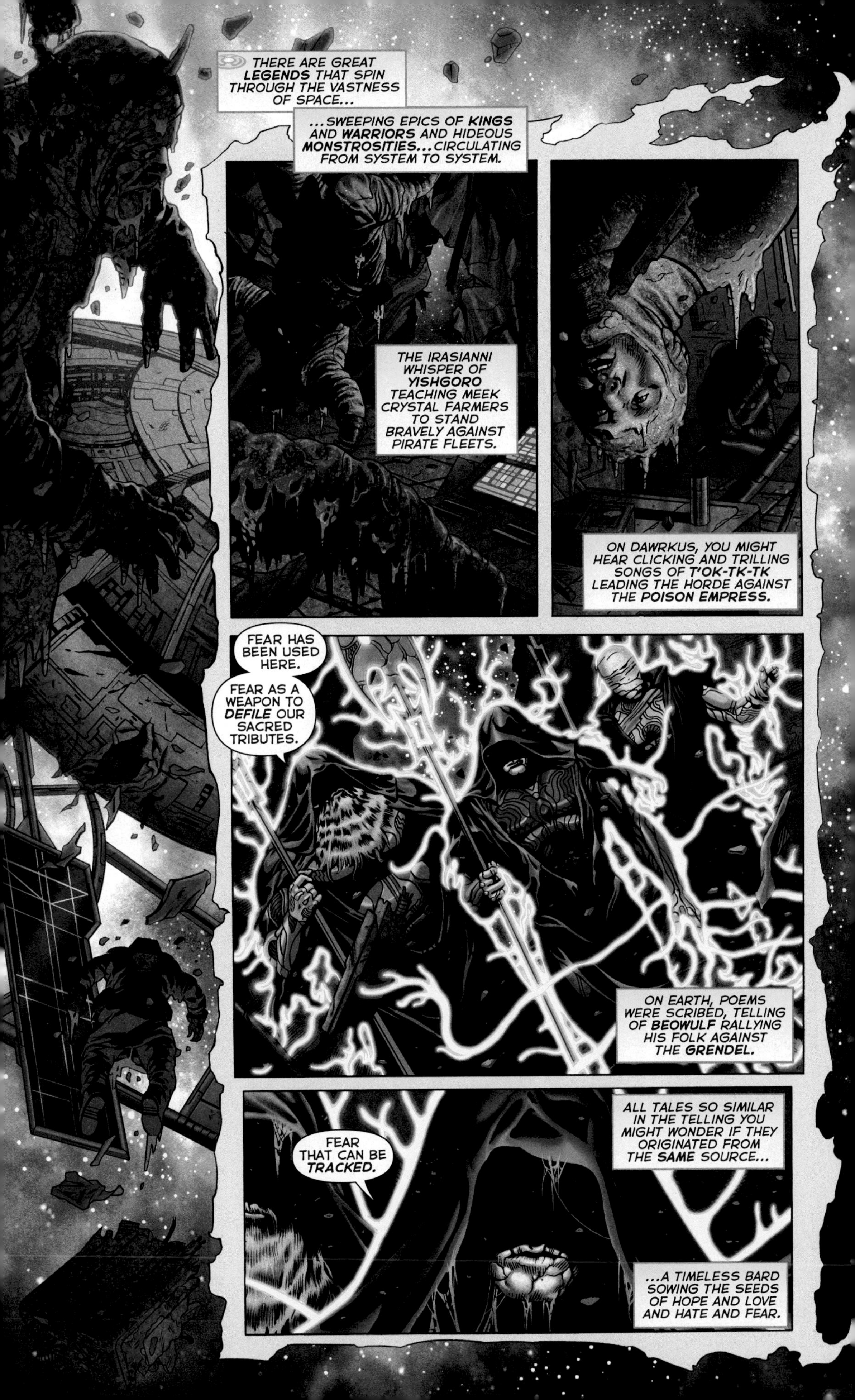
THERE ARE GREAT LEGENDS THAT SPIN THROUGH THE VASTNESS OF SPACE...
...SWEEPING EPICS OF KINGS AND WARRIORS AND HIDEOUS MONSTROSITIES...CIRCULATING FROM SYSTEM TO SYSTEM.
THE IRASIANNI WHISPER OF YISHGORO TEACHING MEEK CRYSTAL FARMERS TO STAND BRAVELY AGAINST PIRATE FLEETS.
ON DAWRKUS, YOU MIGHT HEAR CLICKING AND TRILLING SONGS OF T'OK-TK-TK LEADING THE HORDE AGAINST THE POISON EMPRESS.
FEAR HAS BEEN USED HERE.
FEAR AS A WEAPON TO DEFILE OUR SACRED TRIBUTES.
ON EARTH, POEMS WERE SCRIBED, TELLING OF BEOWULF RALLYING HIS FOLK AGAINST THE GRENDEL.
FEAR THAT CAN BE TRACKED.
ALL TALES SO SIMILAR IN THE TELLING YOU MIGHT WONDER IF THEY ORIGINATED FROM THE SAME SOURCE...
...A TIMELESS BARD SOWING THE SEEDS OF HOPE AND LOVE AND HATE AND FEAR.

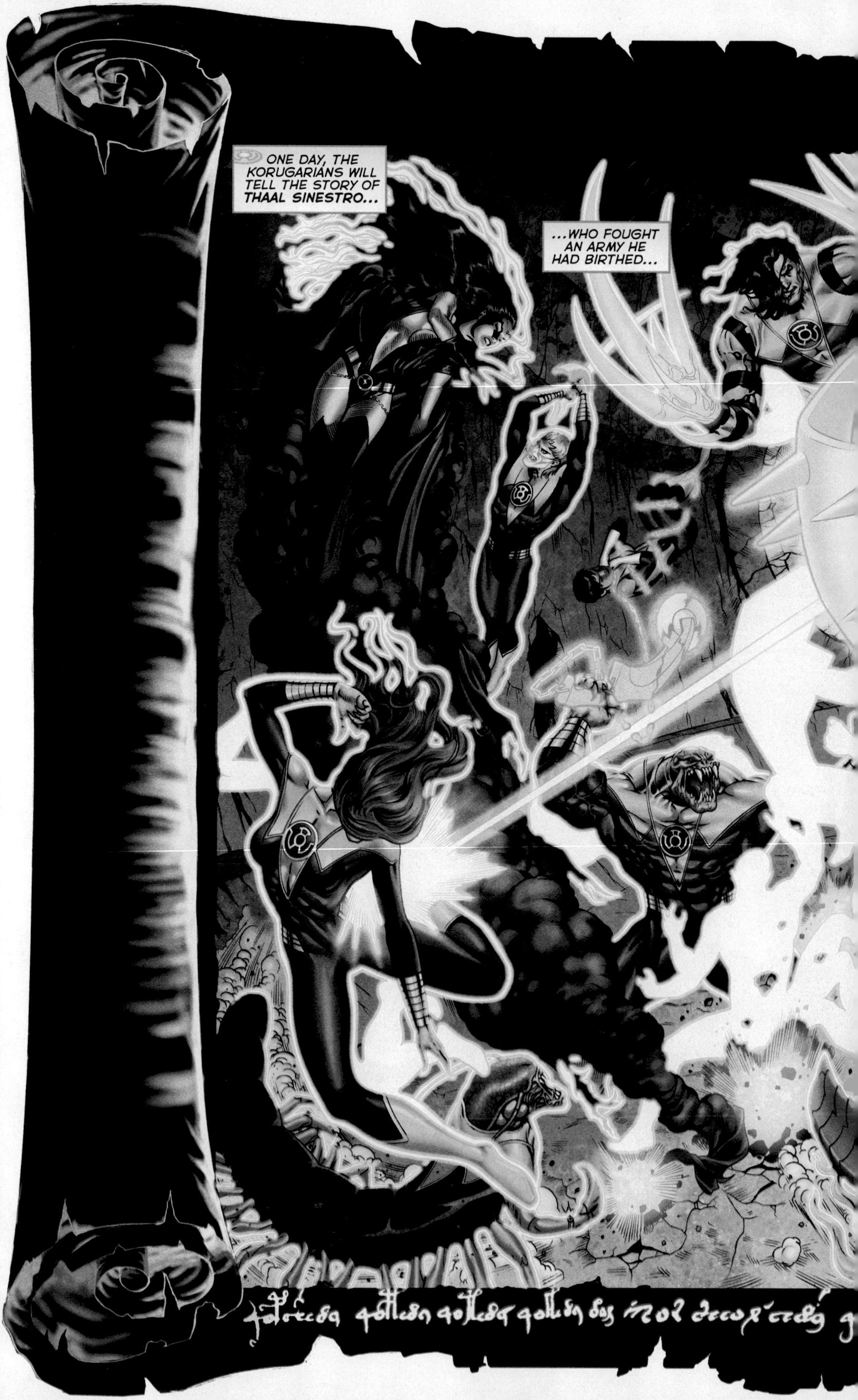
ONE DAY, THE KORUGARIANS WILL TELL THE STORY OF THAAL SINESTRO...
...WHO FOUGHT AN ARMY HE HAD BIRTHED...

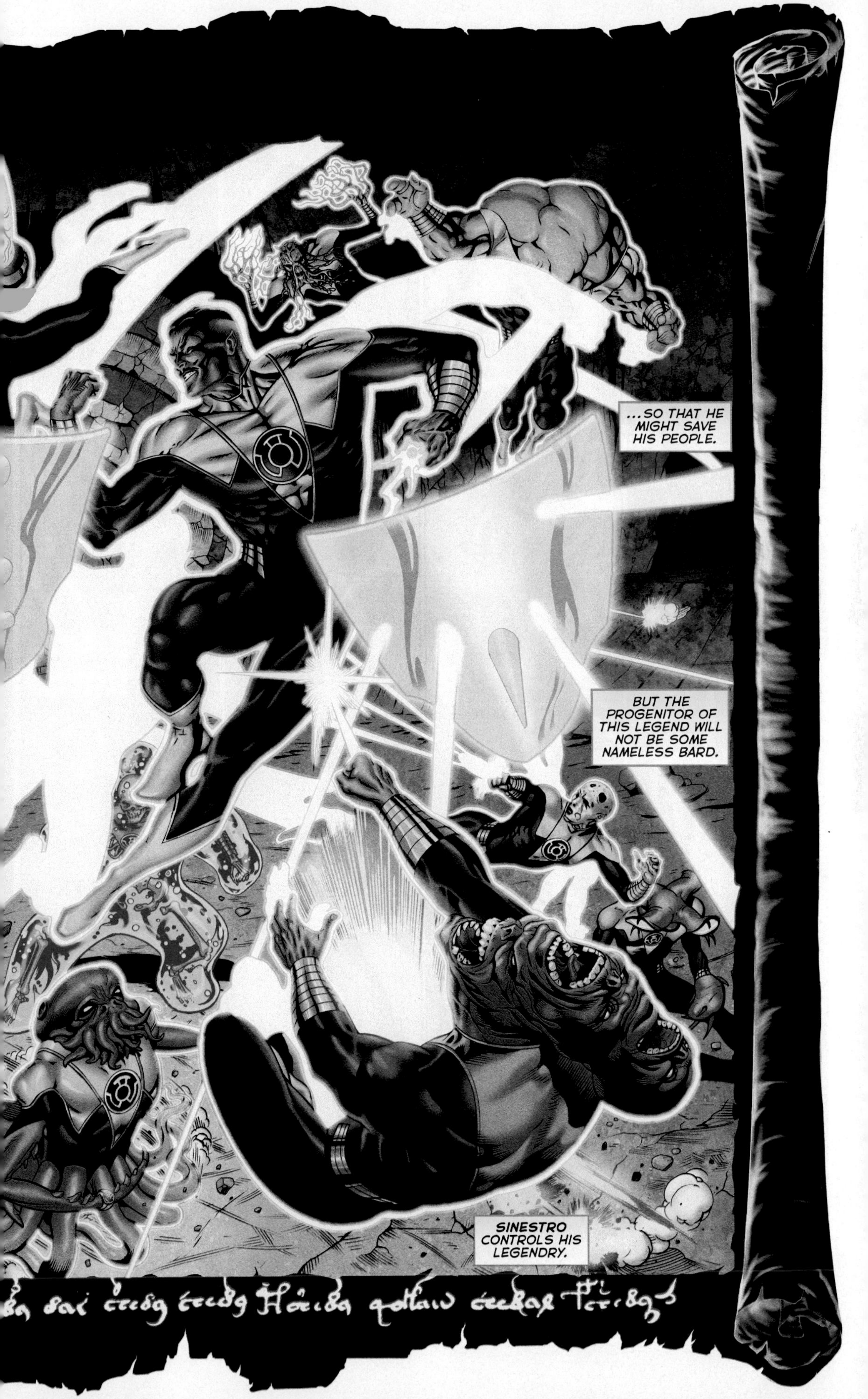
...SO THAT HE MIGHT SAVE HIS PEOPLE.
BUT THE PROGENITOR OF THIS LEGEND WILL NOT BE SOME NAMELESS BARD.
SINESTRO CONTROLS HIS LEGENDRY.

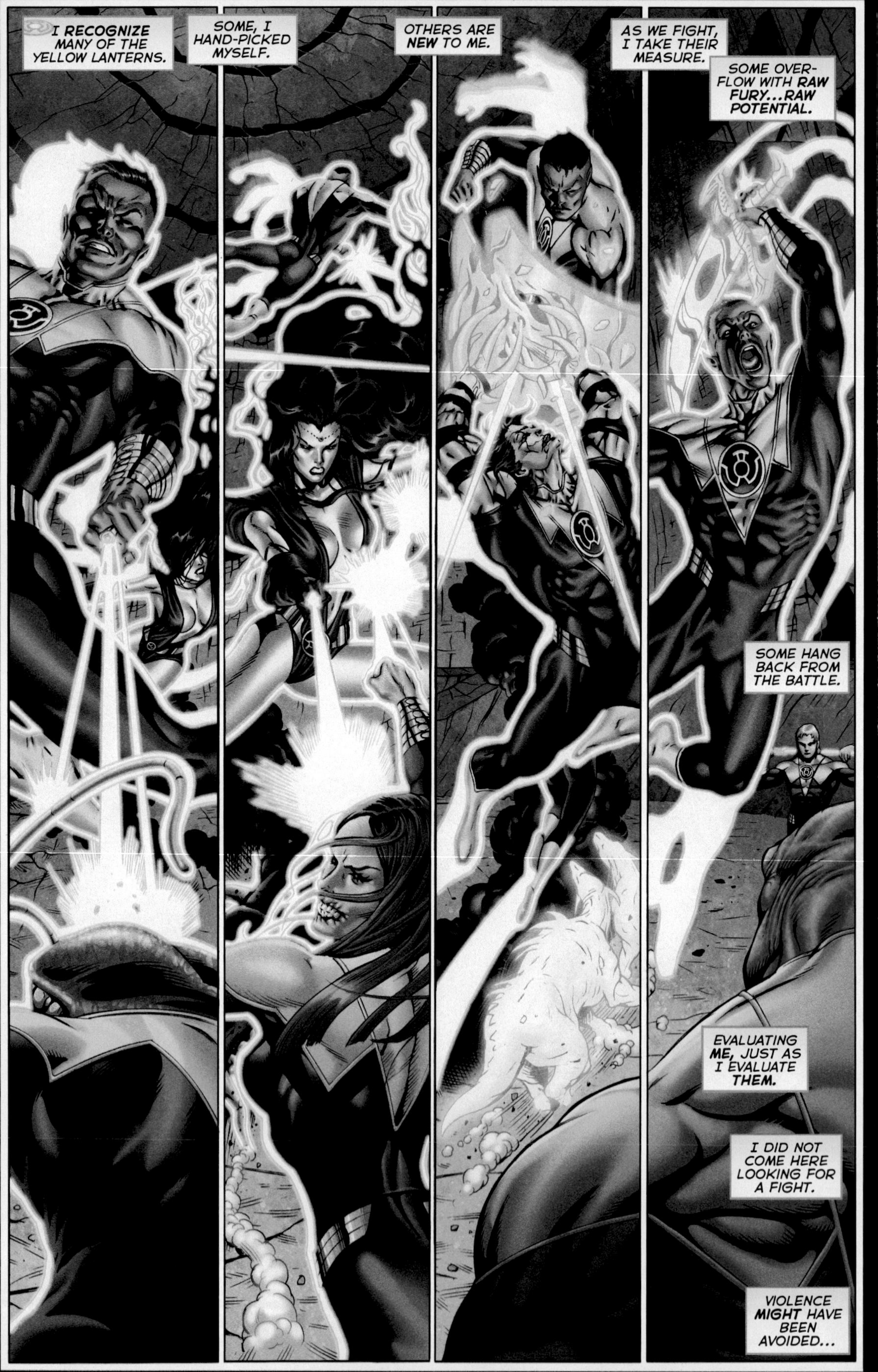
I RECOGNIZE MANY OF THE YELLOW LANTERNS.
SOME, I HAND-PICKED MYSELF.
OTHERS ARE NEW TO ME.
AS WE FIGHT, I TAKE THEIR MEASURE.
SOME OVER-FLOW WITH RAW FURY...RAW POTENTIAL.
SOME HANG BACK FROM THE BATTLE.
EVALUATING ME, JUST AS I EVALUATE THEM.
I DID NOT COME HERE LOOKING FOR A FIGHT.
VIOLENCE MIGHT HAVE BEEN AVOIDED...

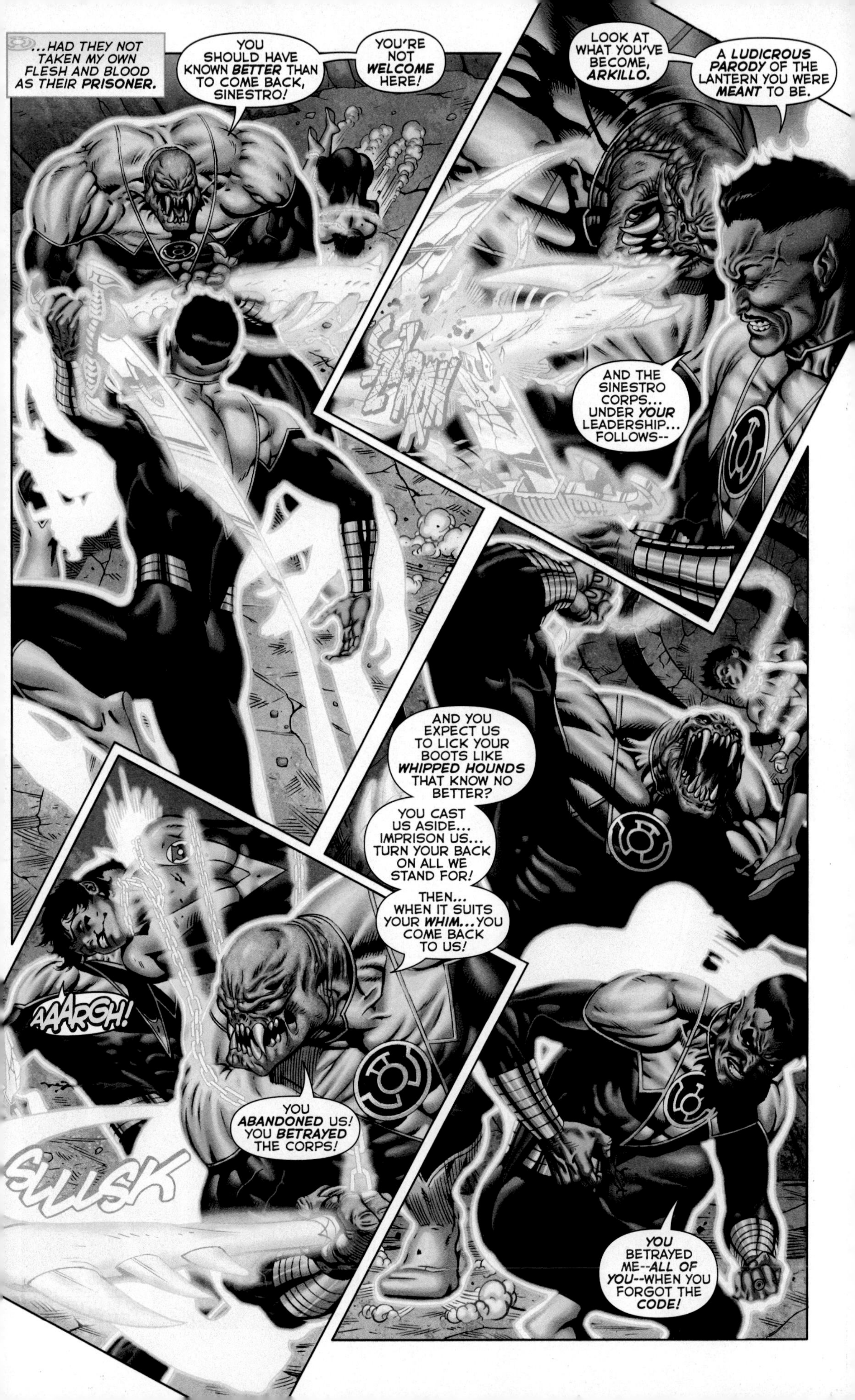

...HAD THEY NOT TAKEN MY OWN FLESH AND BLOOD AS THEIR PRISONER.
YOU SHOULD HAVE KNOWN BETTER THAN TO COME BACK, SINESTRO!
YOU'RE NOT WELCOME HERE!
LOOK AT WHAT YOU'VE BECOME, ARKILLO.
A LUDICROUS PARODY OF THE LANTERN YOU WERE MEANT TO BE.
AND THE SINESTRO CORPS... UNDER YOUR LEADERSHIP... FOLLOWS--
AND YOU EXPECT US TO LICK YOUR BOOTS LIKE WHIPPED HOUNDS THAT KNOW NO BETTER?
YOU CAST US ASIDE... IMPRISON US... TURN YOUR BACK ON ALL WE STAND FOR!
THEN... WHEN IT SUITS YOUR WHIM... YOU COME BACK TO US!
AAARGH!
YOU ABANDONED US! YOU BETRAYED THE CORPS!
SLLISK
YOU BETRAYED ME--ALL OF YOU--WHEN YOU FORGOT THE CODE!

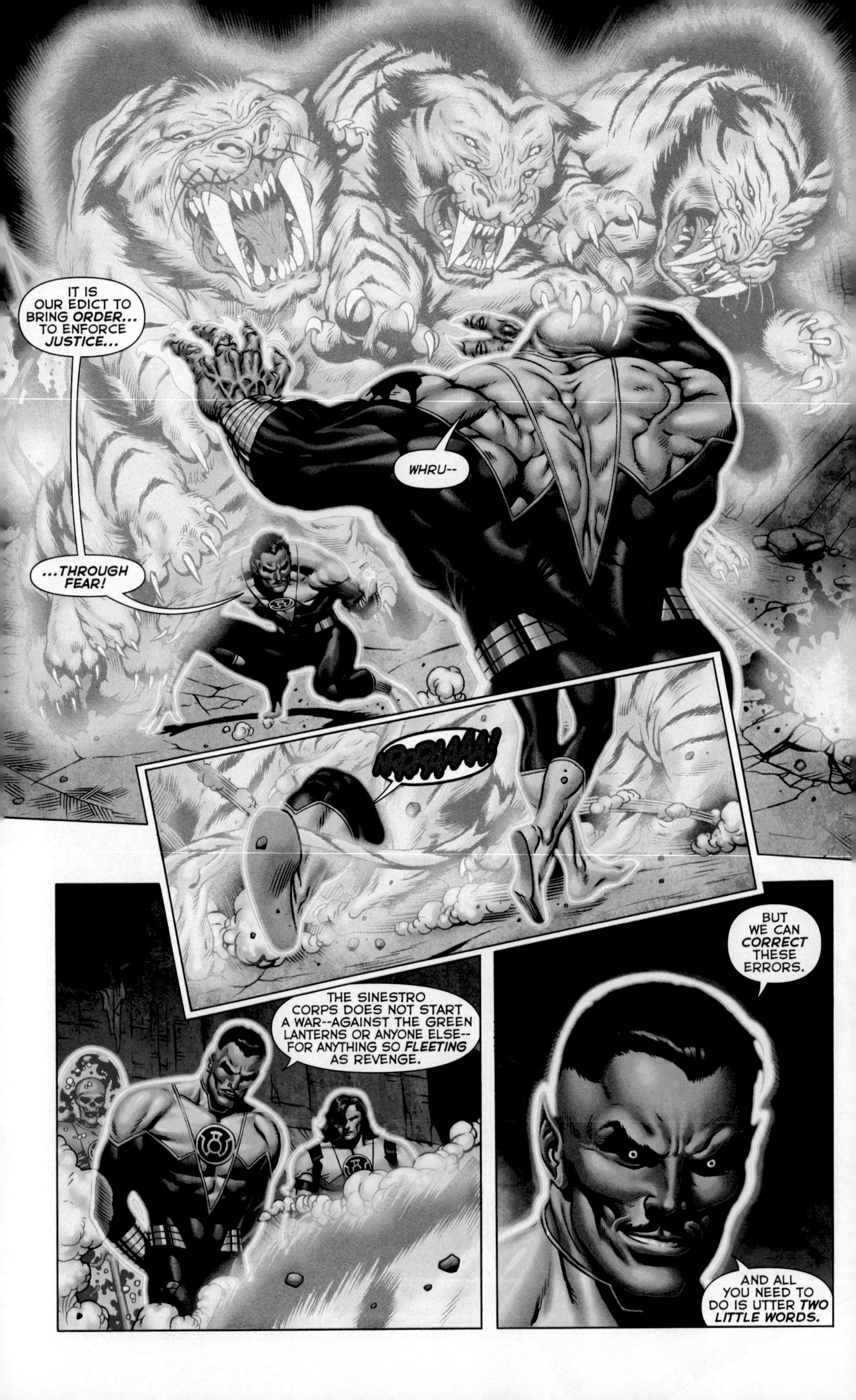
IT IS OUR EDICT TO BRING ORDER... TO ENFORCE JUSTICE...
...THROUGH FEAR!
WHRU--
NRGRAAAA!
THE SINESTRO CORPS DOES NOT START A WAR--AGAINST THE GREEN LANTERNS OR ANYONE ELSE--FOR ANYTHING SO FLEETING AS REVENGE.
BUT WE CAN CORRECT THESE ERRORS.
AND ALL YOU NEED TO DO IS UTTER TWO LITTLE WORDS.

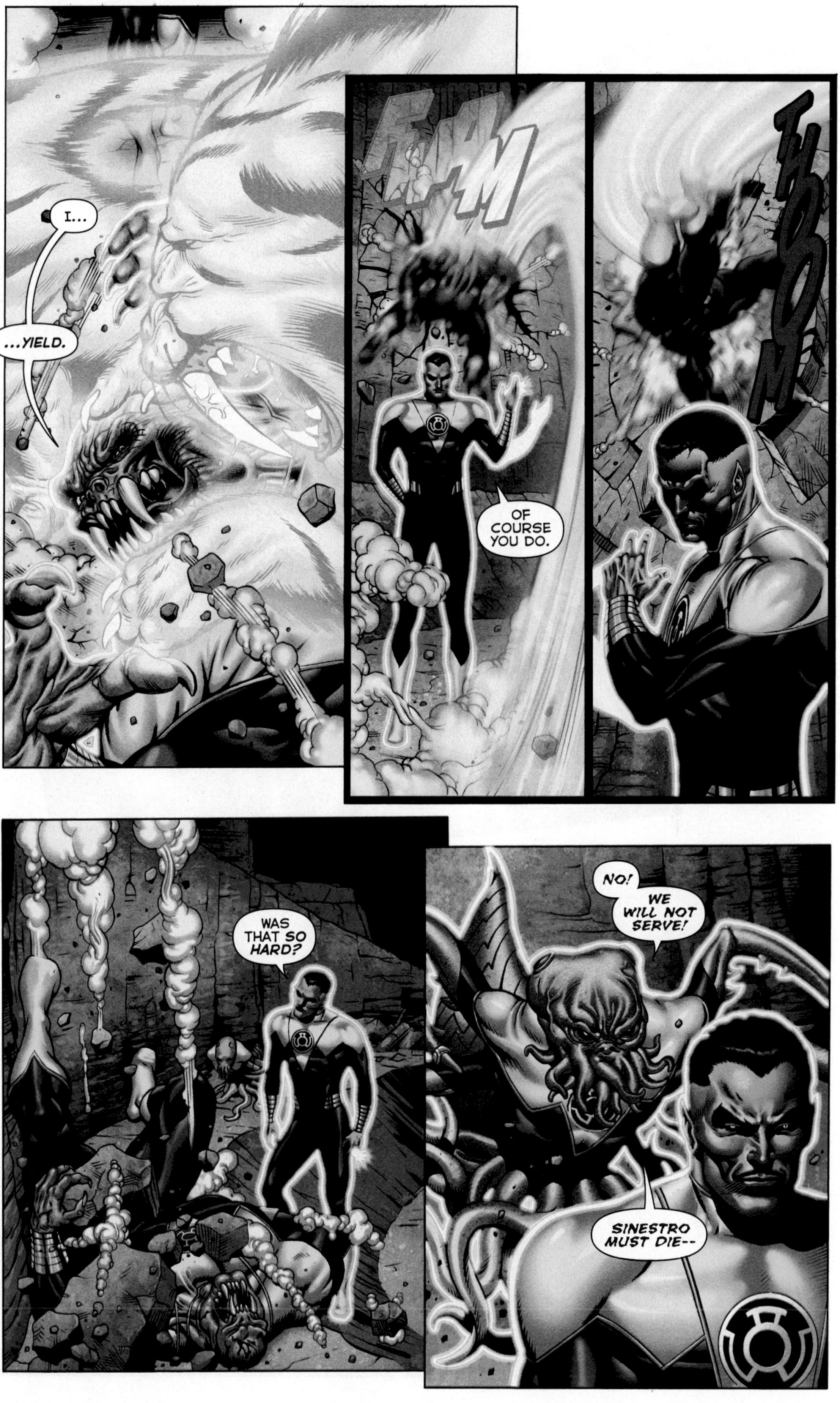
I...
...YIELD.
FLAM
OF COURSE YOU DO.
THOOM
WAS THAT SO HARD?
NO!
WE WILL NOT SERVE!
SINESTRO MUST DIE--

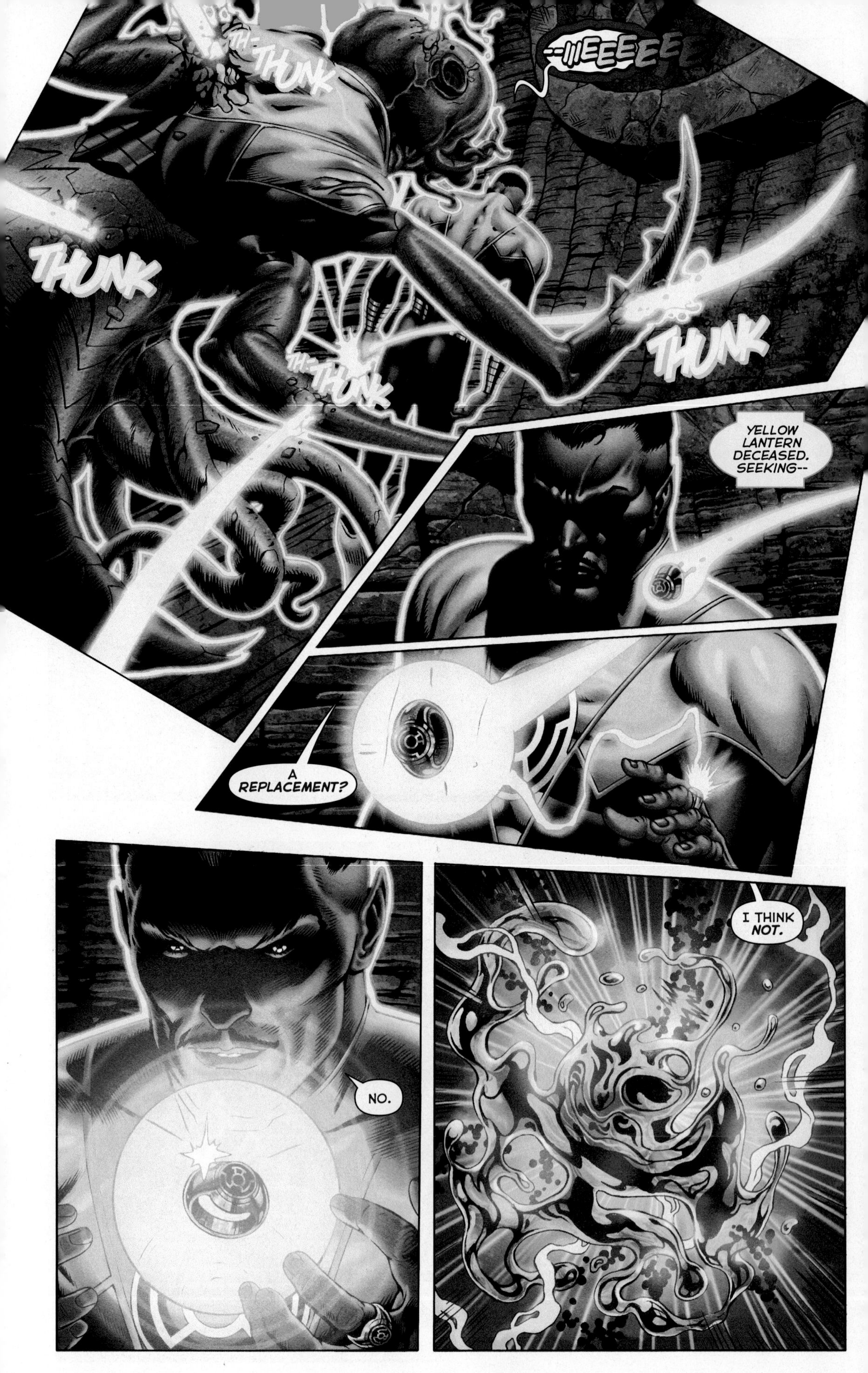
TH-THUNK
--IIIEEEEEE
THUNK
THUNK
TH-THUNK
YELLOW LANTERN DECEASED. SEEKING--
A REPLACEMENT?
NO.
I THINK NOT.

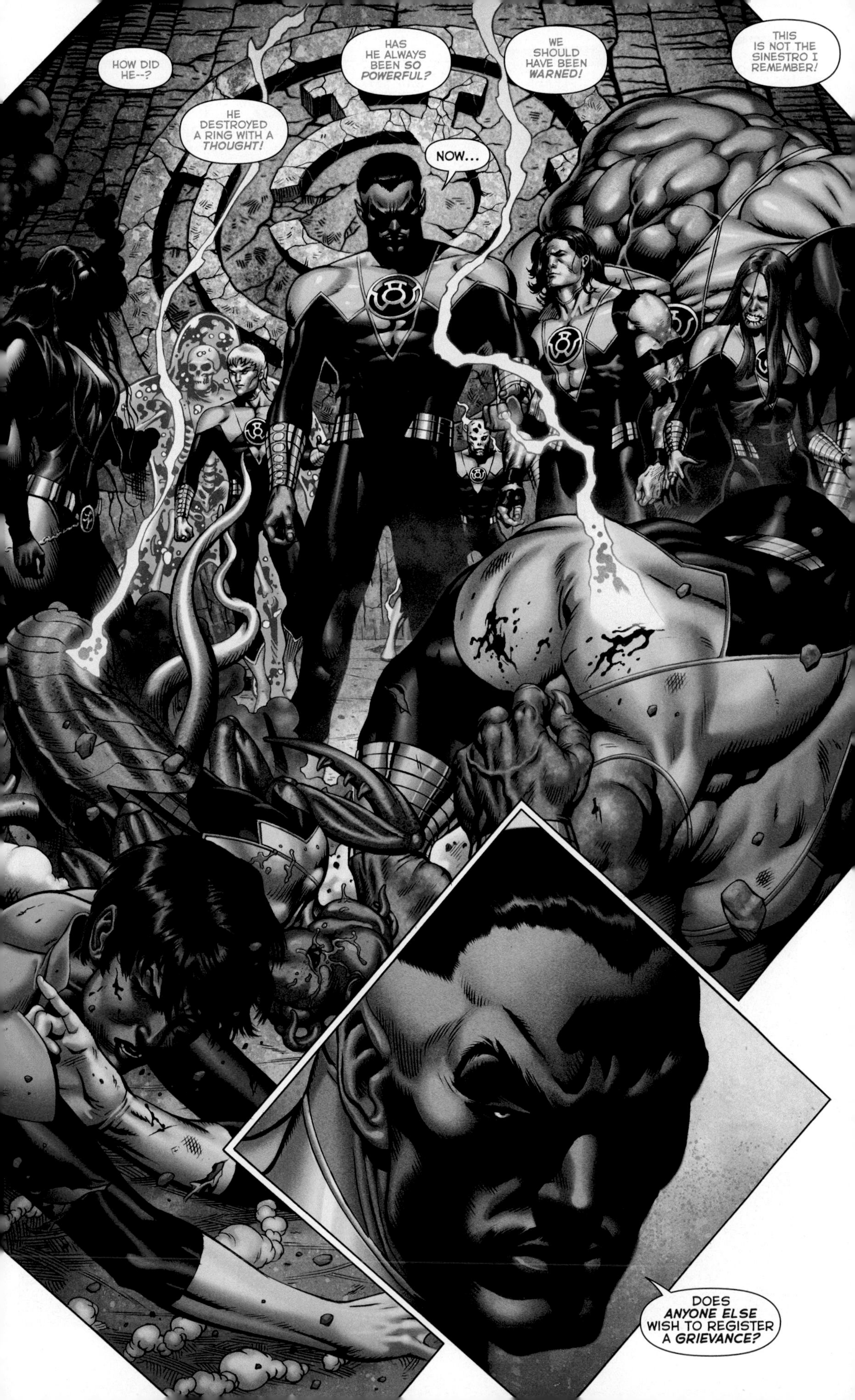
HOW DID HE--?
HE DESTROYED A RING WITH A *THOUGHT!*
HAS HE ALWAYS BEEN *SO POWERFUL?*
WE SHOULD HAVE BEEN *WARNED!*
THIS IS NOT THE SINESTRO I REMEMBER!
NOW...
DOES *ANYONE ELSE* WISH TO REGISTER A *GRIEVANCE?*

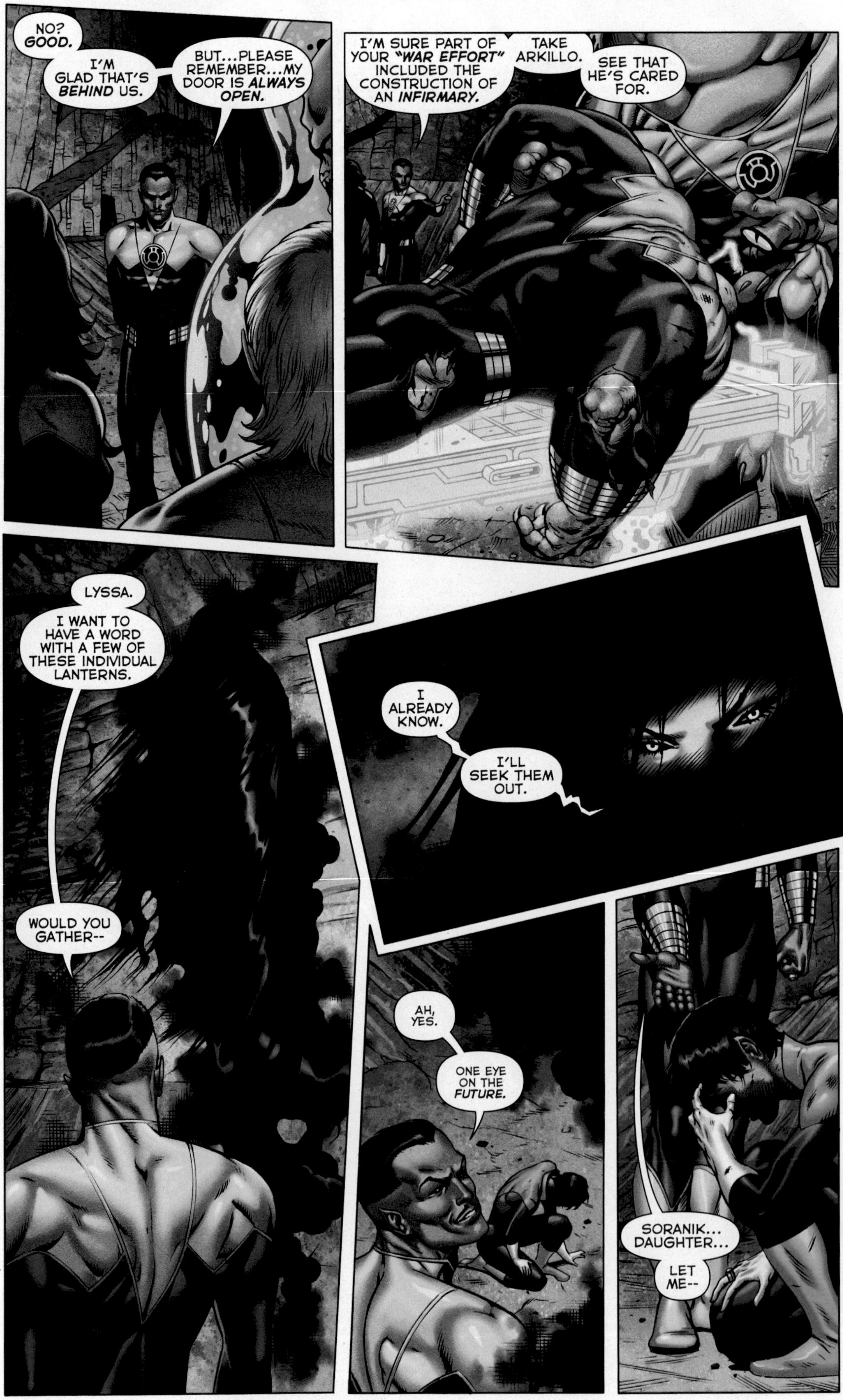

NO? GOOD.
I'M GLAD THAT'S BEHIND US.
BUT...PLEASE REMEMBER...MY DOOR IS ALWAYS OPEN.
I'M SURE PART OF YOUR "WAR EFFORT" INCLUDED THE CONSTRUCTION OF AN INFIRMARY.
TAKE ARKILLO.
SEE THAT HE'S CARED FOR.
LYSSA.
I WANT TO HAVE A WORD WITH A FEW OF THESE INDIVIDUAL LANTERNS.
I ALREADY KNOW.
I'LL SEEK THEM OUT.
WOULD YOU GATHER--
AH, YES.
ONE EYE ON THE FUTURE.
SORANIK... DAUGHTER...
LET ME--

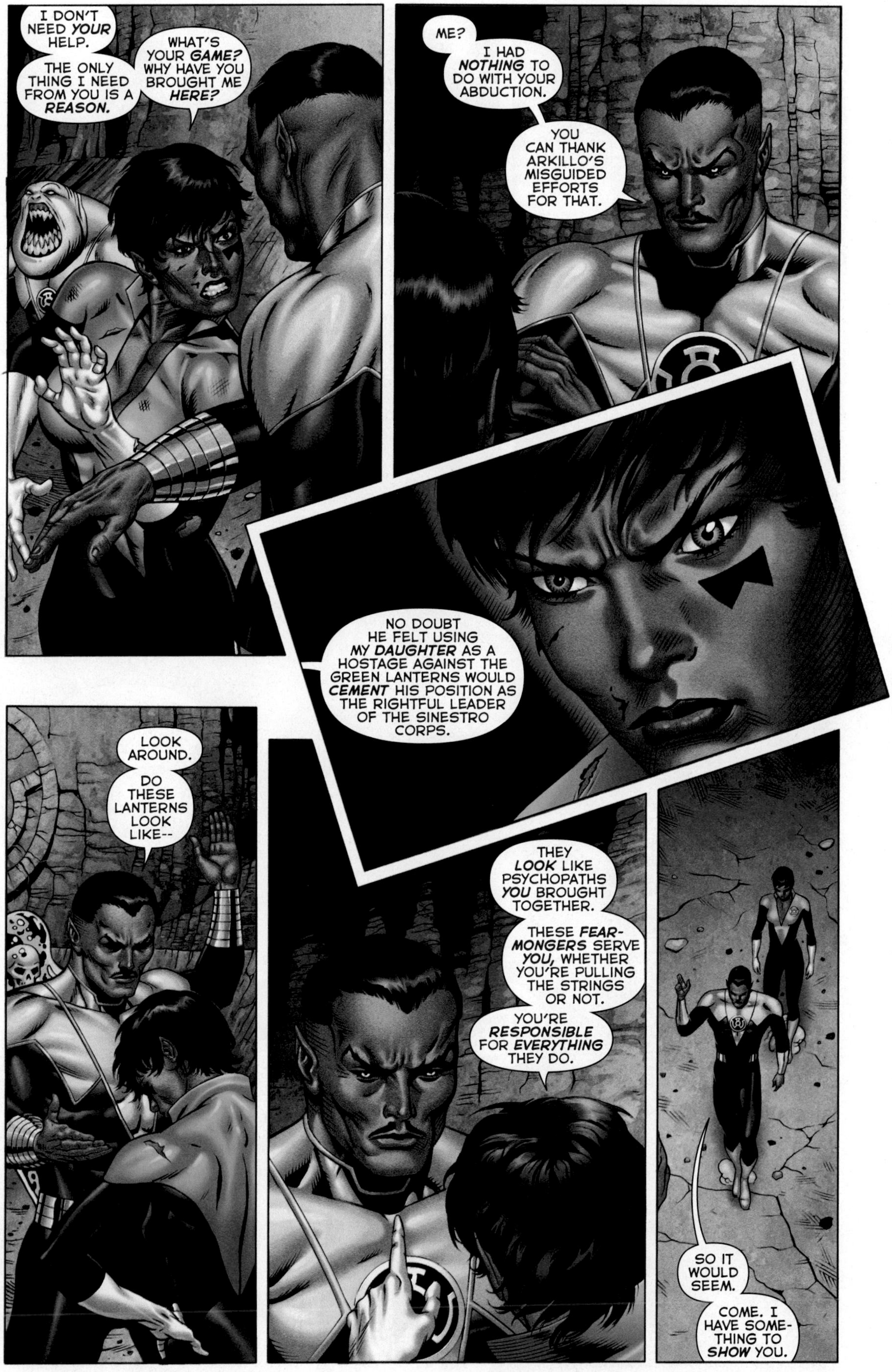
I DON'T NEED YOUR HELP.
THE ONLY THING I NEED FROM YOU IS A REASON.
WHAT'S YOUR GAME? WHY HAVE YOU BROUGHT ME HERE?
ME?
I HAD NOTHING TO DO WITH YOUR ABDUCTION.
YOU CAN THANK ARKILLO'S MISGUIDED EFFORTS FOR THAT.
NO DOUBT HE FELT USING MY DAUGHTER AS A HOSTAGE AGAINST THE GREEN LANTERNS WOULD CEMENT HIS POSITION AS THE RIGHTFUL LEADER OF THE SINESTRO CORPS.
LOOK AROUND.
DO THESE LANTERNS LOOK LIKE--
THEY LOOK LIKE PSYCHOPATHS YOU BROUGHT TOGETHER.
THESE FEAR-MONGERS SERVE YOU, WHETHER YOU'RE PULLING THE STRINGS OR NOT.
YOU'RE RESPONSIBLE FOR EVERYTHING THEY DO.
SO IT WOULD SEEM.
COME. I HAVE SOME-THING TO SHOW YOU.

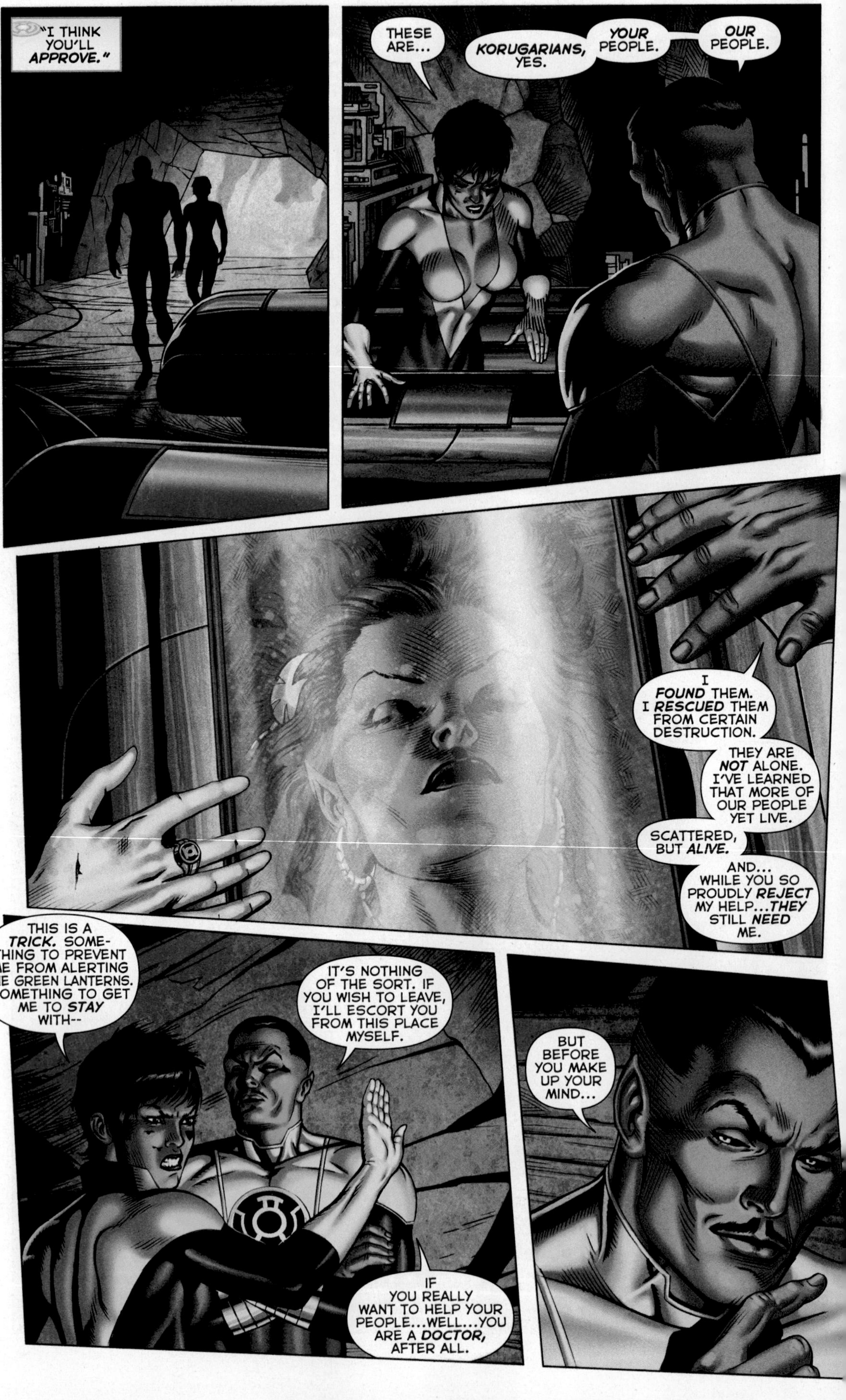
"I THINK YOU'LL APPROVE."
THESE ARE...
KORUGARIANS, YES.
YOUR PEOPLE.
OUR PEOPLE.
I FOUND THEM. I RESCUED THEM FROM CERTAIN DESTRUCTION.
THEY ARE NOT ALONE. I'VE LEARNED THAT MORE OF OUR PEOPLE YET LIVE.
SCATTERED, BUT ALIVE.
AND... WHILE YOU SO PROUDLY REJECT MY HELP...THEY STILL NEED ME.
THIS IS A TRICK. SOMETHING TO PREVENT ME FROM ALERTING THE GREEN LANTERNS. SOMETHING TO GET ME TO STAY WITH--
IT'S NOTHING OF THE SORT. IF YOU WISH TO LEAVE, I'LL ESCORT YOU FROM THIS PLACE MYSELF.
IF YOU REALLY WANT TO HELP YOUR PEOPLE...WELL...YOU ARE A DOCTOR, AFTER ALL.
BUT BEFORE YOU MAKE UP YOUR MIND...

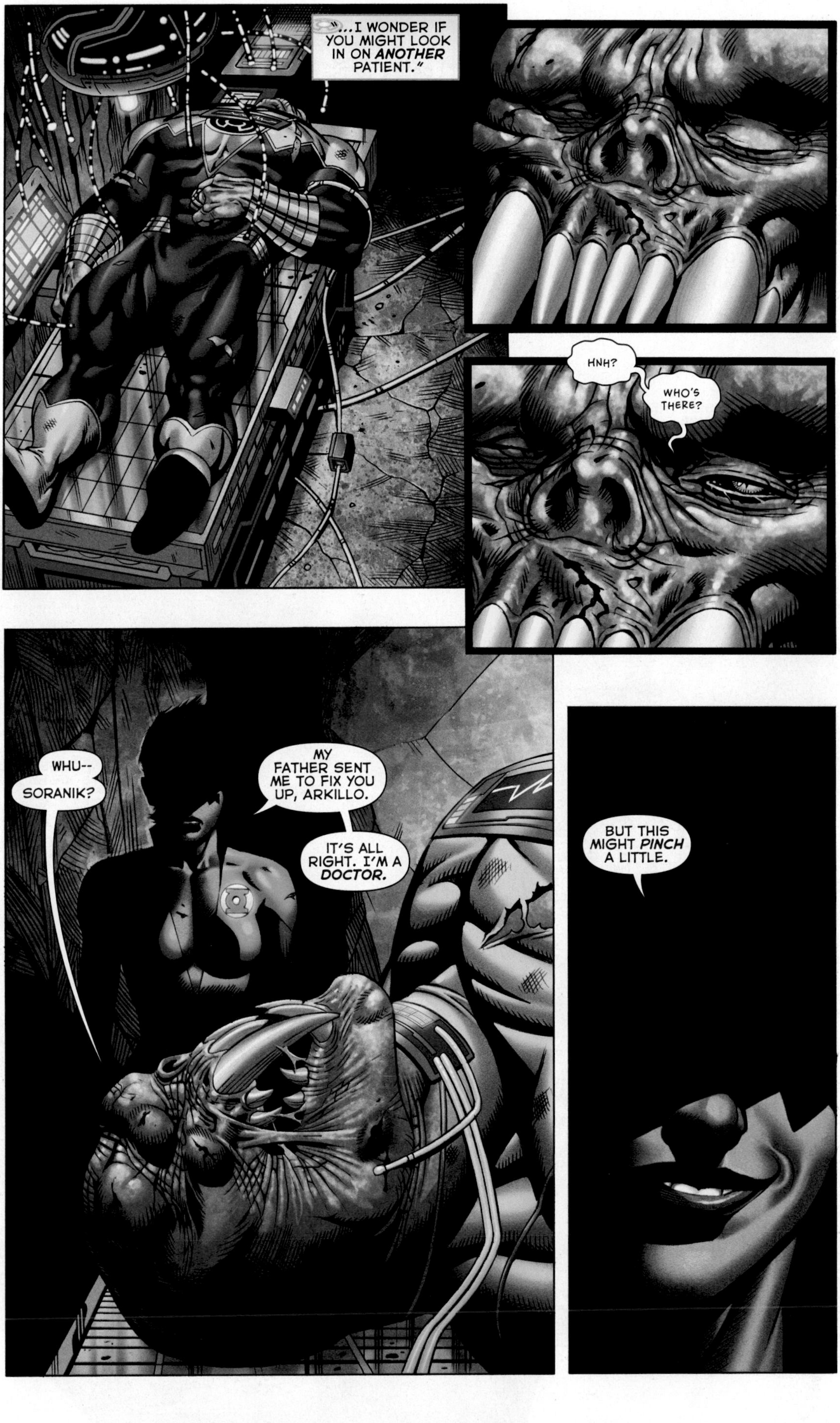
"...I WONDER IF YOU MIGHT LOOK IN ON ANOTHER PATIENT."
HNH?
WHO'S THERE?
WHU-- SORANIK?
MY FATHER SENT ME TO FIX YOU UP, ARKILLO.
IT'S ALL RIGHT. I'M A DOCTOR.
BUT THIS MIGHT PINCH A LITTLE.

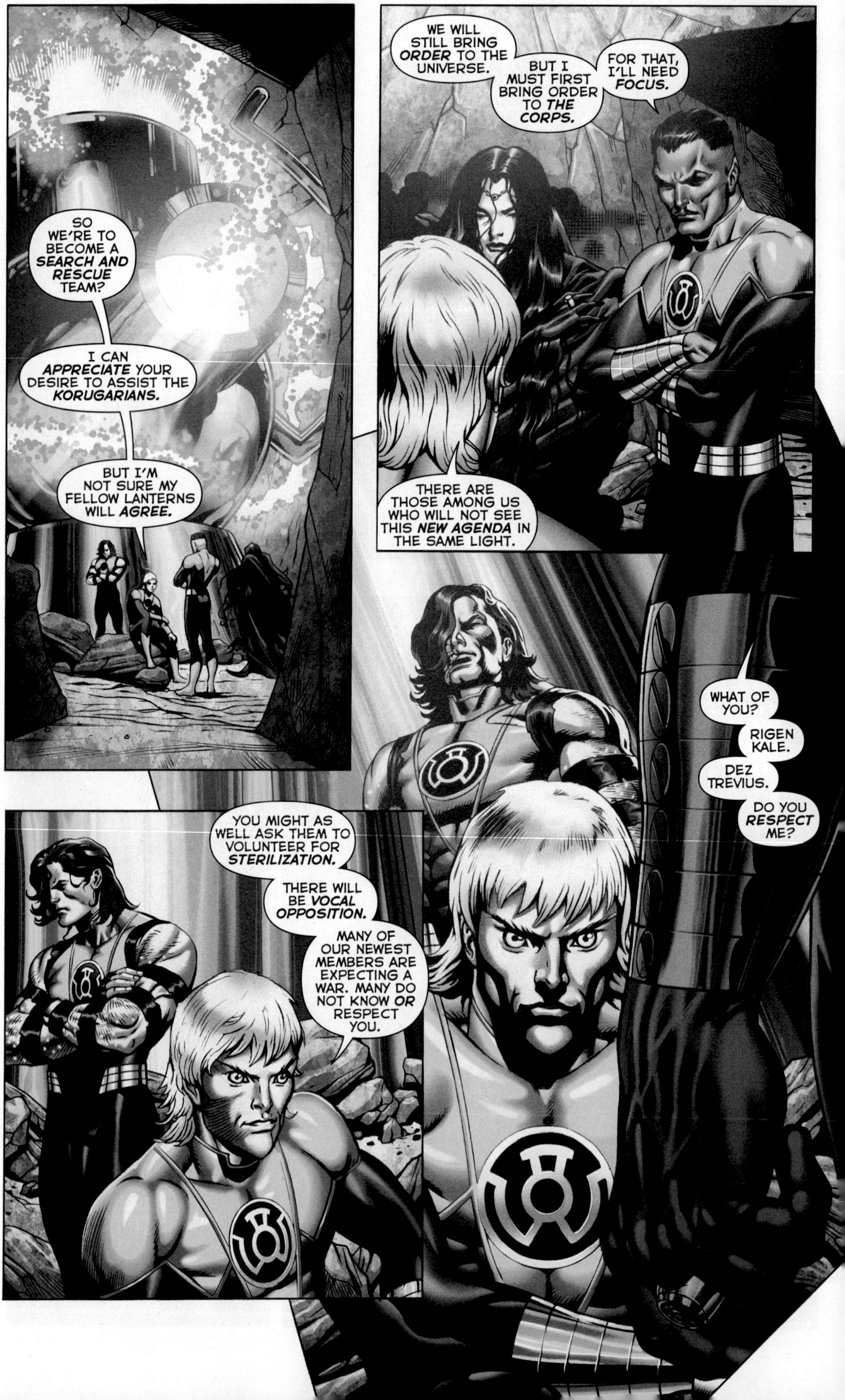
SO WE'RE TO BECOME A SEARCH AND RESCUE TEAM?
I CAN APPRECIATE YOUR DESIRE TO ASSIST THE KORUGARIANS.
BUT I'M NOT SURE MY FELLOW LANTERNS WILL AGREE.
WE WILL STILL BRING ORDER TO THE UNIVERSE.
BUT I MUST FIRST BRING ORDER TO THE CORPS.
FOR THAT, I'LL NEED FOCUS.
THERE ARE THOSE AMONG US WHO WILL NOT SEE THIS NEW AGENDA IN THE SAME LIGHT.
YOU MIGHT AS WELL ASK THEM TO VOLUNTEER FOR STERILIZATION.
THERE WILL BE VOCAL OPPOSITION.
MANY OF OUR NEWEST MEMBERS ARE EXPECTING A WAR. MANY DO NOT KNOW OR RESPECT YOU.
WHAT OF YOU?
RIGEN KALE.
DEZ TREVIUS.
DO YOU RESPECT ME?

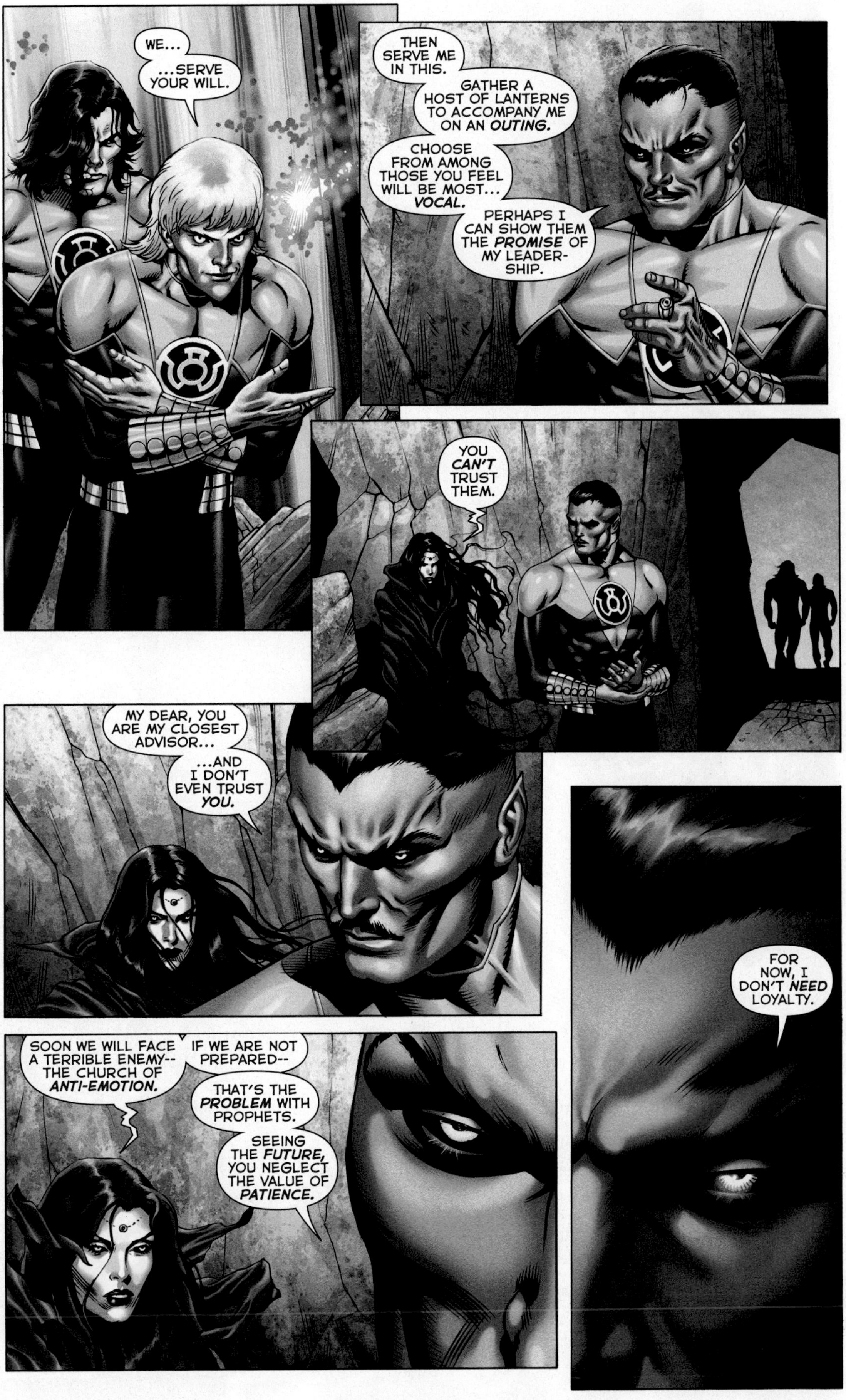

WE...
...SERVE YOUR WILL.
THEN SERVE ME IN THIS.
GATHER A HOST OF LANTERNS TO ACCOMPANY ME ON AN *OUTING.*
CHOOSE FROM AMONG THOSE YOU FEEL WILL BE MOST... *VOCAL.*
PERHAPS I CAN SHOW THEM THE *PROMISE* OF MY LEADER-SHIP.
YOU *CAN'T* TRUST THEM.
MY DEAR, YOU ARE MY CLOSEST ADVISOR...
...AND I DON'T EVEN TRUST *YOU.*
SOON WE WILL FACE A TERRIBLE ENEMY-- THE CHURCH OF *ANTI-EMOTION.*
IF WE ARE NOT PREPARED--
THAT'S THE *PROBLEM* WITH PROPHETS.
SEEING THE *FUTURE,* YOU NEGLECT THE VALUE OF *PATIENCE.*
FOR NOW, I DON'T *NEED* LOYALTY.

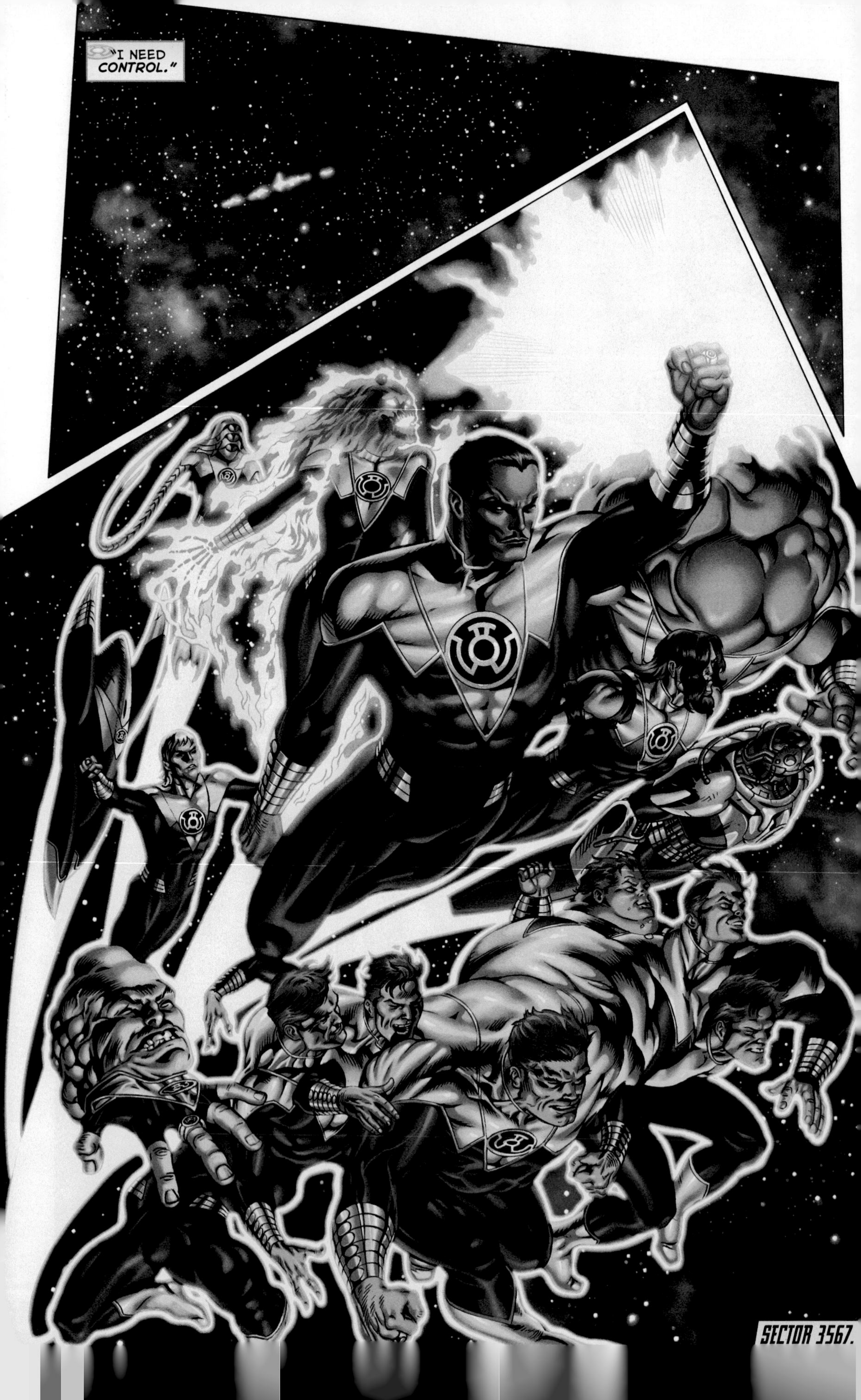
"I NEED CONTROL."
SECTOR 3567.

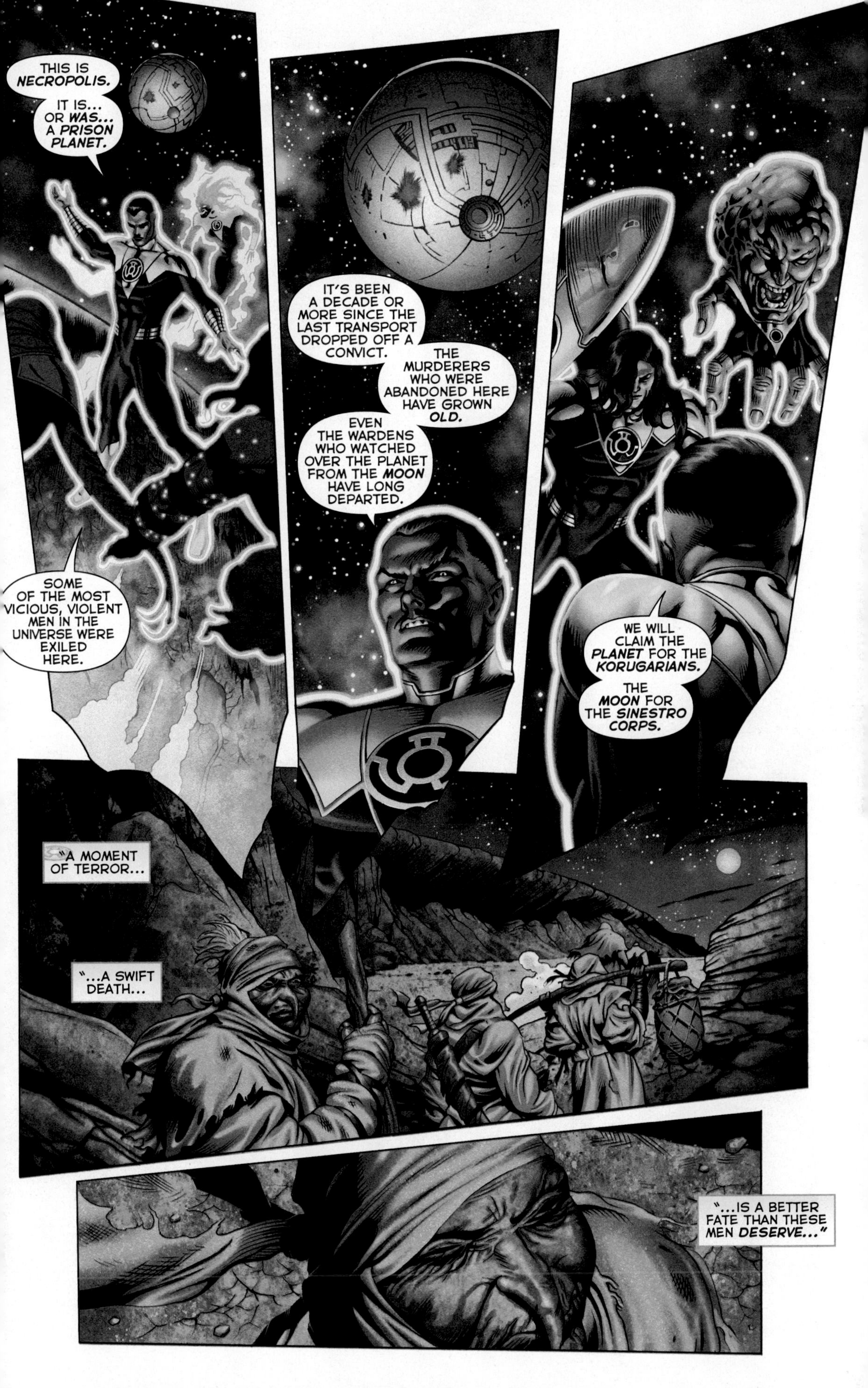
THIS IS NECROPOLIS.
IT IS... OR WAS... A PRISON PLANET.
SOME OF THE MOST VICIOUS, VIOLENT MEN IN THE UNIVERSE WERE EXILED HERE.
IT'S BEEN A DECADE OR MORE SINCE THE LAST TRANSPORT DROPPED OFF A CONVICT.
THE MURDERERS WHO WERE ABANDONED HERE HAVE GROWN OLD.
EVEN THE WARDENS WHO WATCHED OVER THE PLANET FROM THE MOON HAVE LONG DEPARTED.
WE WILL CLAIM THE PLANET FOR THE KORUGARIANS.
THE MOON FOR THE SINESTRO CORPS.
"A MOMENT OF TERROR...
"...A SWIFT DEATH...
"...IS A BETTER FATE THAN THESE MEN DESERVE..."

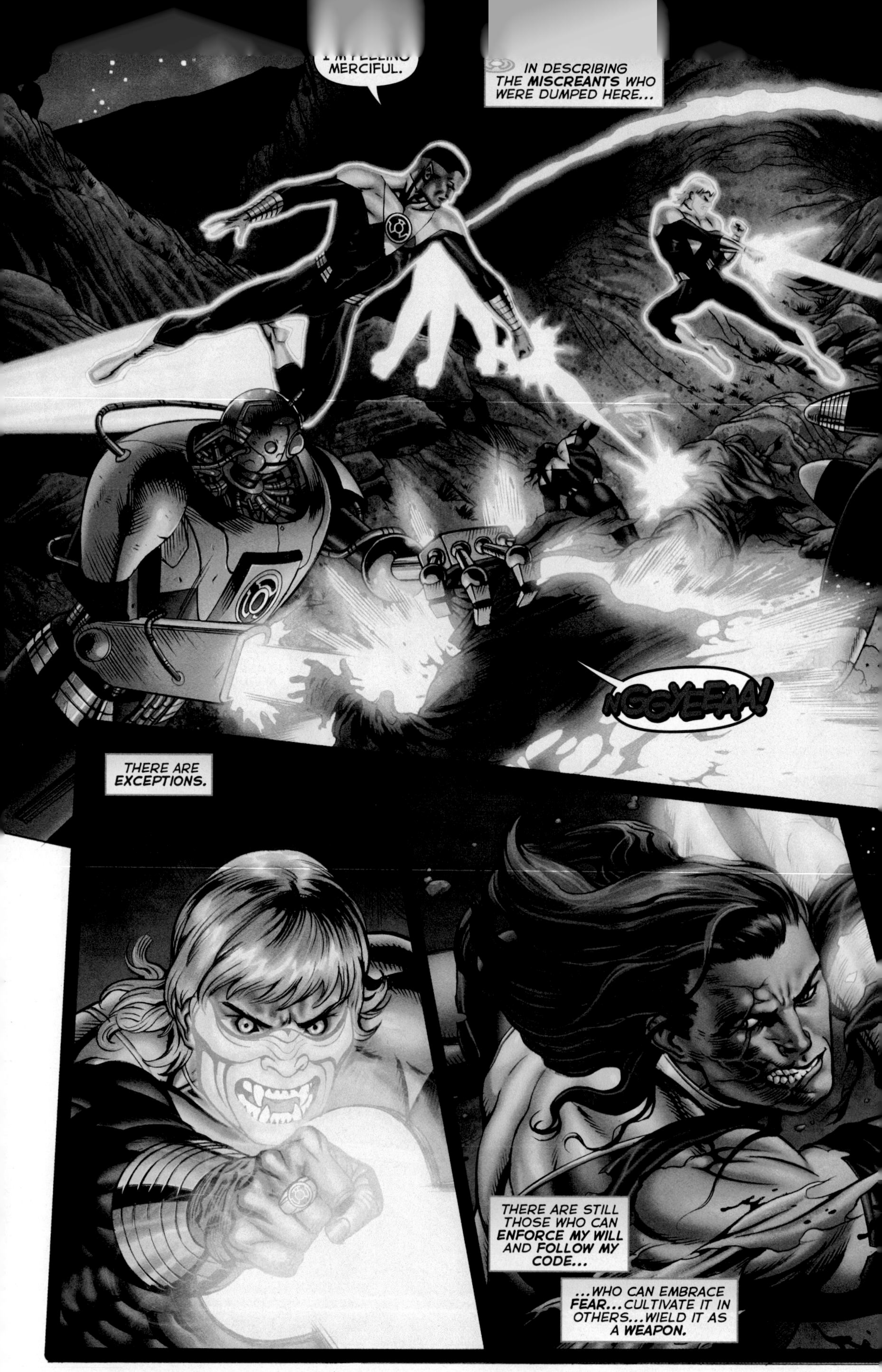
MERCIFUL.
IN DESCRIBING THE MISCREANTS WHO WERE DUMPED HERE...
NGGYEEAA!
THERE ARE EXCEPTIONS.
THERE ARE STILL THOSE WHO CAN ENFORCE MY WILL AND FOLLOW MY CODE...
...WHO CAN EMBRACE FEAR...CULTIVATE IT IN OTHERS...WIELD IT AS A WEAPON.

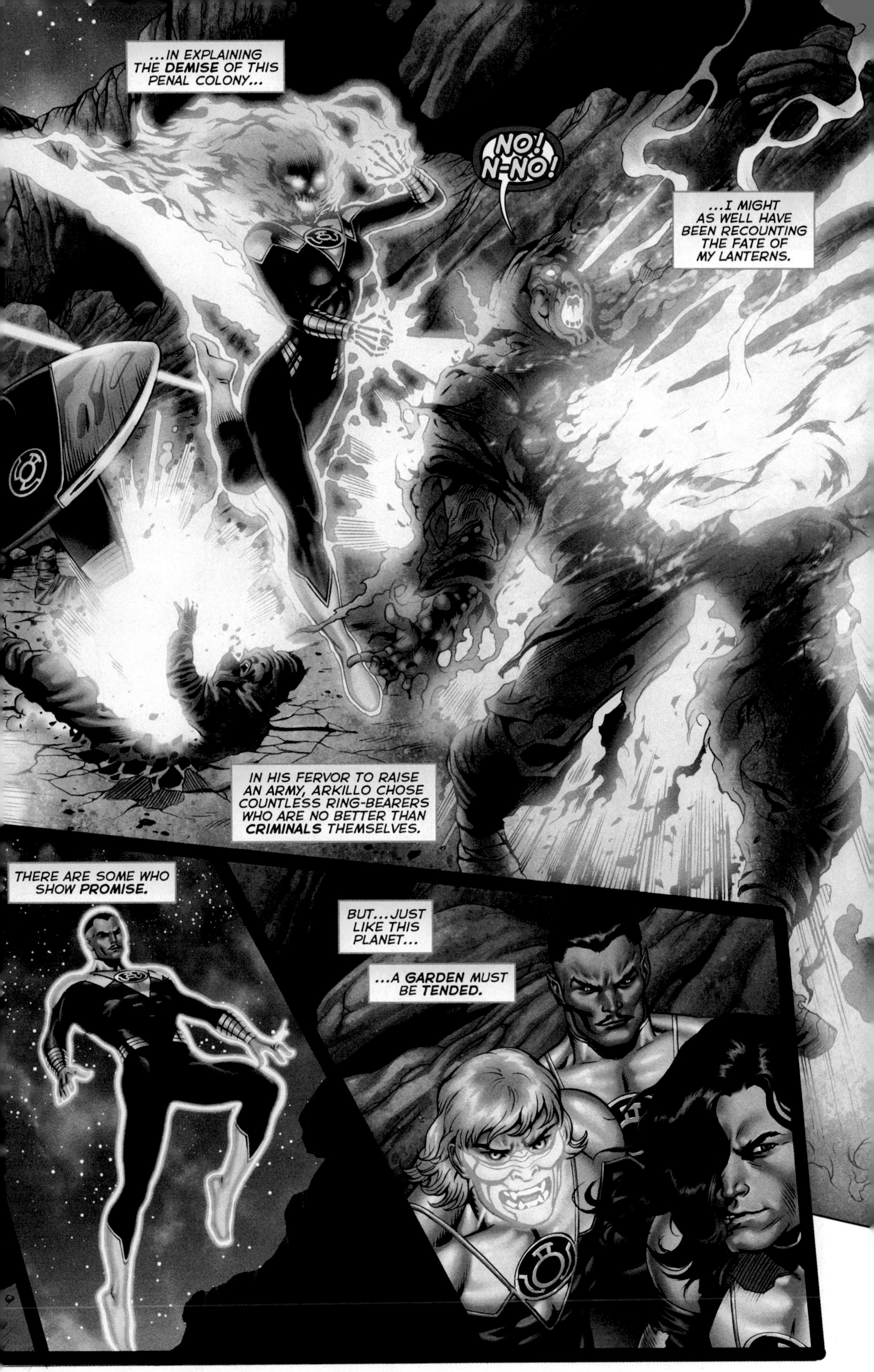
...IN EXPLAINING THE DEMISE OF THIS PENAL COLONY...
NO! N-NO!
...I MIGHT AS WELL HAVE BEEN RECOUNTING THE FATE OF MY LANTERNS.
IN HIS FERVOR TO RAISE AN ARMY, ARKILLO CHOSE COUNTLESS RING-BEARERS WHO ARE NO BETTER THAN CRIMINALS THEMSELVES.
THERE ARE SOME WHO SHOW PROMISE.
BUT...JUST LIKE THIS PLANET...
...A GARDEN MUST BE TENDED.

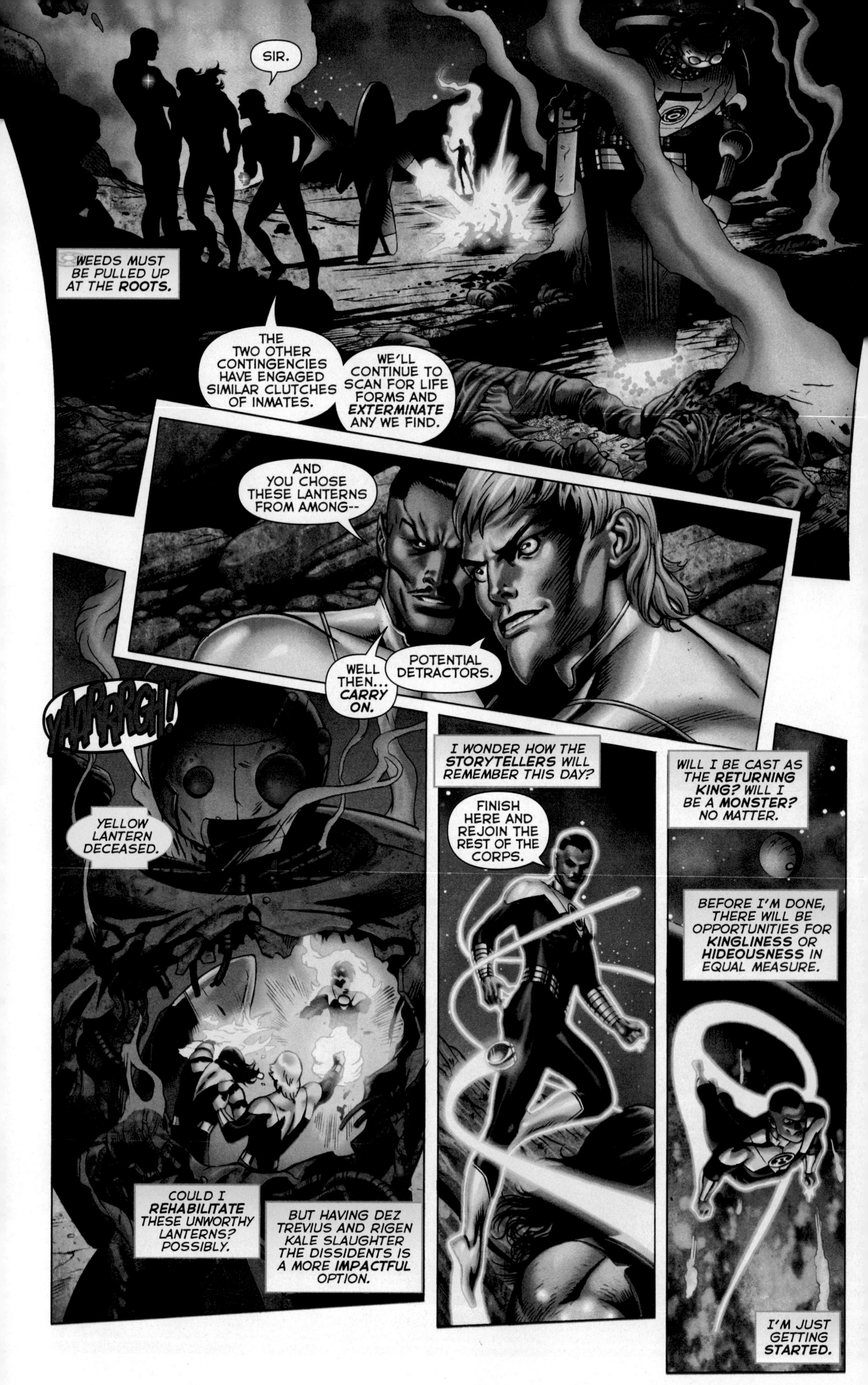
SIR.
WEEDS MUST BE PULLED UP AT THE ROOTS.
THE TWO OTHER CONTINGENCIES HAVE ENGAGED SIMILAR CLUTCHES OF INMATES.
WE'LL CONTINUE TO SCAN FOR LIFE FORMS AND EXTERMINATE ANY WE FIND.
AND YOU CHOSE THESE LANTERNS FROM AMONG--
POTENTIAL DETRACTORS.
WELL THEN... CARRY ON.
YAARRRGH!
YELLOW LANTERN DECEASED.
COULD I REHABILITATE THESE UNWORTHY LANTERNS? POSSIBLY.
BUT HAVING DEZ TREVIUS AND RIGEN KALE SLAUGHTER THE DISSIDENTS IS A MORE IMPACTFUL OPTION.
I WONDER HOW THE STORYTELLERS WILL REMEMBER THIS DAY?
FINISH HERE AND REJOIN THE REST OF THE CORPS.
WILL I BE CAST AS THE RETURNING KING? WILL I BE A MONSTER? NO MATTER.
BEFORE I'M DONE, THERE WILL BE OPPORTUNITIES FOR KINGLINESS OR HIDEOUSNESS IN EQUAL MEASURE.
I'M JUST GETTING STARTED.

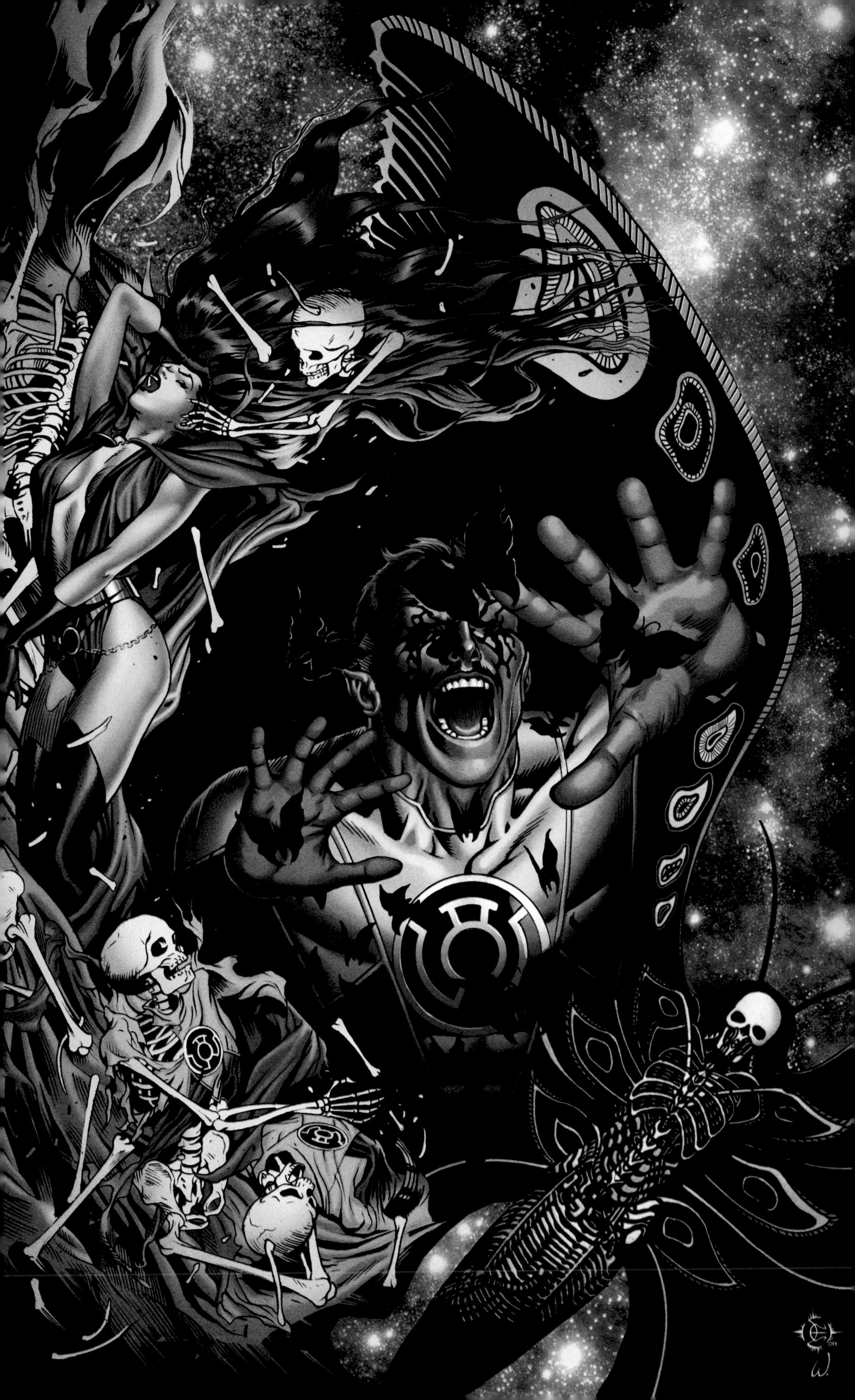

HERESY OF FEAR

CULLEN BUNN writer DALE EAGLESHAM RAGS MORALES artists JASON WRIGHT colorist CARLOS M. MANGUAL letterer
cover art by DALE EAGLESHAM & JASON WRIGHT

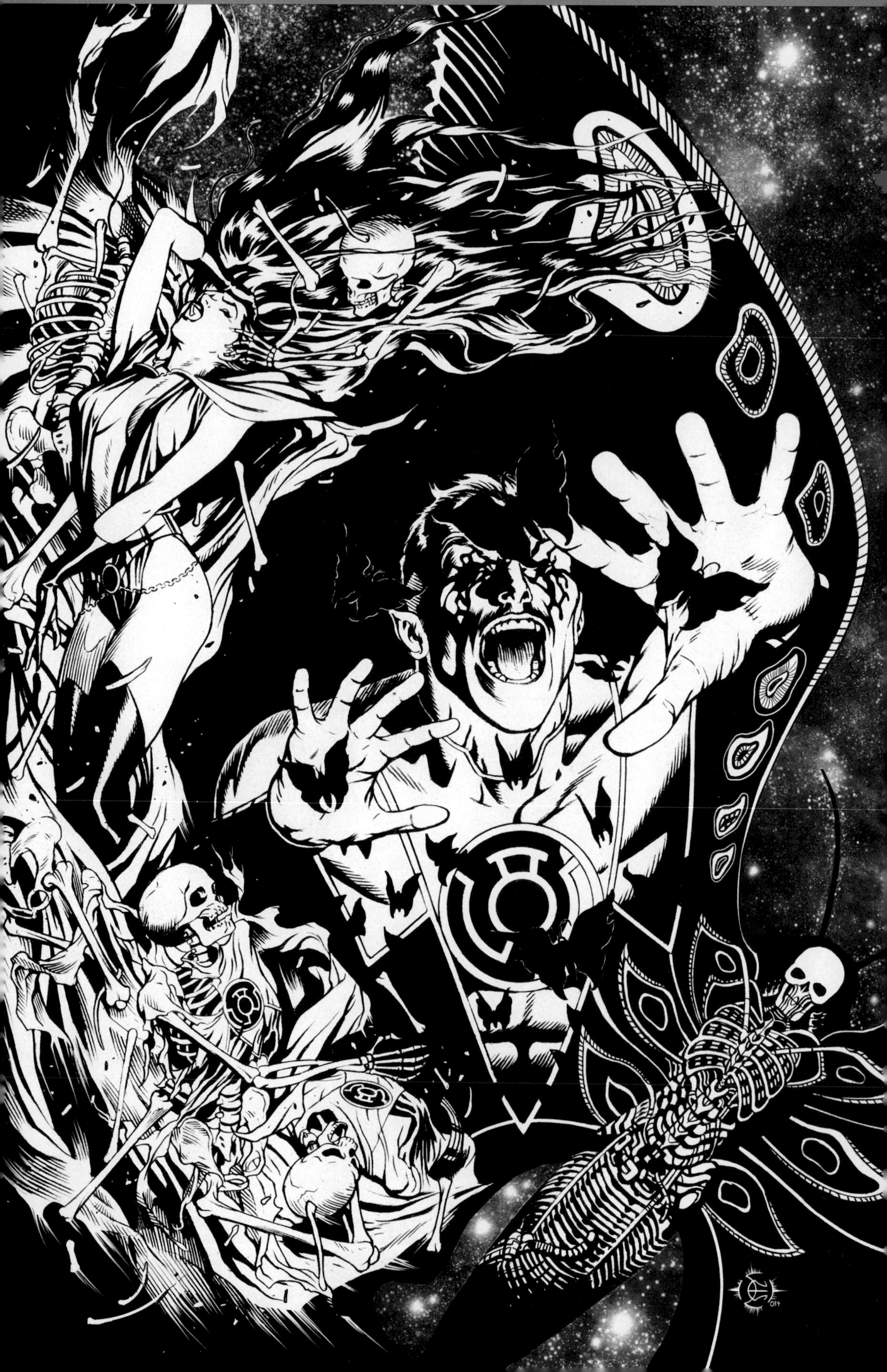

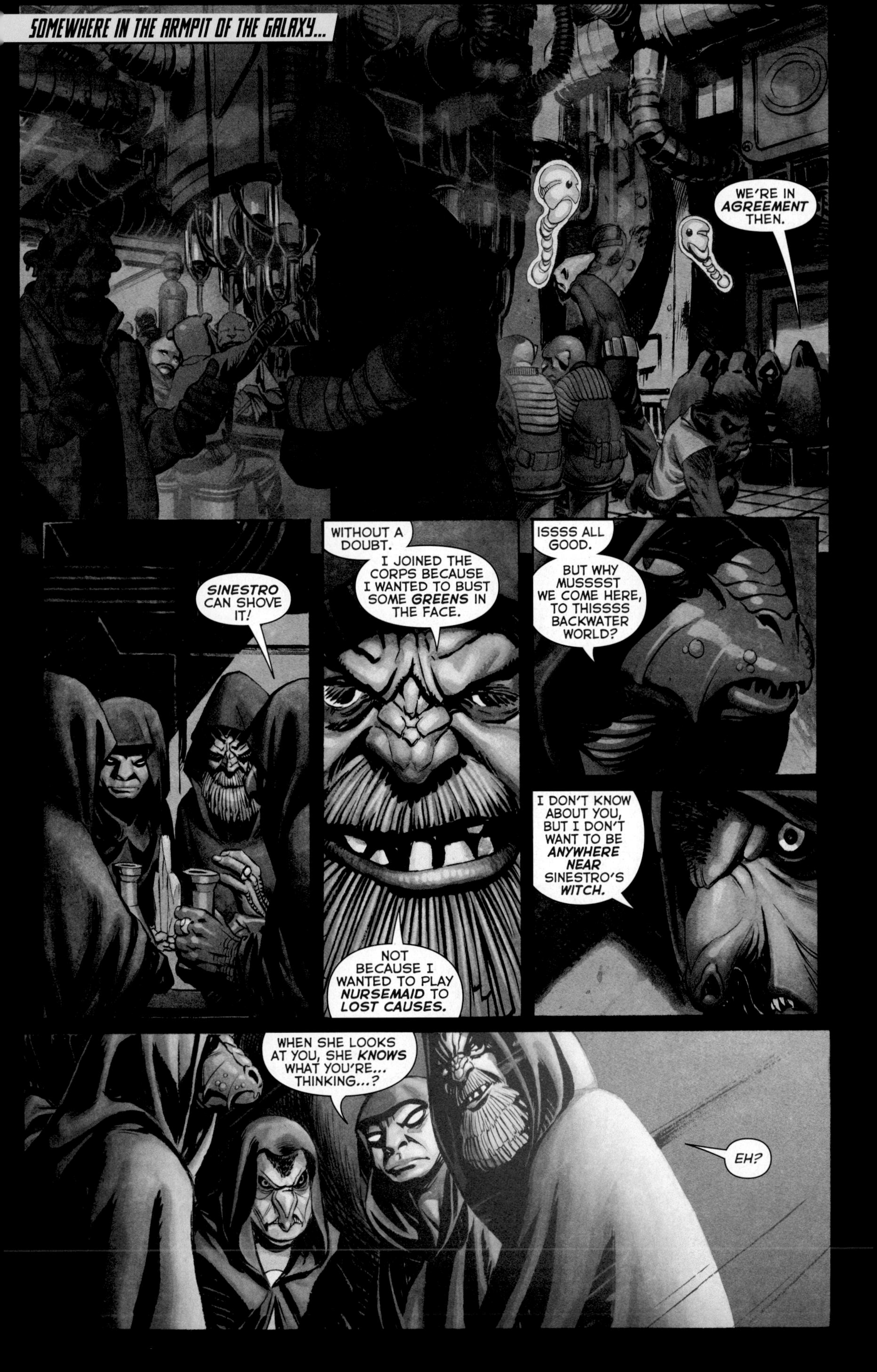
SOMEWHERE IN THE ARMPIT OF THE GALAXY...
WE'RE IN AGREEMENT THEN.
SINESTRO CAN SHOVE IT!
WITHOUT A DOUBT.
I JOINED THE CORPS BECAUSE I WANTED TO BUST SOME GREENS IN THE FACE.
NOT BECAUSE I WANTED TO PLAY NURSEMAID TO LOST CAUSES.
ISSSS ALL GOOD.
BUT WHY MUSSSST WE COME HERE, TO THISSSS BACKWATER WORLD?
I DON'T KNOW ABOUT YOU, BUT I DON'T WANT TO BE ANYWHERE NEAR SINESTRO'S WITCH.
WHEN SHE LOOKS AT YOU, SHE KNOWS WHAT YOU'RE... THINKING...?
EH?

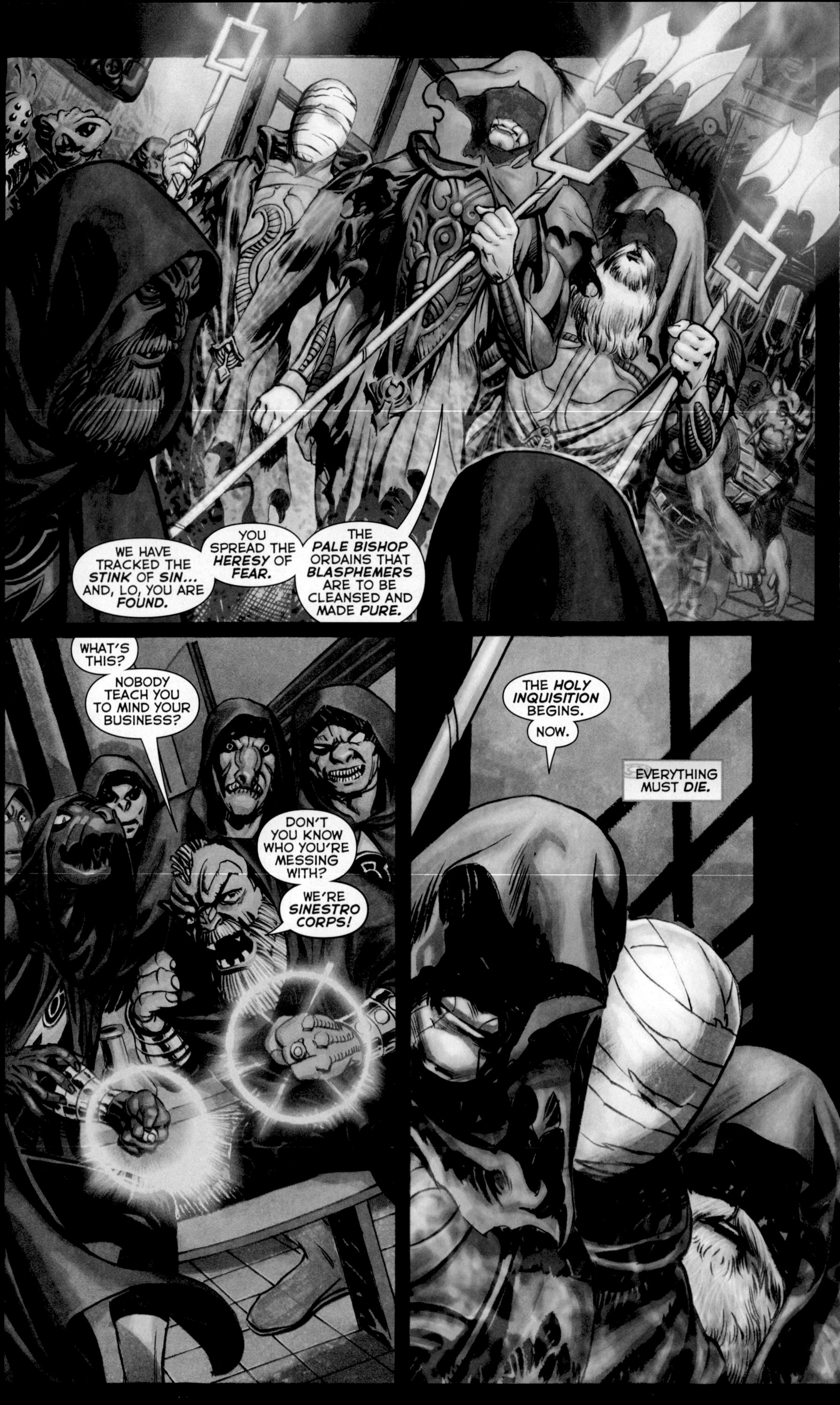

WE HAVE TRACKED THE STINK OF SIN... AND, LO, YOU ARE FOUND.
YOU SPREAD THE HERESY OF FEAR.
THE PALE BISHOP ORDAINS THAT BLASPHEMERS ARE TO BE CLEANSED AND MADE PURE.
WHAT'S THIS?
NOBODY TEACH YOU TO MIND YOUR BUSINESS?
DON'T YOU KNOW WHO YOU'RE MESSING WITH?
WE'RE SINESTRO CORPS!
THE HOLY INQUISITION BEGINS.
NOW.
EVERYTHING MUST DIE.

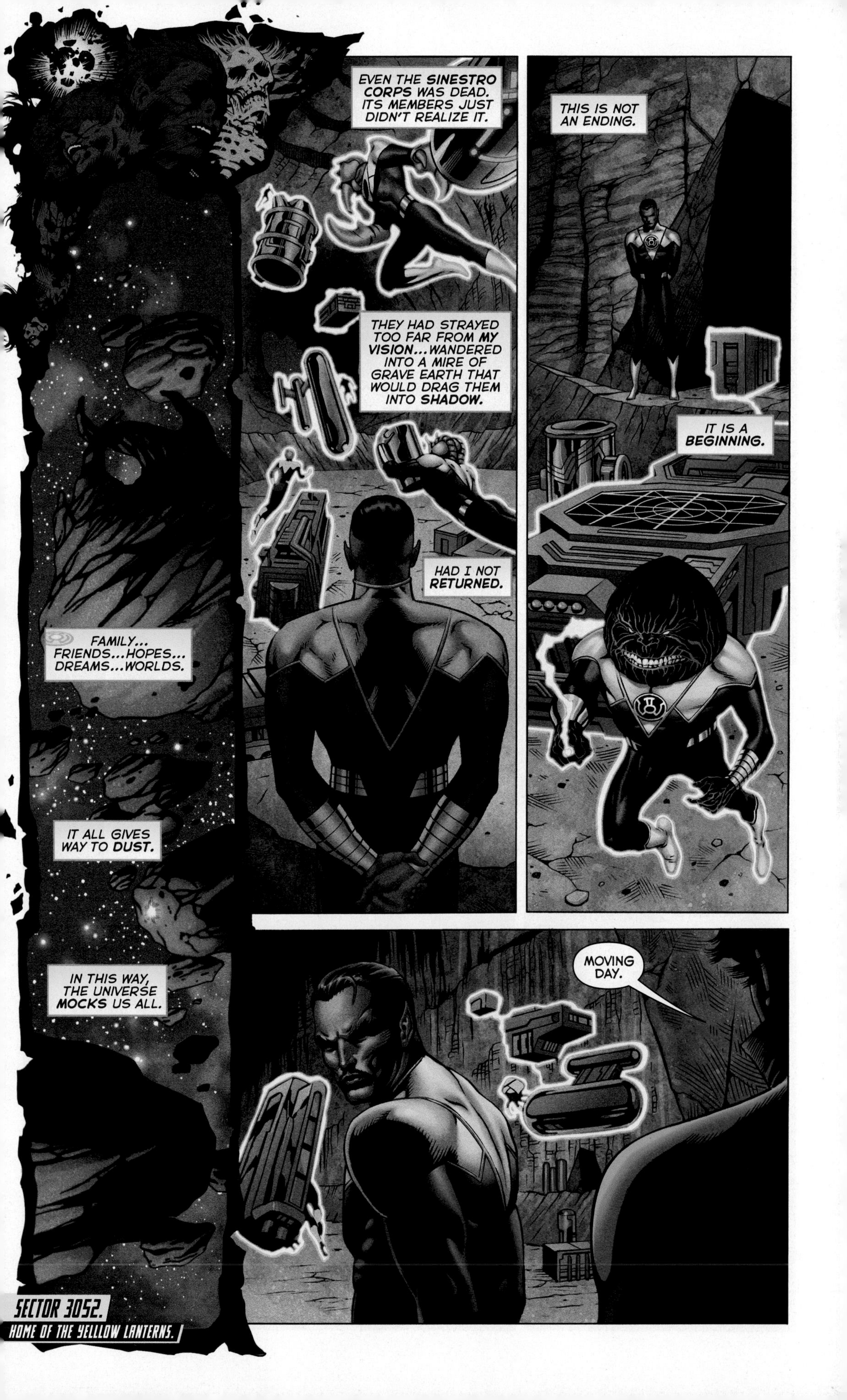

EVEN THE SINESTRO CORPS WAS DEAD. ITS MEMBERS JUST DIDN'T REALIZE IT.
THEY HAD STRAYED TOO FAR FROM MY VISION...WANDERED INTO A MIRE OF GRAVE EARTH THAT WOULD DRAG THEM INTO SHADOW.
HAD I NOT RETURNED.
THIS IS NOT AN ENDING.
IT IS A BEGINNING.
FAMILY... FRIENDS...HOPES... DREAMS...WORLDS.
IT ALL GIVES WAY TO DUST.
IN THIS WAY, THE UNIVERSE MOCKS US ALL.
SECTOR 3052.
HOME OF THE YELLOW LANTERNS.
MOVING DAY.

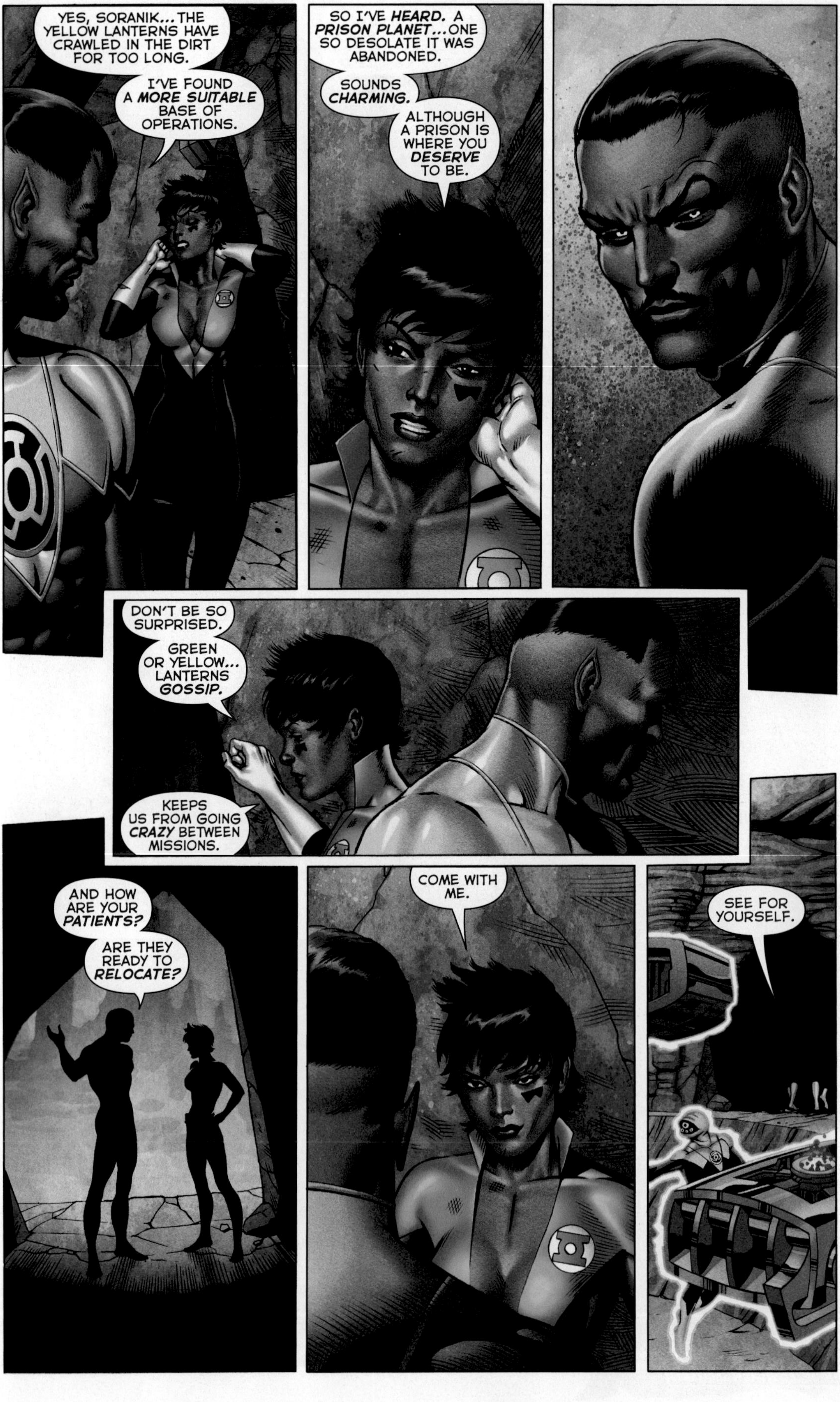
YES, SORANIK... THE YELLOW LANTERNS HAVE CRAWLED IN THE DIRT FOR TOO LONG.
I'VE FOUND A MORE SUITABLE BASE OF OPERATIONS.
SO I'VE HEARD. A PRISON PLANET... ONE SO DESOLATE IT WAS ABANDONED.
SOUNDS CHARMING.
ALTHOUGH A PRISON IS WHERE YOU DESERVE TO BE.
DON'T BE SO SURPRISED.
GREEN OR YELLOW... LANTERNS GOSSIP.
KEEPS US FROM GOING CRAZY BETWEEN MISSIONS.
AND HOW ARE YOUR PATIENTS?
ARE THEY READY TO RELOCATE?
COME WITH ME.
SEE FOR YOURSELF.

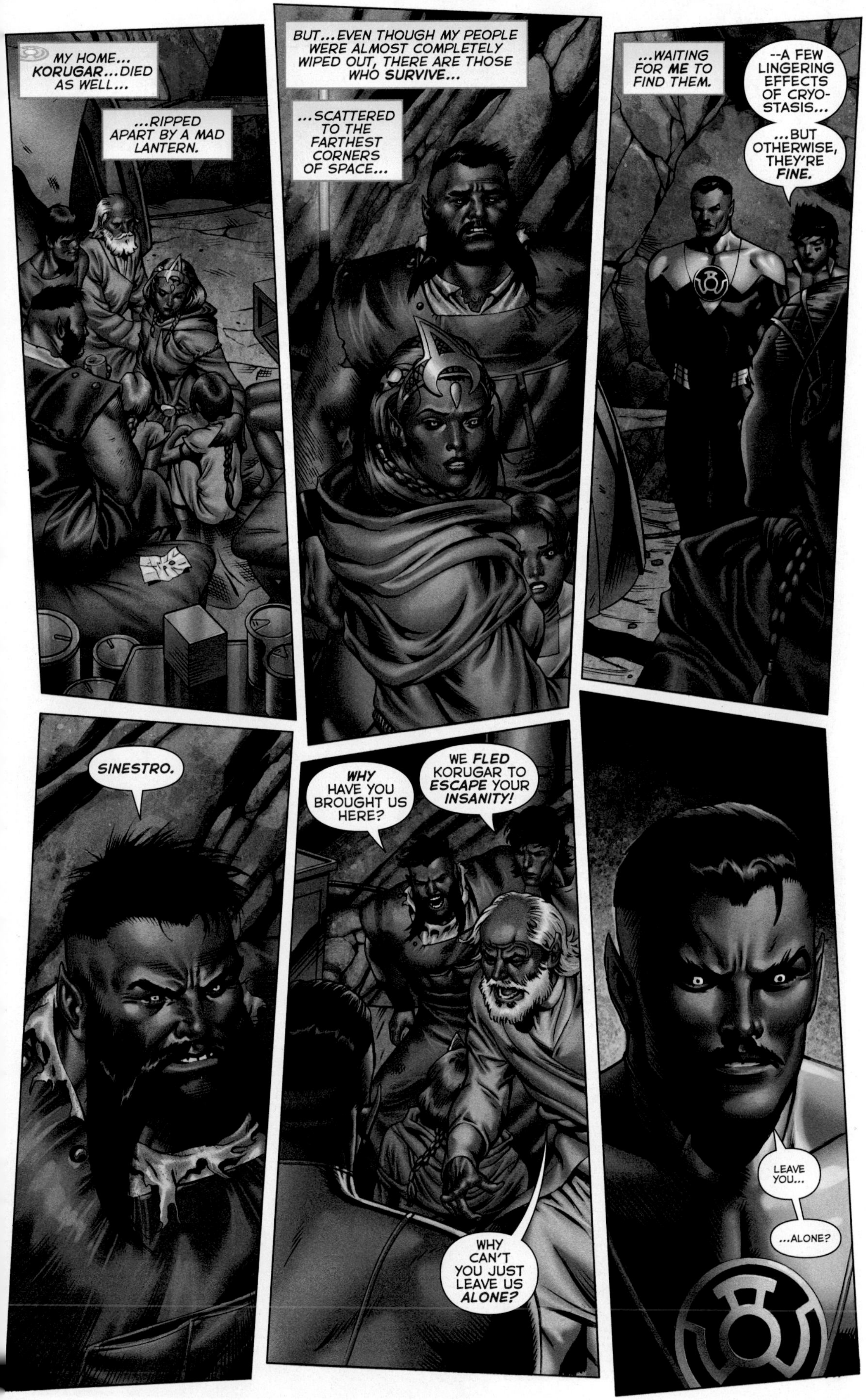
MY HOME... KORUGAR...DIED AS WELL...
...RIPPED APART BY A MAD LANTERN.
BUT...EVEN THOUGH MY PEOPLE WERE ALMOST COMPLETELY WIPED OUT, THERE ARE THOSE WHO SURVIVE...
...SCATTERED TO THE FARTHEST CORNERS OF SPACE...
...WAITING FOR ME TO FIND THEM.
--A FEW LINGERING EFFECTS OF CRYO-STASIS...
...BUT OTHERWISE, THEY'RE FINE.
SINESTRO.
WHY HAVE YOU BROUGHT US HERE?
WE FLED KORUGAR TO ESCAPE YOUR INSANITY!
WHY CAN'T YOU JUST LEAVE US ALONE?
LEAVE YOU...
...ALONE?

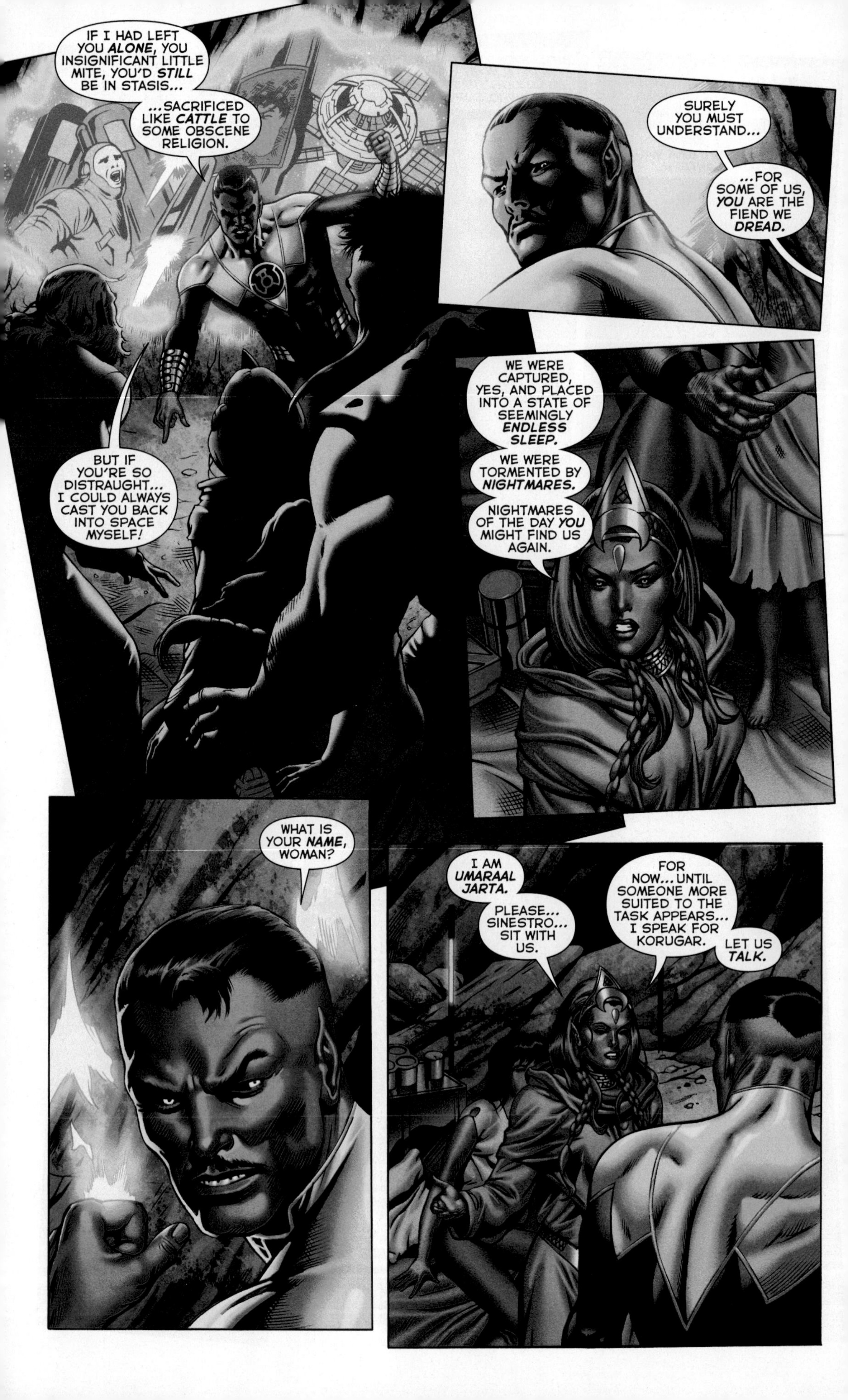
IF I HAD LEFT YOU ALONE, YOU INSIGNIFICANT LITTLE MITE, YOU'D STILL BE IN STASIS...
...SACRIFICED LIKE CATTLE TO SOME OBSCENE RELIGION.
BUT IF YOU'RE SO DISTRAUGHT... I COULD ALWAYS CAST YOU BACK INTO SPACE MYSELF!
SURELY YOU MUST UNDERSTAND...
...FOR SOME OF US, YOU ARE THE FIEND WE DREAD.
WE WERE CAPTURED, YES, AND PLACED INTO A STATE OF SEEMINGLY ENDLESS SLEEP.
WE WERE TORMENTED BY NIGHTMARES.
NIGHTMARES OF THE DAY YOU MIGHT FIND US AGAIN.
WHAT IS YOUR NAME, WOMAN?
I AM UMARAAL JARTA.
PLEASE... SINESTRO... SIT WITH US.
FOR NOW... UNTIL SOMEONE MORE SUITED TO THE TASK APPEARS... I SPEAK FOR KORUGAR.
LET US TALK.

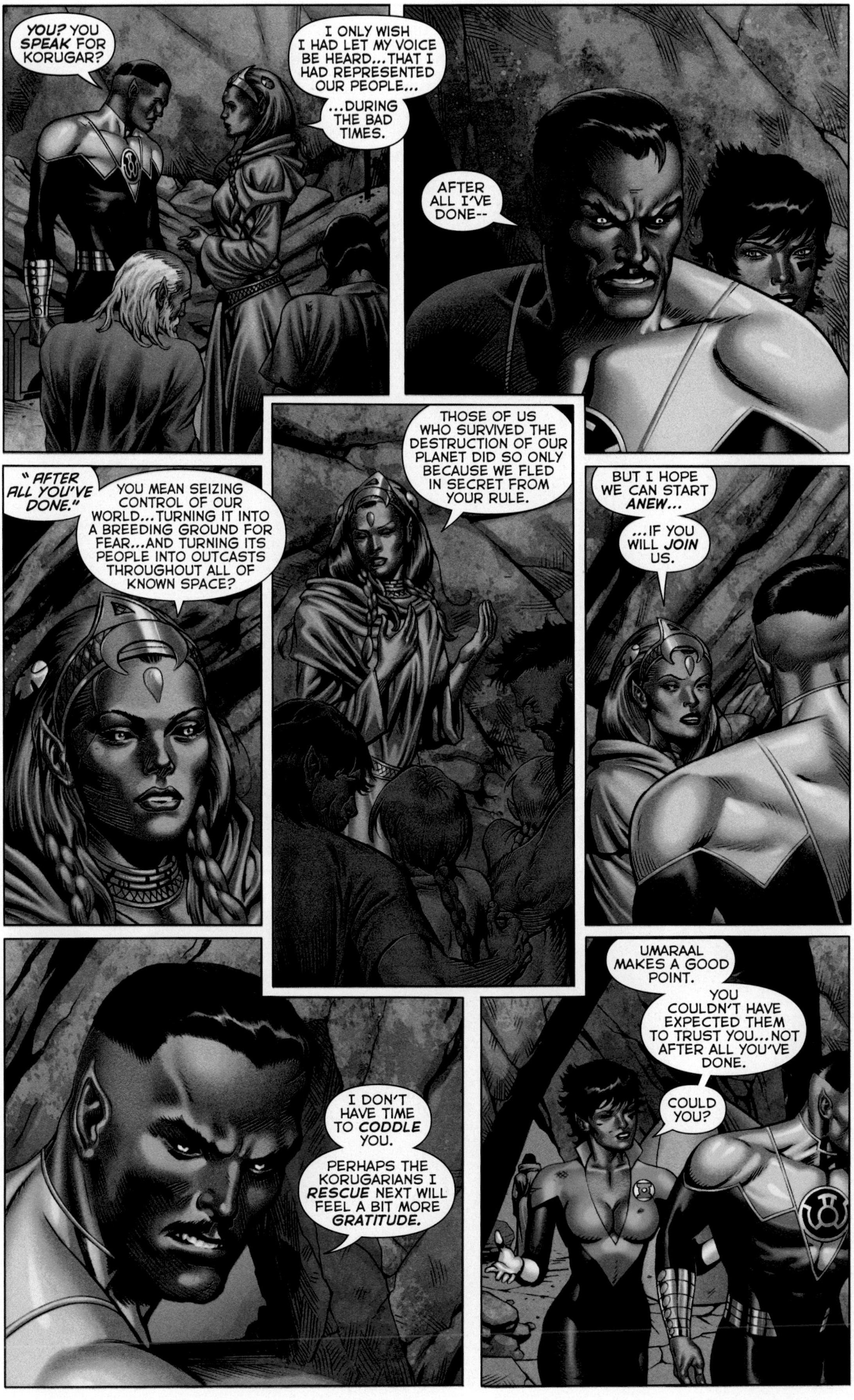
YOU? YOU SPEAK FOR KORUGAR?
I ONLY WISH I HAD LET MY VOICE BE HEARD...THAT I HAD REPRESENTED OUR PEOPLE...
...DURING THE BAD TIMES.
AFTER ALL I'VE DONE--
"AFTER ALL YOU'VE DONE."
YOU MEAN SEIZING CONTROL OF OUR WORLD...TURNING IT INTO A BREEDING GROUND FOR FEAR...AND TURNING ITS PEOPLE INTO OUTCASTS THROUGHOUT ALL OF KNOWN SPACE?
THOSE OF US WHO SURVIVED THE DESTRUCTION OF OUR PLANET DID SO ONLY BECAUSE WE FLED IN SECRET FROM YOUR RULE.
BUT I HOPE WE CAN START ANEW...
...IF YOU WILL JOIN US.
I DON'T HAVE TIME TO CODDLE YOU.
PERHAPS THE KORUGARIANS I RESCUE NEXT WILL FEEL A BIT MORE GRATITUDE.
UMARAAL MAKES A GOOD POINT.
YOU COULDN'T HAVE EXPECTED THEM TO TRUST YOU...NOT AFTER ALL YOU'VE DONE.
COULD YOU?

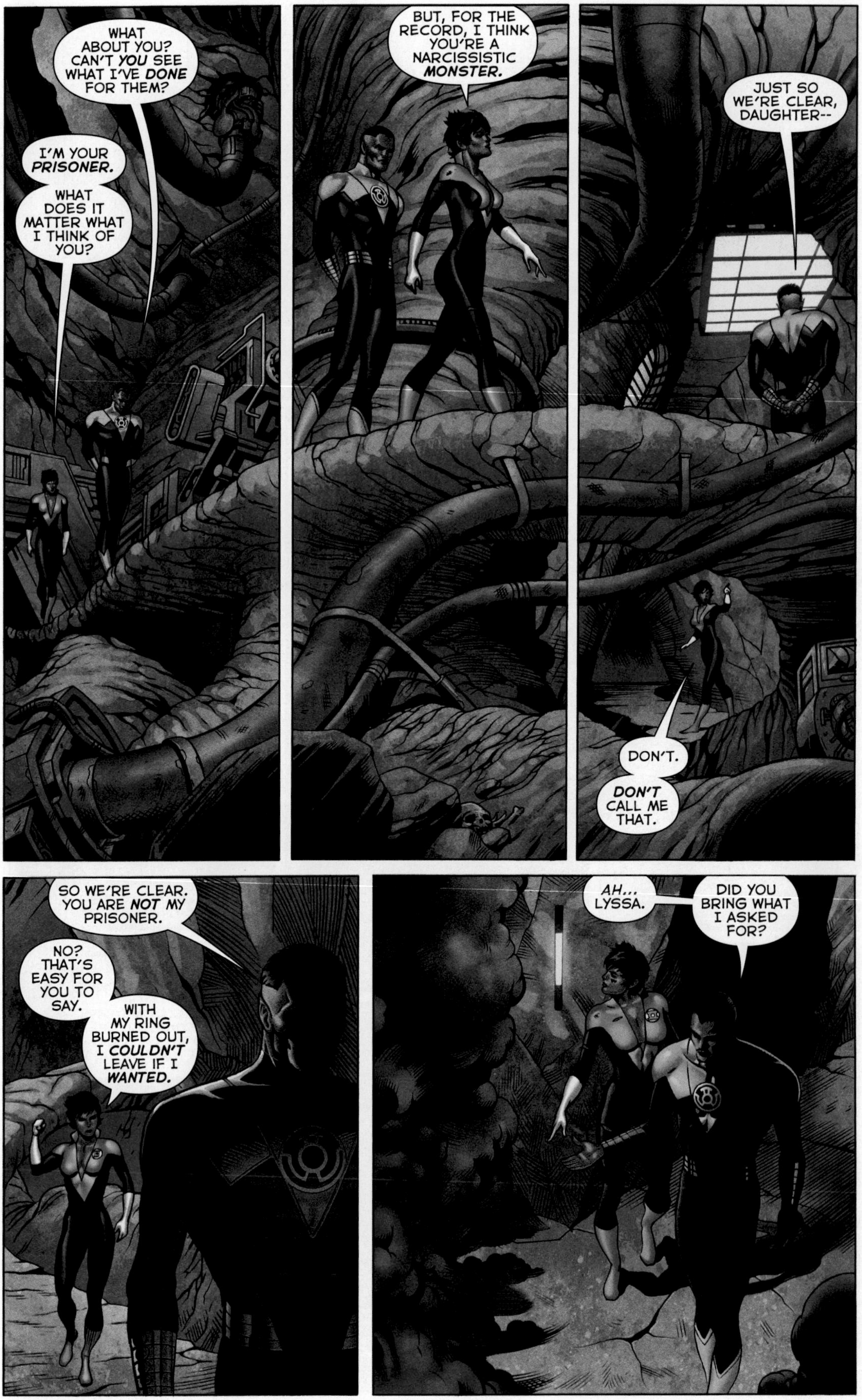
WHAT ABOUT YOU? CAN'T YOU SEE WHAT I'VE DONE FOR THEM?
I'M YOUR PRISONER.
WHAT DOES IT MATTER WHAT I THINK OF YOU?
BUT, FOR THE RECORD, I THINK YOU'RE A NARCISSISTIC MONSTER.
JUST SO WE'RE CLEAR, DAUGHTER--
DON'T.
DON'T CALL ME THAT.
SO WE'RE CLEAR. YOU ARE NOT MY PRISONER.
NO? THAT'S EASY FOR YOU TO SAY.
WITH MY RING BURNED OUT, I COULDN'T LEAVE IF I WANTED.
AH... LYSSA.
DID YOU BRING WHAT I ASKED FOR?

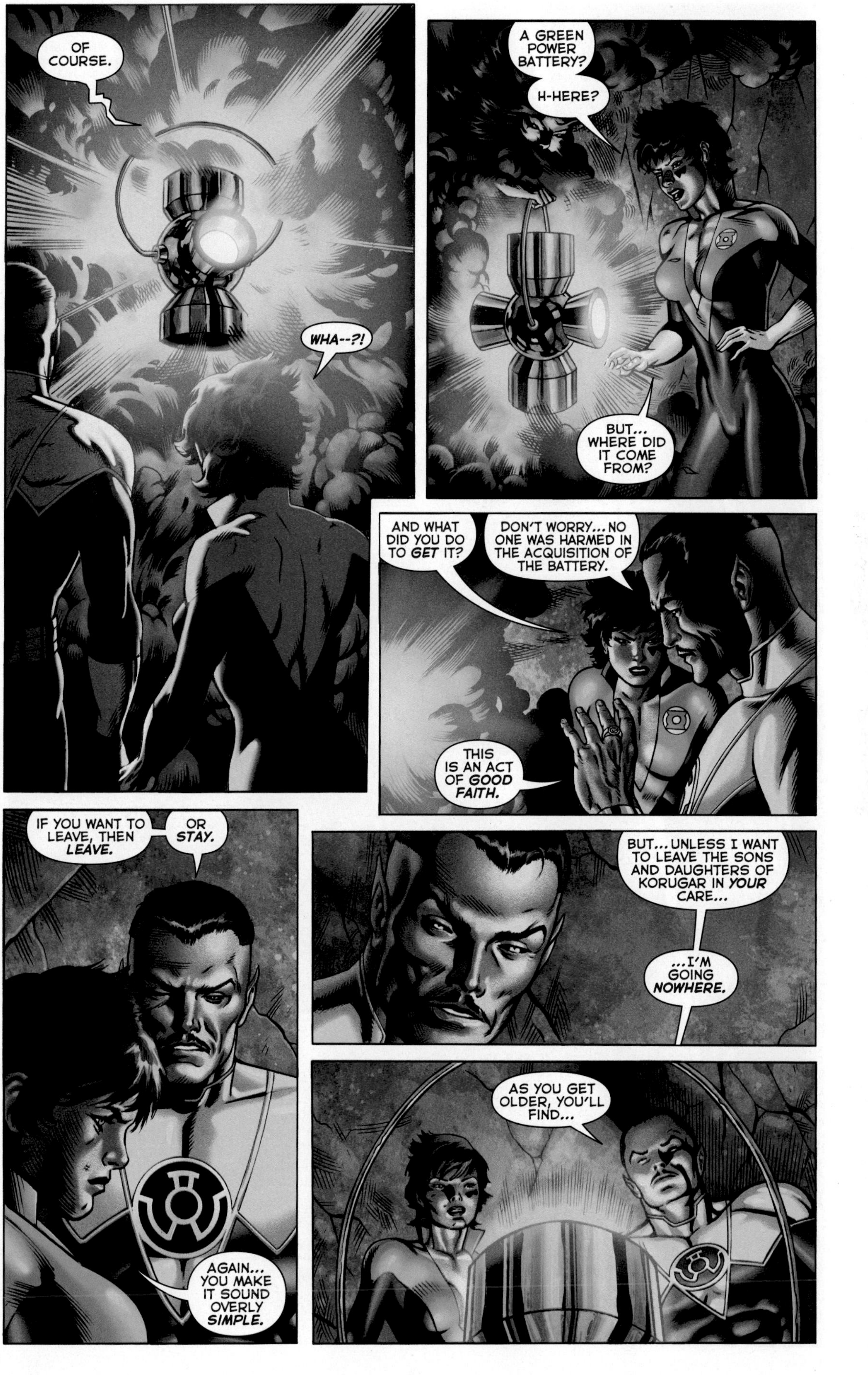
OF COURSE.
WHA--?!
A GREEN POWER BATTERY?
H-HERE?
BUT... WHERE DID IT COME FROM?
AND WHAT DID YOU DO TO GET IT?
DON'T WORRY... NO ONE WAS HARMED IN THE ACQUISITION OF THE BATTERY.
THIS IS AN ACT OF GOOD FAITH.
IF YOU WANT TO LEAVE, THEN LEAVE.
OR STAY.
AGAIN... YOU MAKE IT SOUND OVERLY SIMPLE.
BUT... UNLESS I WANT TO LEAVE THE SONS AND DAUGHTERS OF KORUGAR IN YOUR CARE...
...I'M GOING NOWHERE.
AS YOU GET OLDER, YOU'LL FIND...

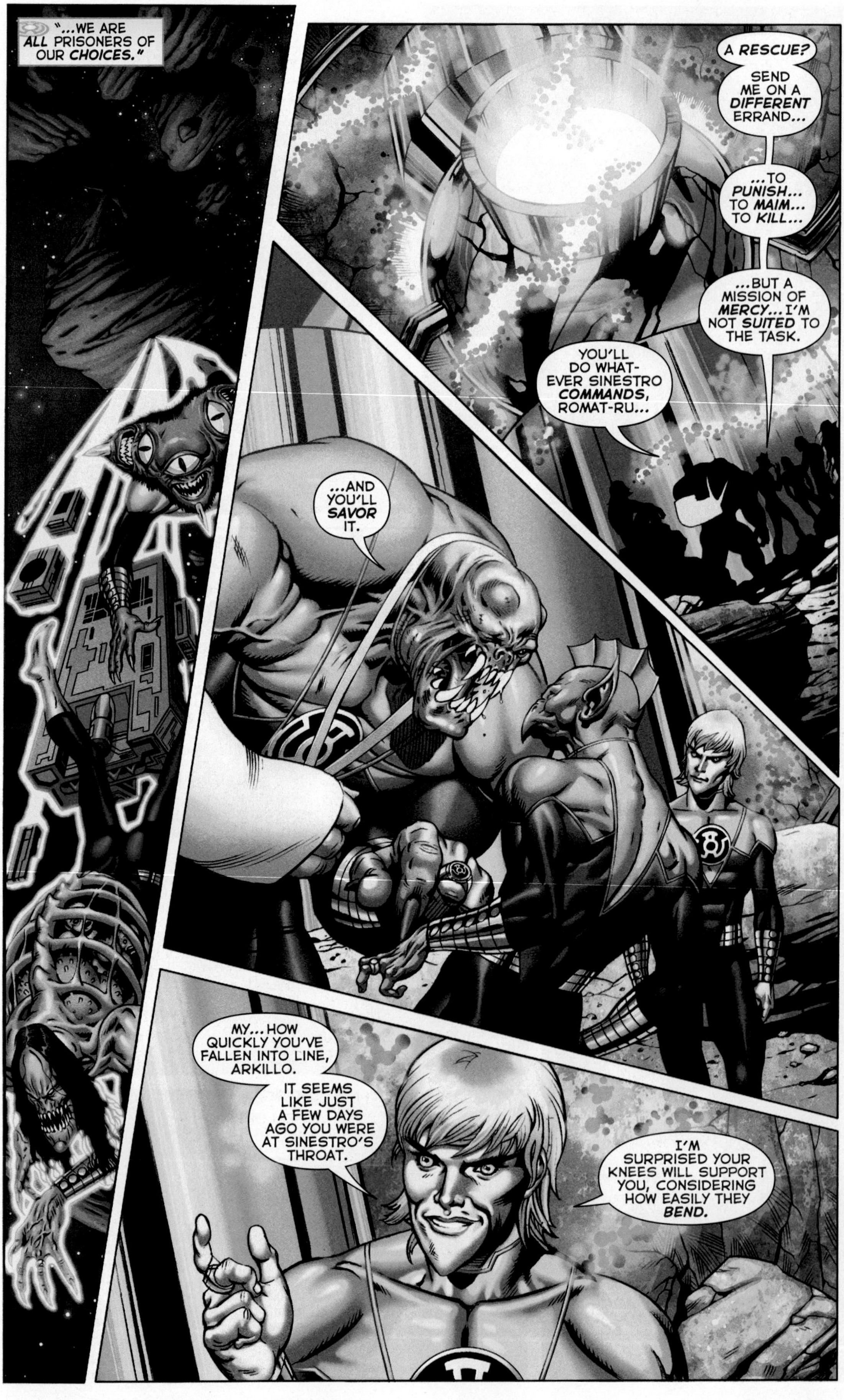
"...WE ARE ALL PRISONERS OF OUR CHOICES."
A RESCUE?
SEND ME ON A DIFFERENT ERRAND...
...TO PUNISH... TO MAIM... TO KILL...
...BUT A MISSION OF MERCY... I'M NOT SUITED TO THE TASK.
YOU'LL DO WHATEVER SINESTRO COMMANDS, ROMAT-RU...
...AND YOU'LL SAVOR IT.
MY... HOW QUICKLY YOU'VE FALLEN INTO LINE, ARKILLO.
IT SEEMS LIKE JUST A FEW DAYS AGO YOU WERE AT SINESTRO'S THROAT.
I'M SURPRISED YOUR KNEES WILL SUPPORT YOU, CONSIDERING HOW EASILY THEY BEND.

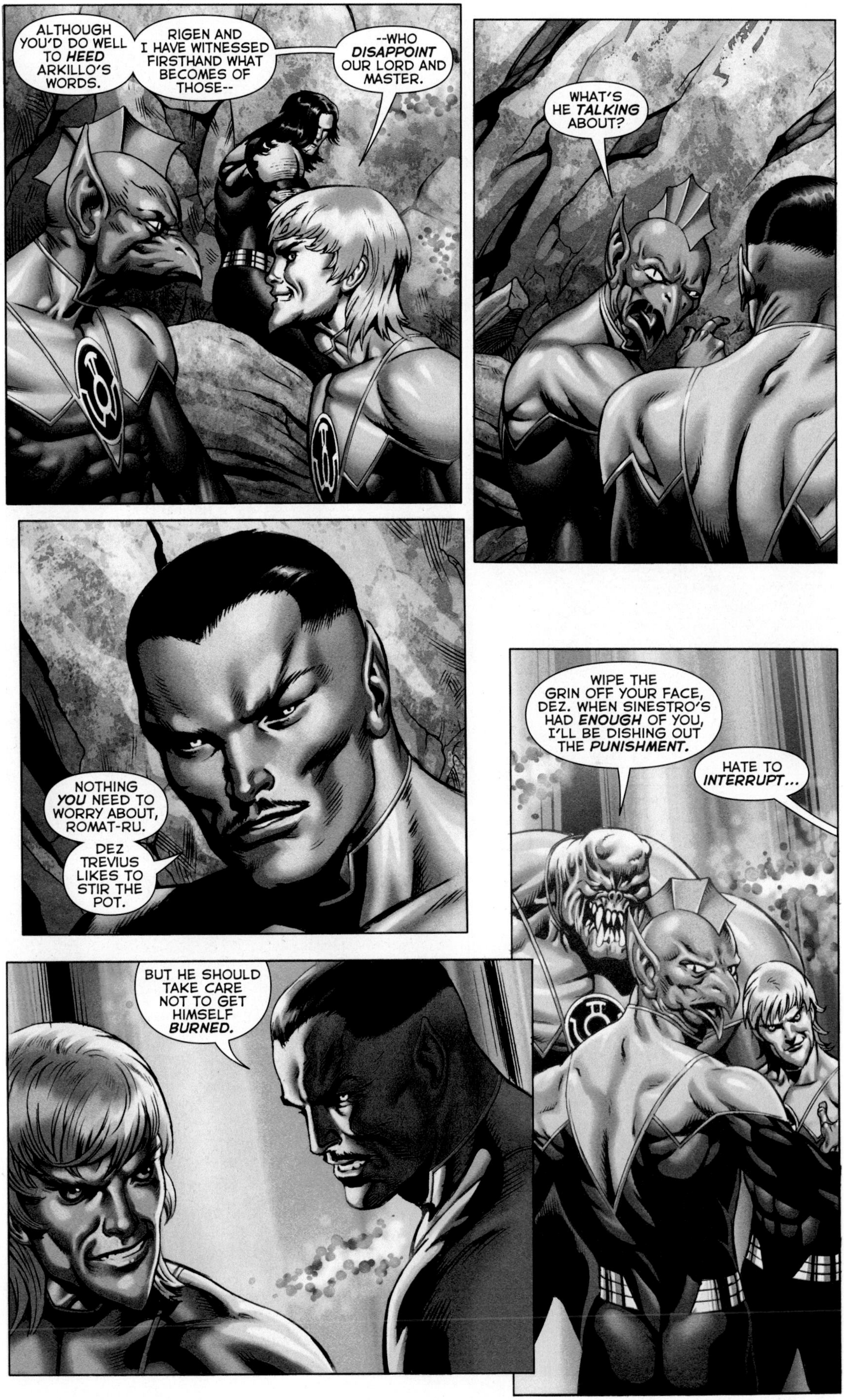
ALTHOUGH YOU'D DO WELL TO HEED ARKILLO'S WORDS.
RIGEN AND I HAVE WITNESSED FIRSTHAND WHAT BECOMES OF THOSE--
--WHO DISAPPOINT OUR LORD AND MASTER.
WHAT'S HE TALKING ABOUT?
NOTHING YOU NEED TO WORRY ABOUT, ROMAT-RU.
DEZ TREVIUS LIKES TO STIR THE POT.
BUT HE SHOULD TAKE CARE NOT TO GET HIMSELF BURNED.
WIPE THE GRIN OFF YOUR FACE, DEZ. WHEN SINESTRO'S HAD ENOUGH OF YOU, I'LL BE DISHING OUT THE PUNISHMENT.
HATE TO INTERRUPT...

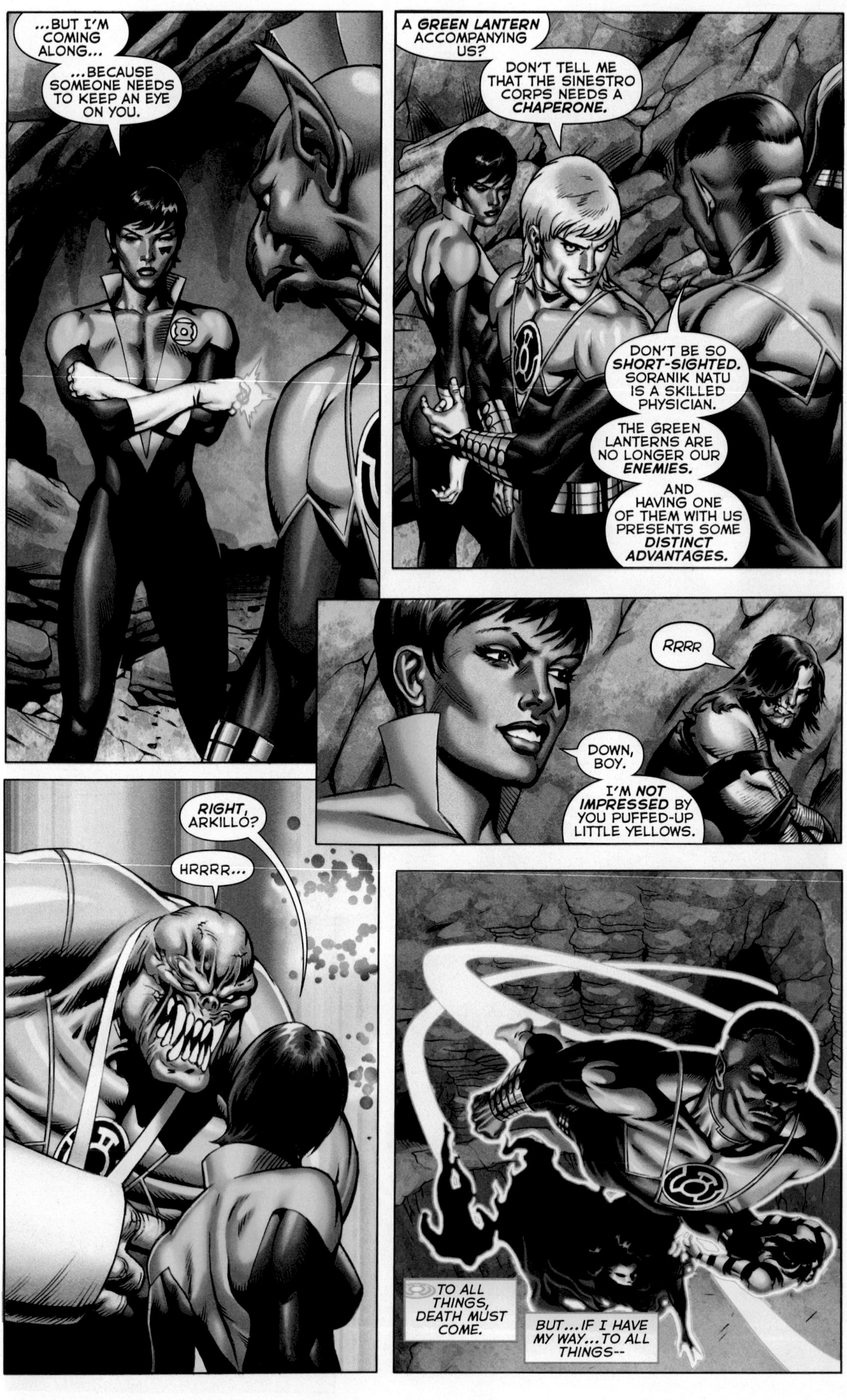
...BUT I'M COMING ALONG...
...BECAUSE SOMEONE NEEDS TO KEEP AN EYE ON YOU.
A GREEN LANTERN ACCOMPANYING US?
DON'T TELL ME THAT THE SINESTRO CORPS NEEDS A CHAPERONE.
DON'T BE SO SHORT-SIGHTED. SORANIK NATU IS A SKILLED PHYSICIAN.
THE GREEN LANTERNS ARE NO LONGER OUR ENEMIES.
AND HAVING ONE OF THEM WITH US PRESENTS SOME DISTINCT ADVANTAGES.
RRRR
DOWN, BOY.
I'M NOT IMPRESSED BY YOU PUFFED-UP LITTLE YELLOWS.
RIGHT, ARKILLO?
HRRRR...
TO ALL THINGS, DEATH MUST COME.
BUT...IF I HAVE MY WAY...TO ALL THINGS--

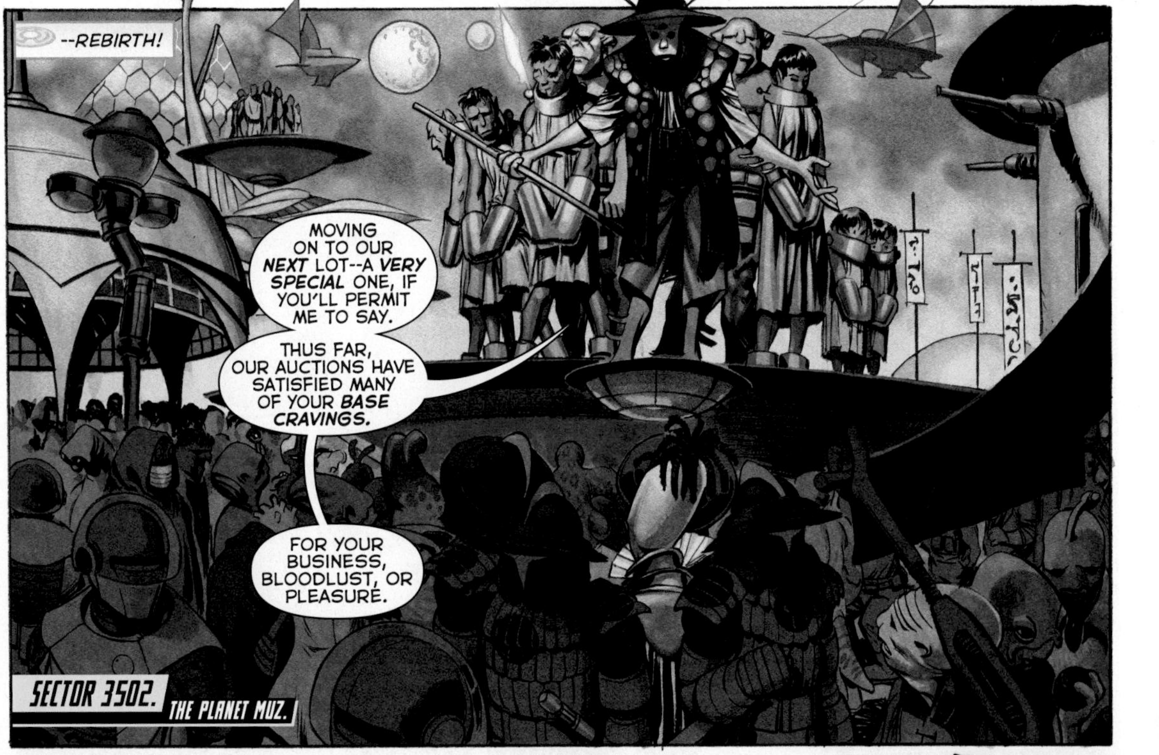

--REBIRTH!
MOVING ON TO OUR NEXT LOT--A VERY SPECIAL ONE, IF YOU'LL PERMIT ME TO SAY.
THUS FAR, OUR AUCTIONS HAVE SATISFIED MANY OF YOUR BASE CRAVINGS.
FOR YOUR BUSINESS, BLOODLUST, OR PLEASURE.
SECTOR 3502.
THE PLANET MUZ.

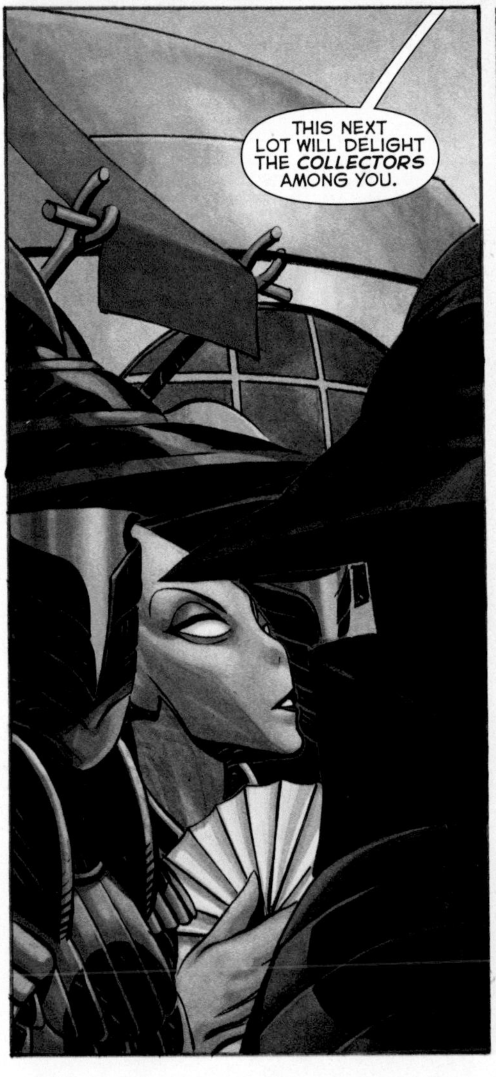

THIS NEXT LOT WILL DELIGHT THE COLLECTORS AMONG YOU.

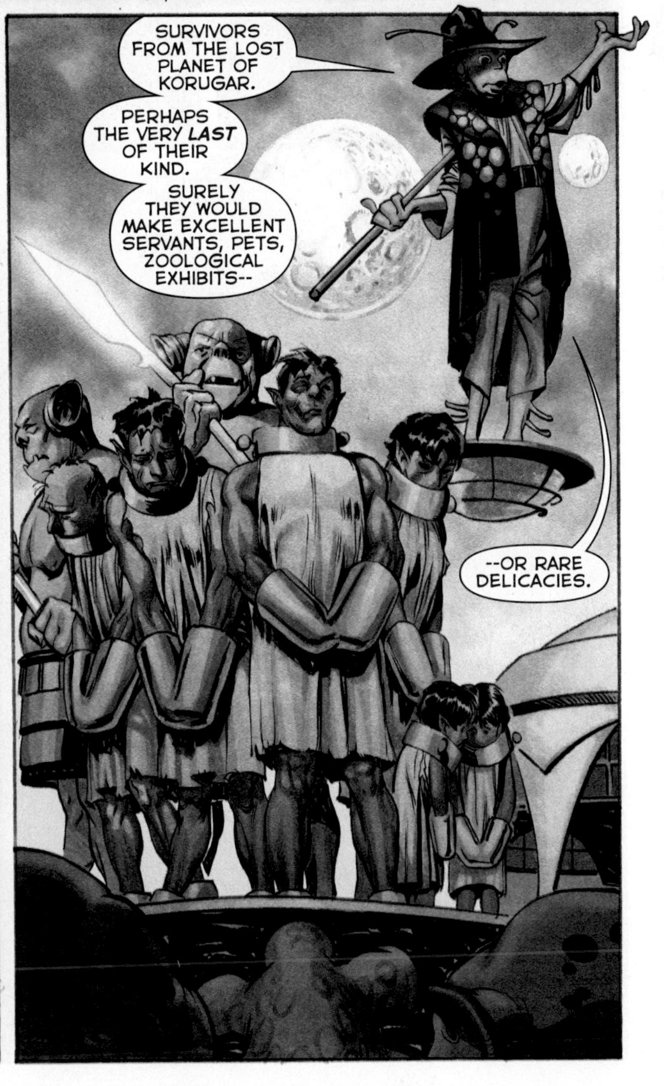

SURVIVORS FROM THE LOST PLANET OF KORUGAR.
PERHAPS THE VERY LAST OF THEIR KIND.
SURELY THEY WOULD MAKE EXCELLENT SERVANTS, PETS, ZOOLOGICAL EXHIBITS--
--OR RARE DELICACIES.

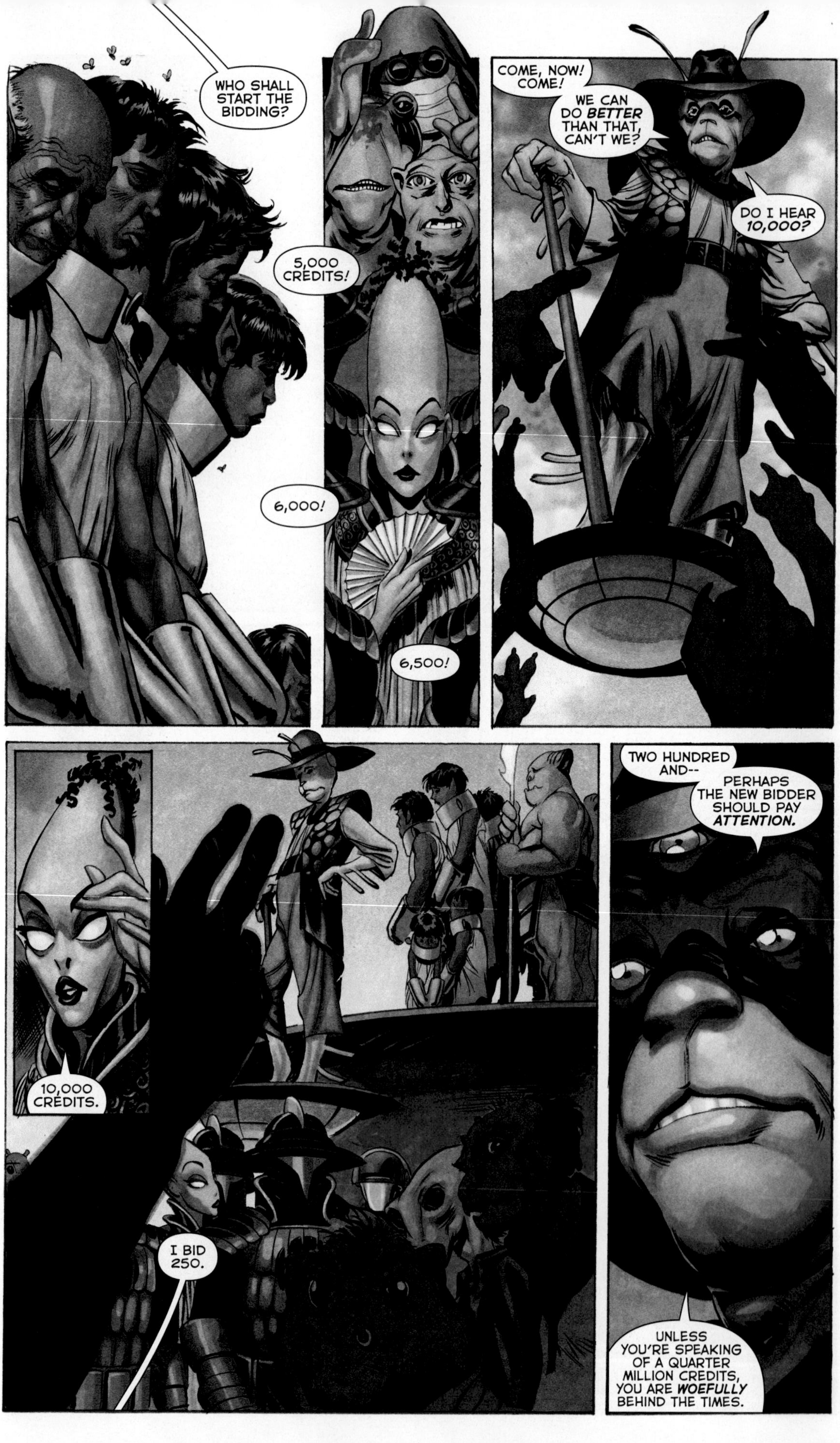
WHO SHALL START THE BIDDING?
5,000 CREDITS!
6,000!
6,500!
COME, NOW! COME!
WE CAN DO BETTER THAN THAT, CAN'T WE?
DO I HEAR 10,000?
10,000 CREDITS.
I BID 250.
TWO HUNDRED AND--
PERHAPS THE NEW BIDDER SHOULD PAY ATTENTION.
UNLESS YOU'RE SPEAKING OF A QUARTER MILLION CREDITS, YOU ARE WOEFULLY BEHIND THE TIMES.

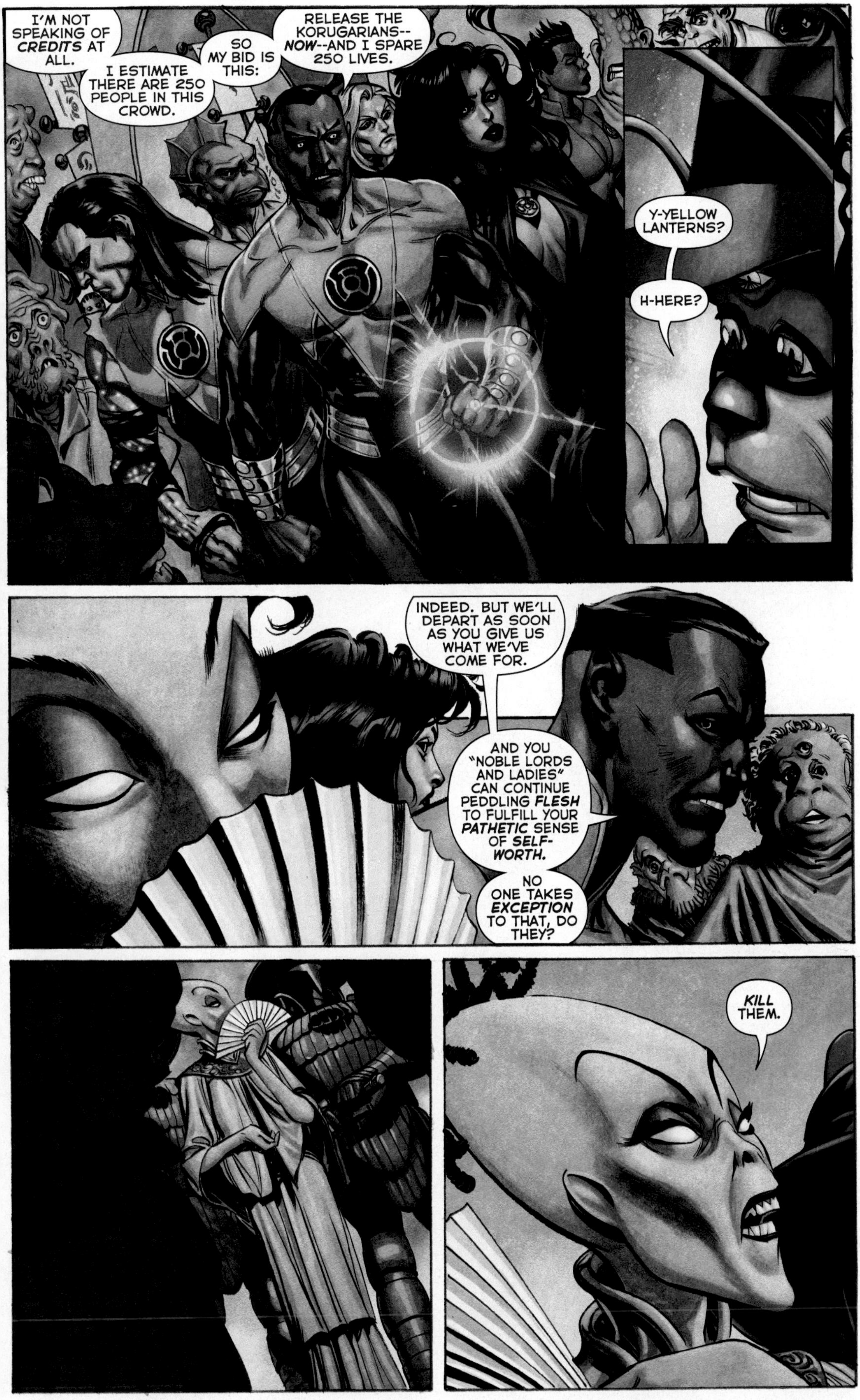
I'M NOT SPEAKING OF CREDITS AT ALL.
I ESTIMATE THERE ARE 250 PEOPLE IN THIS CROWD.
SO MY BID IS THIS:
RELEASE THE KORUGARIANS--NOW--AND I SPARE 250 LIVES.
Y-YELLOW LANTERNS?
H-HERE?
INDEED. BUT WE'LL DEPART AS SOON AS YOU GIVE US WHAT WE'VE COME FOR.
AND YOU "NOBLE LORDS AND LADIES" CAN CONTINUE PEDDLING FLESH TO FULFILL YOUR PATHETIC SENSE OF SELF-WORTH.
NO ONE TAKES EXCEPTION TO THAT, DO THEY?
KILL THEM.

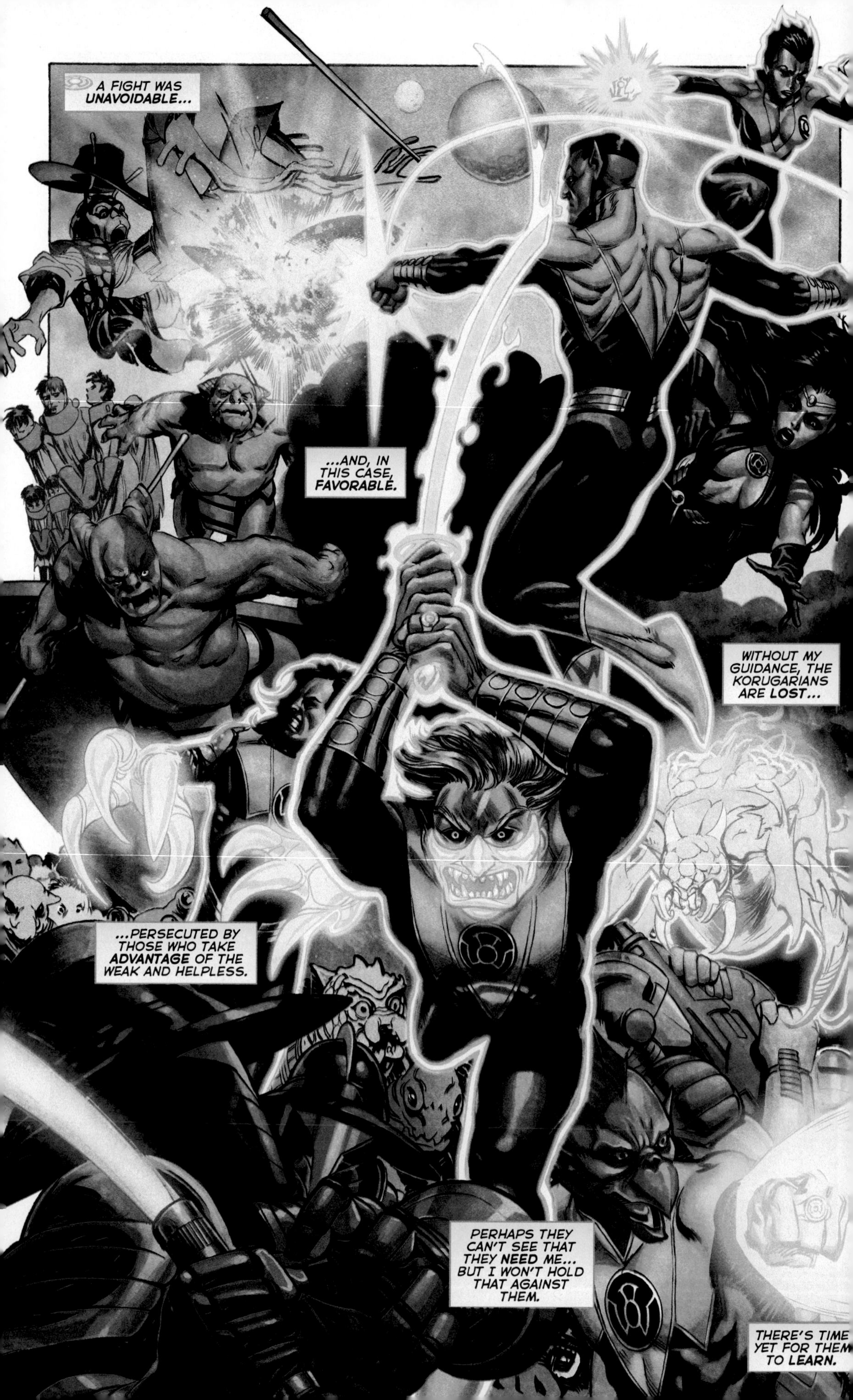
A FIGHT WAS UNAVOIDABLE...
...AND, IN THIS CASE, FAVORABLE.
WITHOUT MY GUIDANCE, THE KORUGARIANS ARE LOST...
...PERSECUTED BY THOSE WHO TAKE ADVANTAGE OF THE WEAK AND HELPLESS.
PERHAPS THEY CAN'T SEE THAT THEY NEED ME... BUT I WON'T HOLD THAT AGAINST THEM.
THERE'S TIME YET FOR THEM TO LEARN.

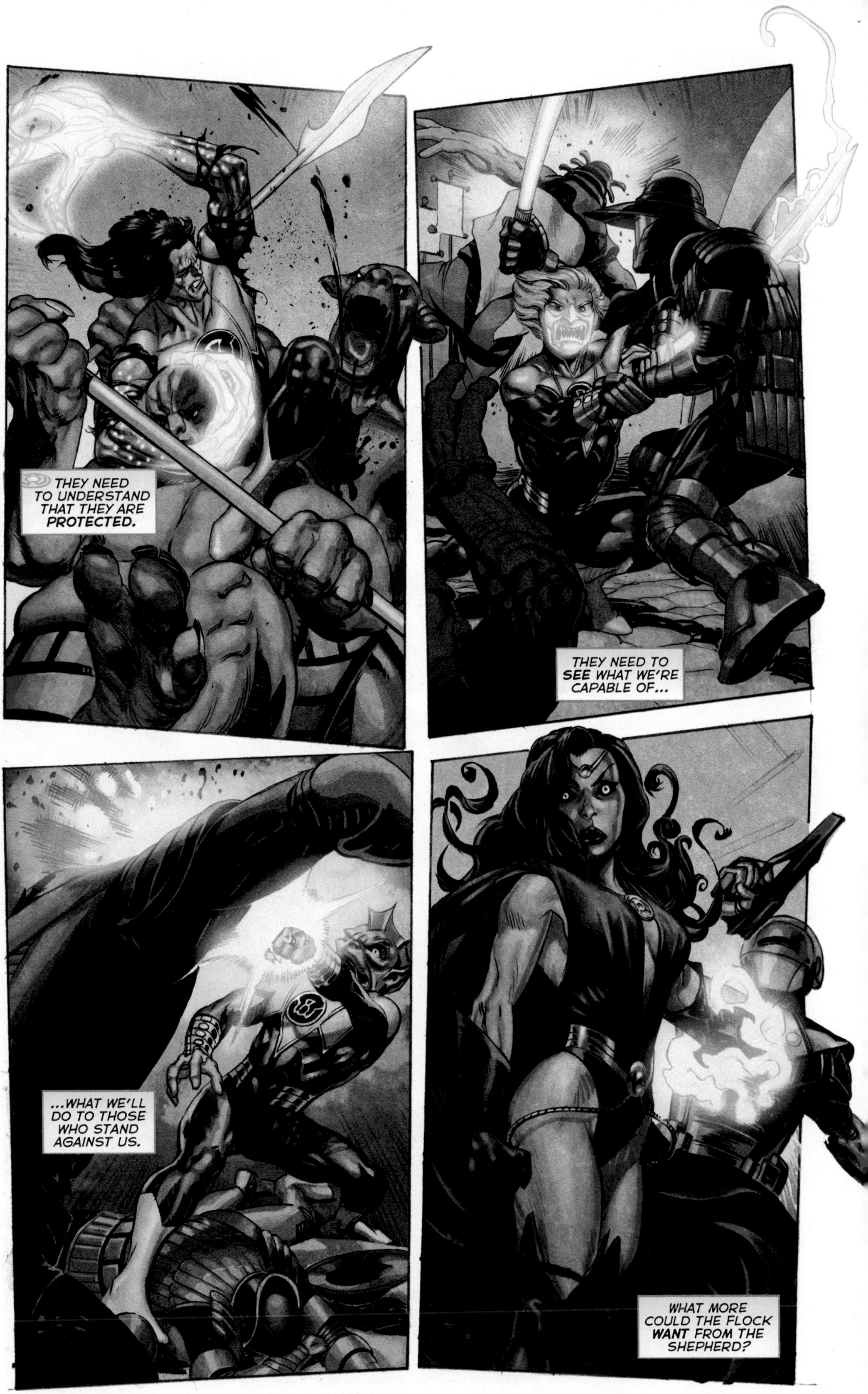

THEY NEED TO UNDERSTAND THAT THEY ARE PROTECTED.
THEY NEED TO SEE WHAT WE'RE CAPABLE OF...
...WHAT WE'LL DO TO THOSE WHO STAND AGAINST US.
WHAT MORE COULD THE FLOCK WANT FROM THE SHEPHERD?

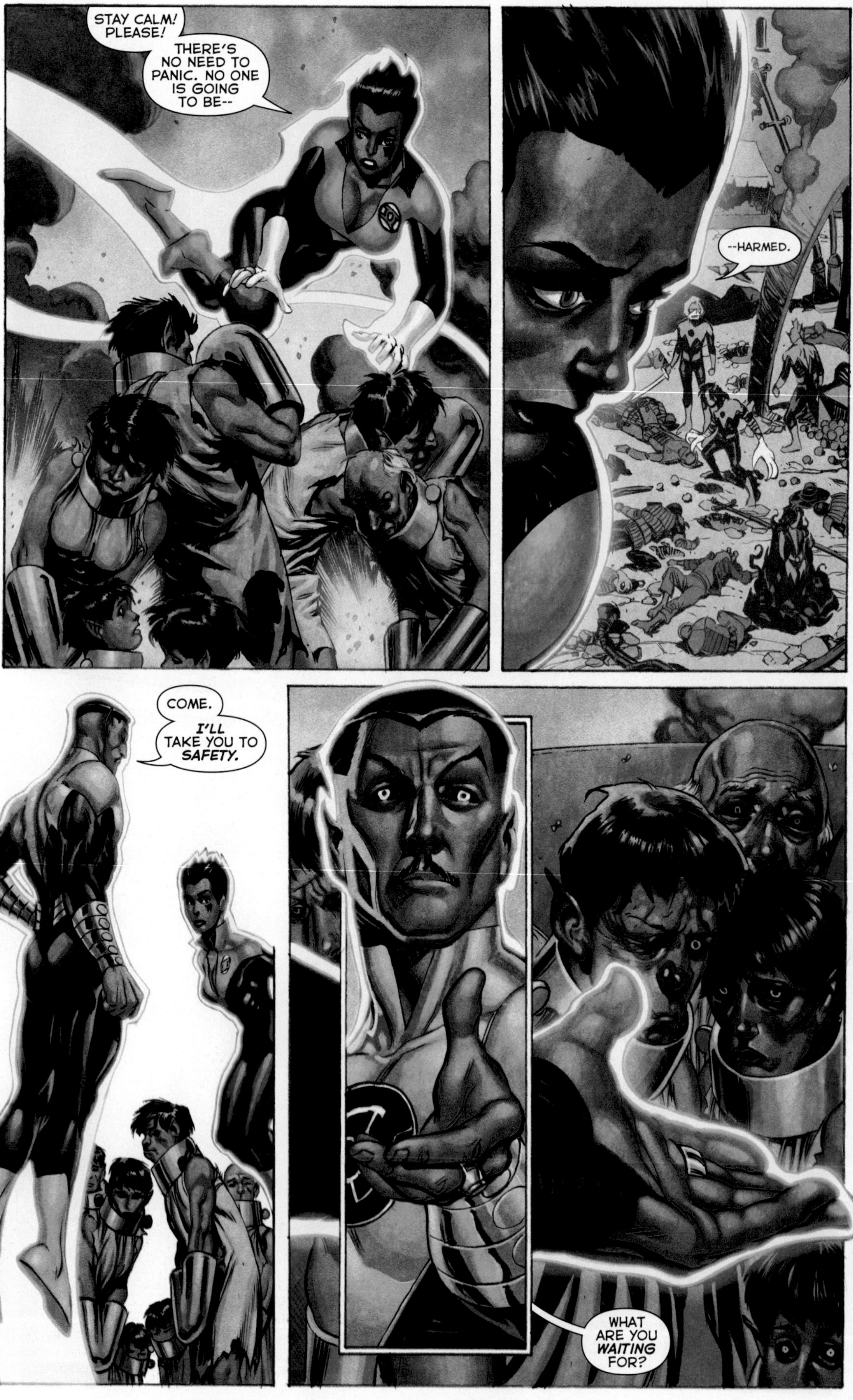
STAY CALM! PLEASE!
THERE'S NO NEED TO PANIC. NO ONE IS GOING TO BE--
--HARMED.
COME. I'LL TAKE YOU TO SAFETY.
WHAT ARE YOU WAITING FOR?

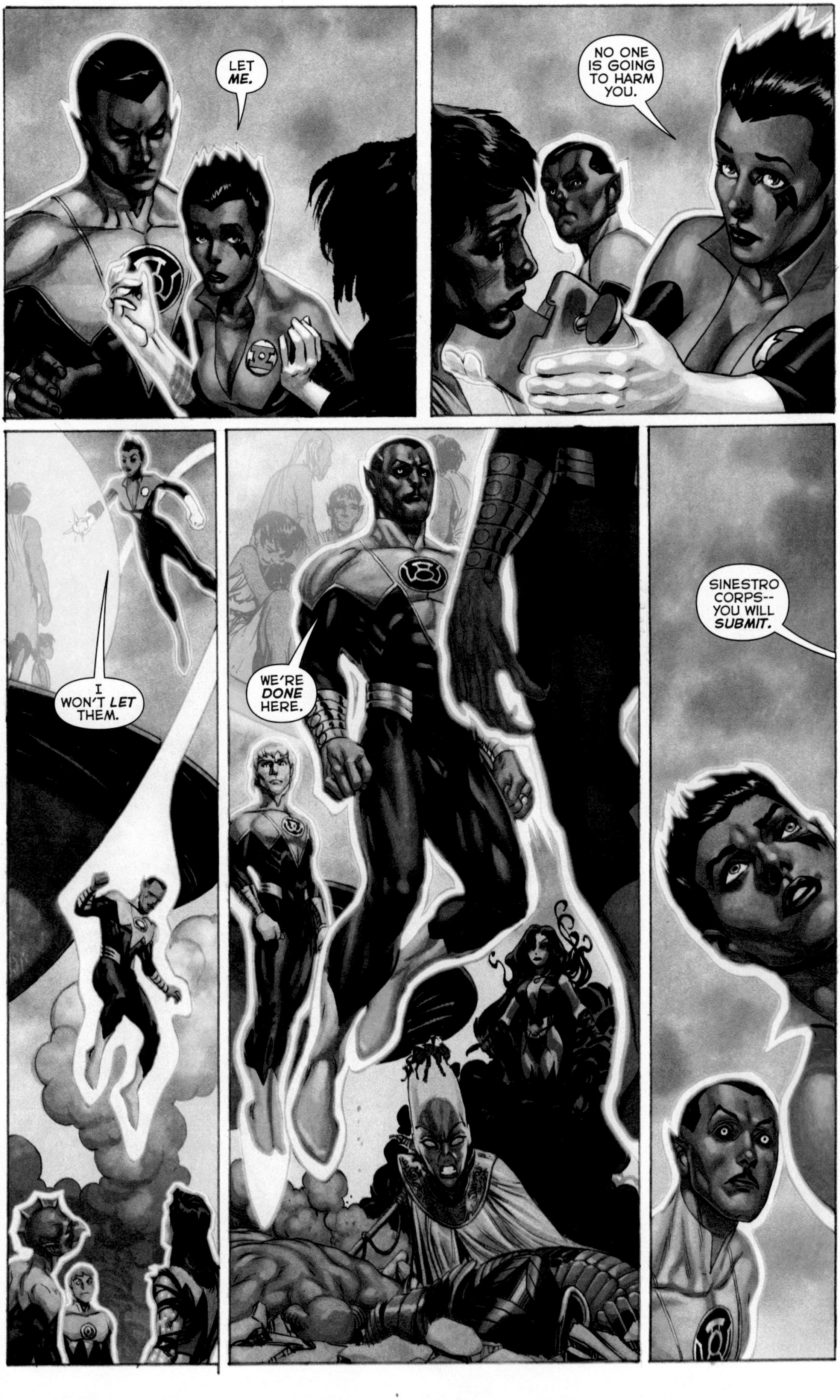
LET ME.
NO ONE IS GOING TO HARM YOU.
I WON'T LET THEM.
WE'RE DONE HERE.
SINESTRO CORPS-- YOU WILL SUBMIT.

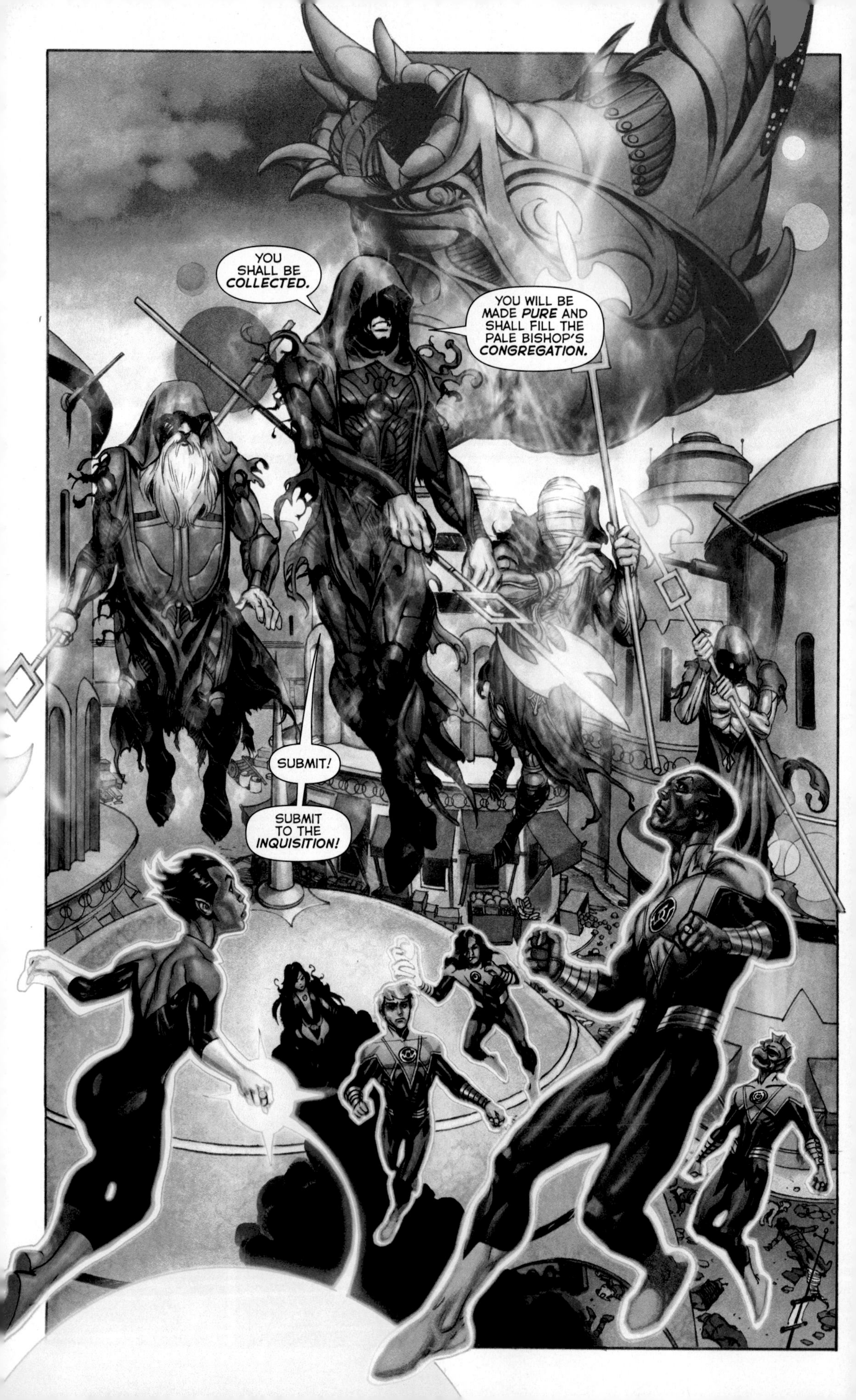
YOU SHALL BE COLLECTED.
YOU WILL BE MADE PURE AND SHALL FILL THE PALE BISHOP'S CONGREGATION.
SUBMIT!
SUBMIT TO THE INQUISITION!

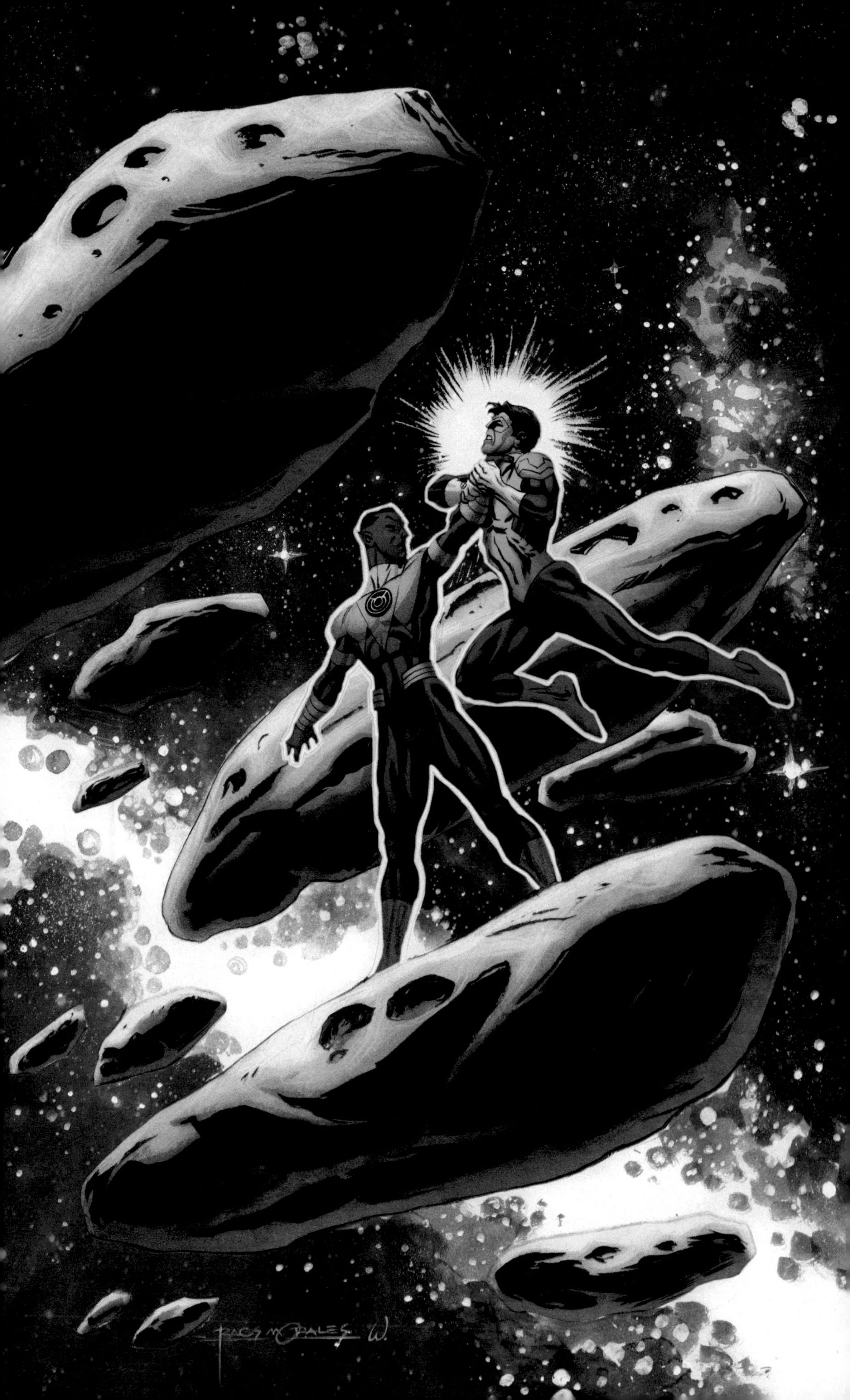

INQUISITION

CULLEN BUNN writer **RAGS MORALES** artist **JASON WRIGHT** colorist **TAYLOR ESPOSITO** letterer
cover art by **RAGS MORALES & JASON WRIGHT**

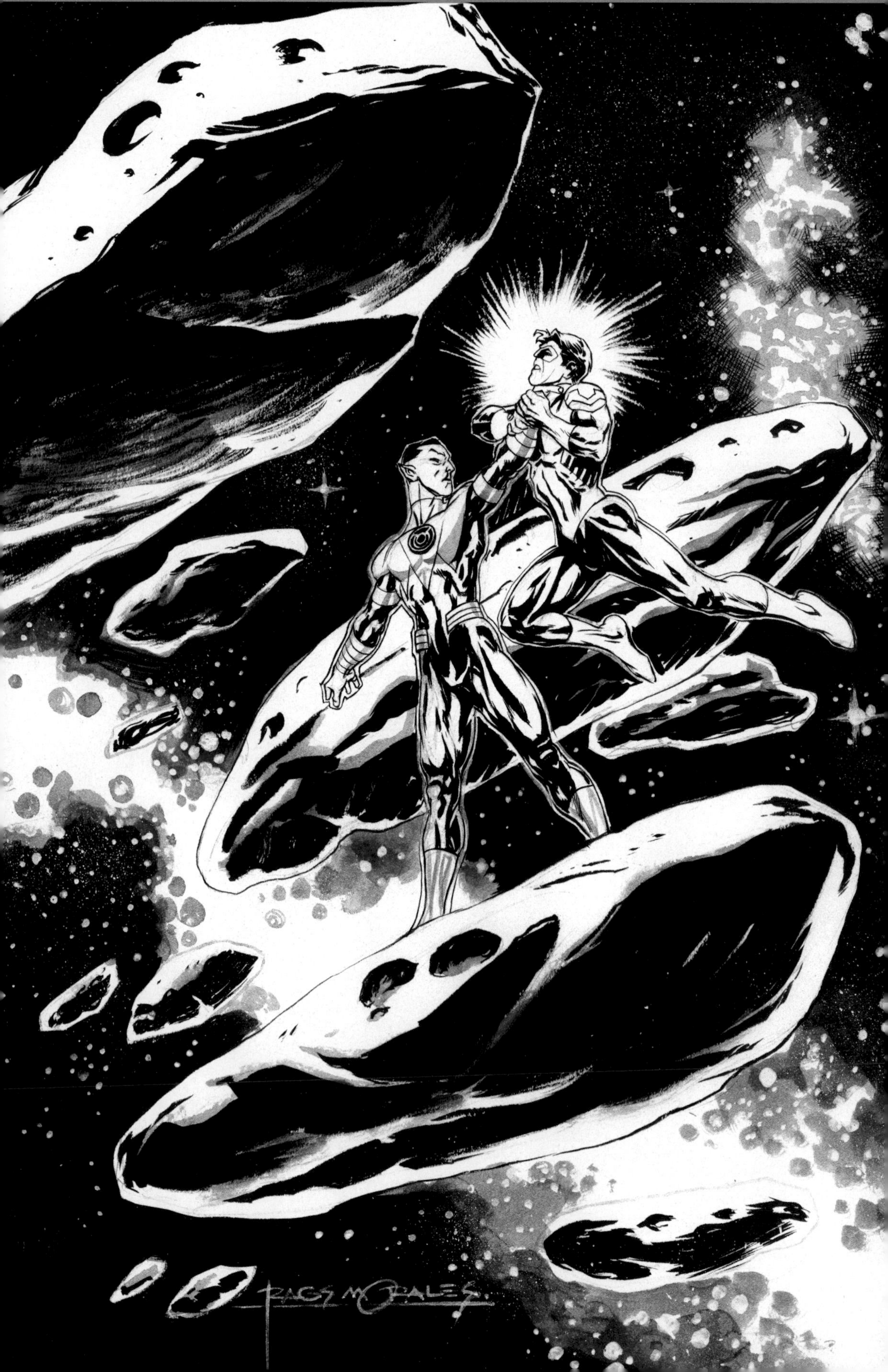
RAGS MORALES

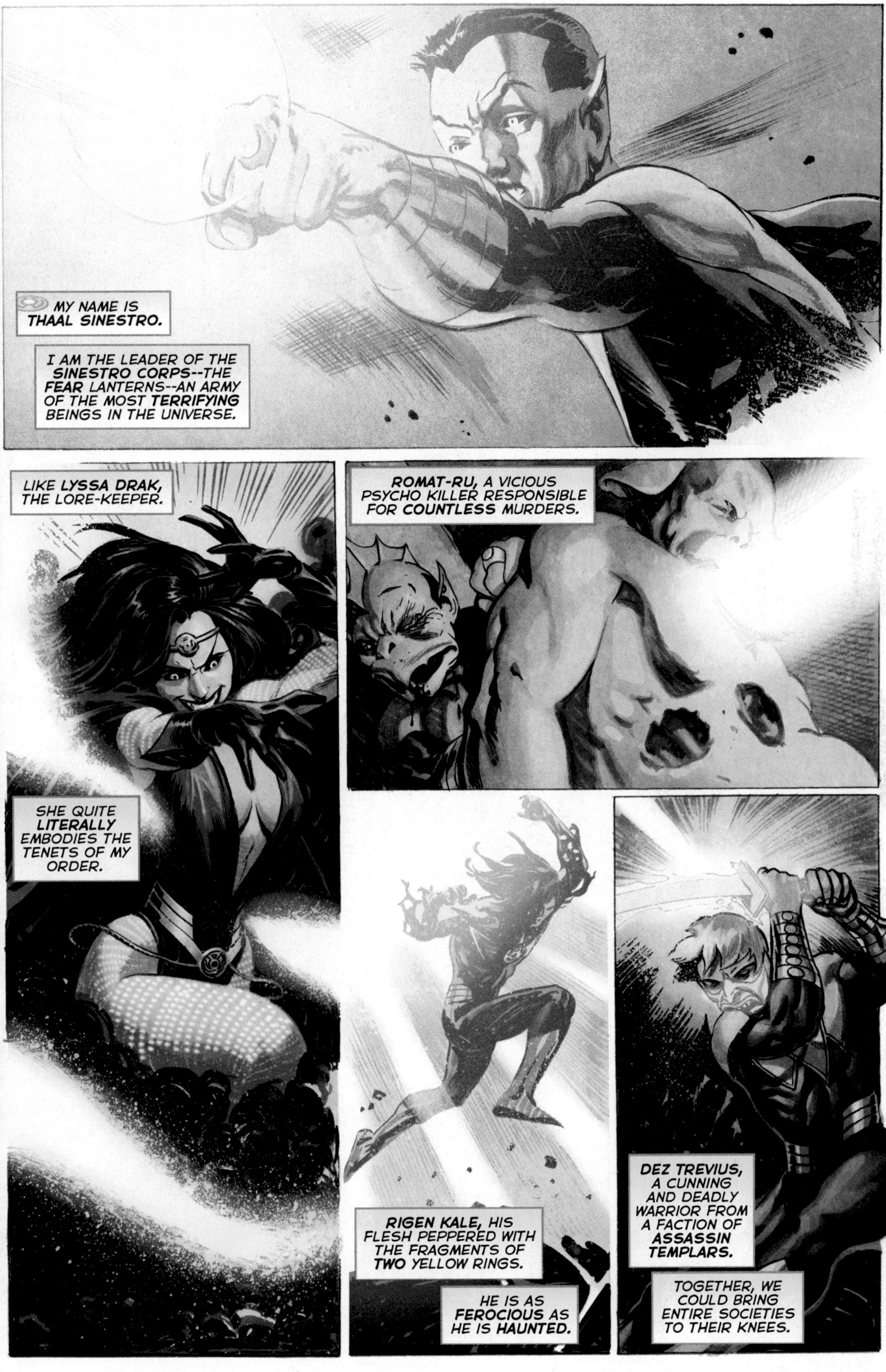
MY NAME IS THAAL SINESTRO.
I AM THE LEADER OF THE SINESTRO CORPS--THE FEAR LANTERNS--AN ARMY OF THE MOST TERRIFYING BEINGS IN THE UNIVERSE.
LIKE LYSSA DRAK, THE LORE-KEEPER.
SHE QUITE LITERALLY EMBODIES THE TENETS OF MY ORDER.
ROMAT-RU, A VICIOUS PSYCHO KILLER RESPONSIBLE FOR COUNTLESS MURDERS.
RIGEN KALE, HIS FLESH PEPPERED WITH THE FRAGMENTS OF TWO YELLOW RINGS.
HE IS AS FEROCIOUS AS HE IS HAUNTED.
DEZ TREVIUS, A CUNNING AND DEADLY WARRIOR FROM A FACTION OF ASSASSIN TEMPLARS.
TOGETHER, WE COULD BRING ENTIRE SOCIETIES TO THEIR KNEES.

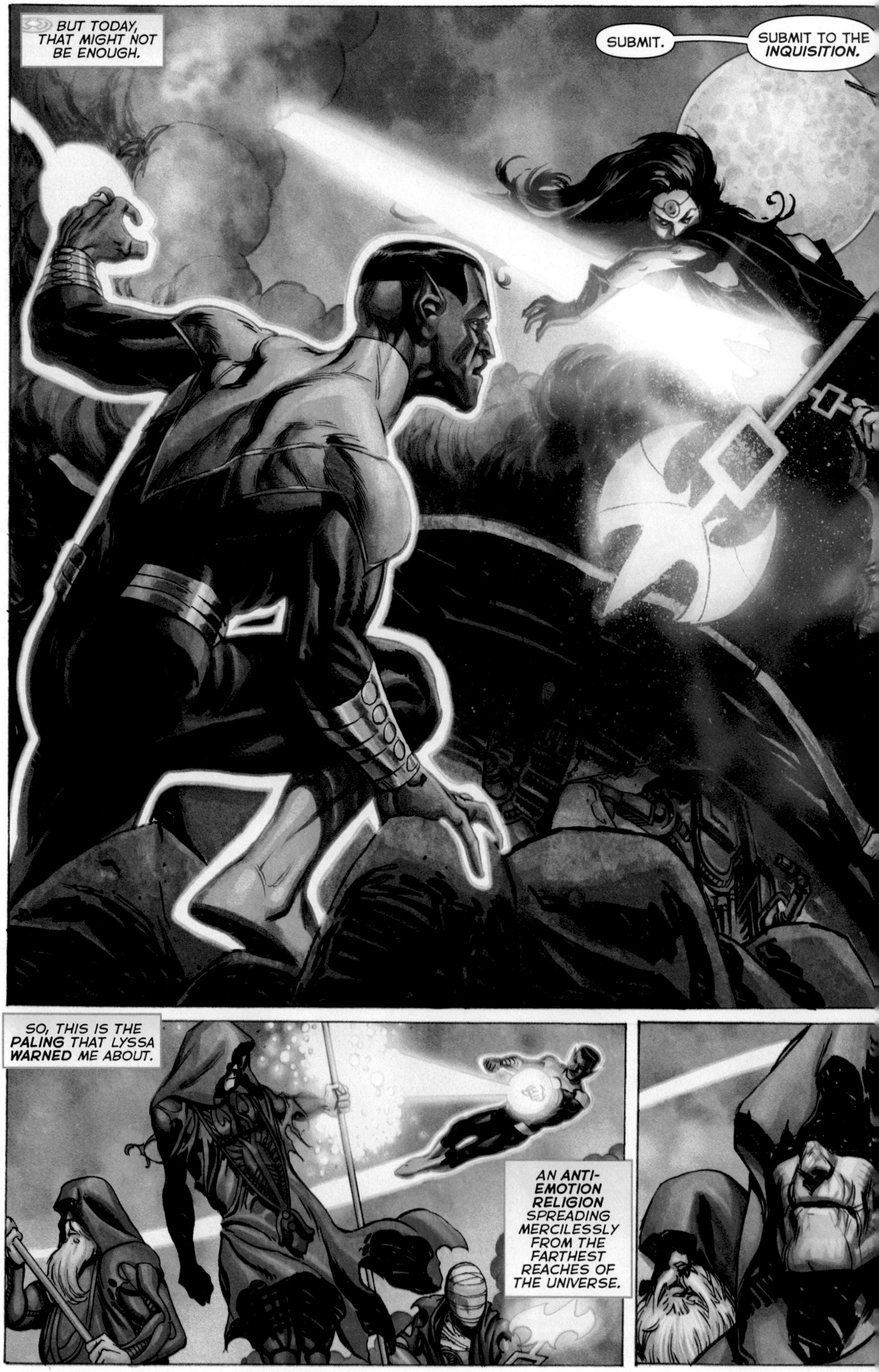
BUT TODAY, THAT MIGHT NOT BE ENOUGH.
SUBMIT.
SUBMIT TO THE INQUISITION.
SO, THIS IS THE PALING THAT LYSSA WARNED ME ABOUT.
AN ANTI-EMOTION RELIGION SPREADING MERCILESSLY FROM THE FARTHEST REACHES OF THE UNIVERSE.

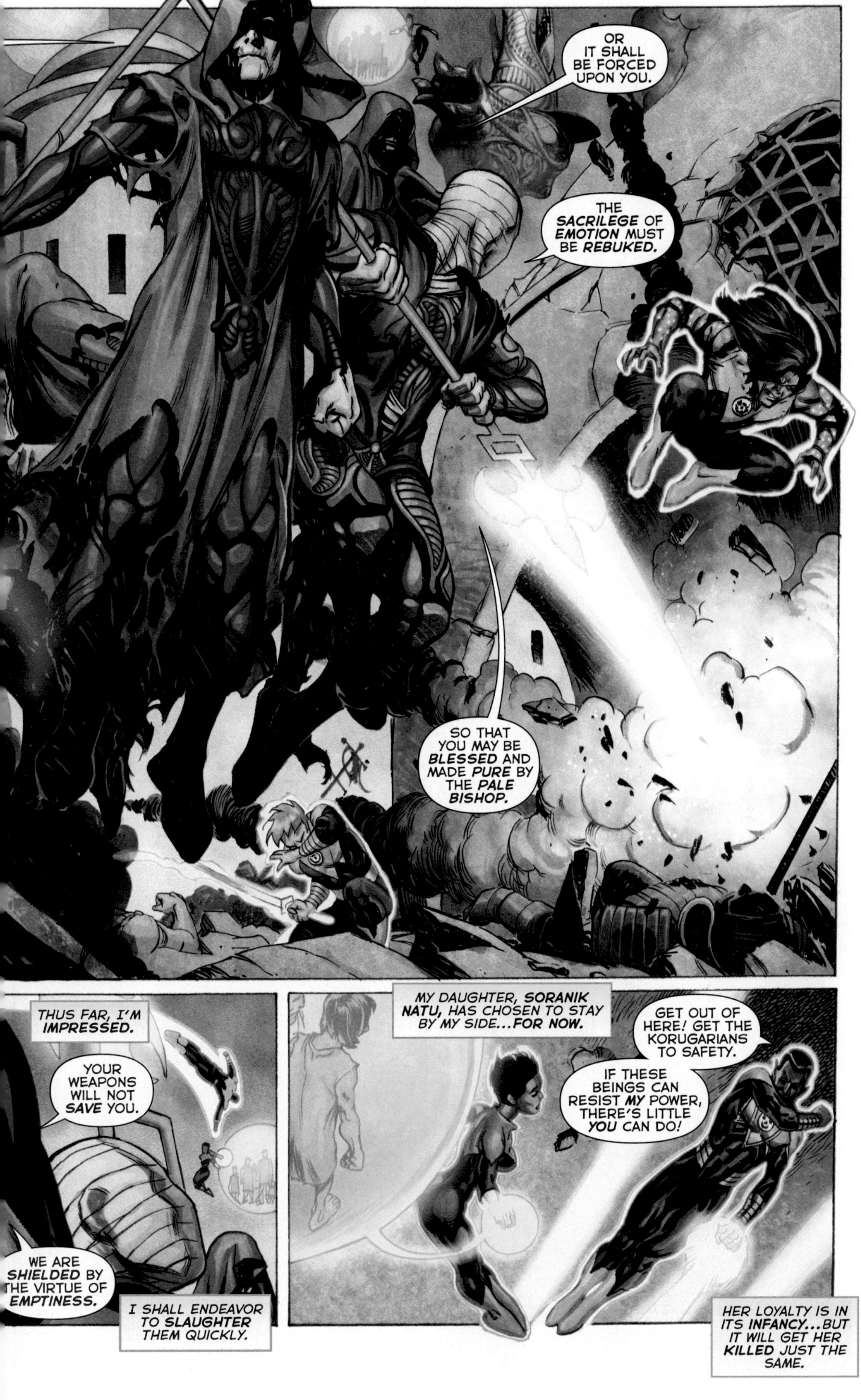
OR IT SHALL BE FORCED UPON YOU.
THE SACRILEGE OF EMOTION MUST BE REBUKED.
SO THAT YOU MAY BE BLESSED AND MADE PURE BY THE PALE BISHOP.
THUS FAR, I'M IMPRESSED.
YOUR WEAPONS WILL NOT SAVE YOU.
WE ARE SHIELDED BY THE VIRTUE OF EMPTINESS.
I SHALL ENDEAVOR TO SLAUGHTER THEM QUICKLY.
MY DAUGHTER, SORANIK NATU, HAS CHOSEN TO STAY BY MY SIDE...FOR NOW.
GET OUT OF HERE! GET THE KORUGARIANS TO SAFETY.
IF THESE BEINGS CAN RESIST MY POWER, THERE'S LITTLE YOU CAN DO!
HER LOYALTY IS IN ITS INFANCY...BUT IT WILL GET HER KILLED JUST THE SAME.

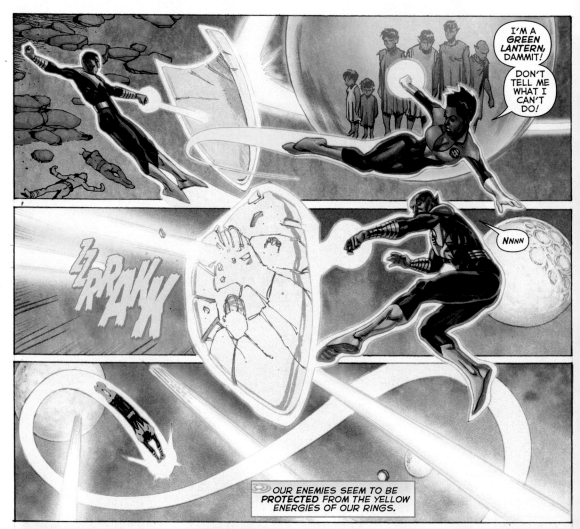

I'M A **GREEN LANTERN,** DAMMIT!

DON'T TELL ME WHAT I CAN'T DO!

Nnnn

ZZRRAWK

OUR ENEMIES SEEM TO BE **PROTECTED** FROM THE YELLOW ENERGIES OF OUR RINGS.

BUT NO WALL IS **IMPENETRABLE.**

KRAWZZZZ

EACH HAS A **WEAKNESS.**

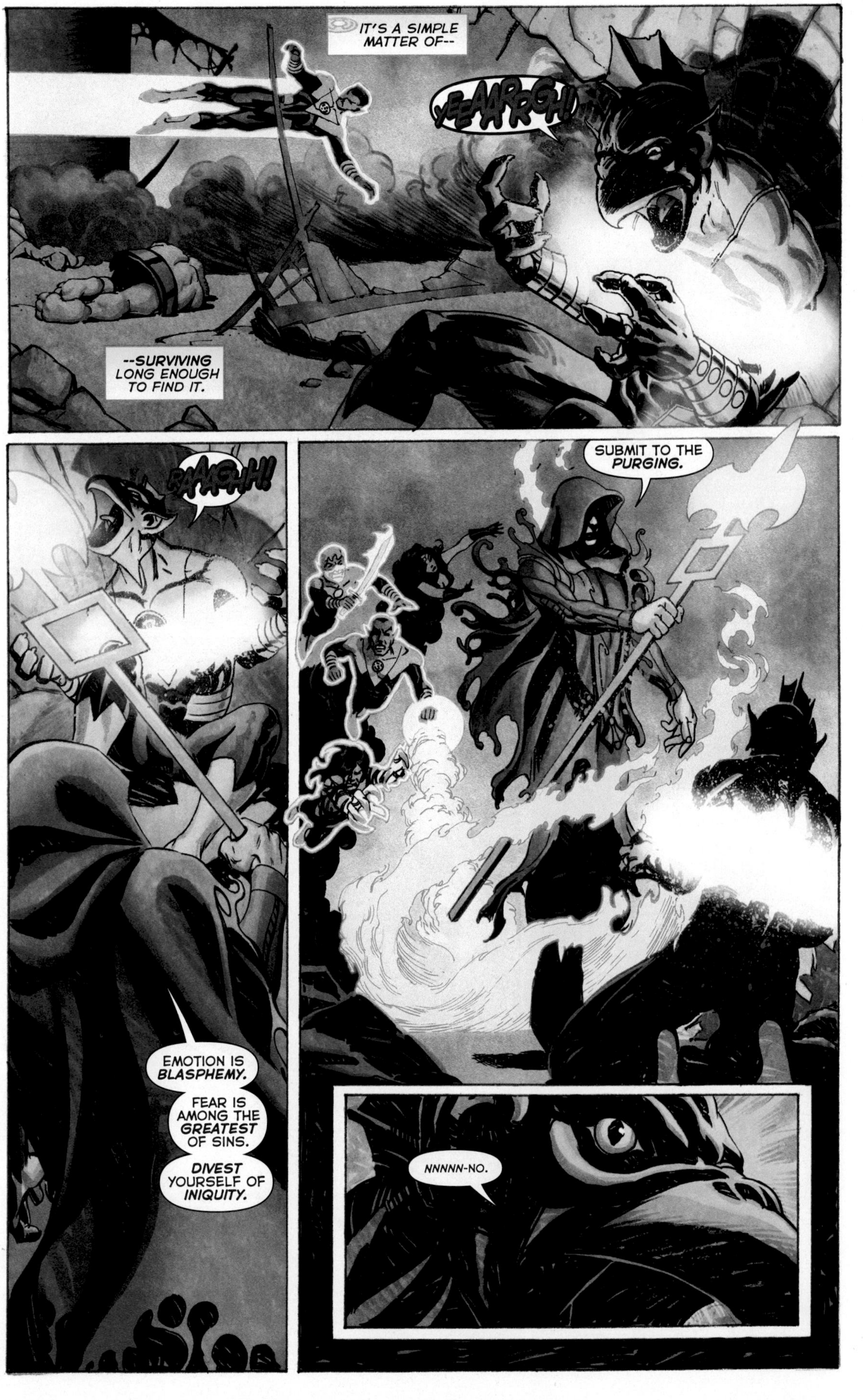
IT'S A SIMPLE MATTER OF--
YEEAARRGH!
--SURVIVING LONG ENOUGH TO FIND IT.
RAAAGHH!
EMOTION IS BLASPHEMY.
FEAR IS AMONG THE GREATEST OF SINS.
DIVEST YOURSELF OF INIQUITY.
SUBMIT TO THE PURGING.
NNNNN-NO.

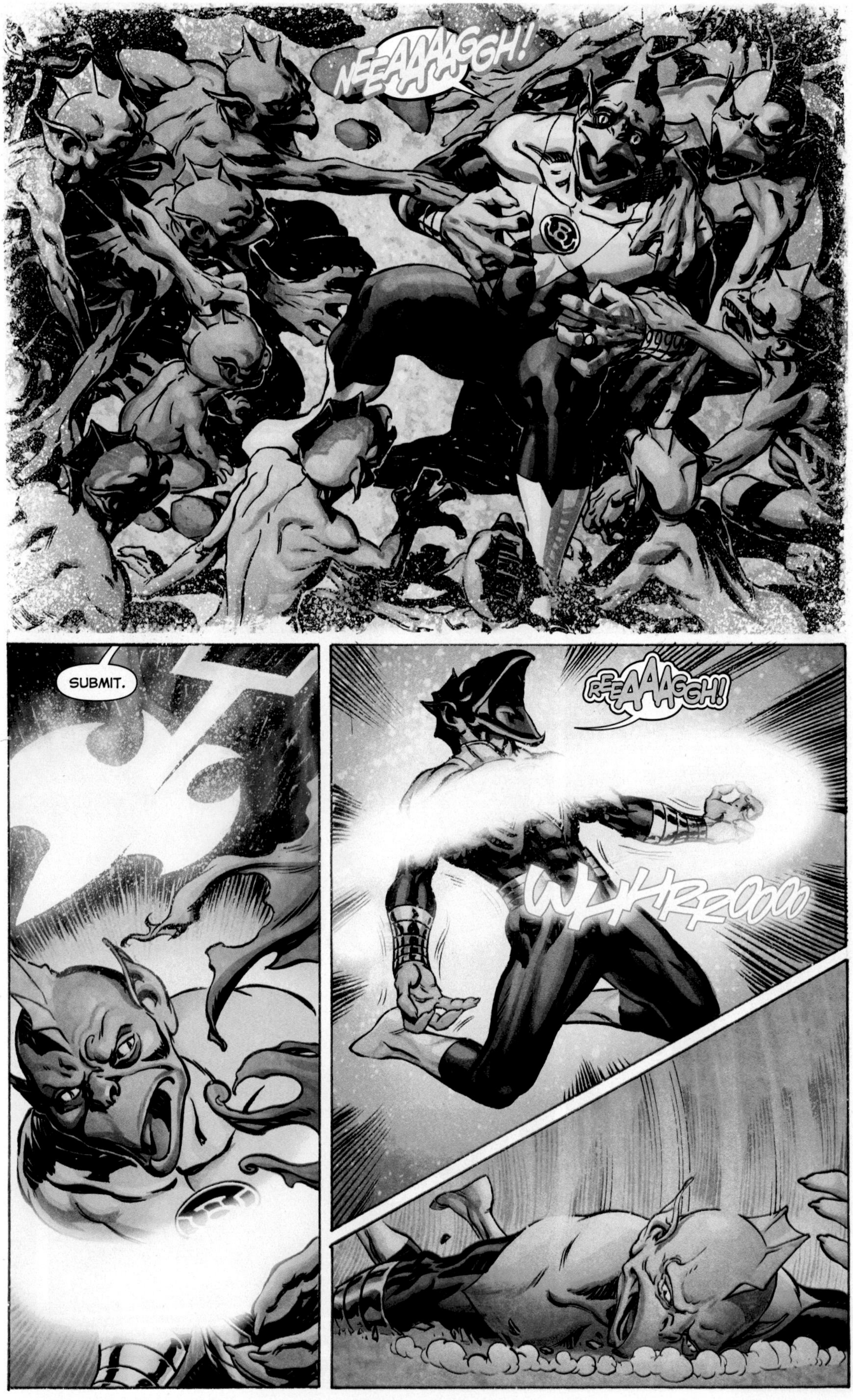
NEEAAAAGGH!
SUBMIT.
REEAAAAGGH!
WHRROOOO

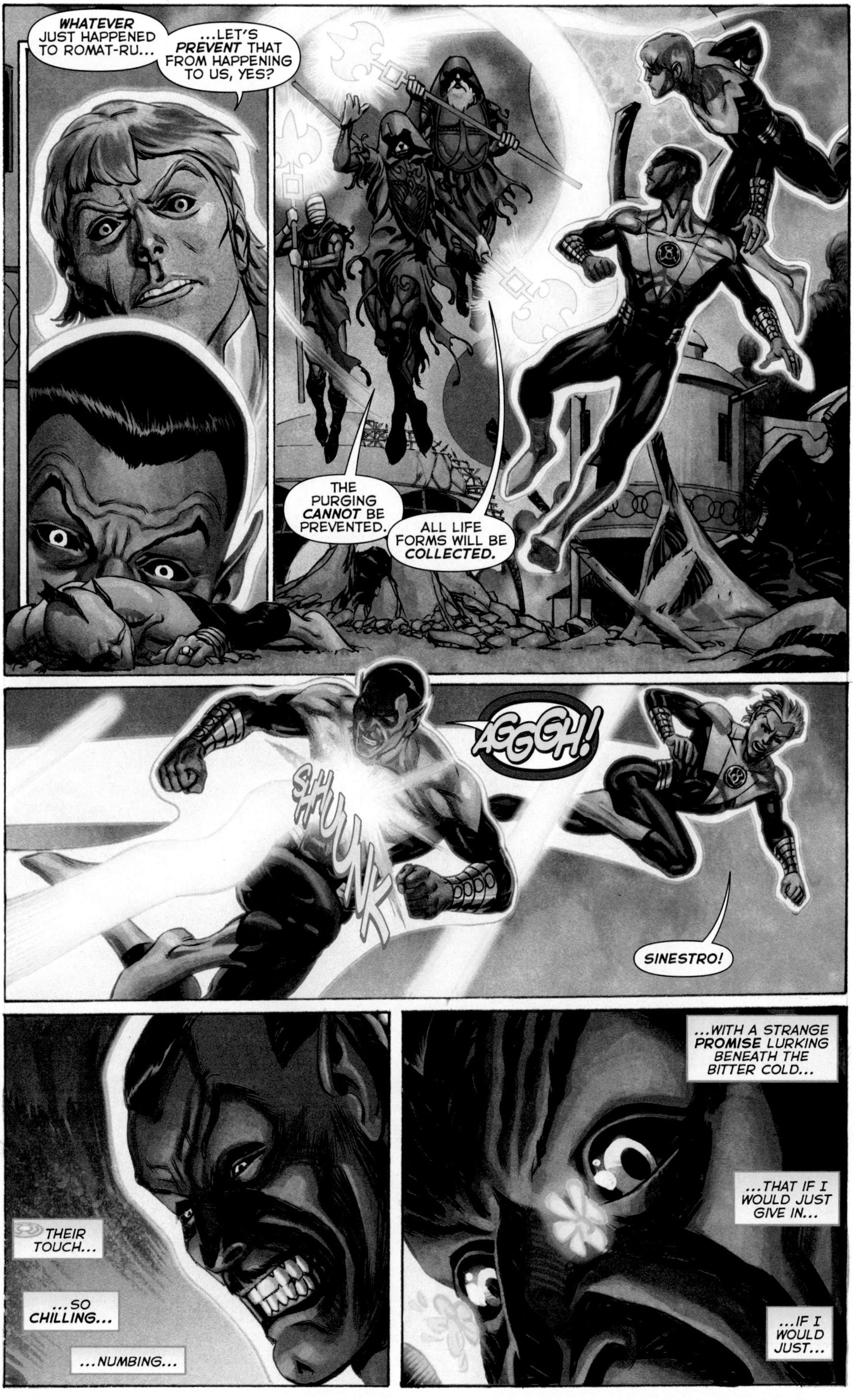
WHATEVER JUST HAPPENED TO ROMAT-RU...
...LET'S PREVENT THAT FROM HAPPENING TO US, YES?
THE PURGING CANNOT BE PREVENTED.
ALL LIFE FORMS WILL BE COLLECTED.
AGGGH!
SHUUNK
SINESTRO!
THEIR TOUCH...
...SO CHILLING...
...NUMBING...
...WITH A STRANGE PROMISE LURKING BENEATH THE BITTER COLD...
...THAT IF I WOULD JUST GIVE IN...
...IF I WOULD JUST...

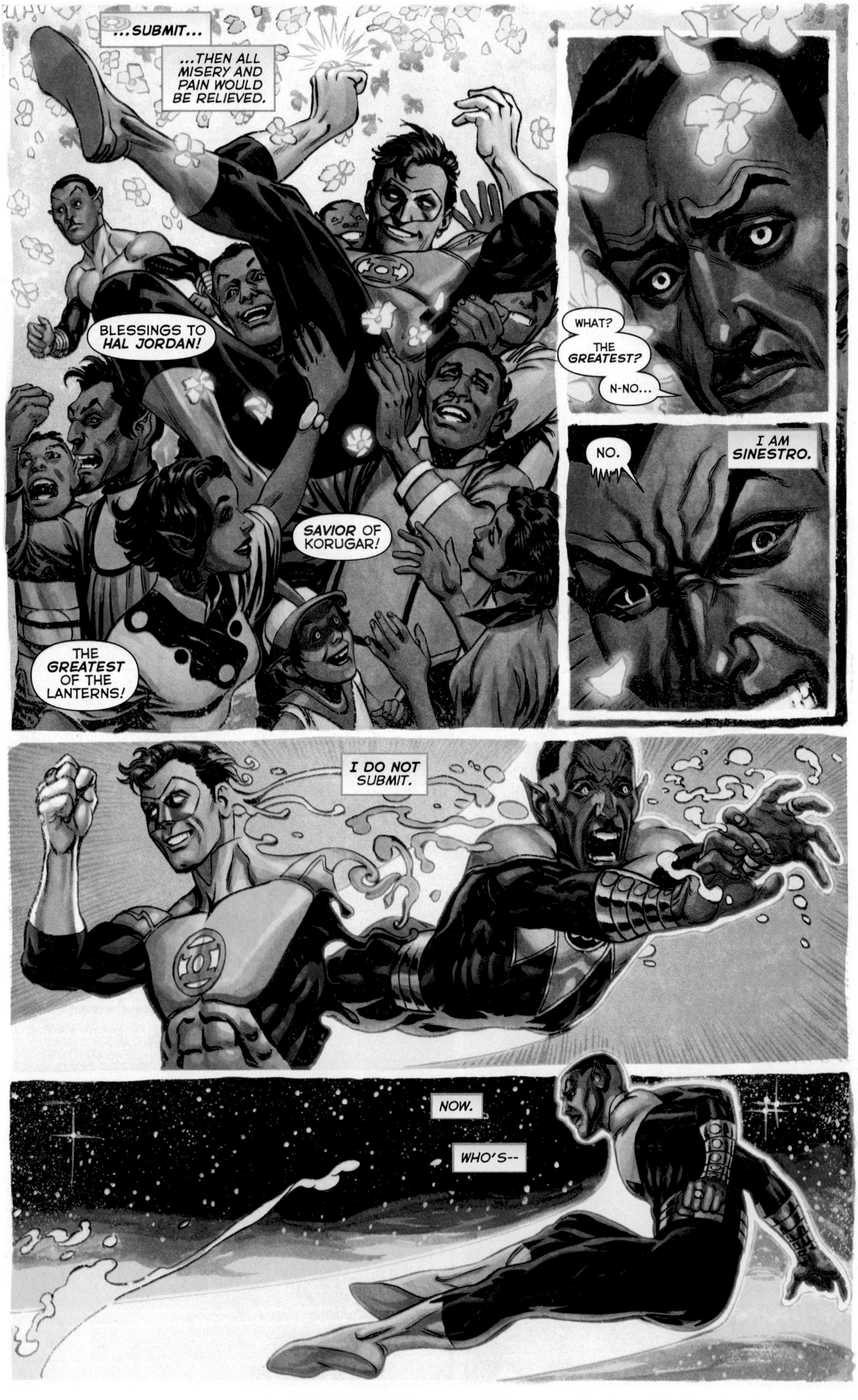
...SUBMIT...
...THEN ALL MISERY AND PAIN WOULD BE RELIEVED.
BLESSINGS TO HAL JORDAN!
SAVIOR OF KORUGAR!
THE GREATEST OF THE LANTERNS!
WHAT? THE GREATEST?
N-NO...
NO.
I AM SINESTRO.
I DO NOT SUBMIT.
NOW.
WHO'S--

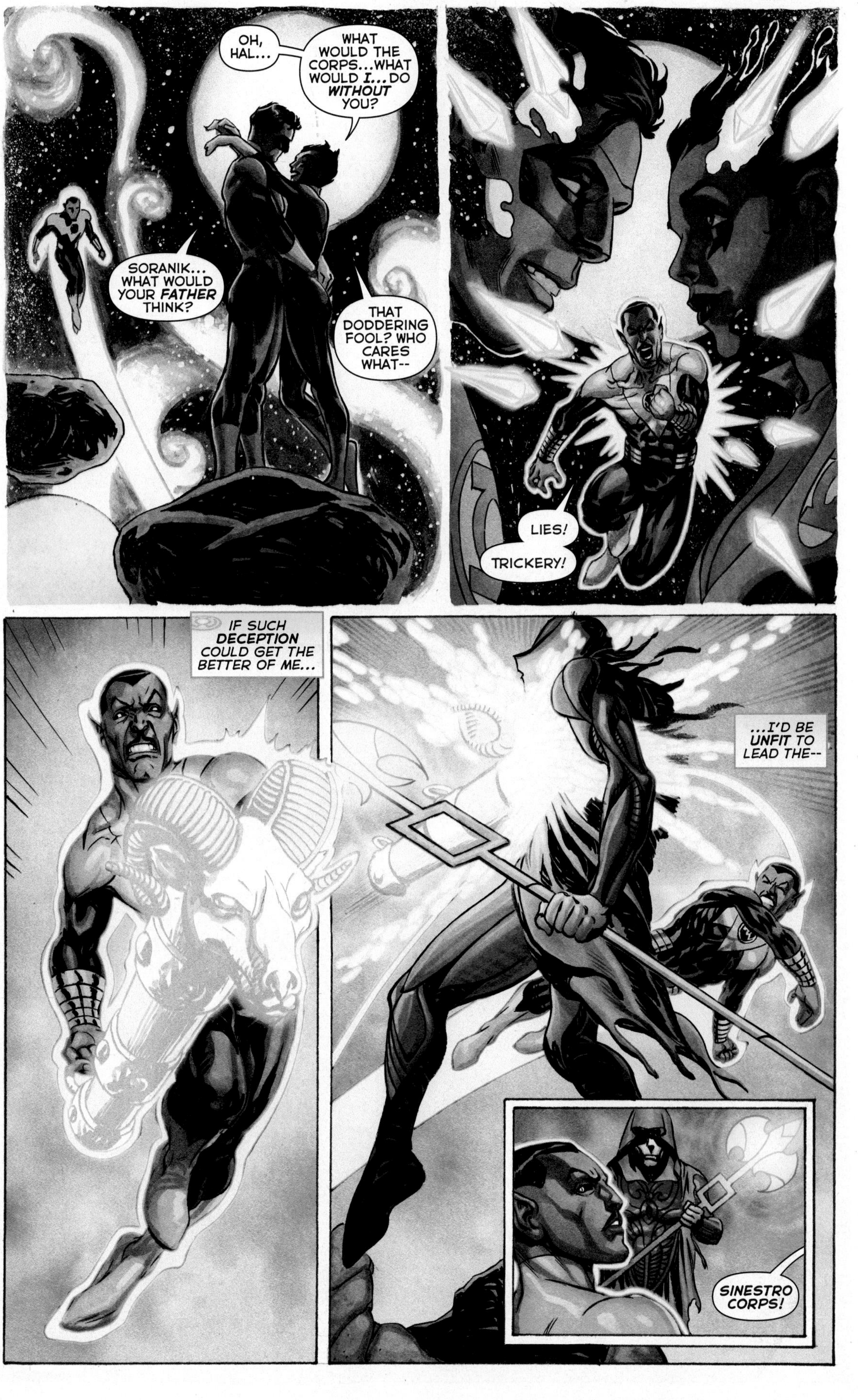
OH, HAL...
WHAT WOULD THE CORPS...WHAT WOULD I...DO WITHOUT YOU?
SORANIK... WHAT WOULD YOUR FATHER THINK?
THAT DODDERING FOOL? WHO CARES WHAT--
LIES!
TRICKERY!
IF SUCH DECEPTION COULD GET THE BETTER OF ME...
...I'D BE UNFIT TO LEAD THE--
SINESTRO CORPS!

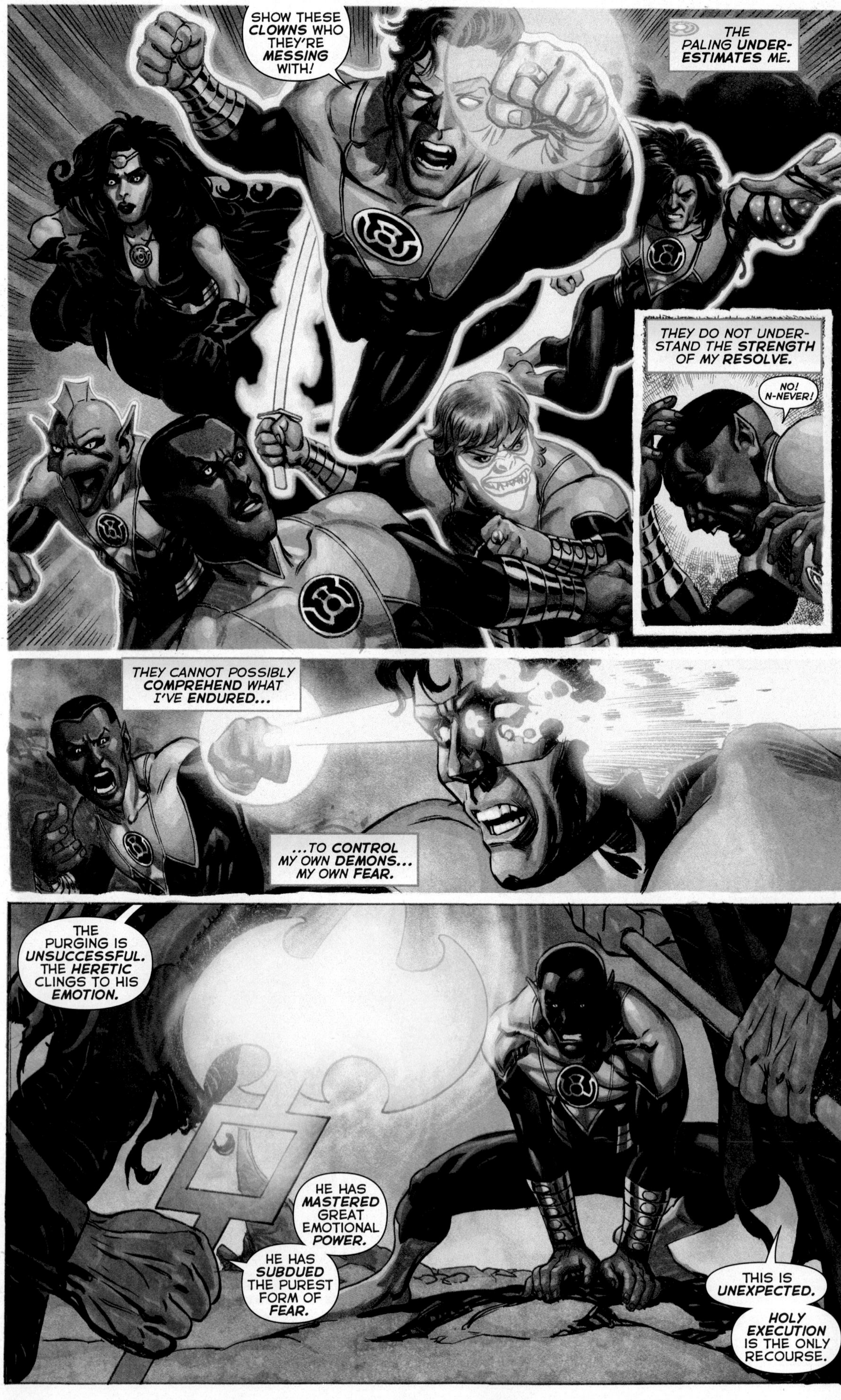
SHOW THESE CLOWNS WHO THEY'RE MESSING WITH!
THE PALING UNDER-ESTIMATES ME.
THEY DO NOT UNDER-STAND THE STRENGTH OF MY RESOLVE.
NO! N-NEVER!
THEY CANNOT POSSIBLY COMPREHEND WHAT I'VE ENDURED...
...TO CONTROL MY OWN DEMONS... MY OWN FEAR.
THE PURGING IS UNSUCCESSFUL. THE HERETIC CLINGS TO HIS EMOTION.
HE HAS MASTERED GREAT EMOTIONAL POWER.
HE HAS SUBDUED THE PUREST FORM OF FEAR.
THIS IS UNEXPECTED.
HOLY EXECUTION IS THE ONLY RECOURSE.

YOU WANT TO KILL MY FATHER?

THE LINE FORMS TO THE *LEFT*.

ZRAKKA ZRAKKA ZRAK ZRAKKA

VRRK VRRK VR-VRRK VR-VRRK

VARIATION IN THE EMOTIONAL SPECTRUM.

COMPENSATE.

RECALIBRATE.

SORANIK?

I KNOW WHAT YOU *SAID*, "DAD."

THERE'S NOTHING I CAN DO TO HELP.

BUT I GUESS IT'S A GOOD THING I *DIDN'T LISTEN*.

SHIELD YOURSELVES FROM THIS *PROFANITY*.

THEIR DEFENSES... GEARED TOWARD PROTECTING THEM FROM *FEAR*.

BUT WITH THEIR ATTENTION *DIVIDED*...

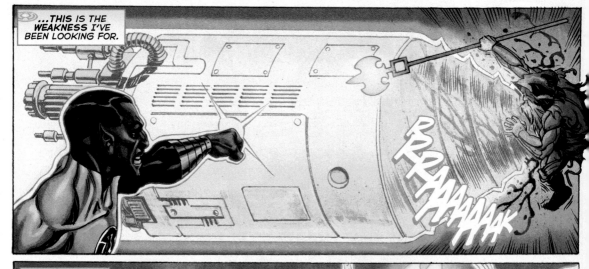

...THIS IS THE WEAKNESS I'VE BEEN LOOKING FOR.

RRRAAAAAAAK

MY ENEMIES MAY HAVE CLEANSED THEMSELVES OF EMOTION.

THAT EMPTINESS AFFORDED THEM SOME PROTECTION.

BUT IN THAT MOMENT...

...WITH EVERYTHING THEY THOUGHT THEY KNEW CRUMBLING AROUND THEM...

...THEY REMEMBERED WHAT IT MEANT TO BE AFRAID.

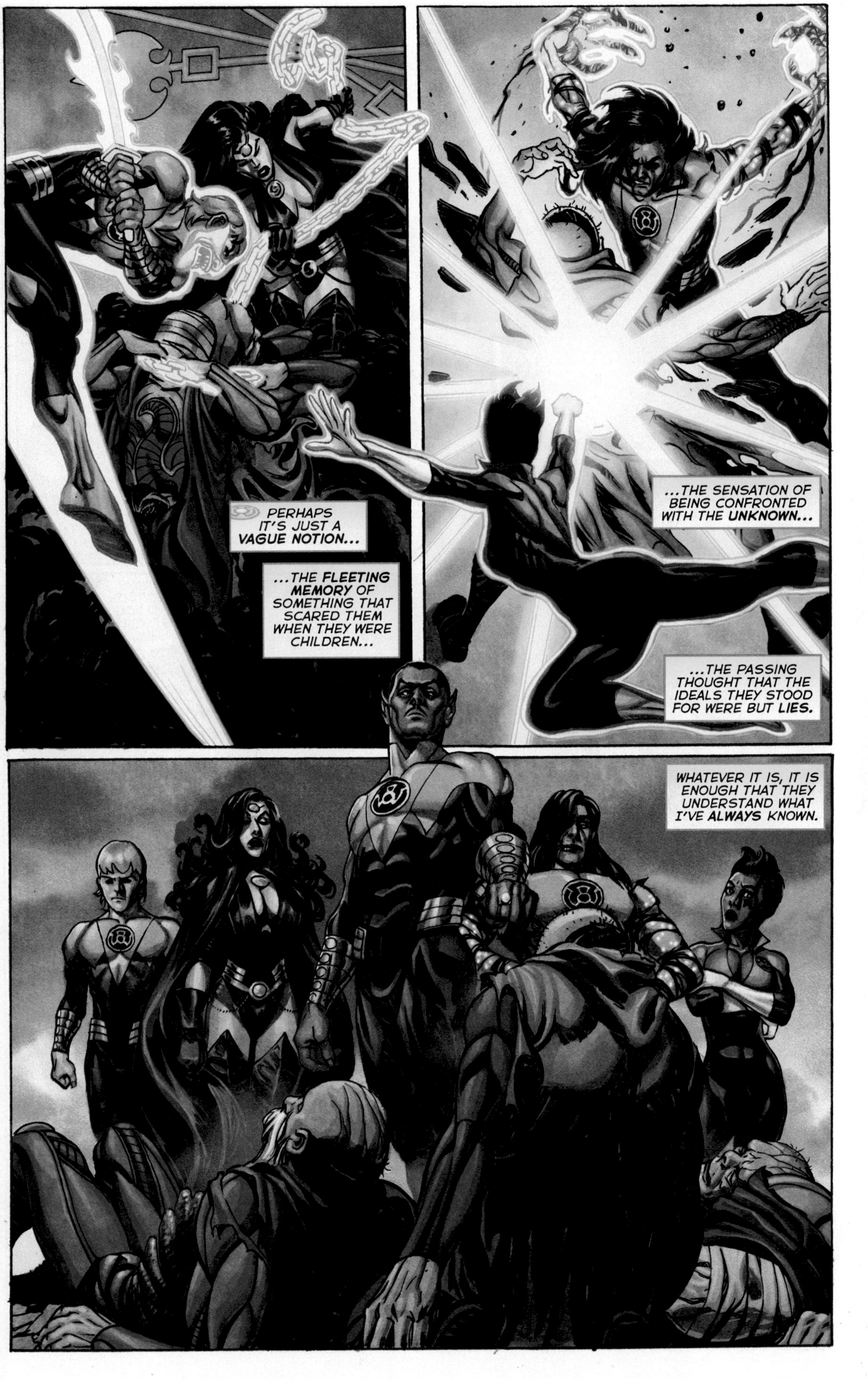
PERHAPS IT'S JUST A VAGUE NOTION...
...THE FLEETING MEMORY OF SOMETHING THAT SCARED THEM WHEN THEY WERE CHILDREN...
...THE SENSATION OF BEING CONFRONTED WITH THE UNKNOWN...
...THE PASSING THOUGHT THAT THE IDEALS THEY STOOD FOR WERE BUT LIES.
WHATEVER IT IS, IT IS ENOUGH THAT THEY UNDERSTAND WHAT I'VE ALWAYS KNOWN.

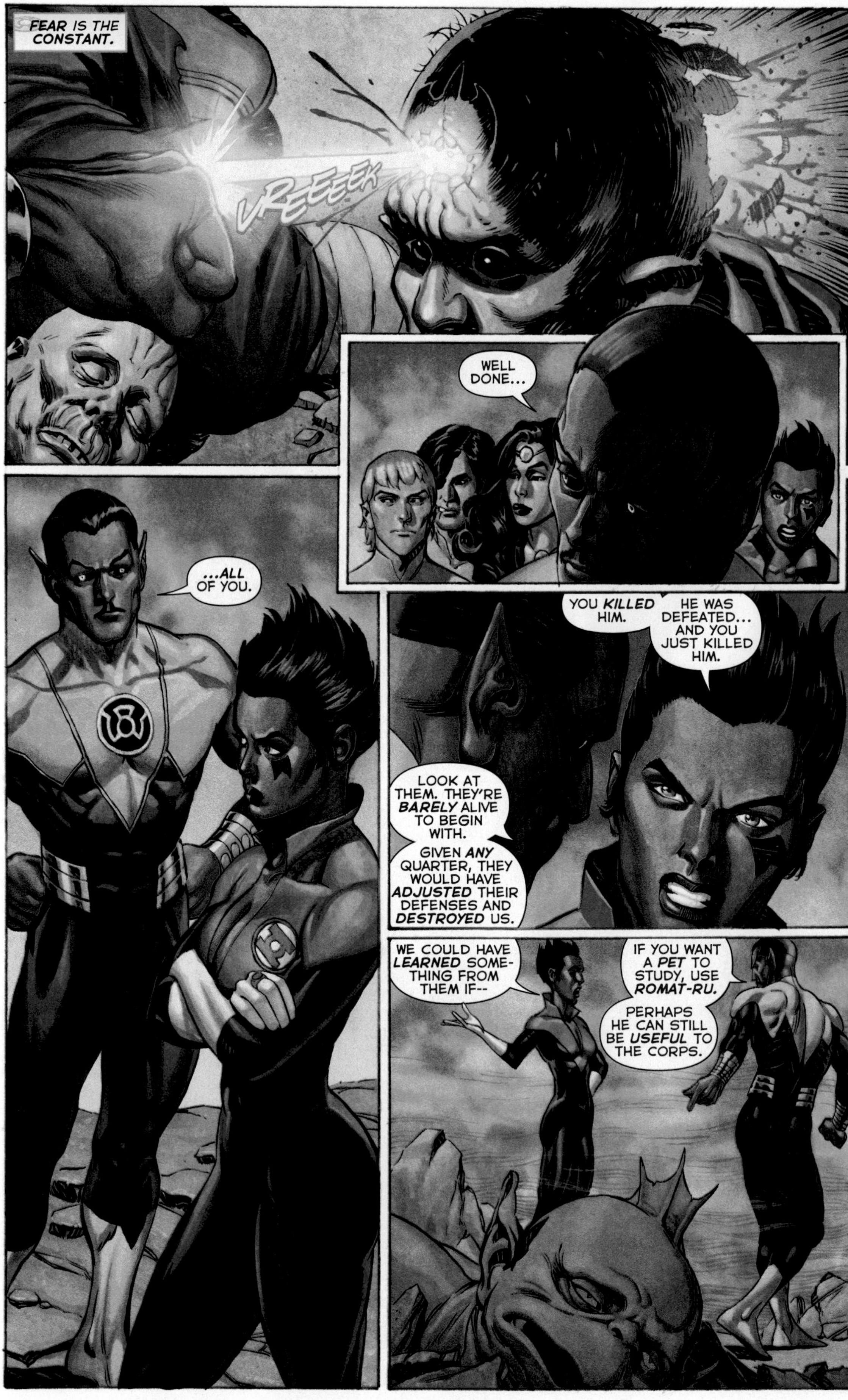
FEAR IS THE CONSTANT.
VREEEEEK
WELL DONE...
...ALL OF YOU.
YOU KILLED HIM.
HE WAS DEFEATED... AND YOU JUST KILLED HIM.
LOOK AT THEM. THEY'RE BARELY ALIVE TO BEGIN WITH.
GIVEN ANY QUARTER, THEY WOULD HAVE ADJUSTED THEIR DEFENSES AND DESTROYED US.
WE COULD HAVE LEARNED SOMETHING FROM THEM IF--
IF YOU WANT A PET TO STUDY, USE ROMAT-RU.
PERHAPS HE CAN STILL BE USEFUL TO THE CORPS.

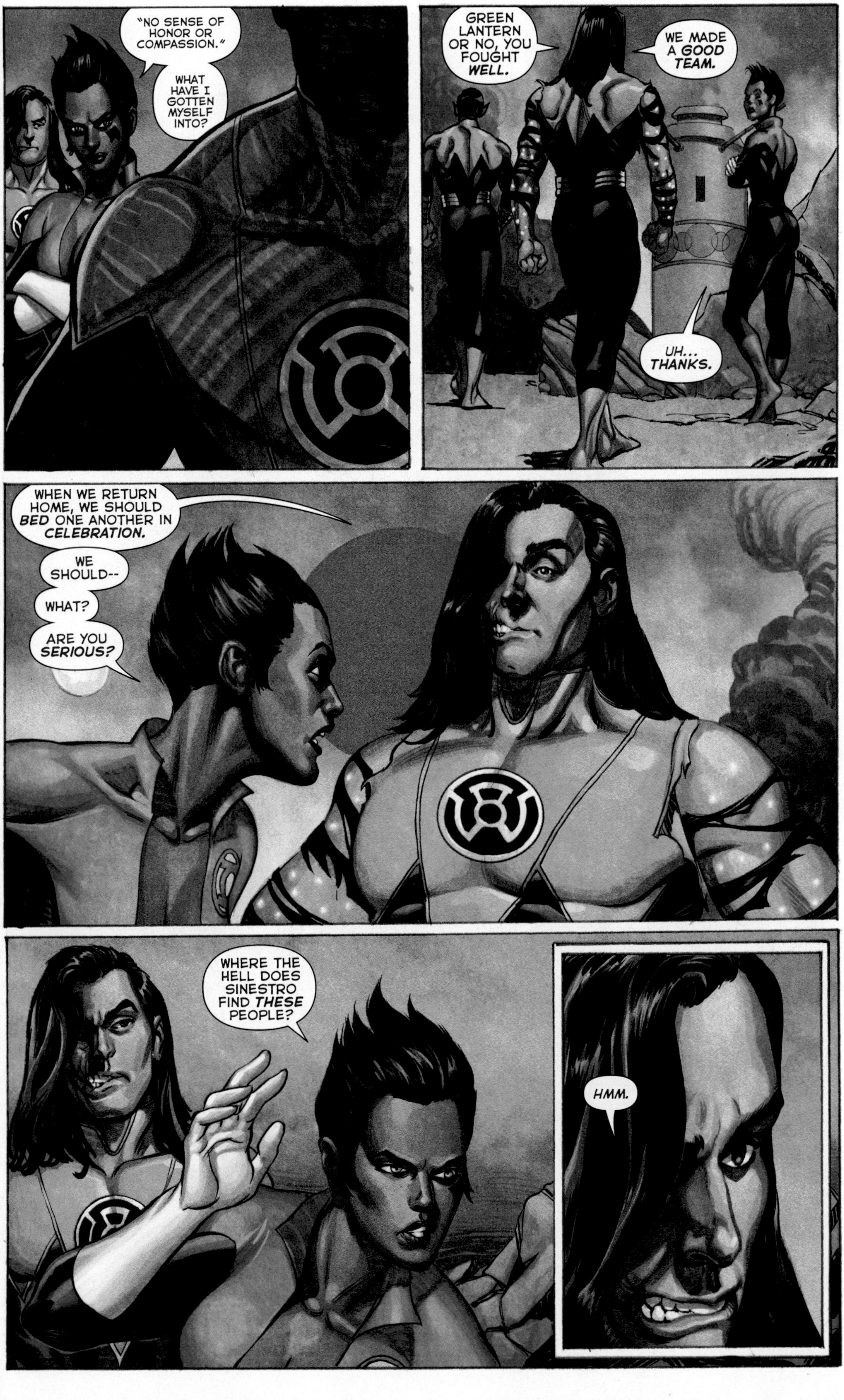
"NO SENSE OF HONOR OR COMPASSION."
WHAT HAVE I GOTTEN MYSELF INTO?
GREEN LANTERN OR NO, YOU FOUGHT WELL.
WE MADE A GOOD TEAM.
UH... THANKS.
WHEN WE RETURN HOME, WE SHOULD BED ONE ANOTHER IN CELEBRATION.
WE SHOULD--
WHAT?
ARE YOU SERIOUS?
WHERE THE HELL DOES SINESTRO FIND THESE PEOPLE?
HMM.

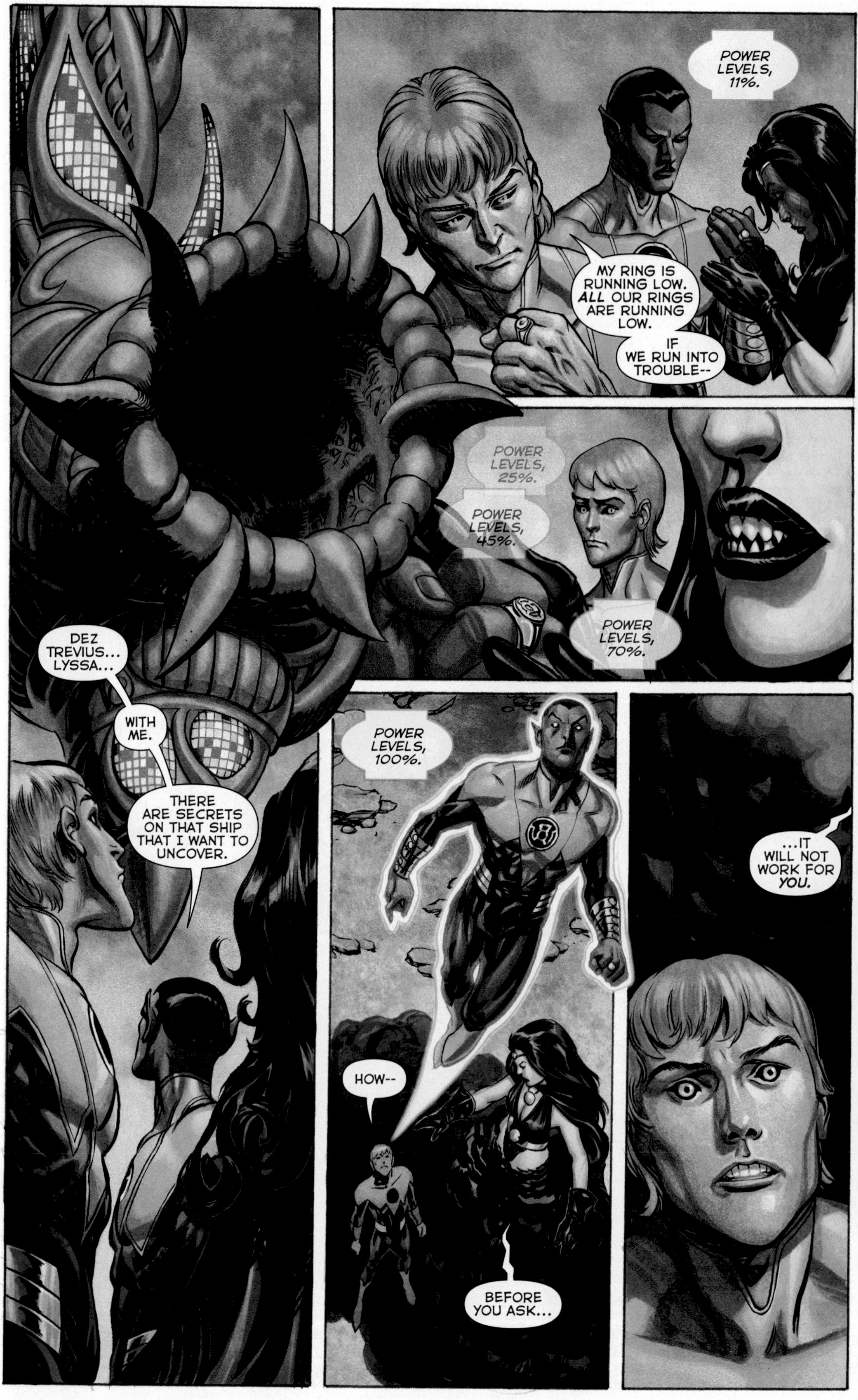
POWER LEVELS, 11%.
MY RING IS RUNNING LOW. ALL OUR RINGS ARE RUNNING LOW.
IF WE RUN INTO TROUBLE--
POWER LEVELS, 25%.
POWER LEVELS, 45%.
POWER LEVELS, 70%.
DEZ TREVIUS... LYSSA...
WITH ME.
THERE ARE SECRETS ON THAT SHIP THAT I WANT TO UNCOVER.
POWER LEVELS, 100%.
HOW--
BEFORE YOU ASK...
...IT WILL NOT WORK FOR YOU.

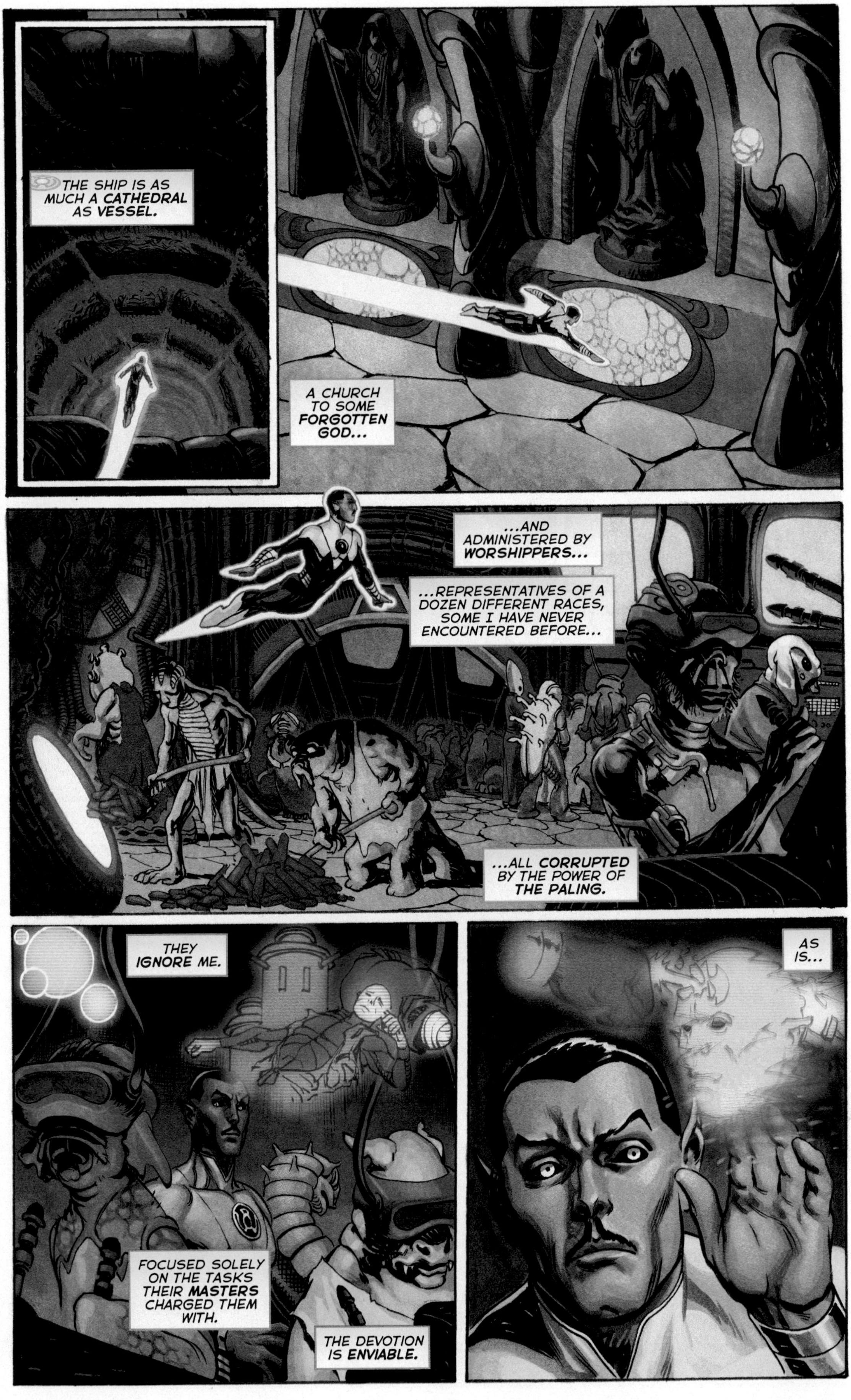
THE SHIP IS AS MUCH A CATHEDRAL AS VESSEL.
A CHURCH TO SOME FORGOTTEN GOD...
...AND ADMINISTERED BY WORSHIPPERS...
...REPRESENTATIVES OF A DOZEN DIFFERENT RACES, SOME I HAVE NEVER ENCOUNTERED BEFORE...
...ALL CORRUPTED BY THE POWER OF THE PALING.
THEY IGNORE ME.
FOCUSED SOLELY ON THE TASKS THEIR MASTERS CHARGED THEM WITH.
THE DEVOTION IS ENVIABLE.
AS IS...

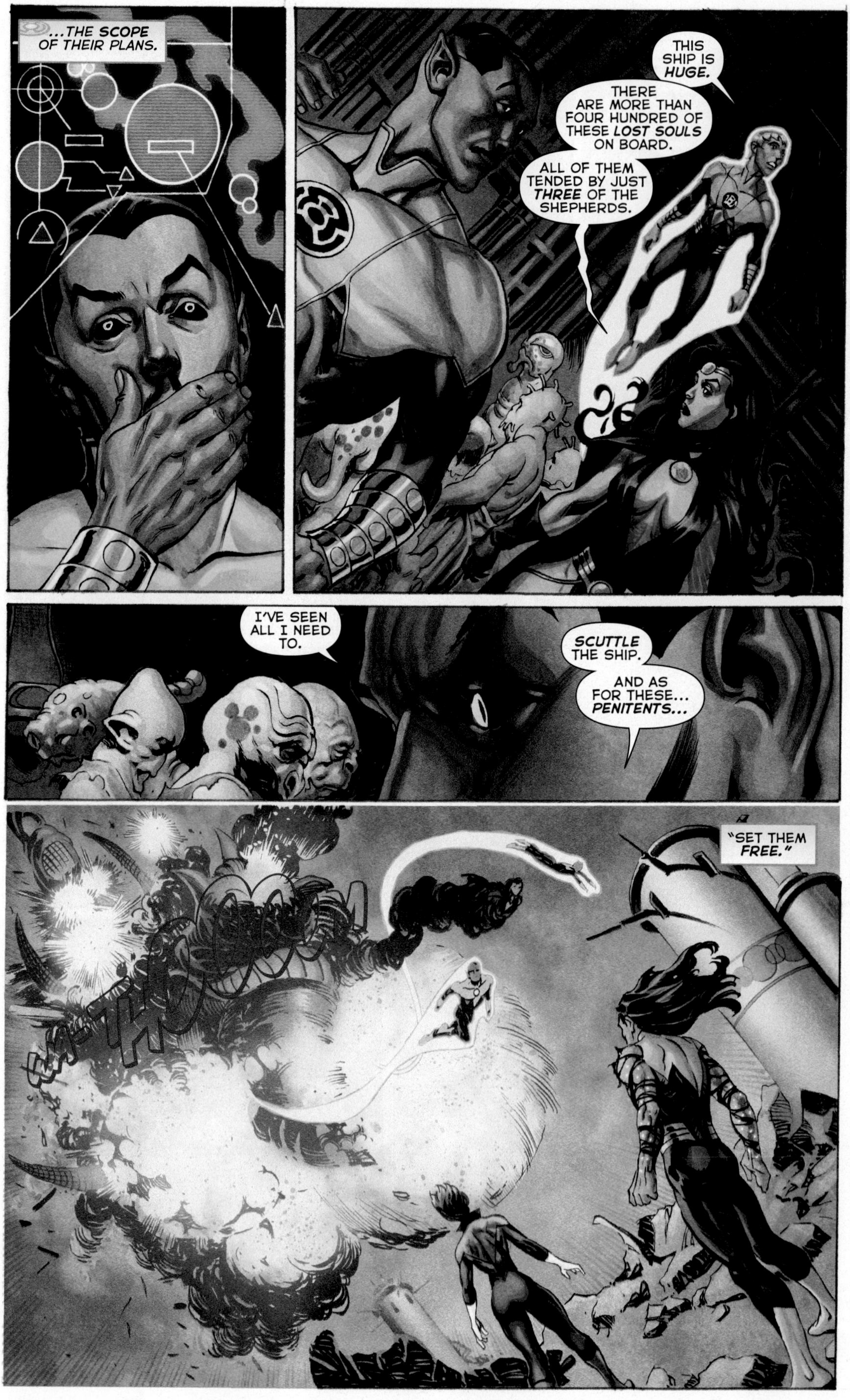
...THE SCOPE OF THEIR PLANS.
THIS SHIP IS HUGE.
THERE ARE MORE THAN FOUR HUNDRED OF THESE LOST SOULS ON BOARD.
ALL OF THEM TENDED BY JUST THREE OF THE SHEPHERDS.
I'VE SEEN ALL I NEED TO.
SCUTTLE THE SHIP.
AND AS FOR THESE... PENITENTS...
"SET THEM FREE."

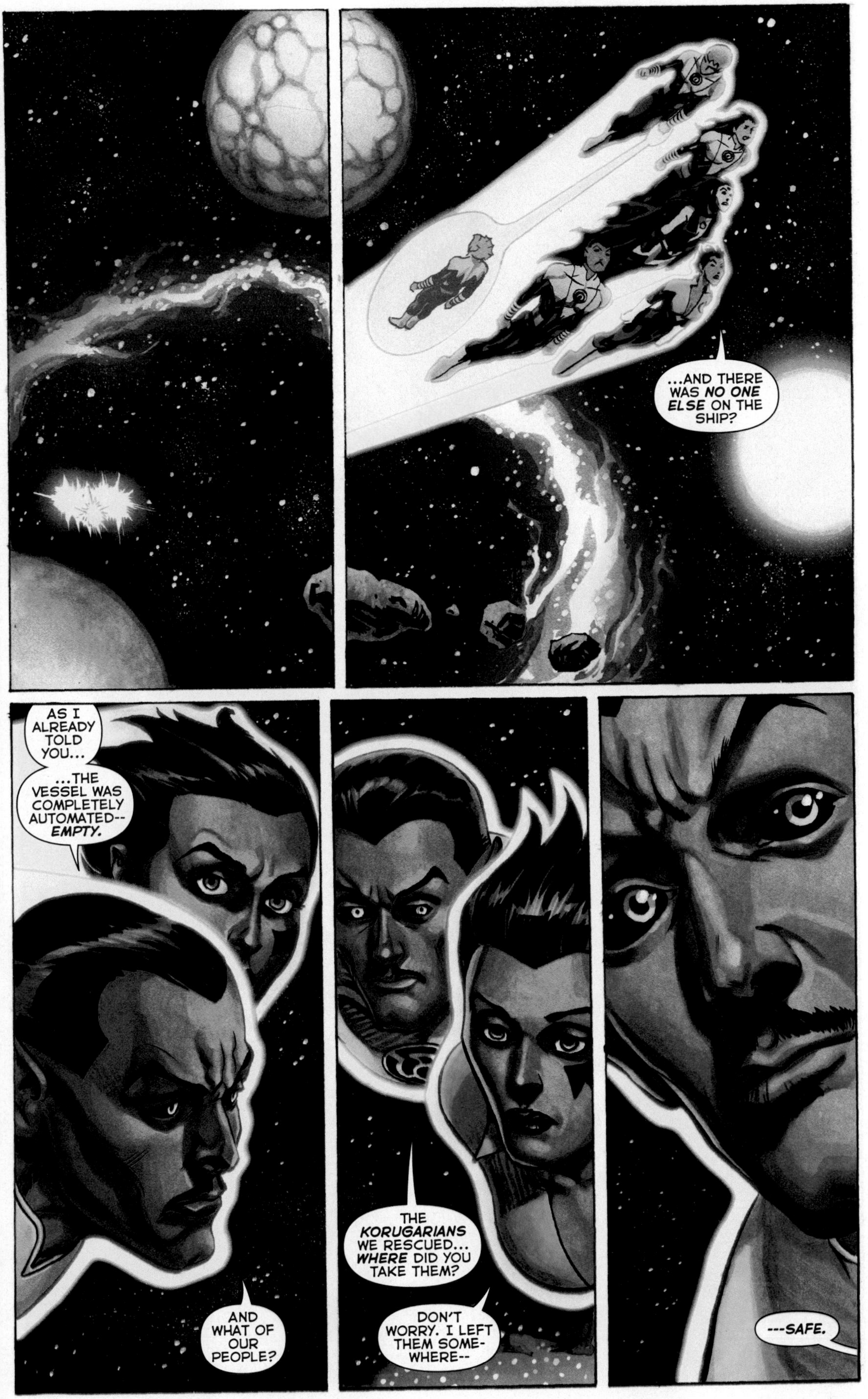
...AND THERE WAS NO ONE ELSE ON THE SHIP?
AS I ALREADY TOLD YOU...
...THE VESSEL WAS COMPLETELY AUTOMATED-- EMPTY.
AND WHAT OF OUR PEOPLE?
THE KORUGARIANS WE RESCUED... WHERE DID YOU TAKE THEM?
DON'T WORRY. I LEFT THEM SOME-WHERE--
---SAFE.

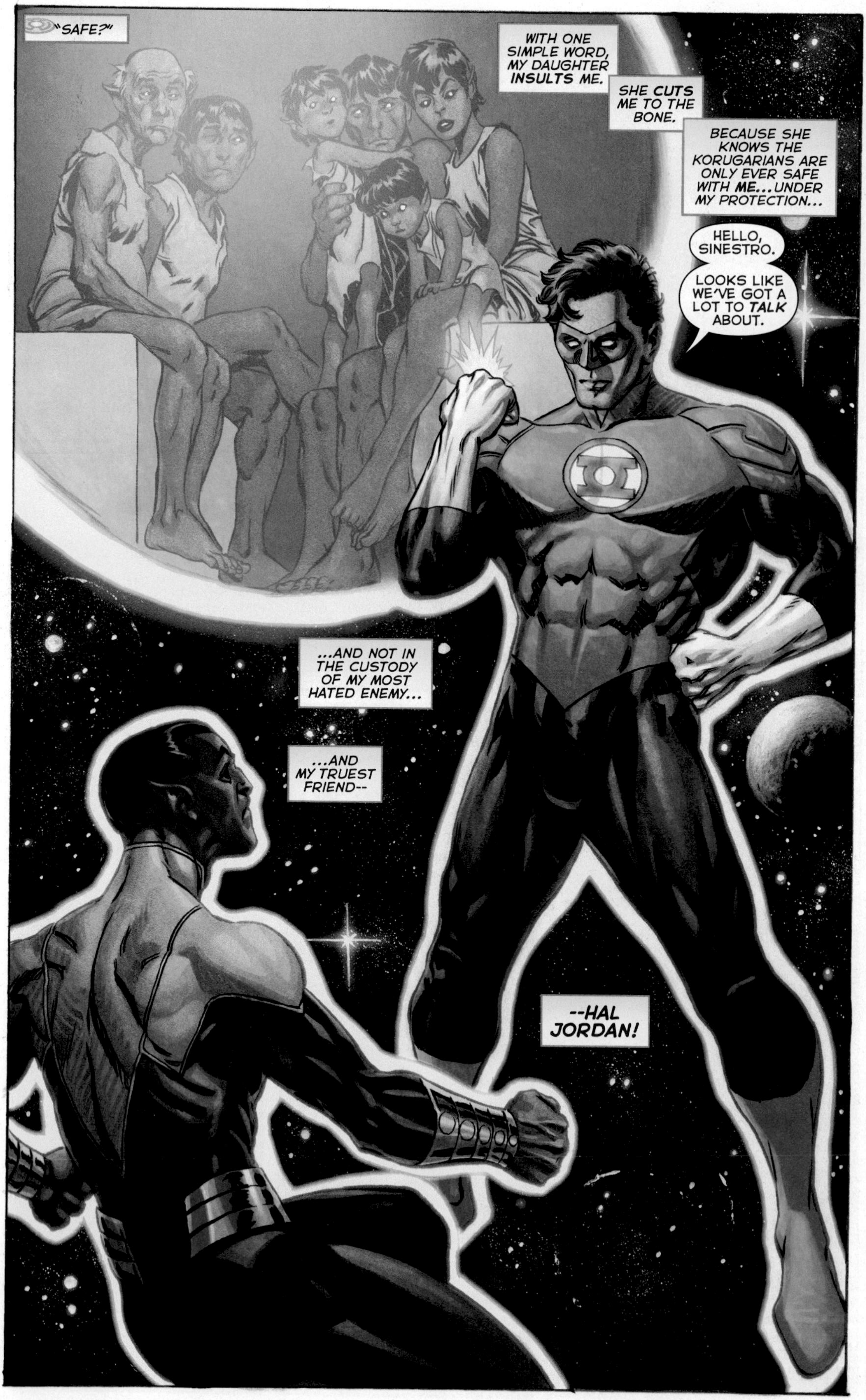
"SAFE?"
WITH ONE SIMPLE WORD, MY DAUGHTER INSULTS ME.
SHE CUTS ME TO THE BONE.
BECAUSE SHE KNOWS THE KORUGARIANS ARE ONLY EVER SAFE WITH ME...UNDER MY PROTECTION...
HELLO, SINESTRO.
LOOKS LIKE WE'VE GOT A LOT TO TALK ABOUT.
...AND NOT IN THE CUSTODY OF MY MOST HATED ENEMY...
...AND MY TRUEST FRIEND--
--HAL JORDAN!

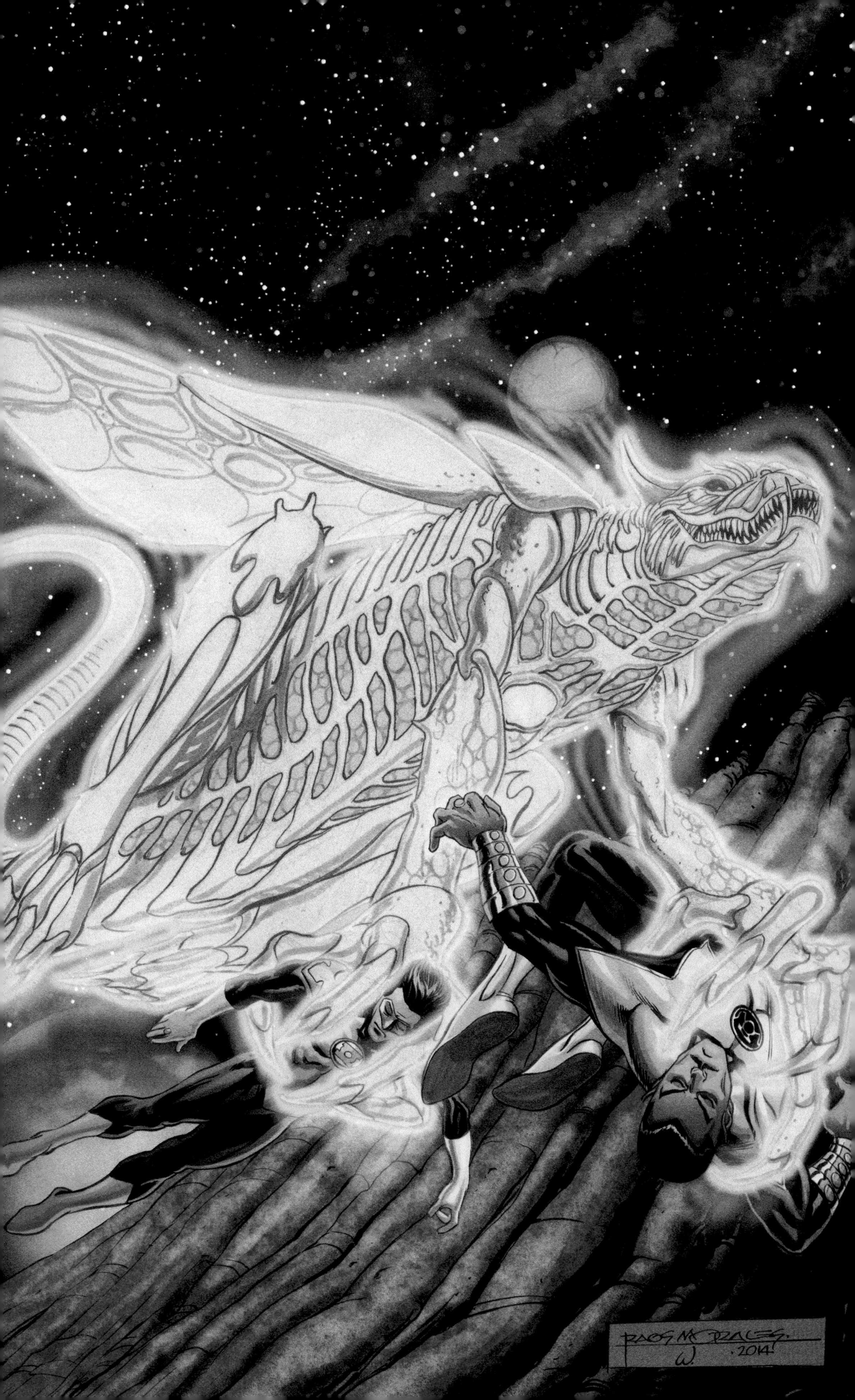
RAGS MORALES
2014

THE DEMON WITHIN

CULLEN BUNN writer **DALE EAGLESHAM** artist **JASON WRIGHT** colorist **DAVE SHARPE** letterer
cover art by **RAGS MORALES & JASON WRIGHT**

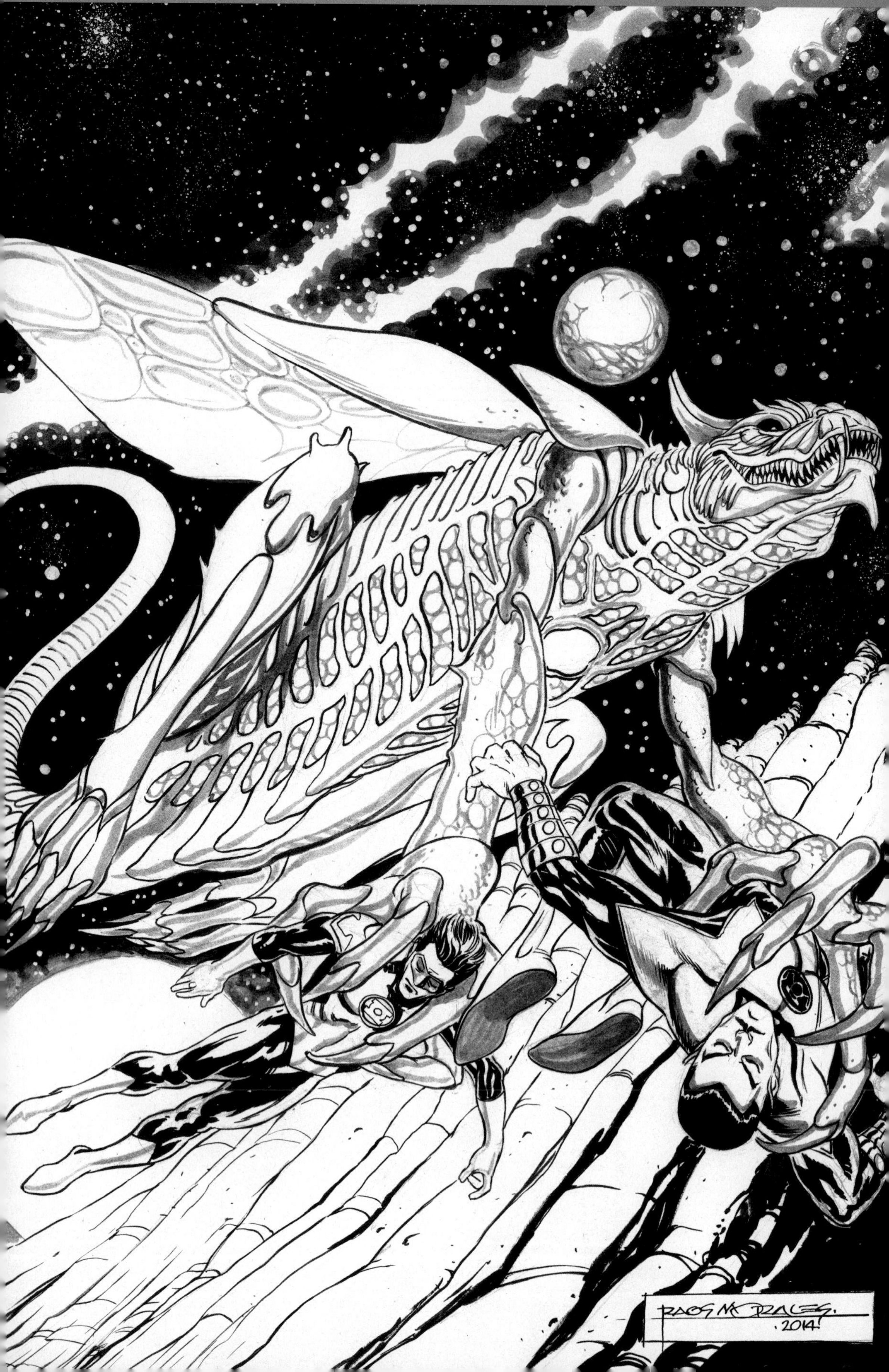
RAGS MORALES
.2014.

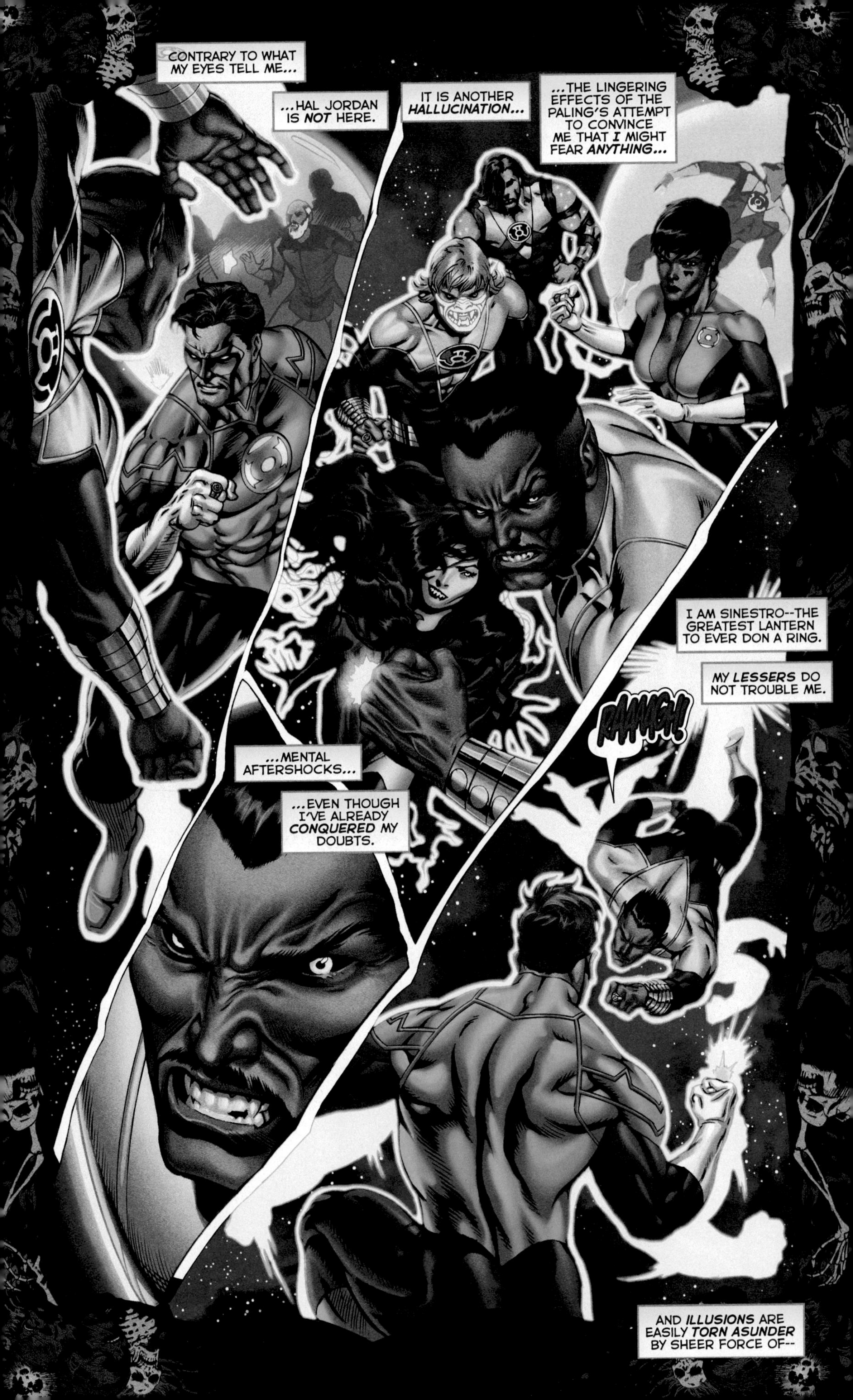
CONTRARY TO WHAT MY EYES TELL ME...
...HAL JORDAN IS NOT HERE.
IT IS ANOTHER HALLUCINATION...
...THE LINGERING EFFECTS OF THE PALING'S ATTEMPT TO CONVINCE ME THAT I MIGHT FEAR ANYTHING...
...MENTAL AFTERSHOCKS...
...EVEN THOUGH I'VE ALREADY CONQUERED MY DOUBTS.
I AM SINESTRO--THE GREATEST LANTERN TO EVER DON A RING.
MY LESSERS DO NOT TROUBLE ME.
RAAAUGH!
AND ILLUSIONS ARE EASILY TORN ASUNDER BY SHEER FORCE OF--

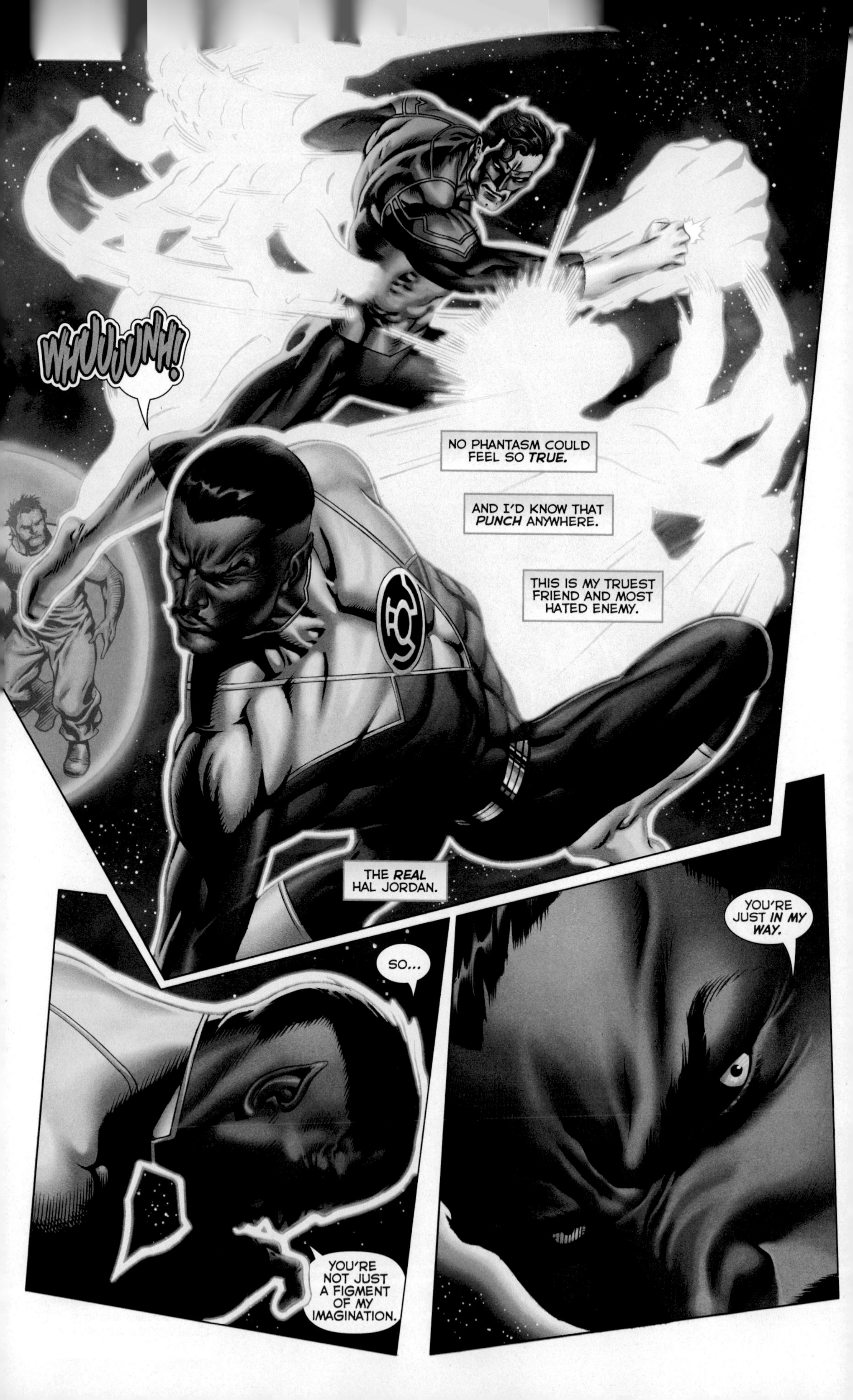
WHUUUUNH!
NO PHANTASM COULD FEEL SO TRUE.
AND I'D KNOW THAT PUNCH ANYWHERE.
THIS IS MY TRUEST FRIEND AND MOST HATED ENEMY.
THE REAL HAL JORDAN.
SO...
YOU'RE NOT JUST A FIGMENT OF MY IMAGINATION.
YOU'RE JUST IN MY WAY.

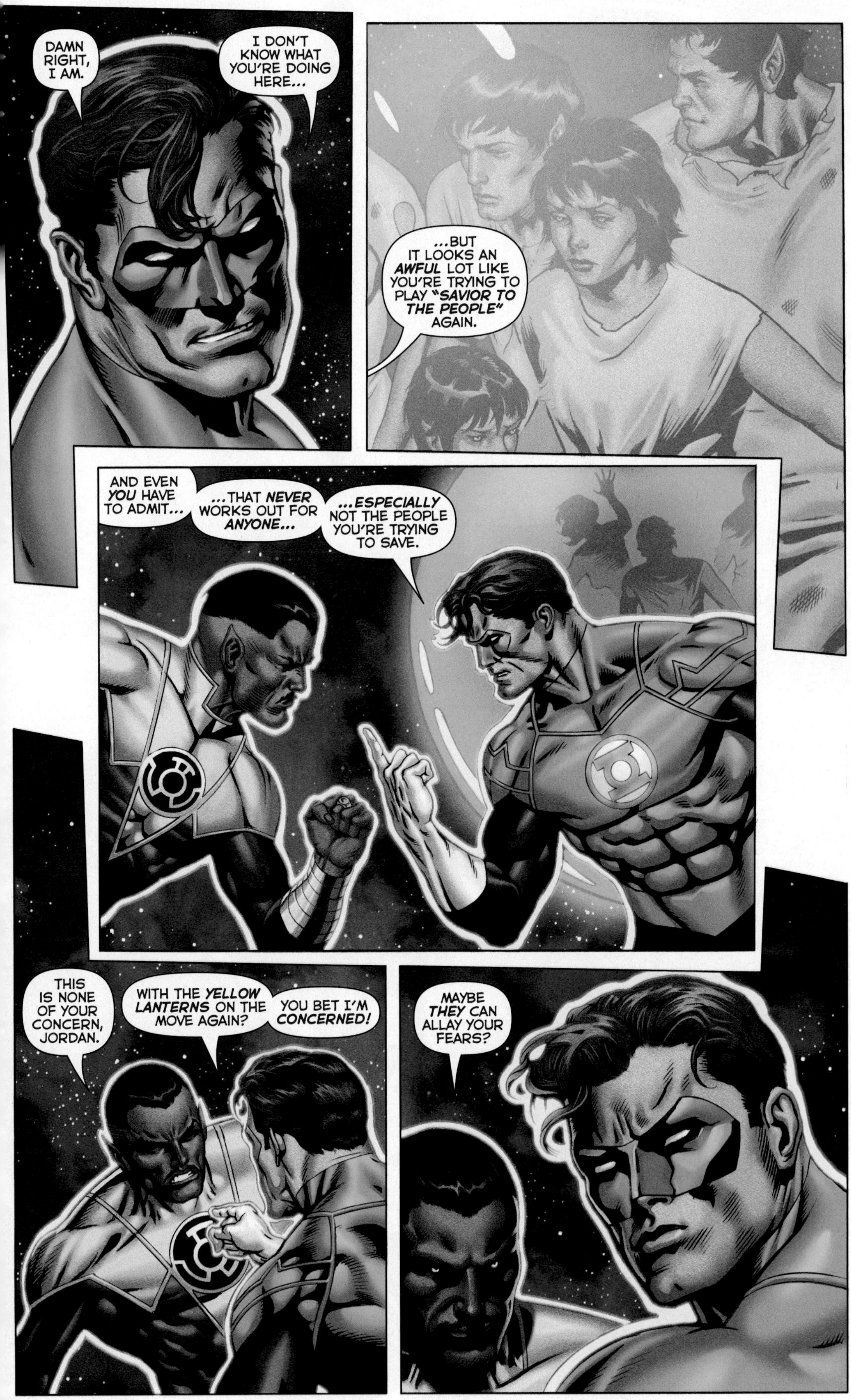
DAMN RIGHT, I AM.
I DON'T KNOW WHAT YOU'RE DOING HERE...
...BUT IT LOOKS AN AWFUL LOT LIKE YOU'RE TRYING TO PLAY "SAVIOR TO THE PEOPLE" AGAIN.
AND EVEN YOU HAVE TO ADMIT...
...THAT NEVER WORKS OUT FOR ANYONE...
...ESPECIALLY NOT THE PEOPLE YOU'RE TRYING TO SAVE.
THIS IS NONE OF YOUR CONCERN, JORDAN.
WITH THE YELLOW LANTERNS ON THE MOVE AGAIN?
YOU BET I'M CONCERNED!
MAYBE THEY CAN ALLAY YOUR FEARS?

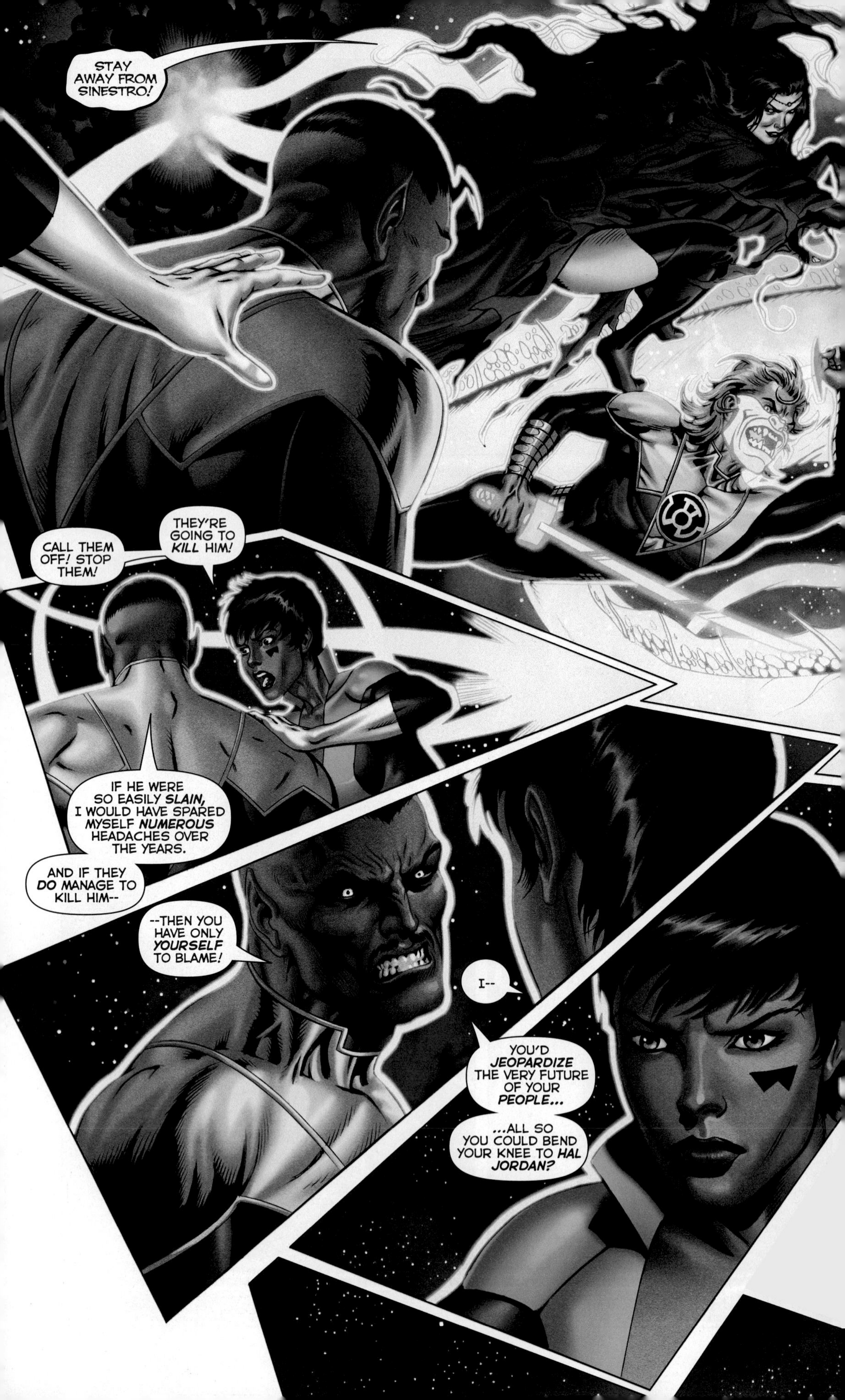
STAY AWAY FROM SINESTRO!
CALL THEM OFF! STOP THEM!
THEY'RE GOING TO KILL HIM!
IF HE WERE SO EASILY SLAIN, I WOULD HAVE SPARED MYSELF NUMEROUS HEADACHES OVER THE YEARS.
AND IF THEY DO MANAGE TO KILL HIM--
--THEN YOU HAVE ONLY YOURSELF TO BLAME!
I--
YOU'D JEOPARDIZE THE VERY FUTURE OF YOUR PEOPLE...
...ALL SO YOU COULD BEND YOUR KNEE TO HAL JORDAN?

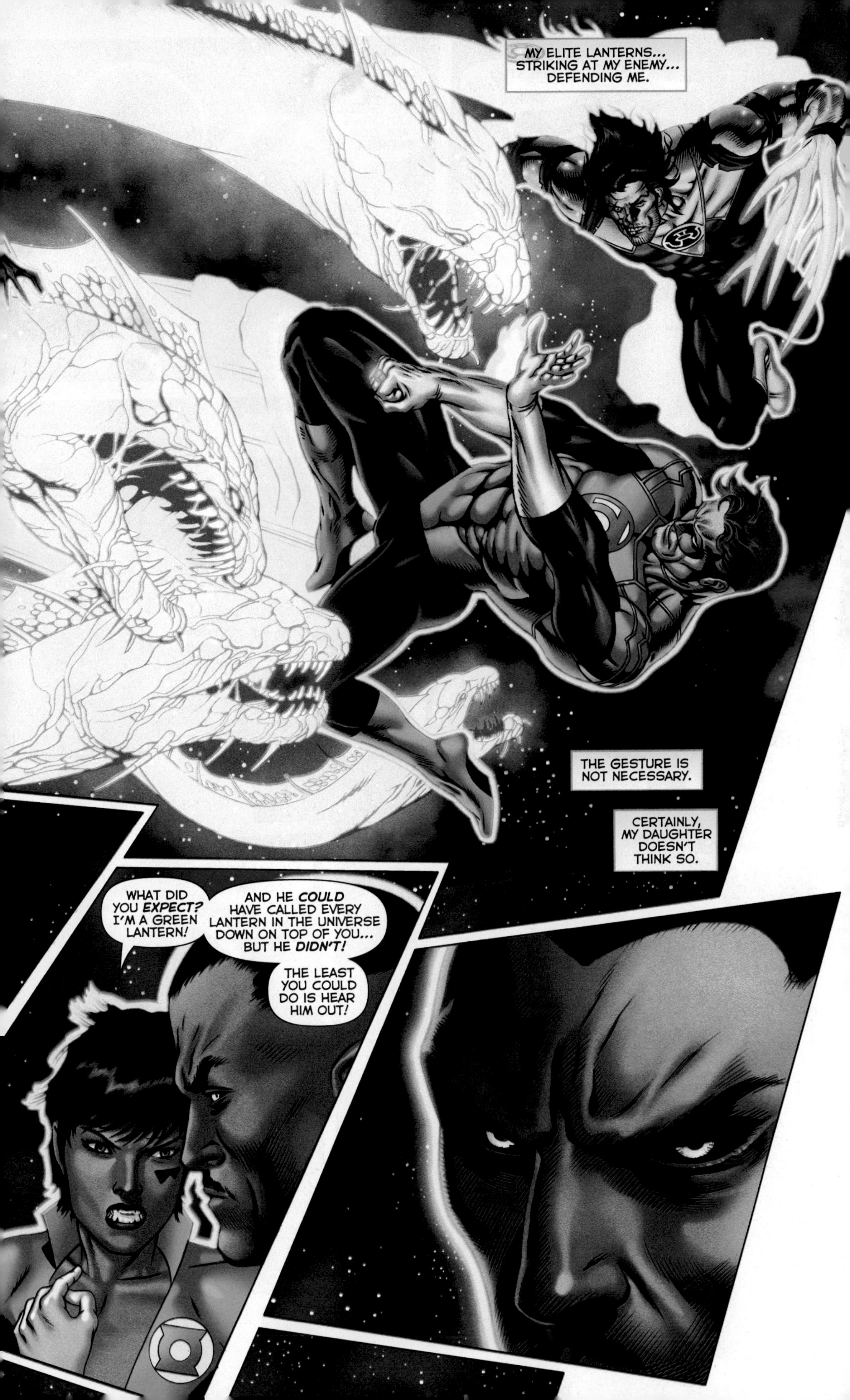
MY ELITE LANTERNS... STRIKING AT MY ENEMY... DEFENDING ME.
THE GESTURE IS NOT NECESSARY.
CERTAINLY, MY DAUGHTER DOESN'T THINK SO.
WHAT DID YOU *EXPECT?* I'M A GREEN LANTERN!
AND HE *COULD* HAVE CALLED EVERY LANTERN IN THE UNIVERSE DOWN ON TOP OF YOU... BUT HE *DIDN'T!*
THE LEAST YOU COULD DO IS HEAR HIM OUT!

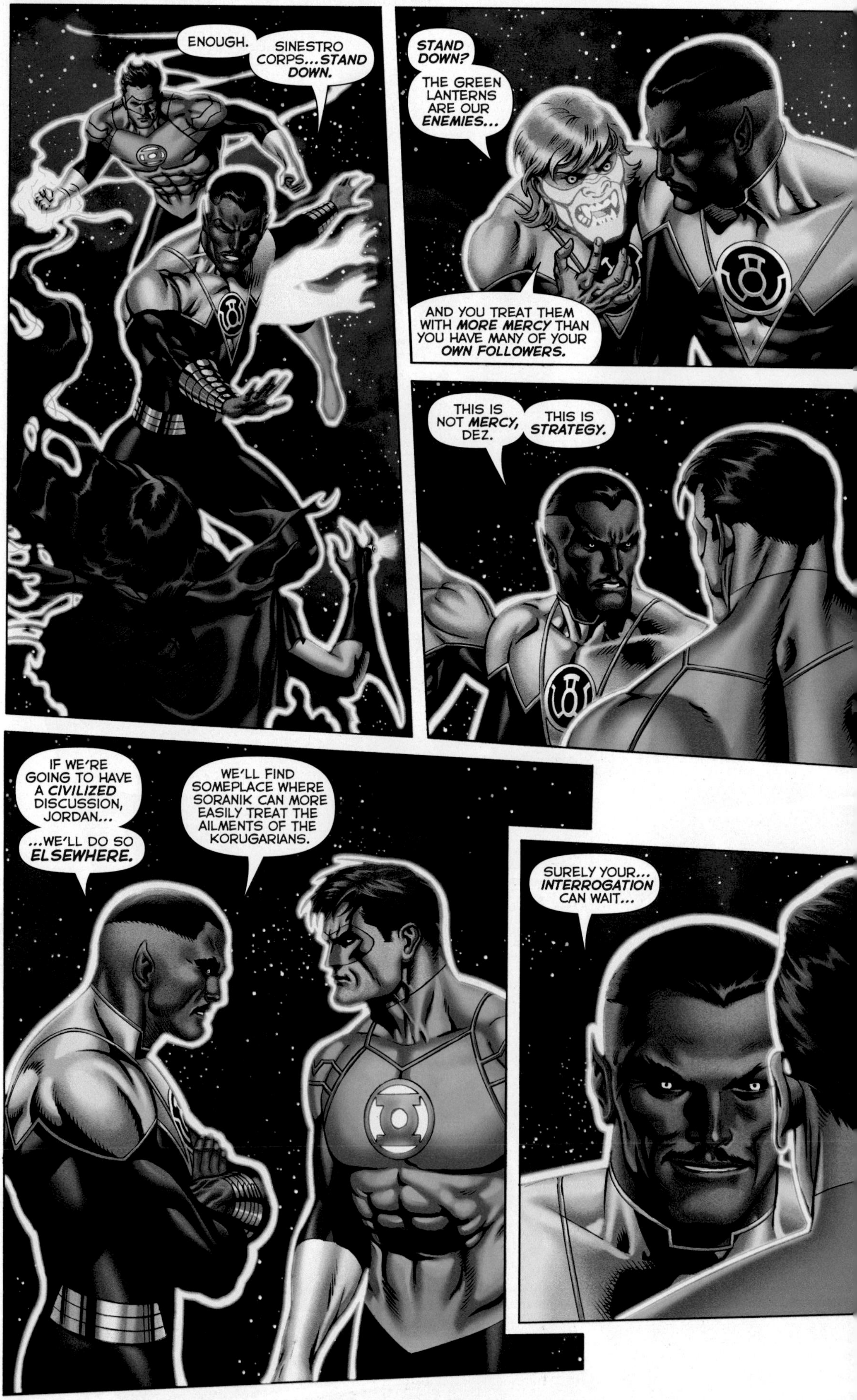
ENOUGH.
SINESTRO CORPS...STAND DOWN.
STAND DOWN?
THE GREEN LANTERNS ARE OUR ENEMIES...
AND YOU TREAT THEM WITH MORE MERCY THAN YOU HAVE MANY OF YOUR OWN FOLLOWERS.
THIS IS NOT MERCY, DEZ.
THIS IS STRATEGY.
IF WE'RE GOING TO HAVE A CIVILIZED DISCUSSION, JORDAN...
...WE'LL DO SO ELSEWHERE.
WE'LL FIND SOMEPLACE WHERE SORANIK CAN MORE EASILY TREAT THE AILMENTS OF THE KORUGARIANS.
SURELY YOUR... INTERROGATION CAN WAIT...

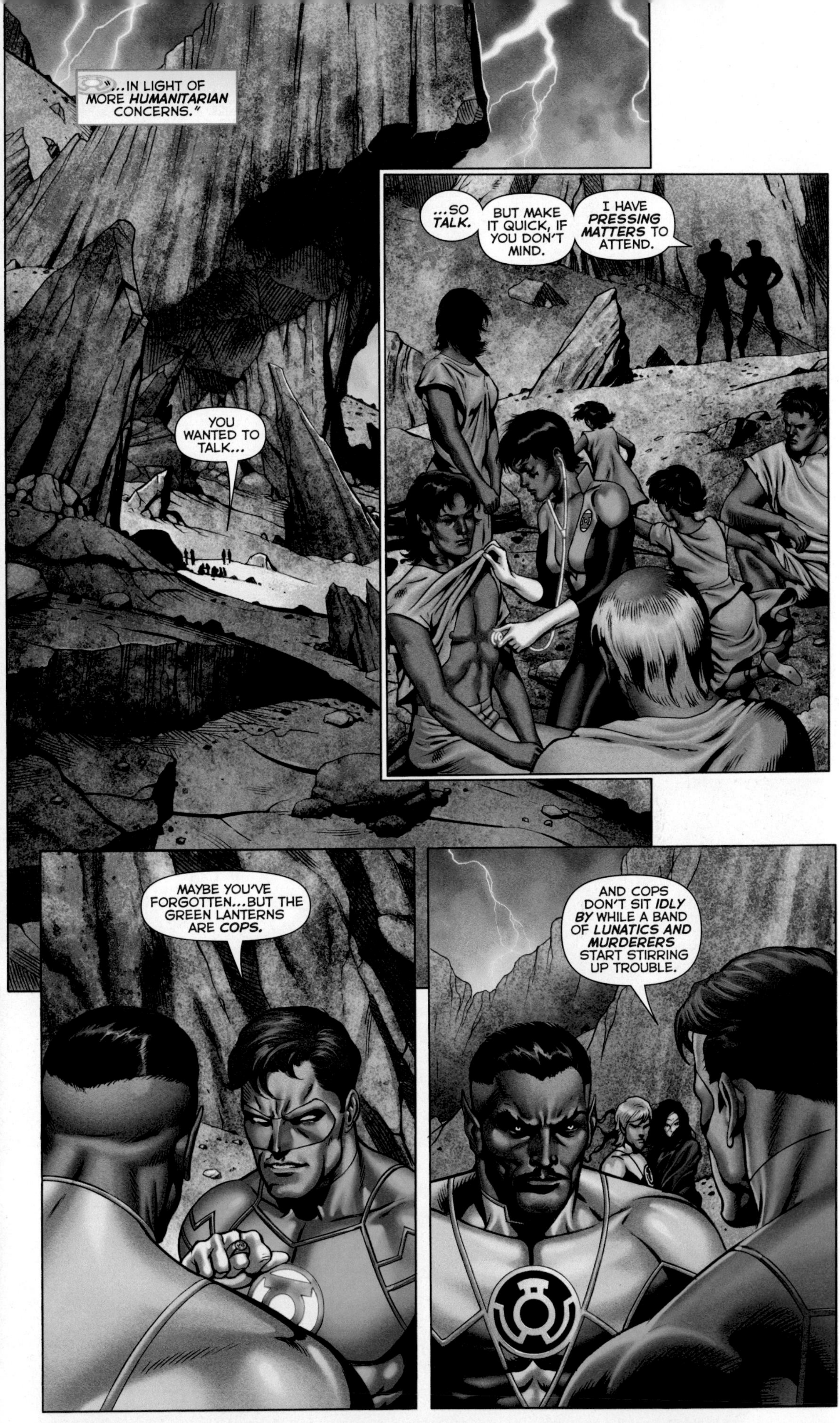
"...IN LIGHT OF MORE HUMANITARIAN CONCERNS."
YOU WANTED TO TALK...
...SO TALK.
BUT MAKE IT QUICK, IF YOU DON'T MIND.
I HAVE PRESSING MATTERS TO ATTEND.
MAYBE YOU'VE FORGOTTEN...BUT THE GREEN LANTERNS ARE COPS.
AND COPS DON'T SIT IDLY BY WHILE A BAND OF LUNATICS AND MURDERERS START STIRRING UP TROUBLE.

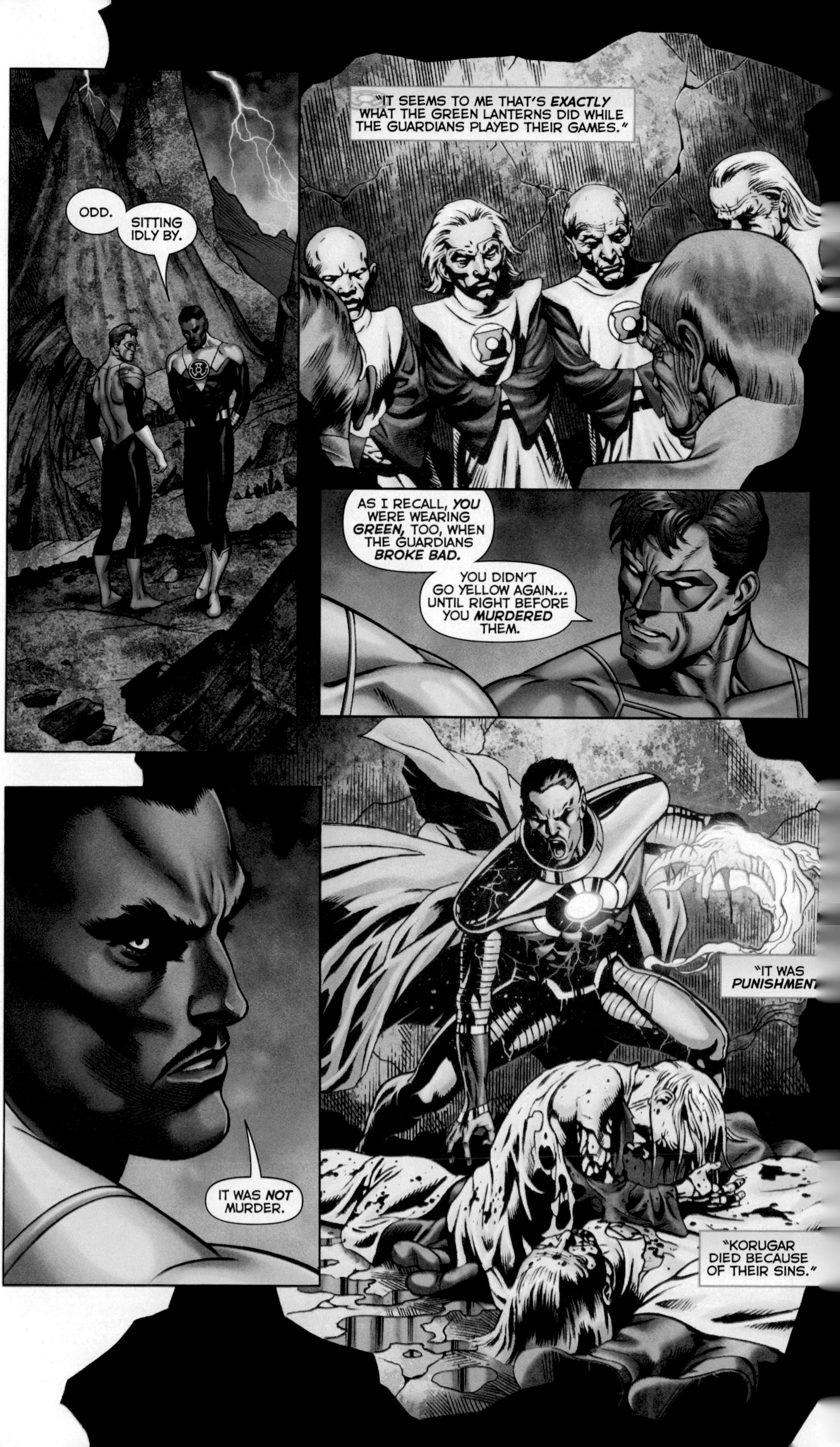
ODD.
SITTING IDLY BY.
"IT SEEMS TO ME THAT'S EXACTLY WHAT THE GREEN LANTERNS DID WHILE THE GUARDIANS PLAYED THEIR GAMES."
AS I RECALL, YOU WERE WEARING GREEN, TOO, WHEN THE GUARDIANS BROKE BAD.
YOU DIDN'T GO YELLOW AGAIN... UNTIL RIGHT BEFORE YOU MURDERED THEM.
IT WAS NOT MURDER.
"IT WAS PUNISHMENT
"KORUGAR DIED BECAUSE OF THEIR SINS."

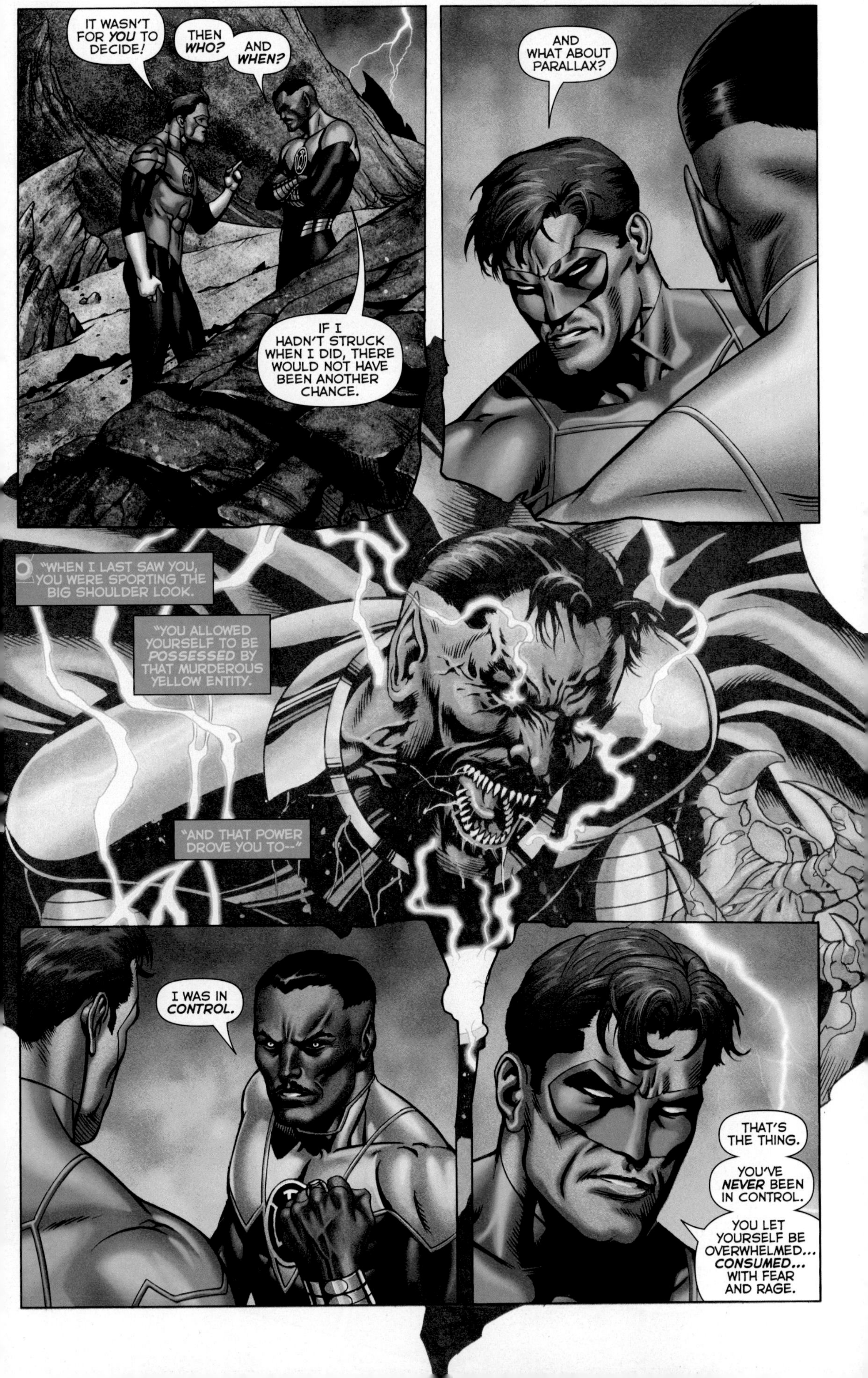

IT WASN'T FOR *YOU* TO DECIDE!
THEN *WHO?*
AND *WHEN?*
IF I HADN'T STRUCK WHEN I DID, THERE WOULD NOT HAVE BEEN ANOTHER CHANCE.
AND WHAT ABOUT PARALLAX?
"WHEN I LAST SAW YOU, YOU WERE SPORTING THE BIG SHOULDER LOOK.
"YOU ALLOWED YOURSELF TO BE *POSSESSED* BY THAT MURDEROUS YELLOW ENTITY.
"AND THAT POWER DROVE YOU TO--"
I WAS IN *CONTROL.*
THAT'S THE THING.
YOU'VE *NEVER* BEEN IN CONTROL.
YOU LET YOURSELF BE OVERWHELMED... *CONSUMED...* WITH FEAR AND RAGE.

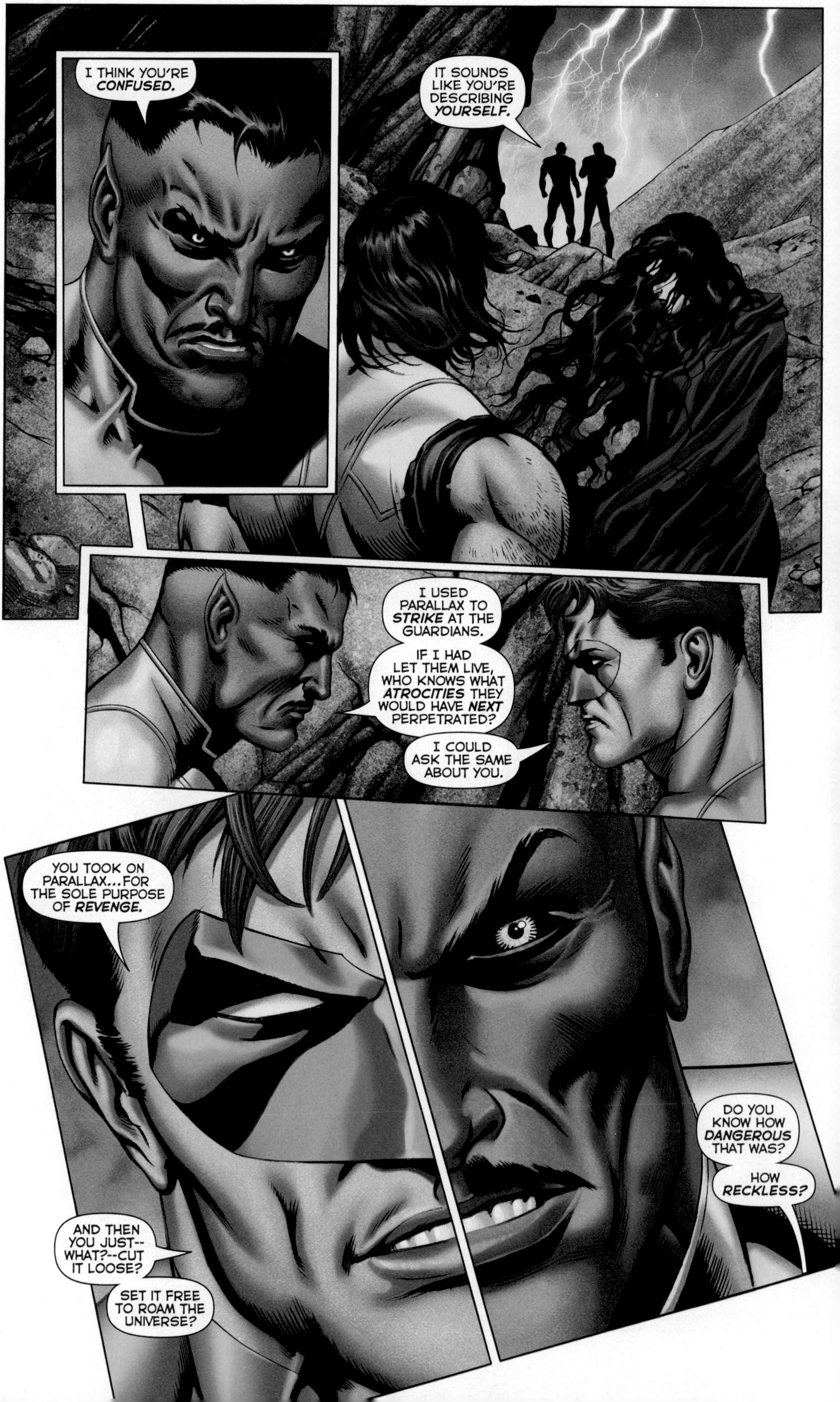

I THINK YOU'RE *CONFUSED.*
IT SOUNDS LIKE YOU'RE DESCRIBING *YOURSELF.*
I USED PARALLAX TO *STRIKE* AT THE GUARDIANS.
IF I HAD LET THEM LIVE, WHO KNOWS WHAT *ATROCITIES* THEY WOULD HAVE *NEXT* PERPETRATED?
I COULD ASK THE SAME ABOUT YOU.
YOU TOOK ON PARALLAX...FOR THE SOLE PURPOSE OF *REVENGE.*
DO YOU KNOW HOW *DANGEROUS* THAT WAS?
HOW *RECKLESS?*
AND THEN YOU JUST--WHAT?--CUT IT LOOSE?
SET IT FREE TO ROAM THE UNIVERSE?

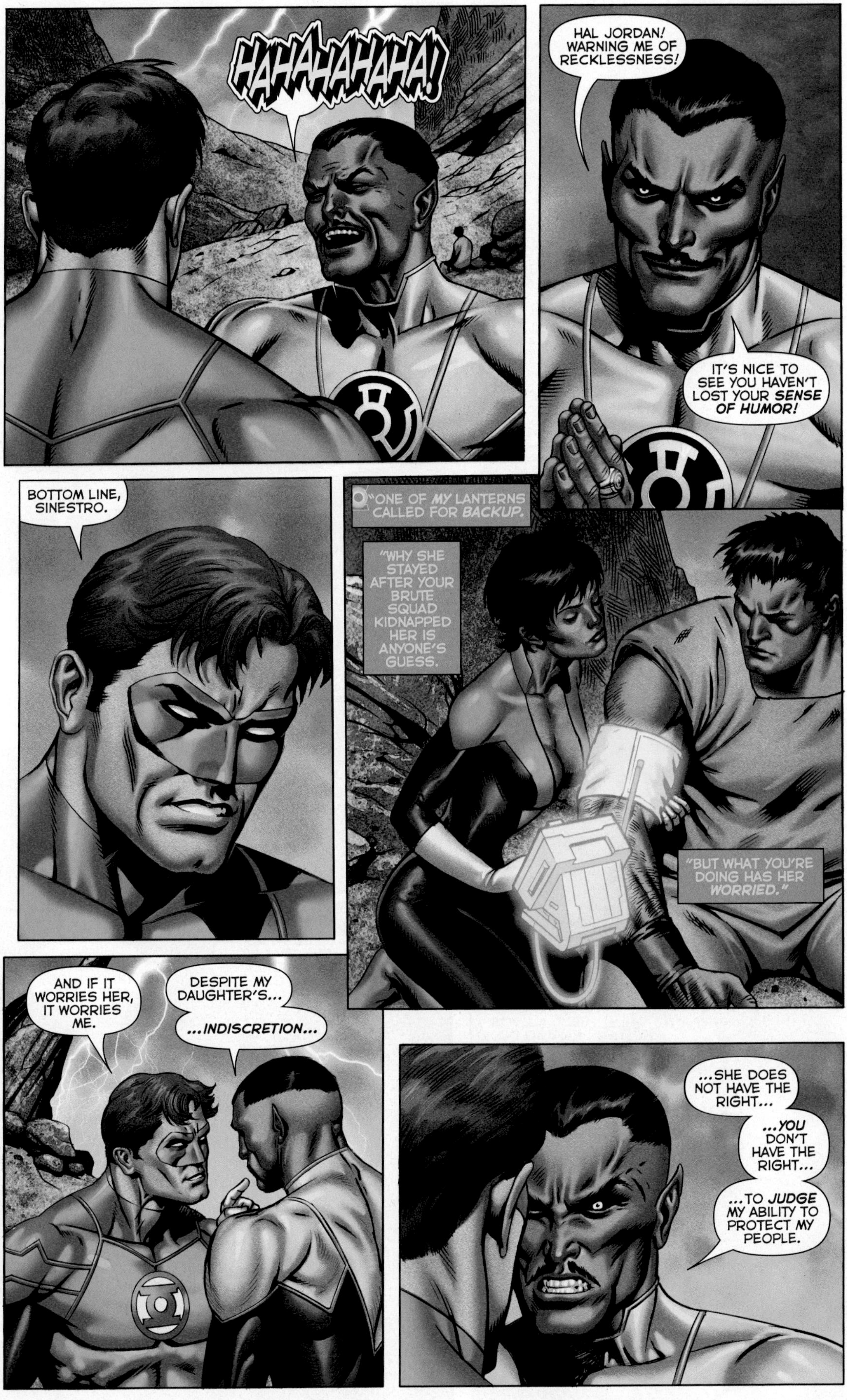
HAHAHAHAHA!
HAL JORDAN! WARNING ME OF RECKLESSNESS!
IT'S NICE TO SEE YOU HAVEN'T LOST YOUR SENSE OF HUMOR!
BOTTOM LINE, SINESTRO.
"ONE OF MY LANTERNS CALLED FOR BACKUP.
"WHY SHE STAYED AFTER YOUR BRUTE SQUAD KIDNAPPED HER IS ANYONE'S GUESS.
"BUT WHAT YOU'RE DOING HAS HER WORRIED."
AND IF IT WORRIES HER, IT WORRIES ME.
DESPITE MY DAUGHTER'S...
...INDISCRETION...
...SHE DOES NOT HAVE THE RIGHT...
...YOU DON'T HAVE THE RIGHT...
...TO JUDGE MY ABILITY TO PROTECT MY PEOPLE.

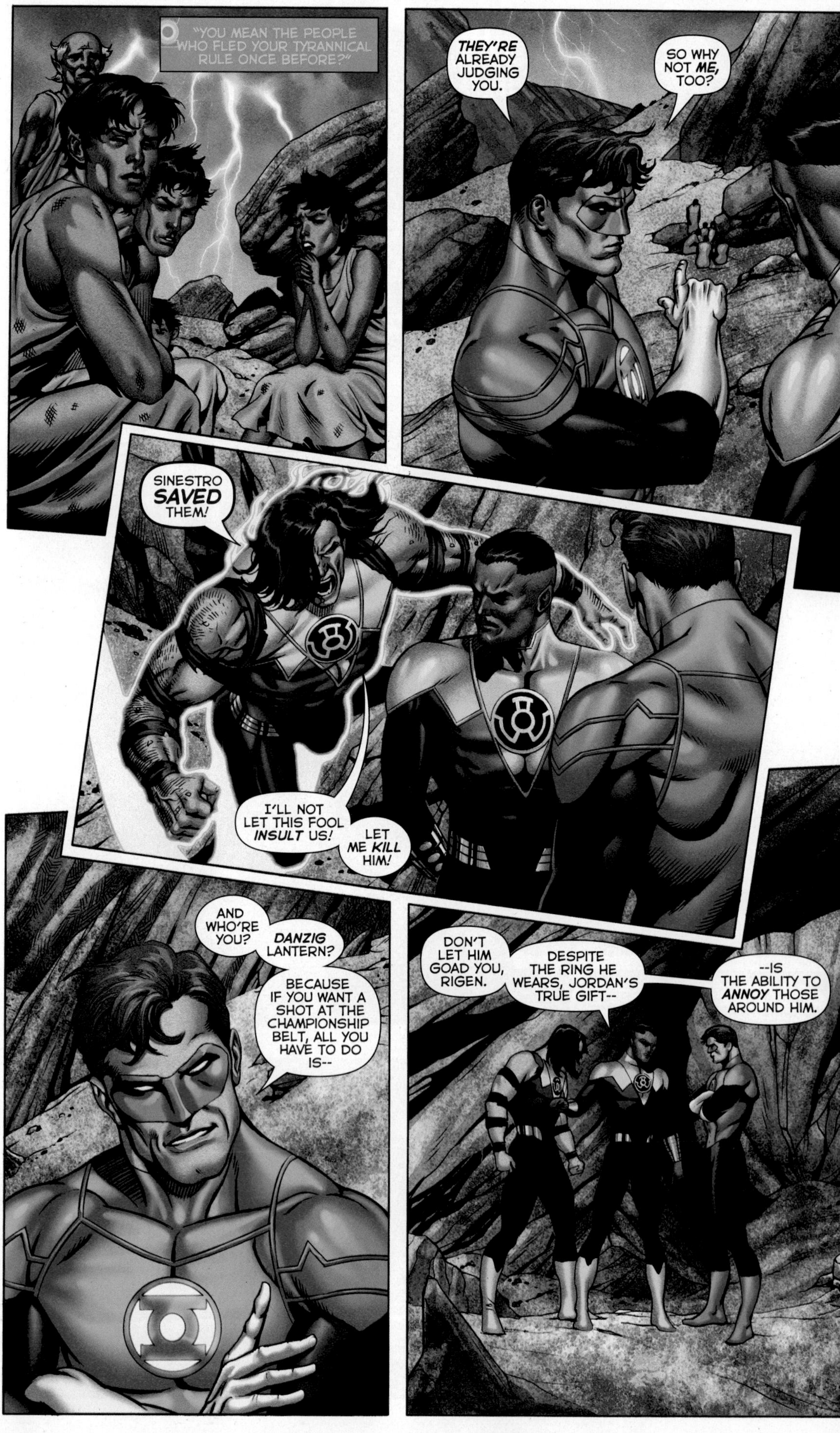
"YOU MEAN THE PEOPLE WHO FLED YOUR TYRANNICAL RULE ONCE BEFORE?"
THEY'RE ALREADY JUDGING YOU.
SO WHY NOT ME, TOO?
SINESTRO SAVED THEM!
I'LL NOT LET THIS FOOL INSULT US!
LET ME KILL HIM!
AND WHO'RE YOU? DANZIG LANTERN?
BECAUSE IF YOU WANT A SHOT AT THE CHAMPIONSHIP BELT, ALL YOU HAVE TO DO IS--
DON'T LET HIM GOAD YOU, RIGEN.
DESPITE THE RING HE WEARS, JORDAN'S TRUE GIFT--
--IS THE ABILITY TO ANNOY THOSE AROUND HIM.

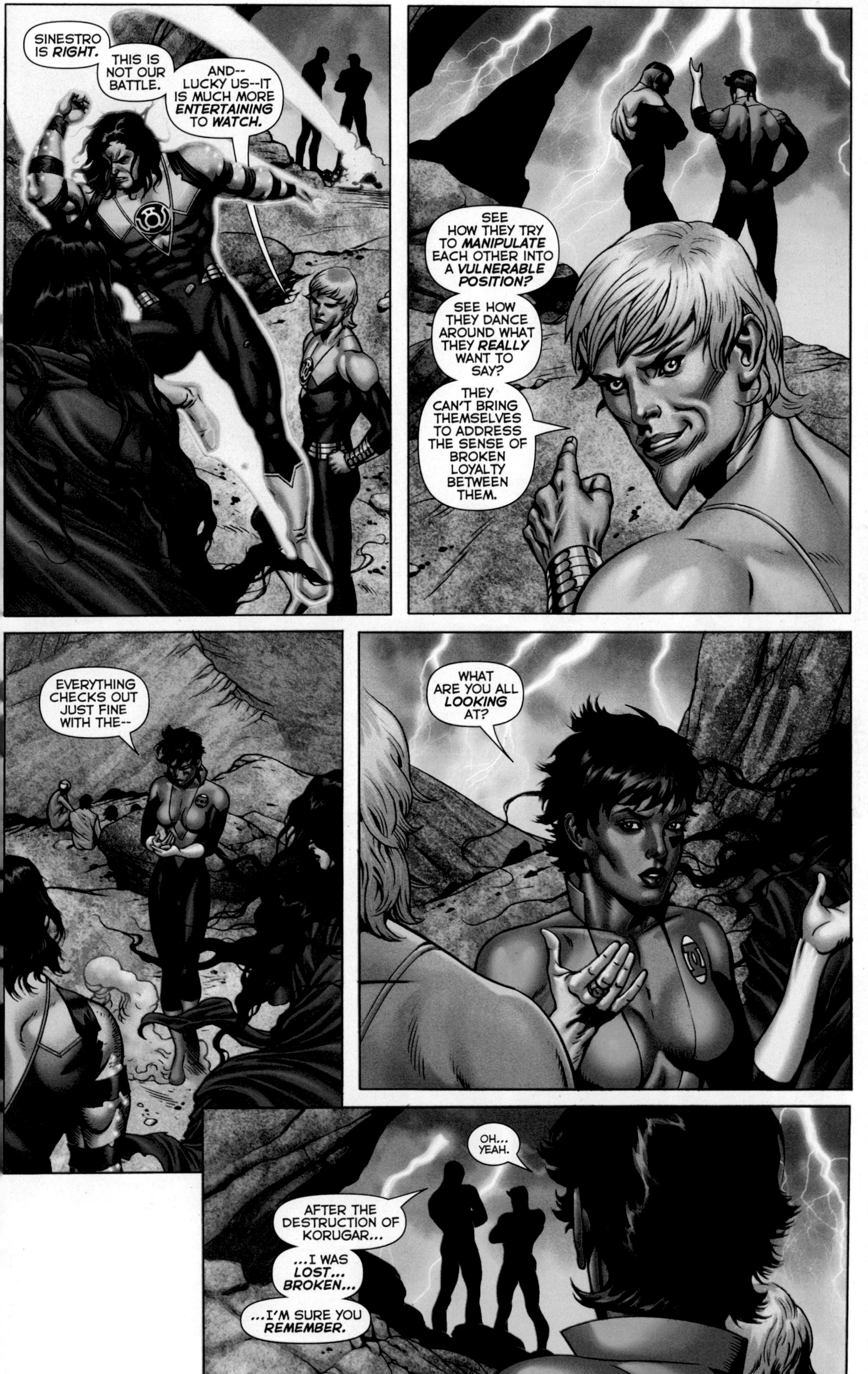
SINESTRO IS RIGHT.
THIS IS NOT OUR BATTLE.
AND-- LUCKY US--IT IS MUCH MORE ENTERTAINING TO WATCH.
SEE HOW THEY TRY TO MANIPULATE EACH OTHER INTO A VULNERABLE POSITION?
SEE HOW THEY DANCE AROUND WHAT THEY REALLY WANT TO SAY?
THEY CAN'T BRING THEMSELVES TO ADDRESS THE SENSE OF BROKEN LOYALTY BETWEEN THEM.
EVERYTHING CHECKS OUT JUST FINE WITH THE--
WHAT ARE YOU ALL LOOKING AT?
OH... YEAH.
AFTER THE DESTRUCTION OF KORUGAR...
...I WAS LOST... BROKEN...
...I'M SURE YOU REMEMBER.

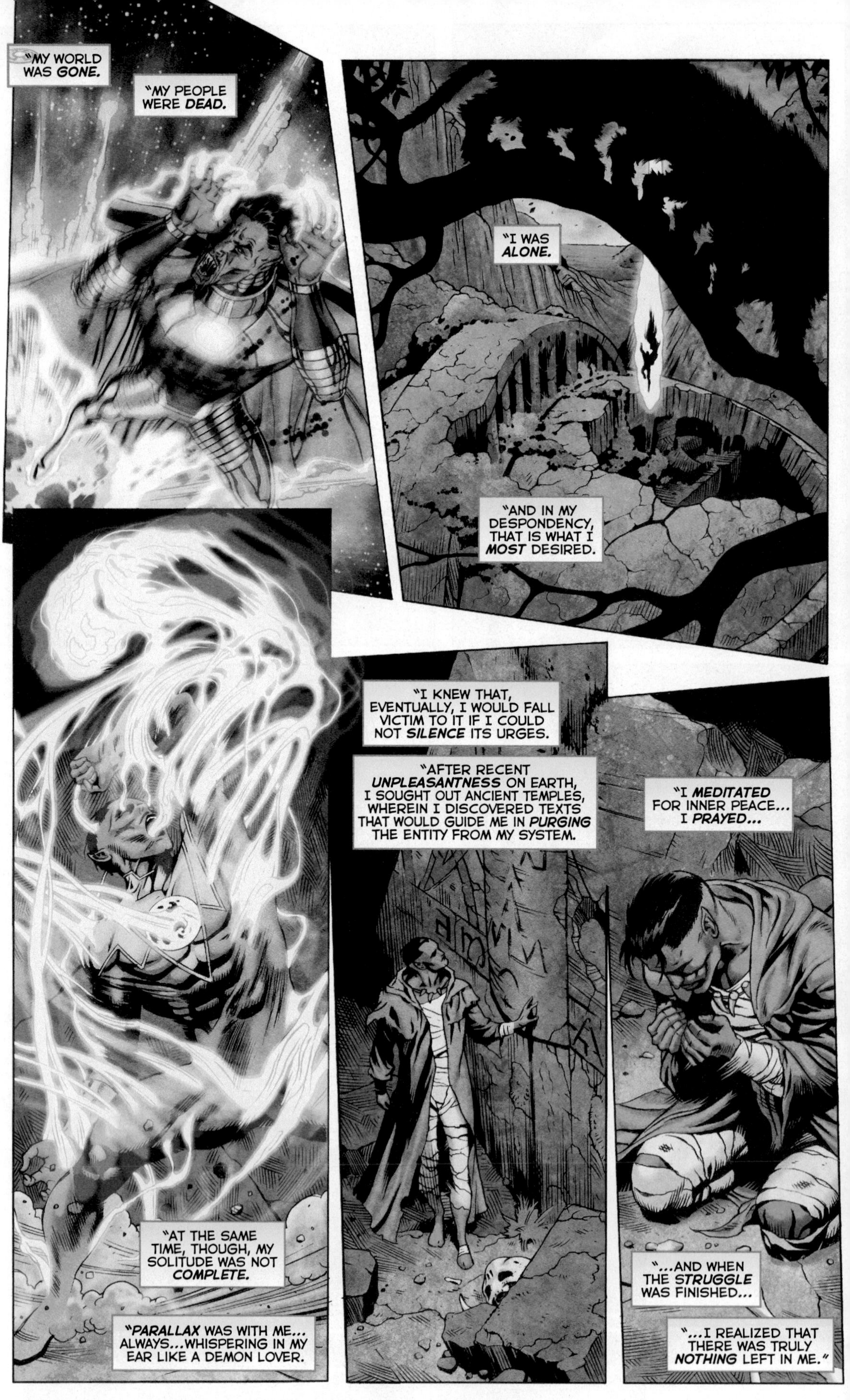
"MY WORLD WAS GONE.
"MY PEOPLE WERE DEAD.
"I WAS ALONE.
"AND IN MY DESPONDENCY, THAT IS WHAT I MOST DESIRED.
"AT THE SAME TIME, THOUGH, MY SOLITUDE WAS NOT COMPLETE.
"PARALLAX WAS WITH ME... ALWAYS...WHISPERING IN MY EAR LIKE A DEMON LOVER.
"I KNEW THAT, EVENTUALLY, I WOULD FALL VICTIM TO IT IF I COULD NOT SILENCE ITS URGES.
"AFTER RECENT UNPLEASANTNESS ON EARTH, I SOUGHT OUT ANCIENT TEMPLES, WHEREIN I DISCOVERED TEXTS THAT WOULD GUIDE ME IN PURGING THE ENTITY FROM MY SYSTEM.
"I MEDITATED FOR INNER PEACE... I PRAYED...
"...AND WHEN THE STRUGGLE WAS FINISHED...
"...I REALIZED THAT THERE WAS TRULY NOTHING LEFT IN ME."

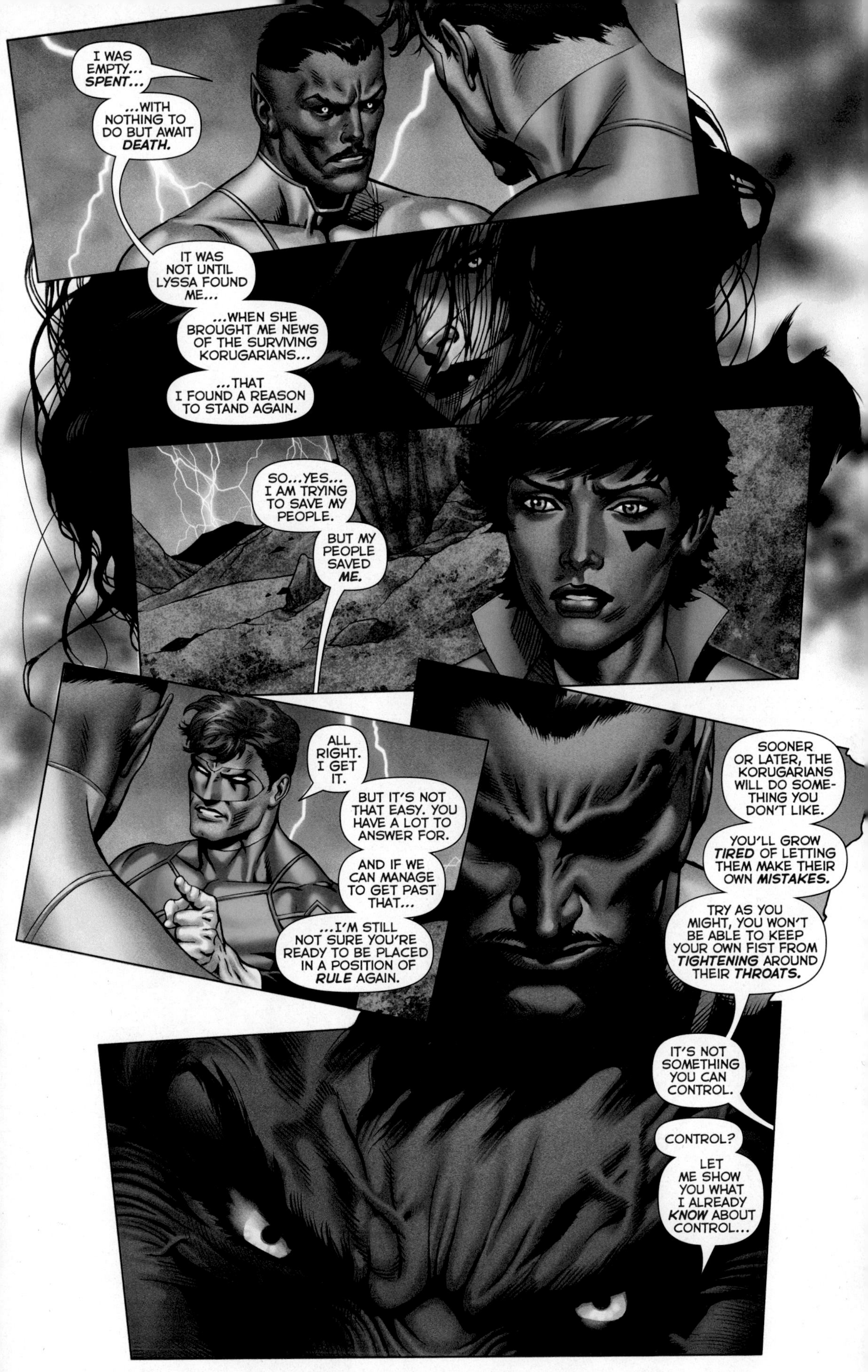

I WAS EMPTY... SPENT...
...WITH NOTHING TO DO BUT AWAIT DEATH.
IT WAS NOT UNTIL LYSSA FOUND ME...
...WHEN SHE BROUGHT ME NEWS OF THE SURVIVING KORUGARIANS...
...THAT I FOUND A REASON TO STAND AGAIN.
SO...YES... I AM TRYING TO SAVE MY PEOPLE.
BUT MY PEOPLE SAVED ME.
ALL RIGHT. I GET IT.
BUT IT'S NOT THAT EASY. YOU HAVE A LOT TO ANSWER FOR.
AND IF WE CAN MANAGE TO GET PAST THAT...
...I'M STILL NOT SURE YOU'RE READY TO BE PLACED IN A POSITION OF RULE AGAIN.
SOONER OR LATER, THE KORUGARIANS WILL DO SOMETHING YOU DON'T LIKE.
YOU'LL GROW TIRED OF LETTING THEM MAKE THEIR OWN MISTAKES.
TRY AS YOU MIGHT, YOU WON'T BE ABLE TO KEEP YOUR OWN FIST FROM TIGHTENING AROUND THEIR THROATS.
IT'S NOT SOMETHING YOU CAN CONTROL.
CONTROL?
LET ME SHOW YOU WHAT I ALREADY KNOW ABOUT CONTROL...

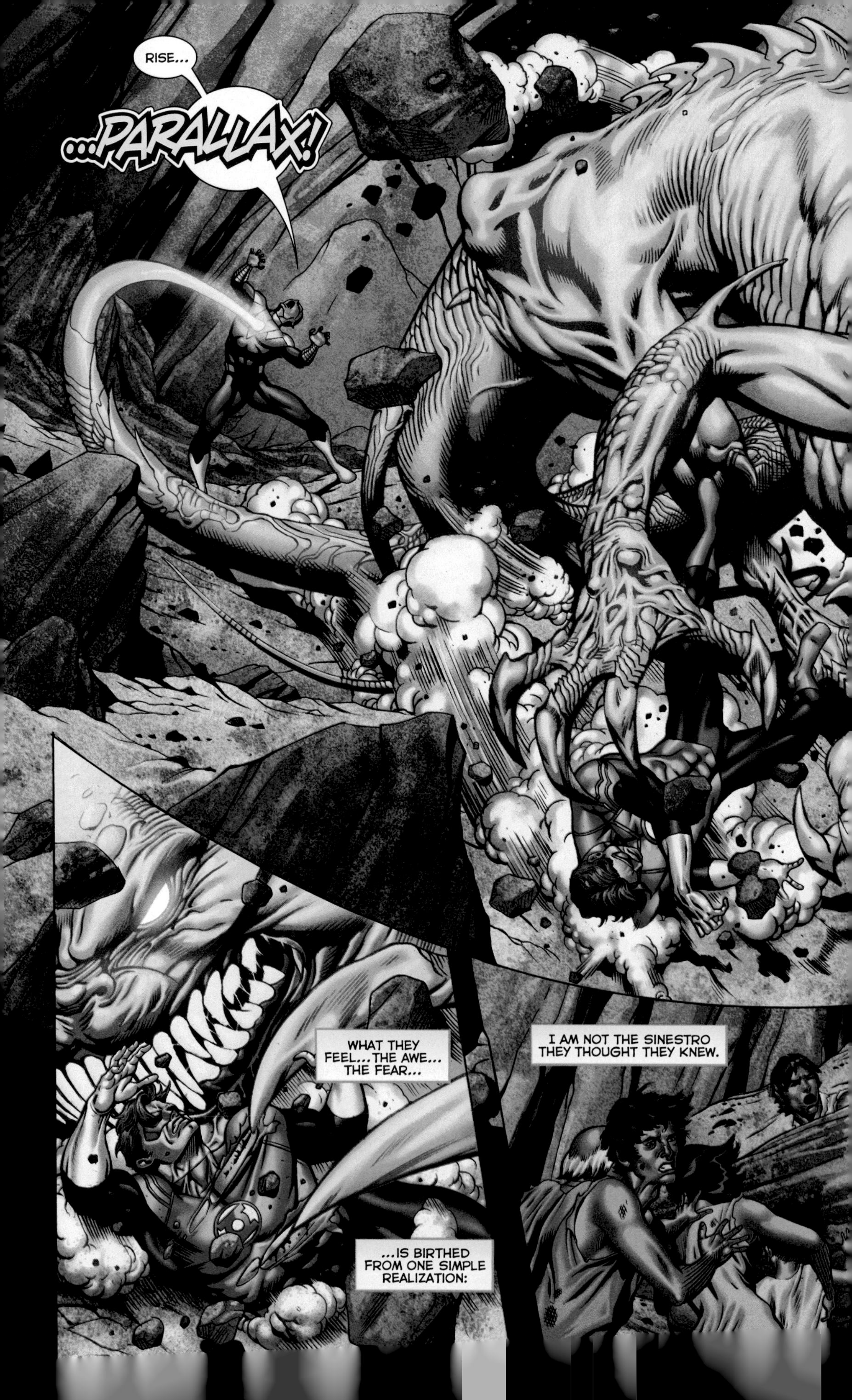
RISE...
...PARALLAX!
WHAT THEY FEEL...THE AWE... THE FEAR...
...IS BIRTHED FROM ONE SIMPLE REALIZATION:
I AM NOT THE SINESTRO THEY THOUGHT THEY KNEW.

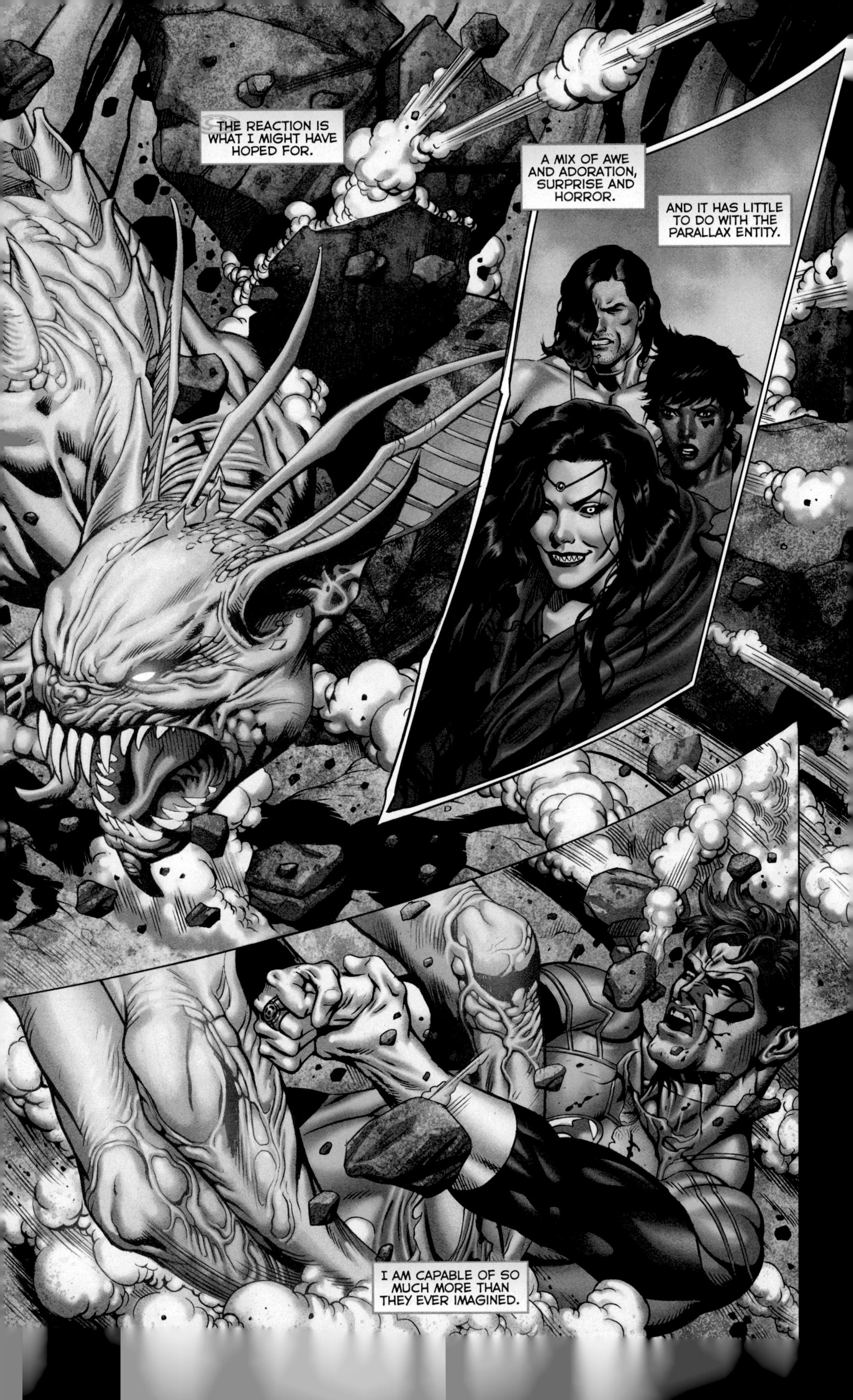
THE REACTION IS WHAT I MIGHT HAVE HOPED FOR.
A MIX OF AWE AND ADORATION, SURPRISE AND HORROR.
AND IT HAS LITTLE TO DO WITH THE PARALLAX ENTITY.
I AM CAPABLE OF SO MUCH MORE THAN THEY EVER IMAGINED.

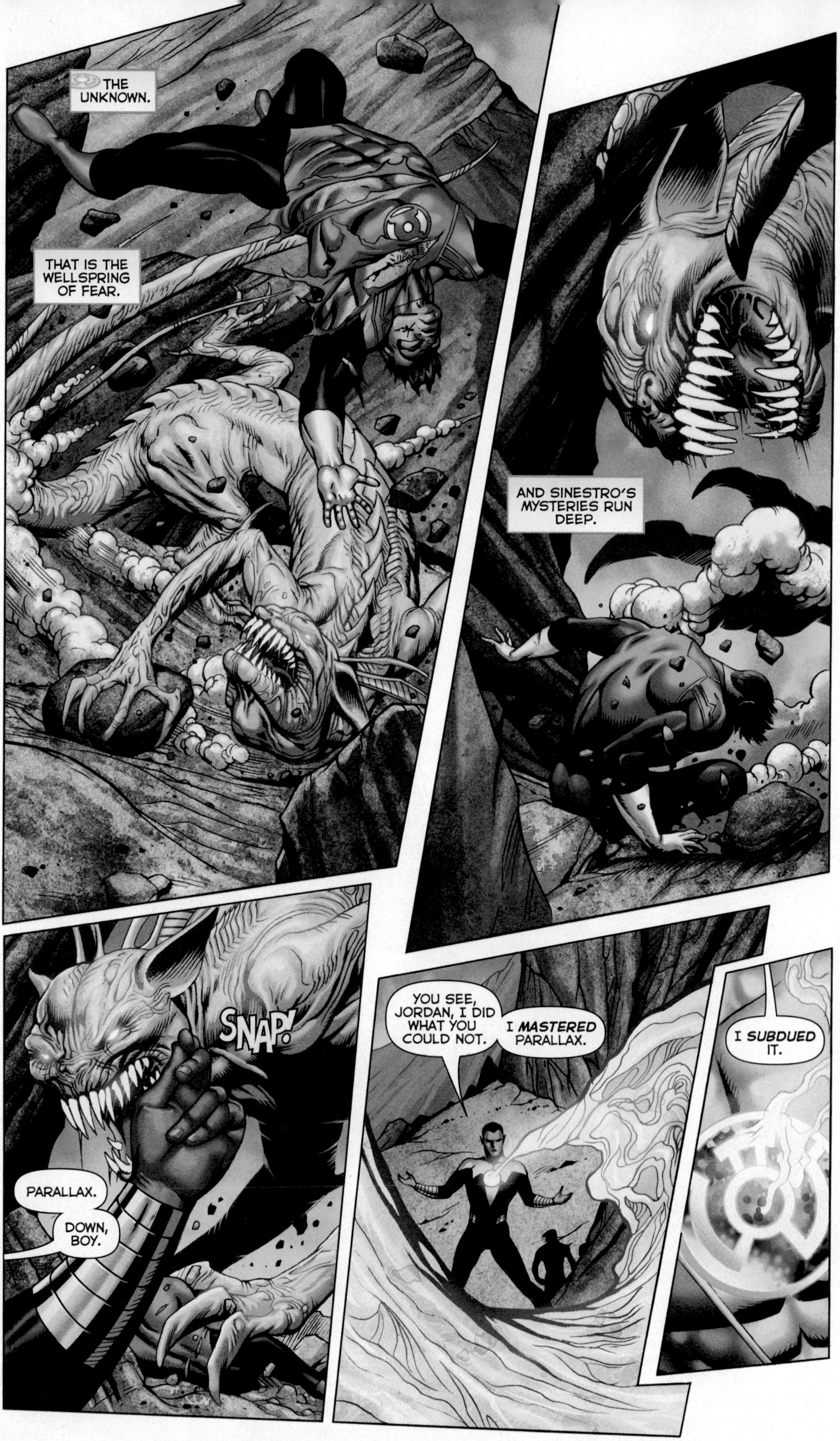
THE UNKNOWN.
THAT IS THE WELLSPRING OF FEAR.
AND SINESTRO'S MYSTERIES RUN DEEP.
SNAP!
PARALLAX.
DOWN, BOY.
YOU SEE, JORDAN, I DID WHAT YOU COULD NOT.
I *MASTERED* PARALLAX.
I *SUBDUED* IT.

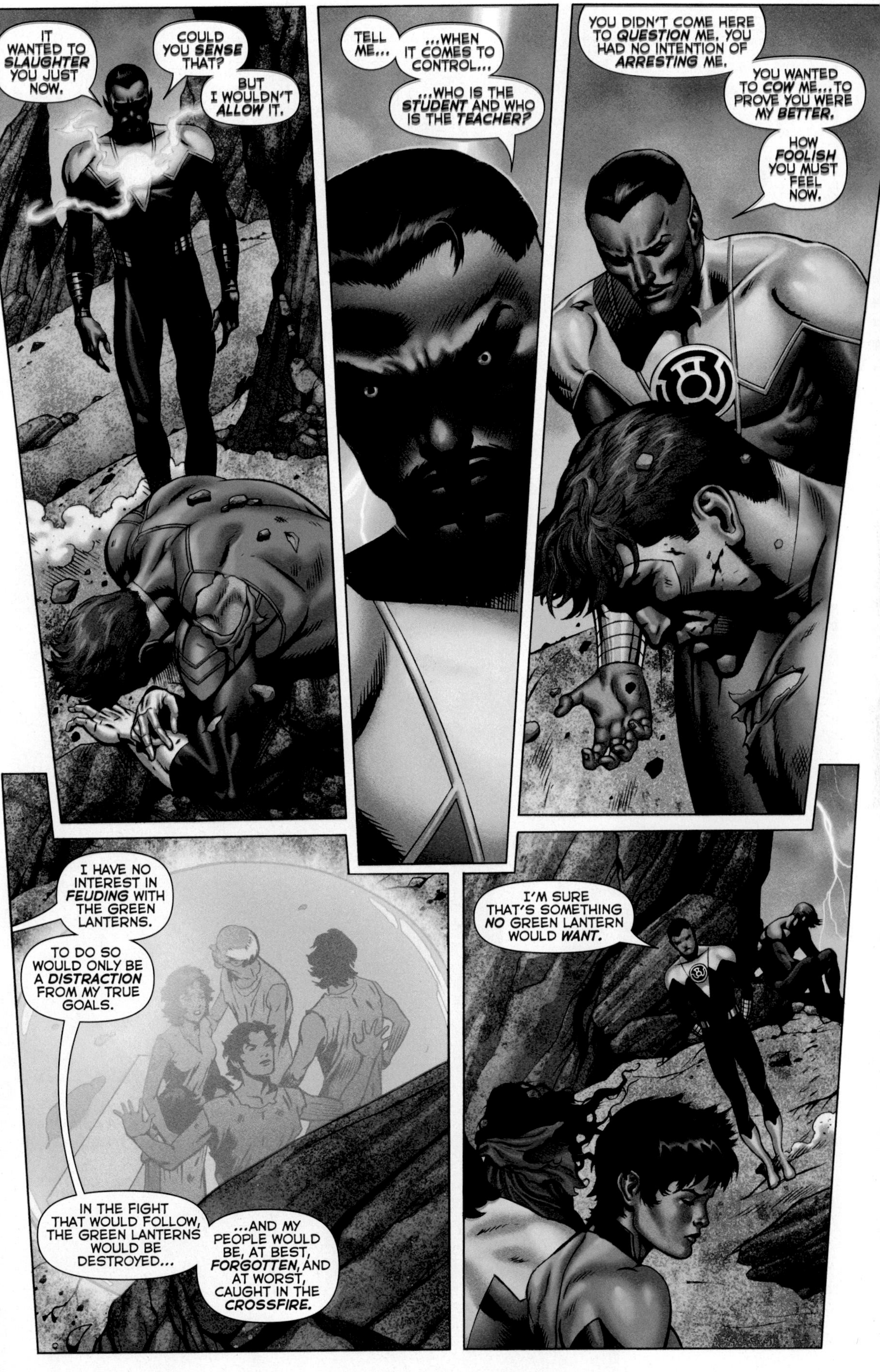
IT WANTED TO SLAUGHTER YOU JUST NOW.
COULD YOU SENSE THAT?
BUT I WOULDN'T ALLOW IT.
TELL ME...
...WHEN IT COMES TO CONTROL...
...WHO IS THE STUDENT AND WHO IS THE TEACHER?
YOU DIDN'T COME HERE TO QUESTION ME. YOU HAD NO INTENTION OF ARRESTING ME.
YOU WANTED TO COW ME...TO PROVE YOU WERE MY BETTER.
HOW FOOLISH YOU MUST FEEL NOW.
I HAVE NO INTEREST IN FEUDING WITH THE GREEN LANTERNS.
TO DO SO WOULD ONLY BE A DISTRACTION FROM MY TRUE GOALS.
IN THE FIGHT THAT WOULD FOLLOW, THE GREEN LANTERNS WOULD BE DESTROYED...
...AND MY PEOPLE WOULD BE, AT BEST, FORGOTTEN, AND AT WORST, CAUGHT IN THE CROSSFIRE.
I'M SURE THAT'S SOMETHING NO GREEN LANTERN WOULD WANT.

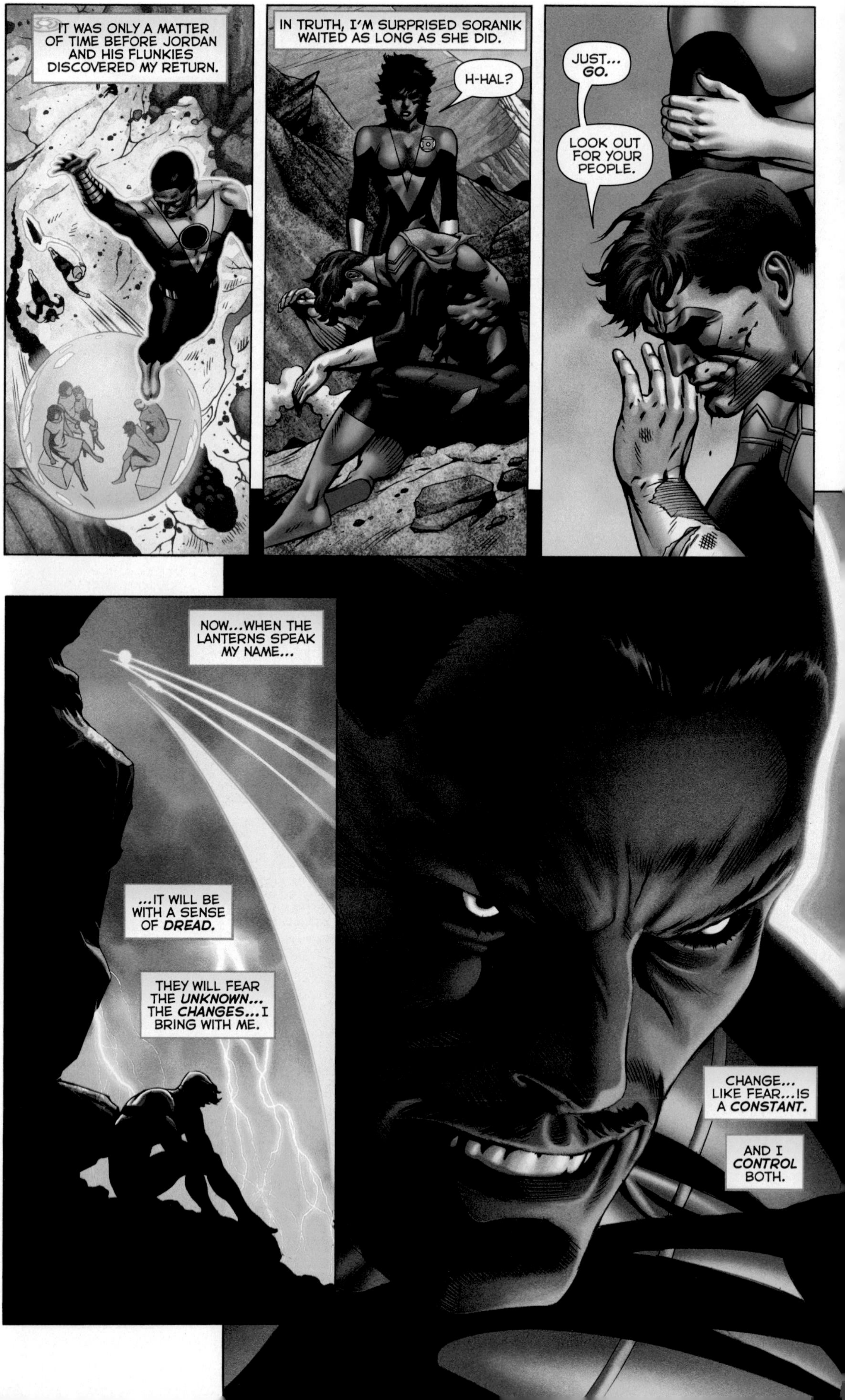
IT WAS ONLY A MATTER OF TIME BEFORE JORDAN AND HIS FLUNKIES DISCOVERED MY RETURN.
IN TRUTH, I'M SURPRISED SORANIK WAITED AS LONG AS SHE DID.
H-HAL?
JUST... GO.
LOOK OUT FOR YOUR PEOPLE.
NOW...WHEN THE LANTERNS SPEAK MY NAME...
...IT WILL BE WITH A SENSE OF DREAD.
THEY WILL FEAR THE UNKNOWN... THE CHANGES... I BRING WITH ME.
CHANGE... LIKE FEAR...IS A CONSTANT.
AND I CONTROL BOTH.

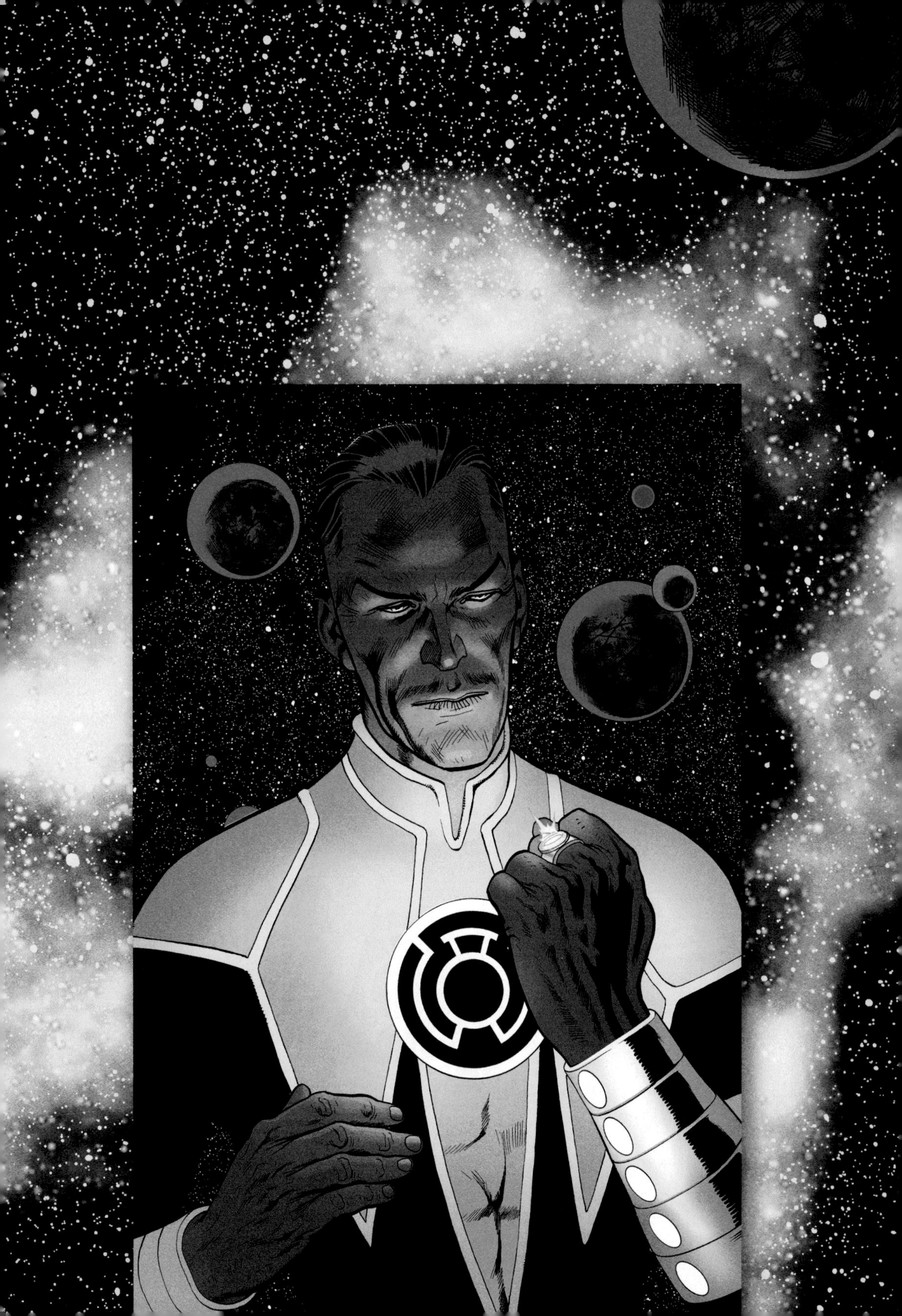

THE NIGHT, BOTH FEARFUL AND DARK

CULLEN BUNN writer **IGOR LIMA** penciller **RUY JOSÉ** inker **JASON WRIGHT** colorist **DAVE SHARPE** letterer
cover art by **KEVIN NOWLAN**

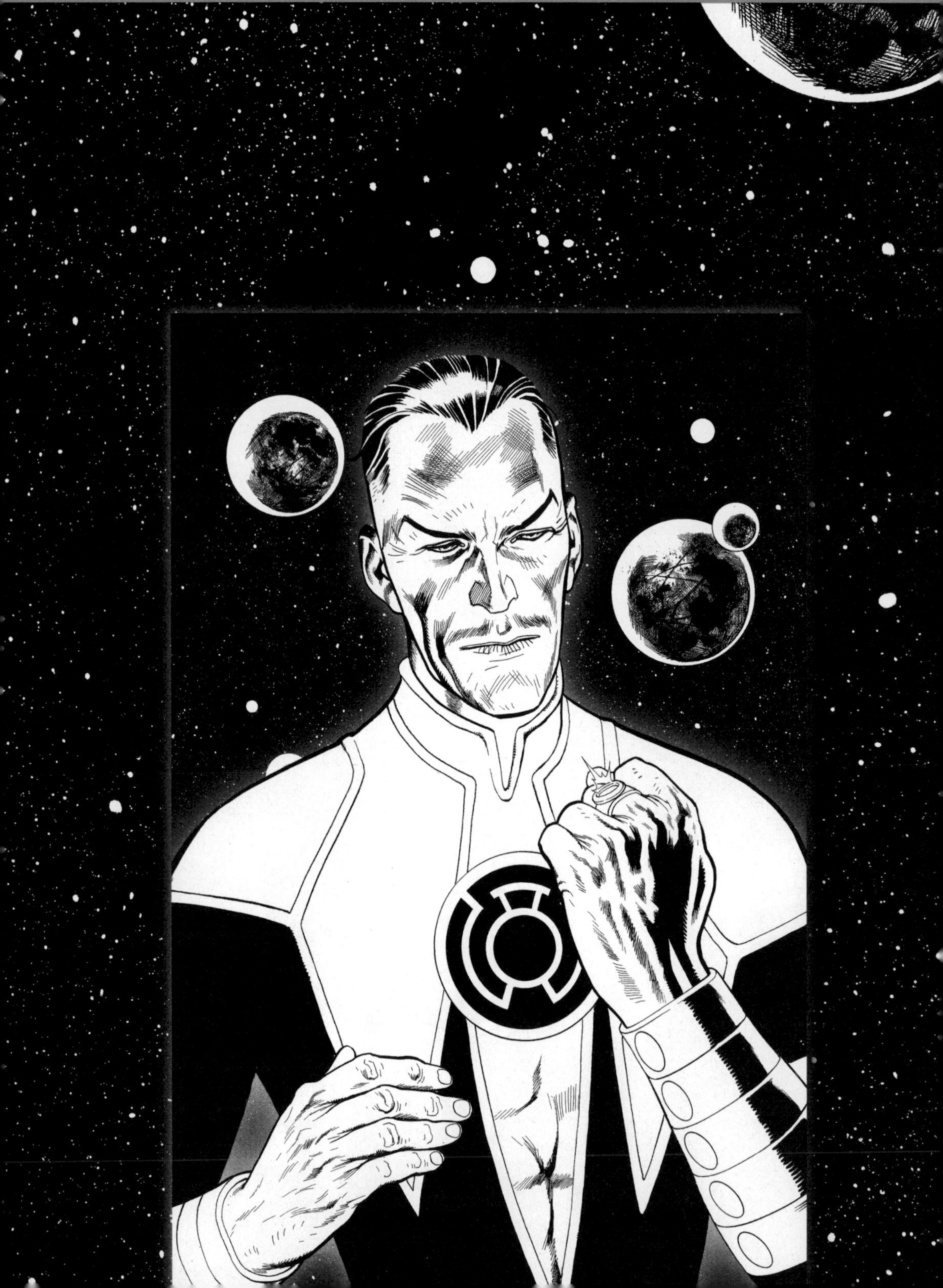

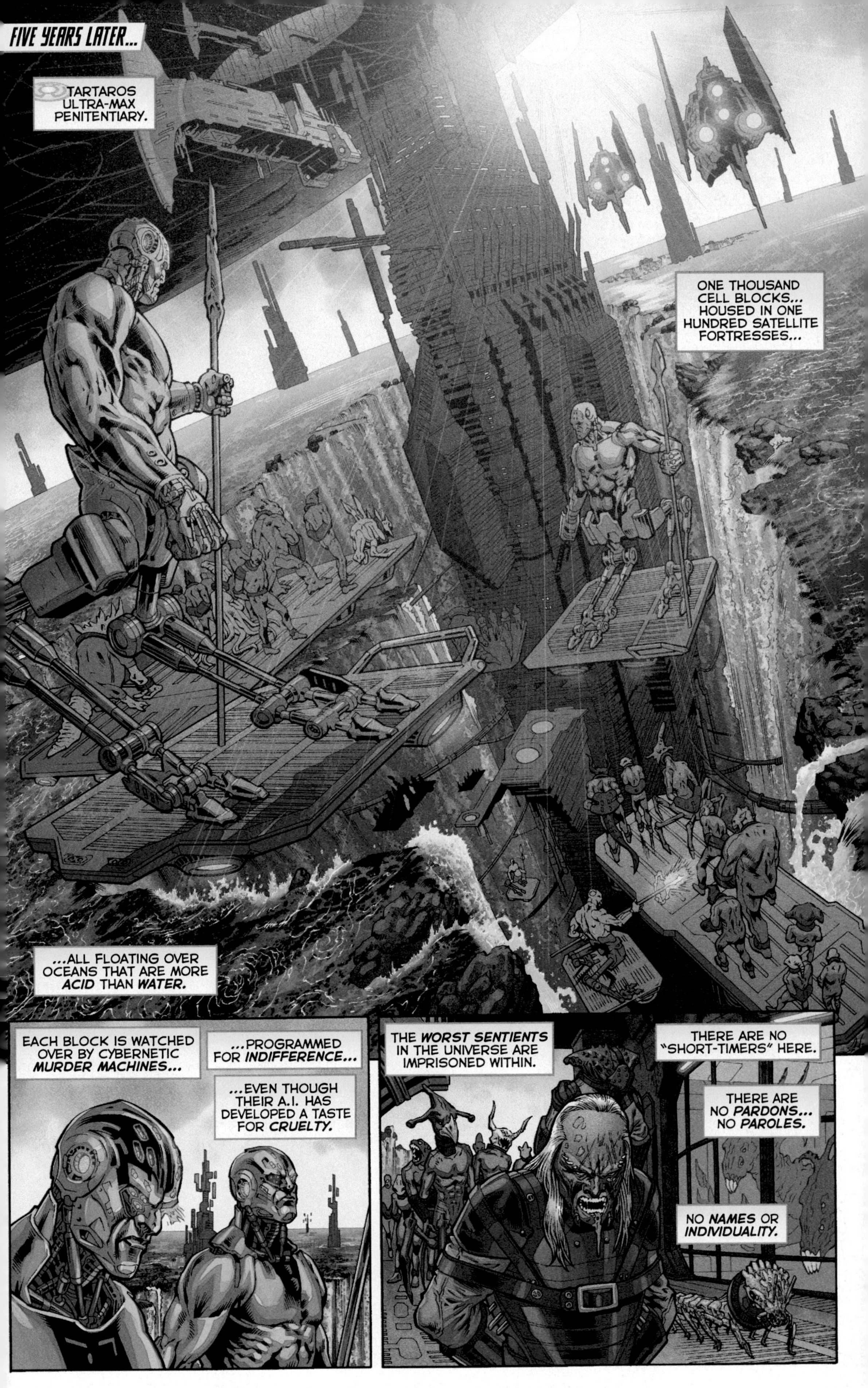
FIVE YEARS LATER...
TARTAROS ULTRA-MAX PENITENTIARY.
ONE THOUSAND CELL BLOCKS... HOUSED IN ONE HUNDRED SATELLITE FORTRESSES...
...ALL FLOATING OVER OCEANS THAT ARE MORE ACID THAN WATER.
EACH BLOCK IS WATCHED OVER BY CYBERNETIC MURDER MACHINES...
...PROGRAMMED FOR INDIFFERENCE...
...EVEN THOUGH THEIR A.I. HAS DEVELOPED A TASTE FOR CRUELTY.
THE WORST SENTIENTS IN THE UNIVERSE ARE IMPRISONED WITHIN.
THERE ARE NO "SHORT-TIMERS" HERE.
THERE ARE NO PARDONS... NO PAROLES.
NO NAMES OR INDIVIDUALITY.

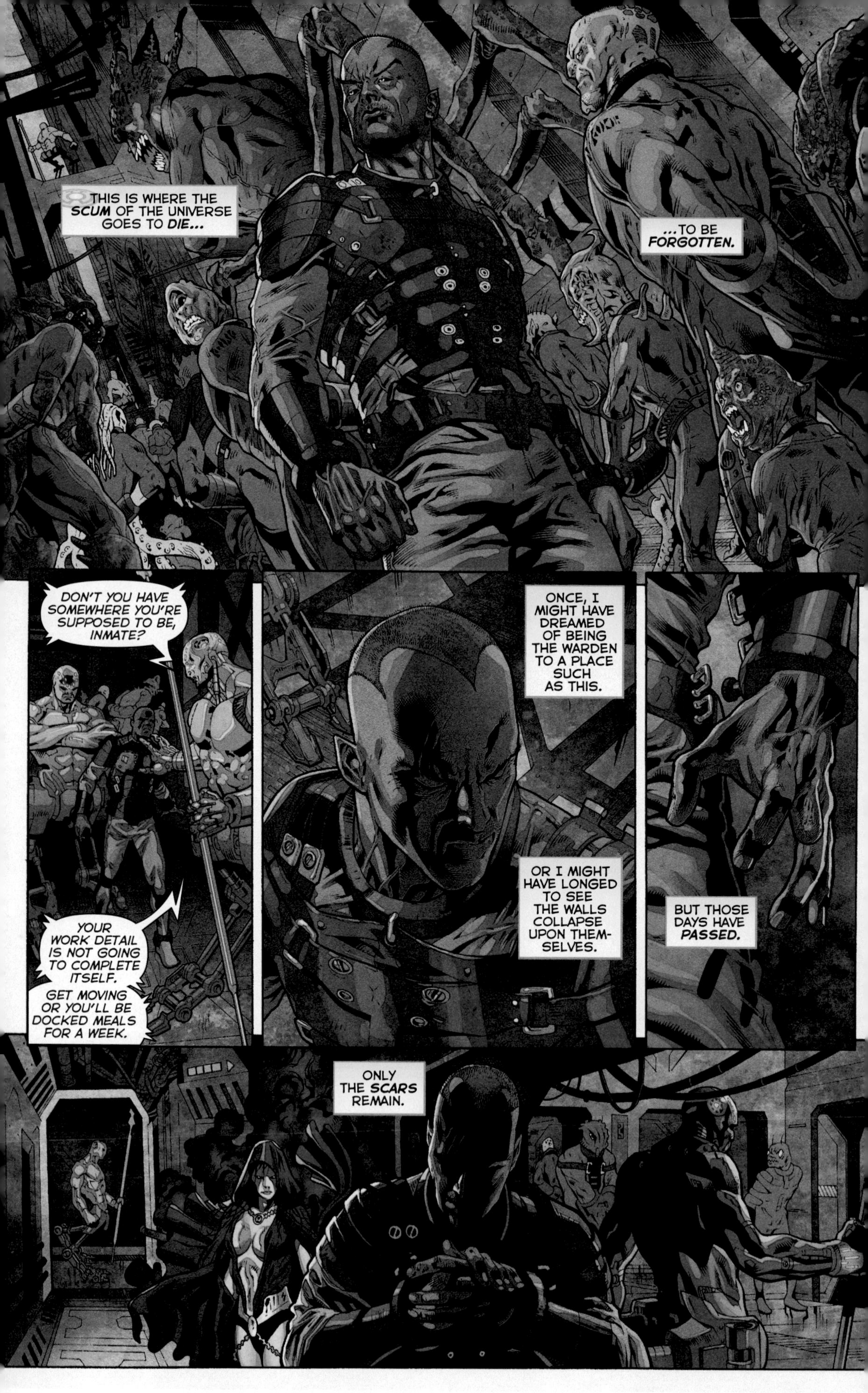
THIS IS WHERE THE SCUM OF THE UNIVERSE GOES TO DIE...
...TO BE FORGOTTEN.
DON'T YOU HAVE SOMEWHERE YOU'RE SUPPOSED TO BE, INMATE?
YOUR WORK DETAIL IS NOT GOING TO COMPLETE ITSELF.
GET MOVING OR YOU'LL BE DOCKED MEALS FOR A WEEK.
ONCE, I MIGHT HAVE DREAMED OF BEING THE WARDEN TO A PLACE SUCH AS THIS.
OR I MIGHT HAVE LONGED TO SEE THE WALLS COLLAPSE UPON THEM-SELVES.
BUT THOSE DAYS HAVE PASSED.
ONLY THE SCARS REMAIN.

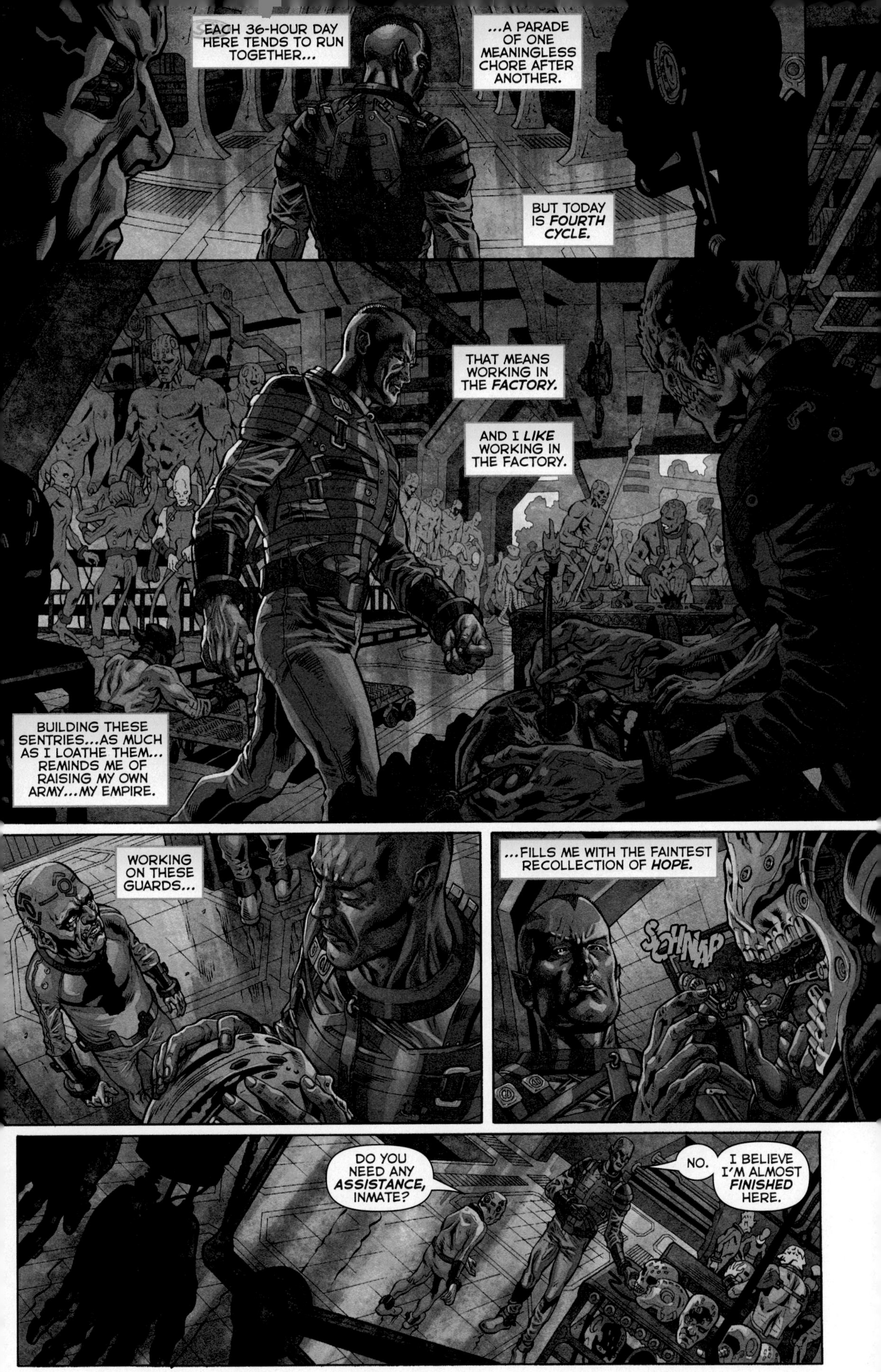
EACH 36-HOUR DAY HERE TENDS TO RUN TOGETHER...
...A PARADE OF ONE MEANINGLESS CHORE AFTER ANOTHER.
BUT TODAY IS FOURTH CYCLE.
THAT MEANS WORKING IN THE FACTORY.
AND I LIKE WORKING IN THE FACTORY.
BUILDING THESE SENTRIES...AS MUCH AS I LOATHE THEM... REMINDS ME OF RAISING MY OWN ARMY...MY EMPIRE.
WORKING ON THESE GUARDS...
...FILLS ME WITH THE FAINTEST RECOLLECTION OF HOPE.
SCHNAP
DO YOU NEED ANY ASSISTANCE, INMATE?
NO.
I BELIEVE I'M ALMOST FINISHED HERE.

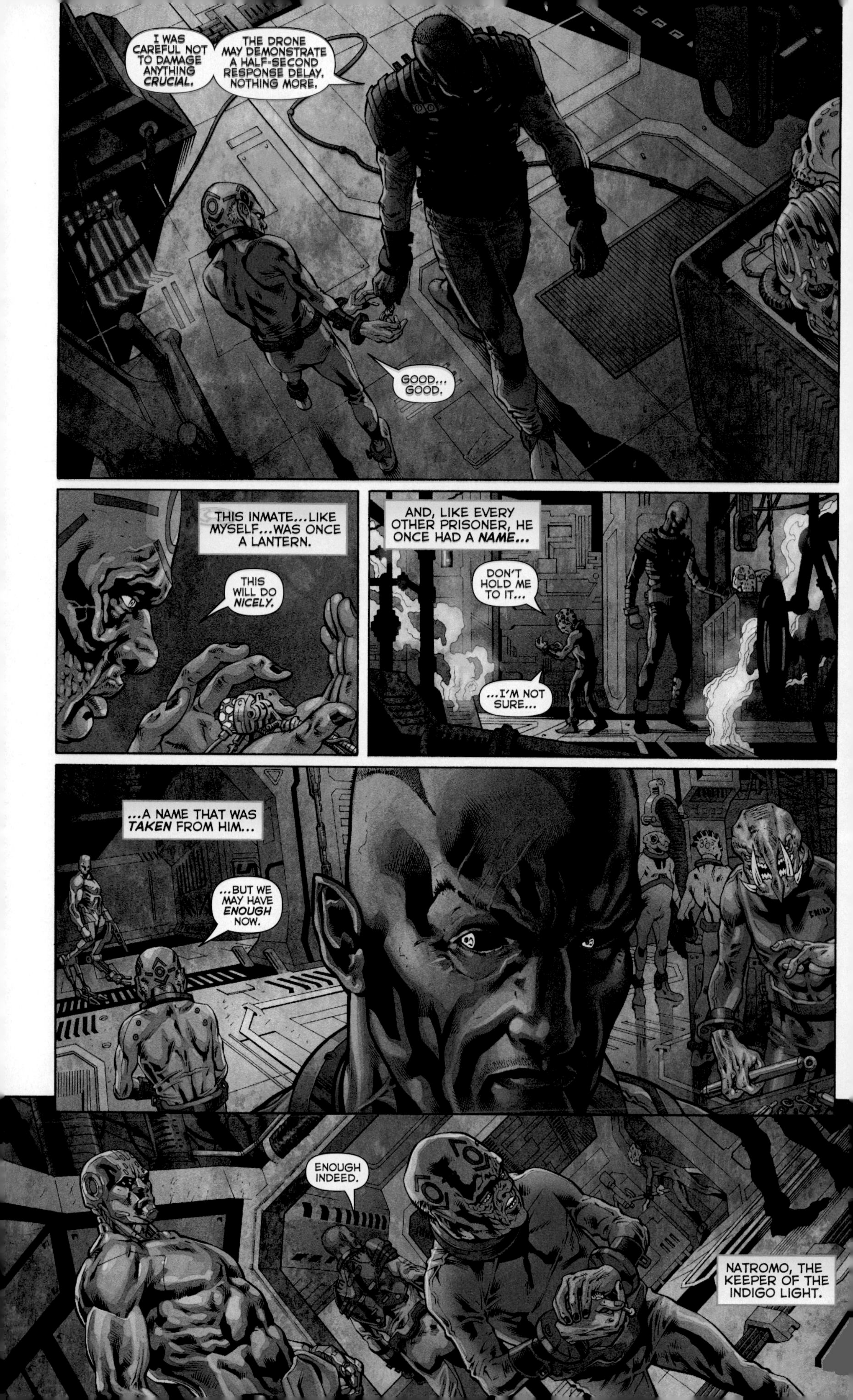
I WAS CAREFUL NOT TO DAMAGE ANYTHING CRUCIAL.
THE DRONE MAY DEMONSTRATE A HALF-SECOND RESPONSE DELAY. NOTHING MORE.
GOOD... GOOD.
THIS INMATE...LIKE MYSELF...WAS ONCE A LANTERN.
THIS WILL DO NICELY.
AND, LIKE EVERY OTHER PRISONER, HE ONCE HAD A NAME...
DON'T HOLD ME TO IT...
...I'M NOT SURE...
...A NAME THAT WAS TAKEN FROM HIM...
...BUT WE MAY HAVE ENOUGH NOW.
ENOUGH INDEED.
NATROMO, THE KEEPER OF THE INDIGO LIGHT.

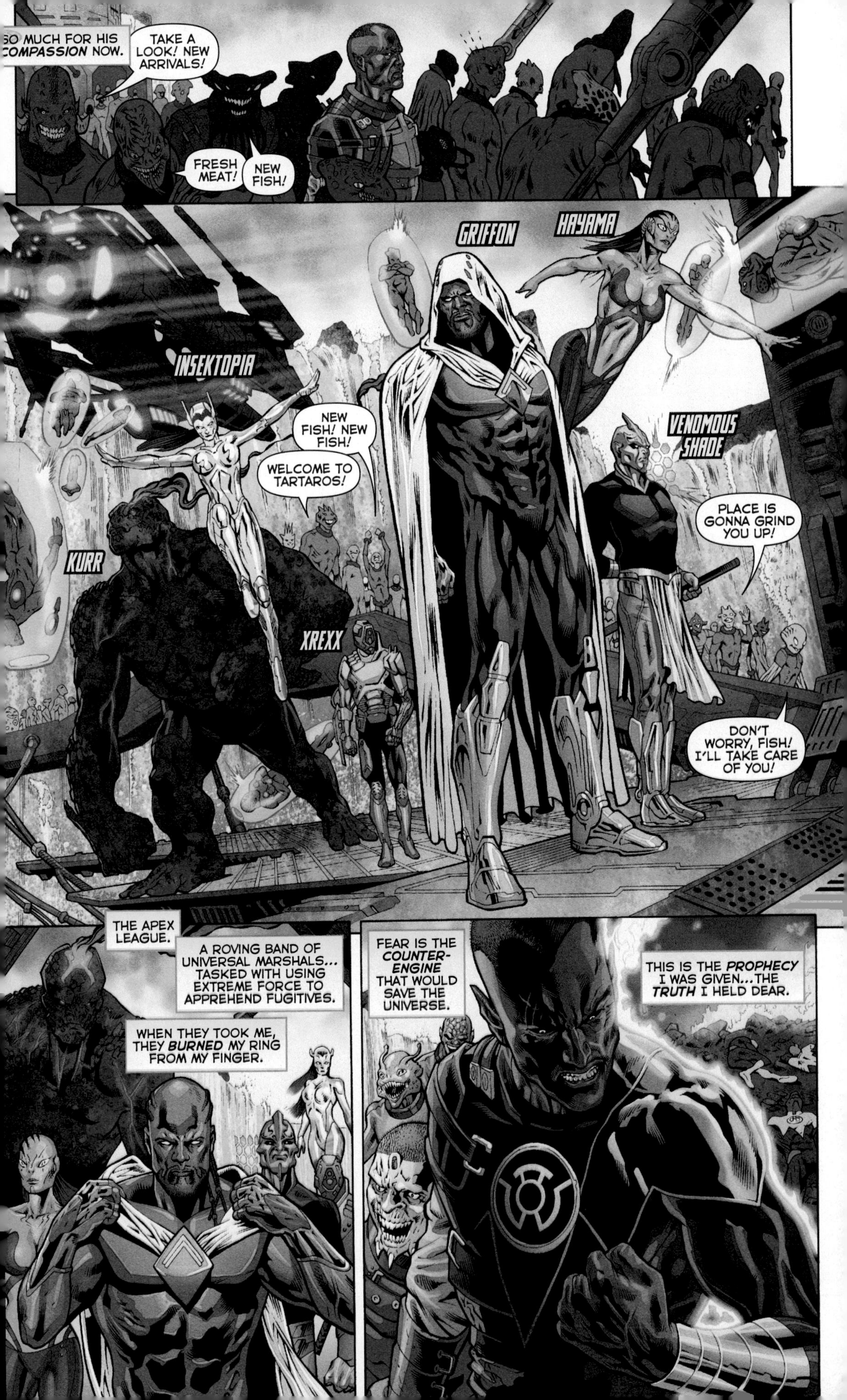
SO MUCH FOR HIS COMPASSION NOW.
TAKE A LOOK! NEW ARRIVALS!
FRESH MEAT!
NEW FISH!
GRIFFON
HAYAMA
INSEKTOPIA
VENOMOUS SHADE
NEW FISH! NEW FISH!
WELCOME TO TARTAROS!
KURR
XREXX
PLACE IS GONNA GRIND YOU UP!
DON'T WORRY, FISH! I'LL TAKE CARE OF YOU!
THE APEX LEAGUE.
A ROVING BAND OF UNIVERSAL MARSHALS... TASKED WITH USING EXTREME FORCE TO APPREHEND FUGITIVES.
WHEN THEY TOOK ME, THEY BURNED MY RING FROM MY FINGER.
FEAR IS THE COUNTER-ENGINE THAT WOULD SAVE THE UNIVERSE.
THIS IS THE PROPHECY I WAS GIVEN...THE TRUTH I HELD DEAR.

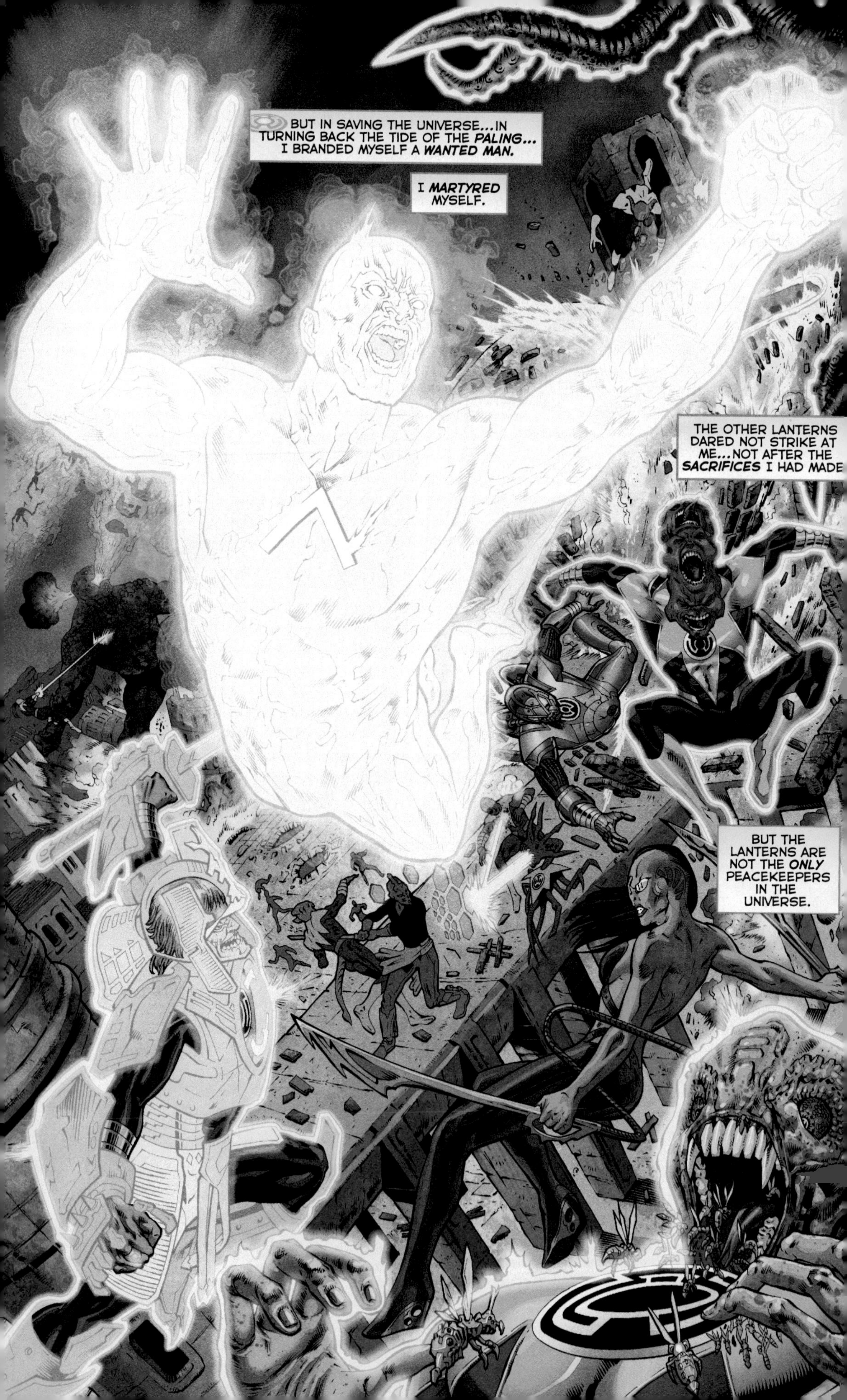
BUT IN SAVING THE UNIVERSE...IN TURNING BACK THE TIDE OF THE *PALING*... I BRANDED MYSELF A *WANTED MAN.*
I *MARTYRED* MYSELF.
THE OTHER LANTERNS DARED NOT STRIKE AT ME...NOT AFTER THE *SACRIFICES* I HAD MADE
BUT THE LANTERNS ARE NOT THE *ONLY* PEACEKEEPERS IN THE UNIVERSE.

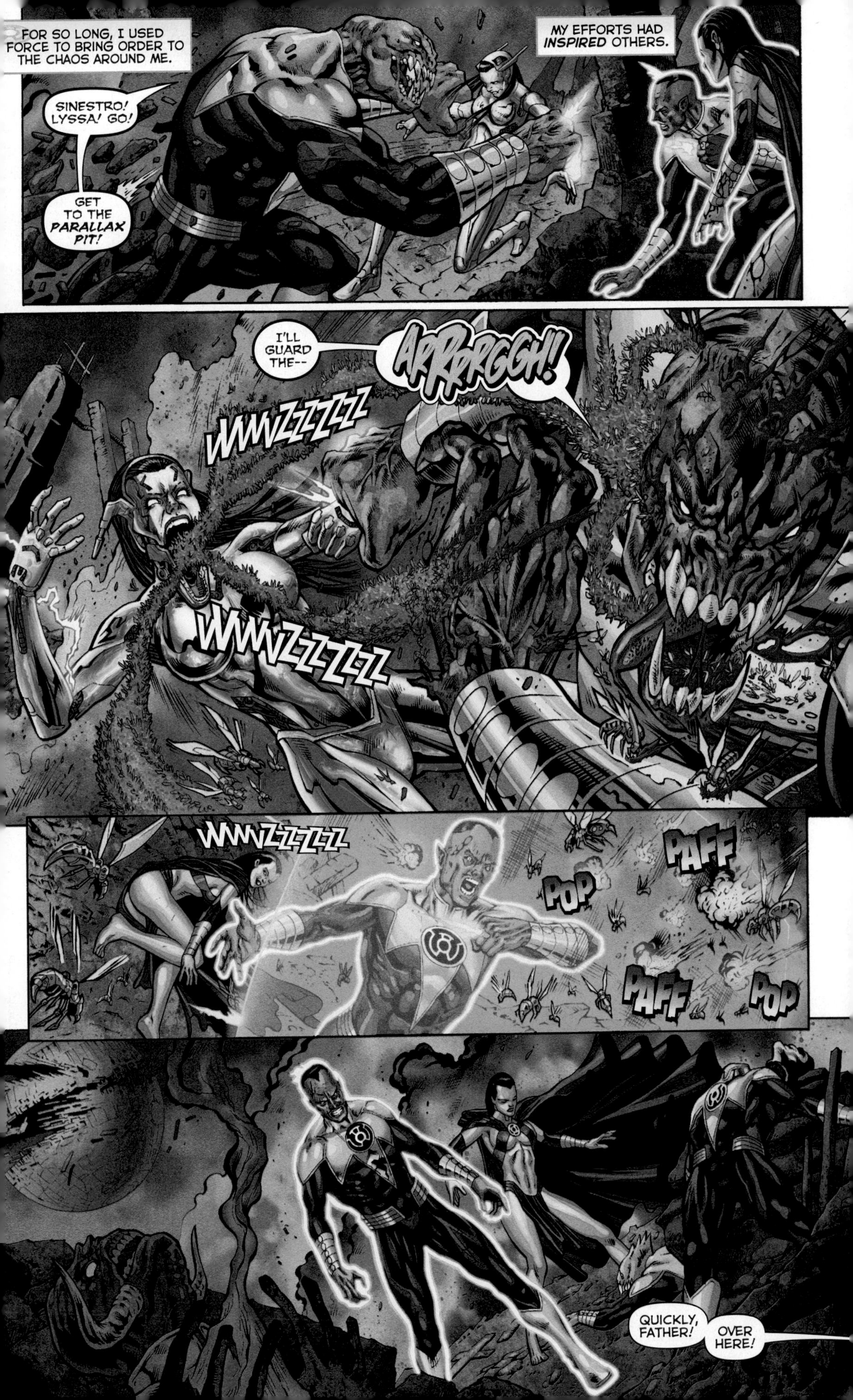
FOR SO LONG, I USED FORCE TO BRING ORDER TO THE CHAOS AROUND ME.
SINESTRO! LYSSA! GO!
GET TO THE PARALLAX PIT!
MY EFFORTS HAD INSPIRED OTHERS.
I'LL GUARD THE--
ARRRRGGH!
WWWZZZZZZ
WWWZZZZZZ
WWWZZZZZZ
PAFF
POP
PAFF
POP
QUICKLY, FATHER!
OVER HERE!

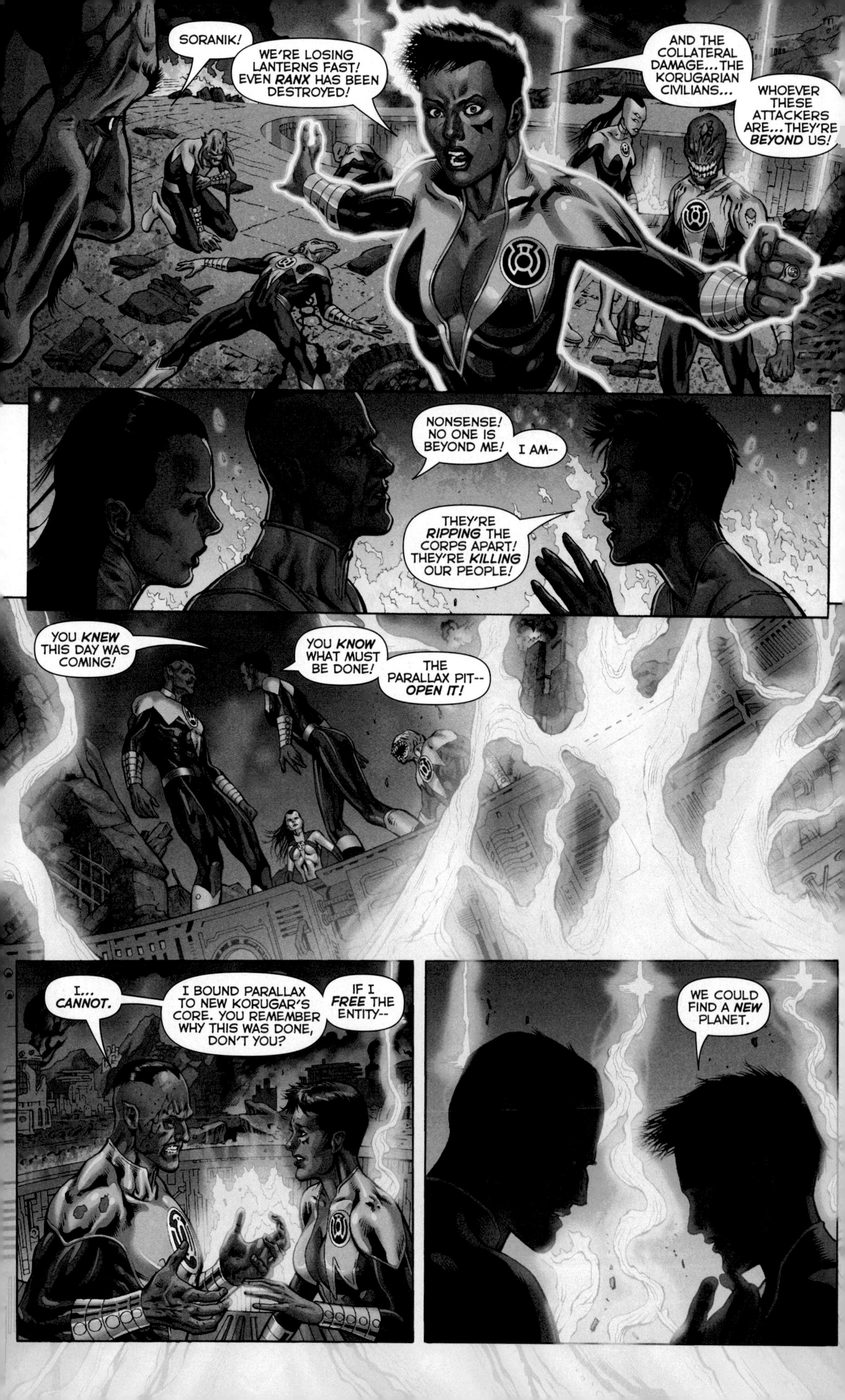
SORANIK!
WE'RE LOSING LANTERNS FAST! EVEN RANX HAS BEEN DESTROYED!
AND THE COLLATERAL DAMAGE... THE KORUGARIAN CIVILIANS...
WHOEVER THESE ATTACKERS ARE... THEY'RE BEYOND US!
NONSENSE! NO ONE IS BEYOND ME!
I AM--
THEY'RE RIPPING THE CORPS APART! THEY'RE KILLING OUR PEOPLE!
YOU KNEW THIS DAY WAS COMING!
YOU KNOW WHAT MUST BE DONE!
THE PARALLAX PIT-- OPEN IT!
I... CANNOT.
I BOUND PARALLAX TO NEW KORUGAR'S CORE. YOU REMEMBER WHY THIS WAS DONE, DON'T YOU?
IF I FREE THE ENTITY--
WE COULD FIND A NEW PLANET.

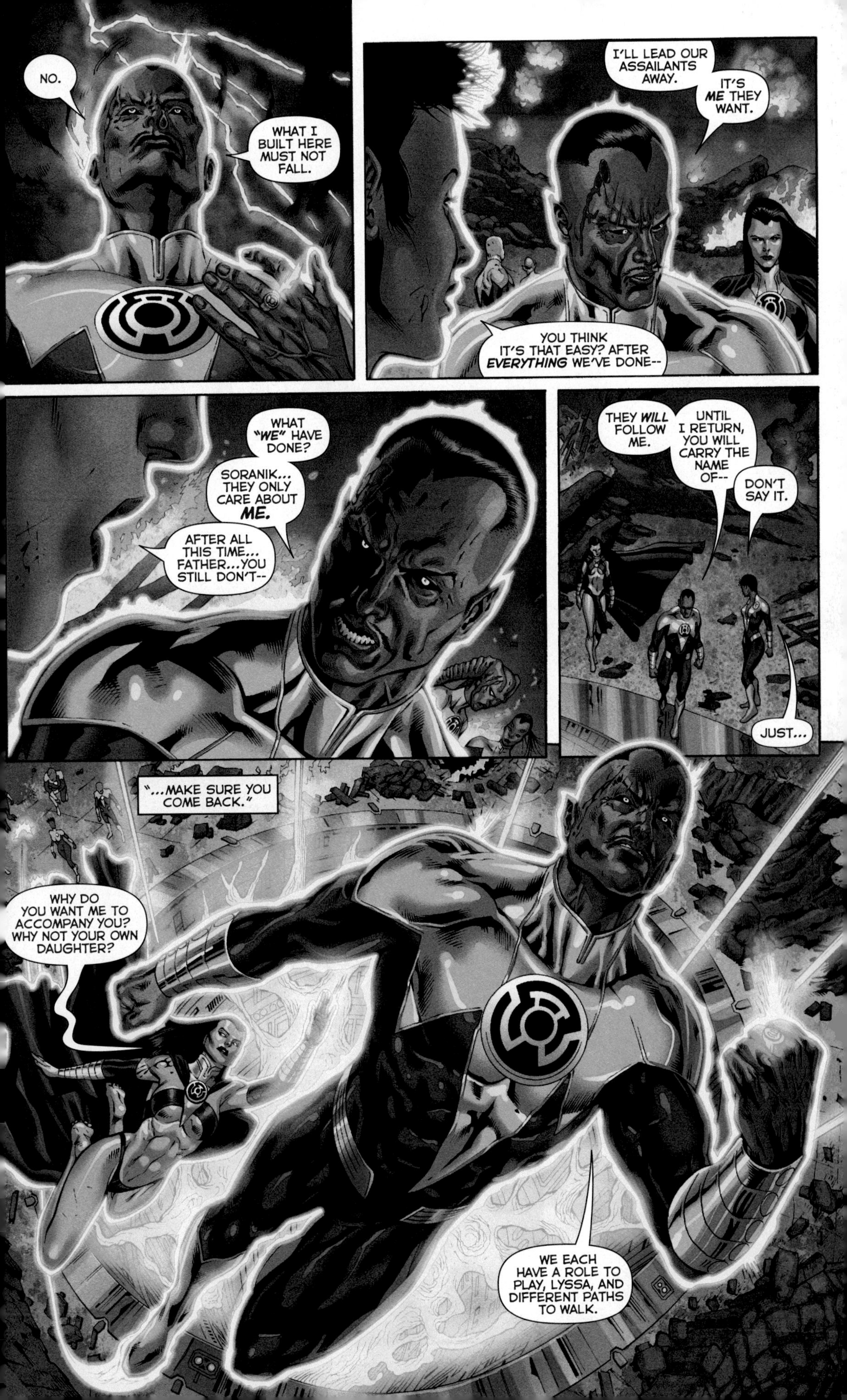
NO.
WHAT I BUILT HERE MUST NOT FALL.
I'LL LEAD OUR ASSAILANTS AWAY.
IT'S ME THEY WANT.
YOU THINK IT'S THAT EASY? AFTER EVERYTHING WE'VE DONE--
WHAT "WE" HAVE DONE?
SORANIK... THEY ONLY CARE ABOUT ME.
AFTER ALL THIS TIME... FATHER...YOU STILL DON'T--
THEY WILL FOLLOW ME.
UNTIL I RETURN, YOU WILL CARRY THE NAME OF--
DON'T SAY IT.
JUST...
"...MAKE SURE YOU COME BACK."
WHY DO YOU WANT ME TO ACCOMPANY YOU? WHY NOT YOUR OWN DAUGHTER?
WE EACH HAVE A ROLE TO PLAY, LYSSA, AND DIFFERENT PATHS TO WALK.

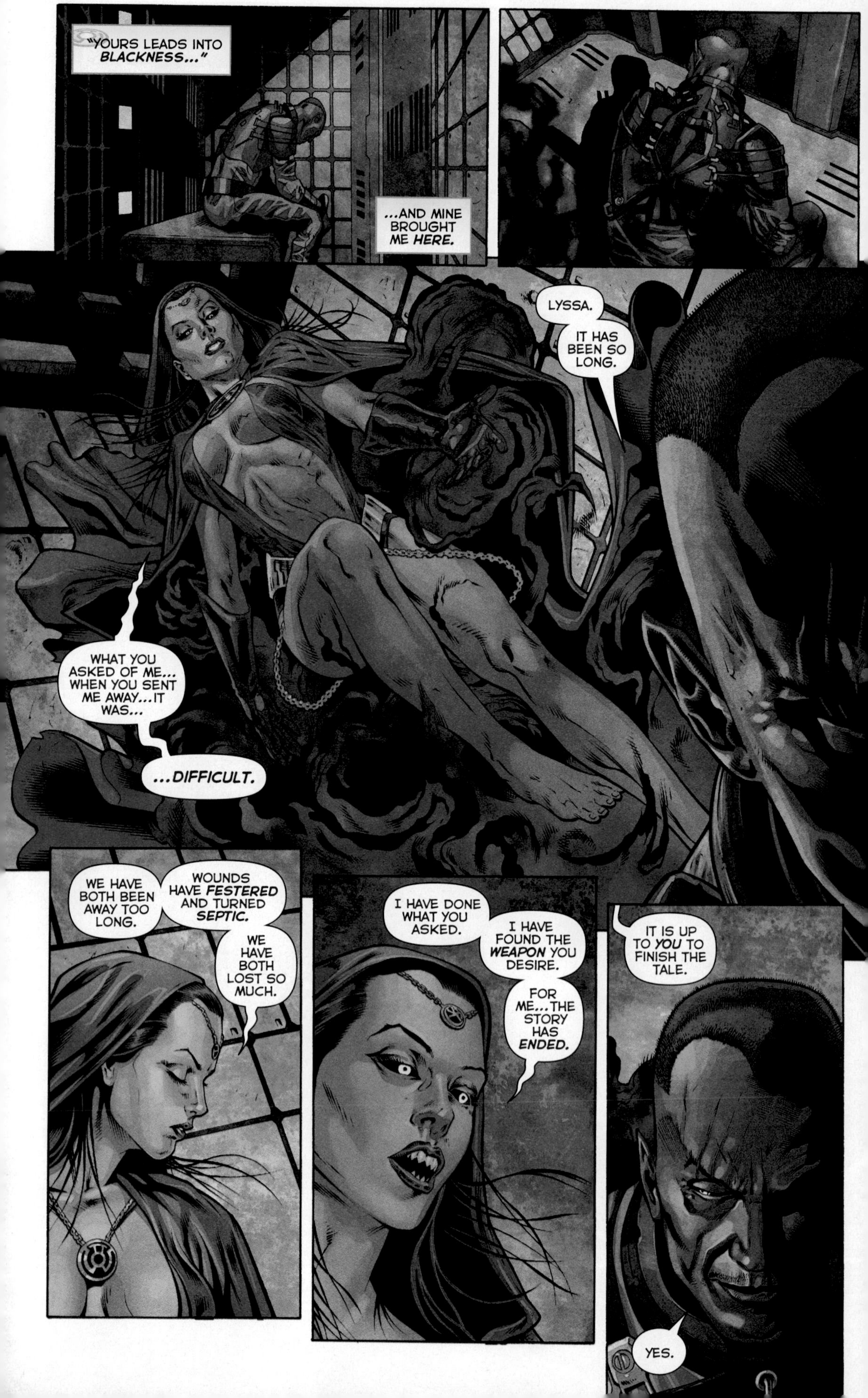
"YOURS LEADS INTO BLACKNESS..."
...AND MINE BROUGHT ME HERE.
LYSSA.
IT HAS BEEN SO LONG.
WHAT YOU ASKED OF ME... WHEN YOU SENT ME AWAY...IT WAS...
...DIFFICULT.
WE HAVE BOTH BEEN AWAY TOO LONG.
WOUNDS HAVE FESTERED AND TURNED SEPTIC.
WE HAVE BOTH LOST SO MUCH.
I HAVE DONE WHAT YOU ASKED.
I HAVE FOUND THE WEAPON YOU DESIRE.
FOR ME...THE STORY HAS ENDED.
IT IS UP TO YOU TO FINISH THE TALE.
YES.

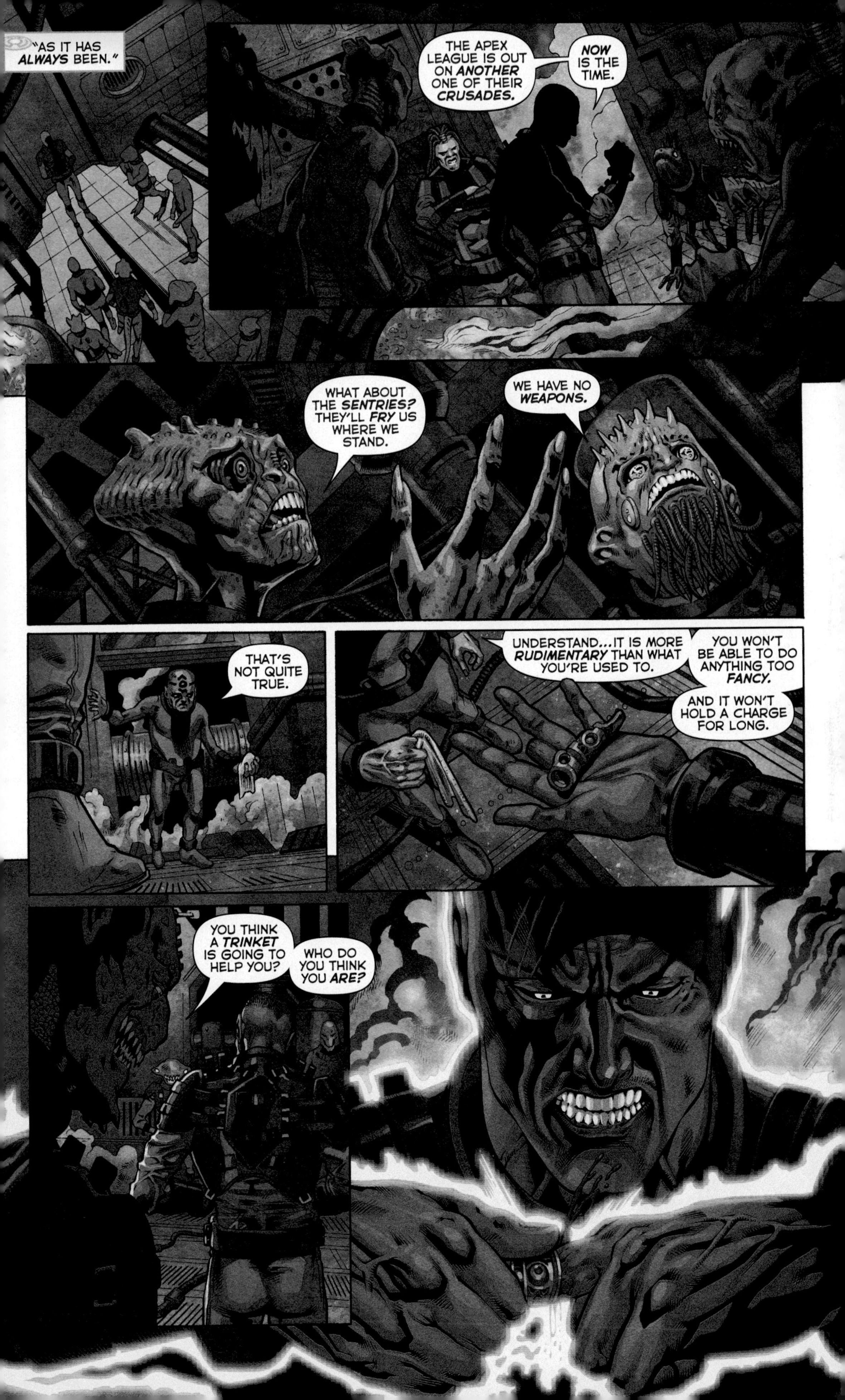
"AS IT HAS ALWAYS BEEN."
THE APEX LEAGUE IS OUT ON ANOTHER ONE OF THEIR CRUSADES.
NOW IS THE TIME.
WHAT ABOUT THE SENTRIES? THEY'LL FRY US WHERE WE STAND.
WE HAVE NO WEAPONS.
THAT'S NOT QUITE TRUE.
UNDERSTAND... IT IS MORE RUDIMENTARY THAN WHAT YOU'RE USED TO.
YOU WON'T BE ABLE TO DO ANYTHING TOO FANCY.
AND IT WON'T HOLD A CHARGE FOR LONG.
YOU THINK A TRINKET IS GOING TO HELP YOU?
WHO DO YOU THINK YOU ARE?

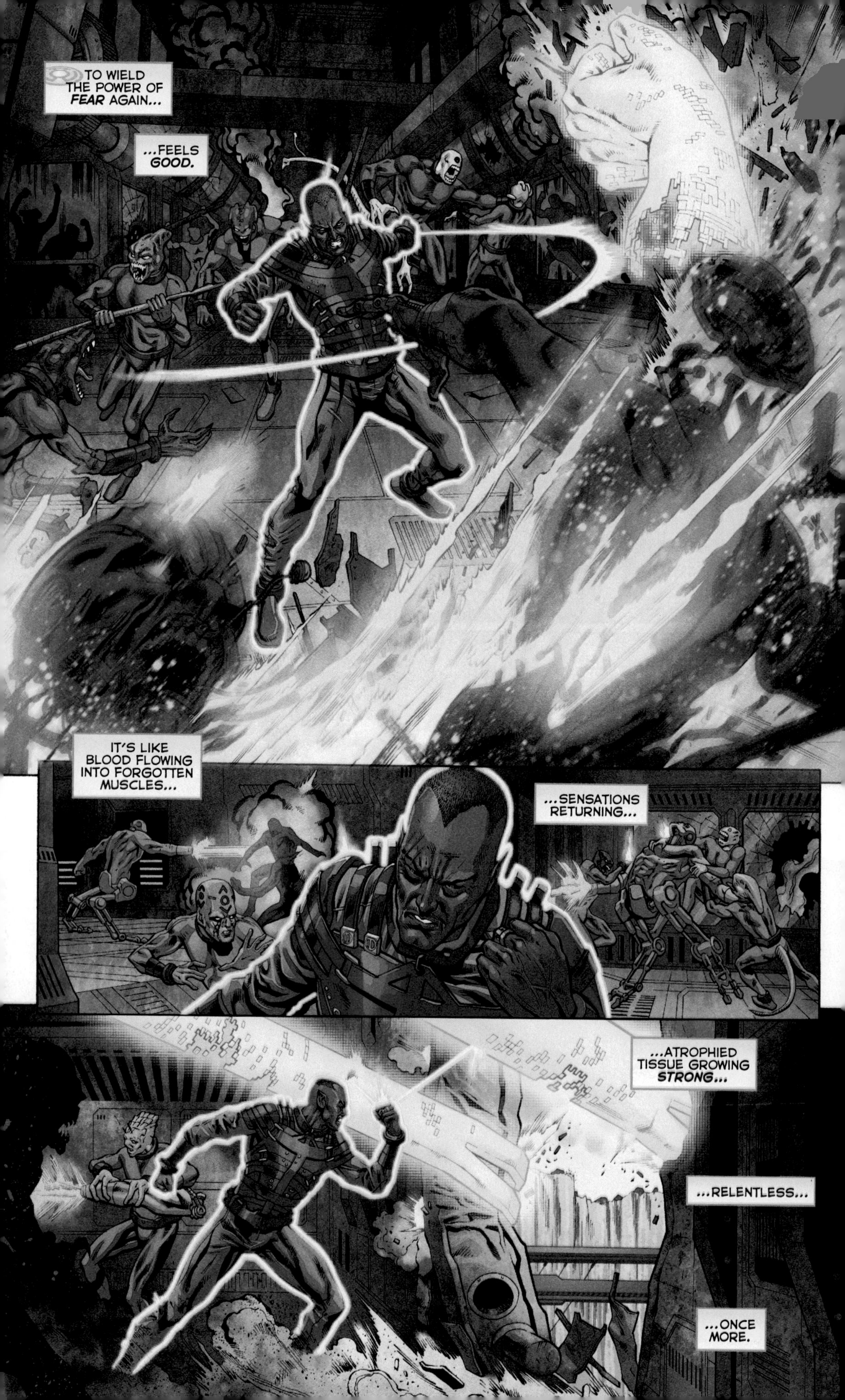
TO WIELD THE POWER OF FEAR AGAIN...
...FEELS GOOD.
IT'S LIKE BLOOD FLOWING INTO FORGOTTEN MUSCLES...
...SENSATIONS RETURNING...
...ATROPHIED TISSUE GROWING STRONG...
...RELENTLESS...
...ONCE MORE.

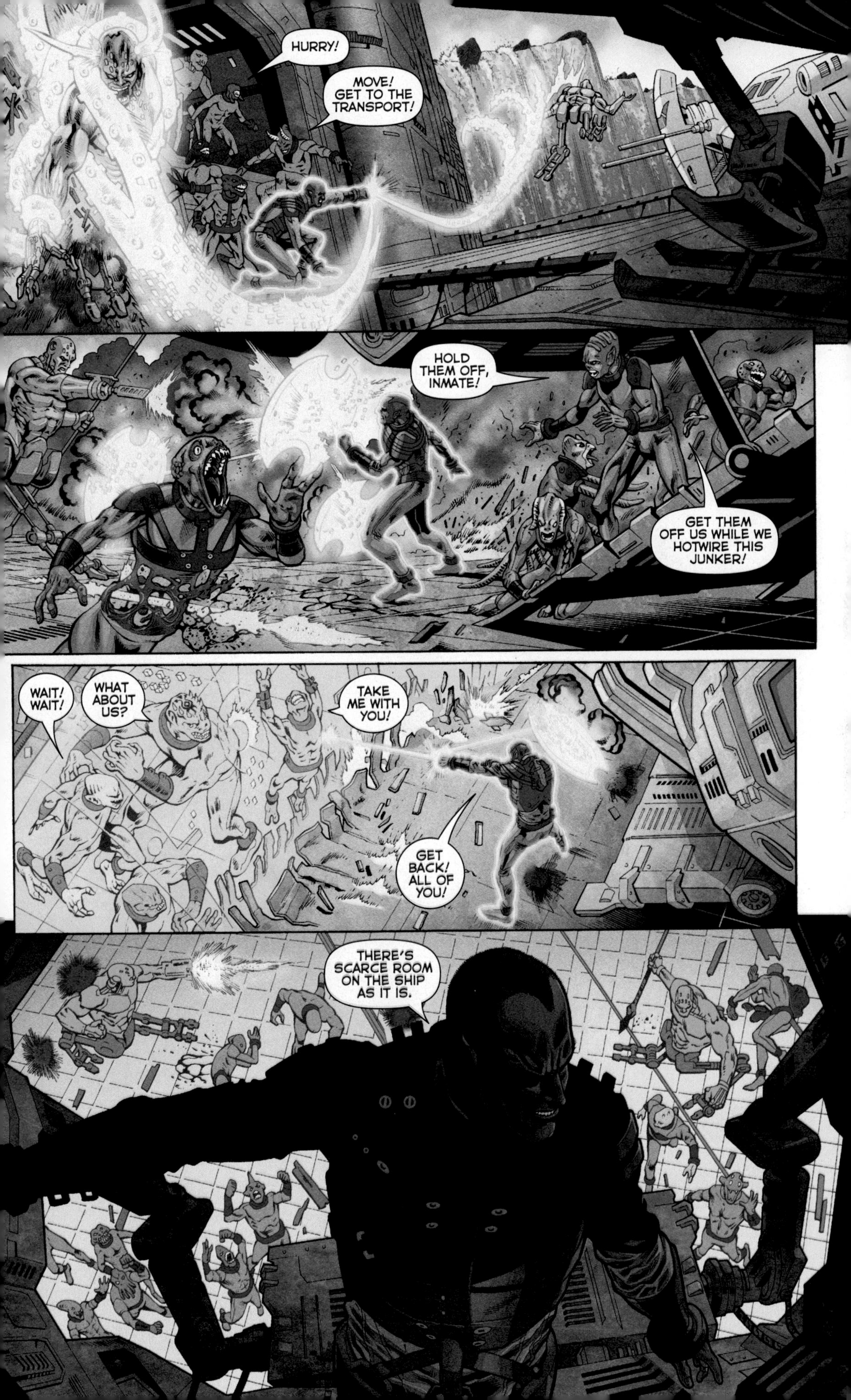
HURRY!
MOVE! GET TO THE TRANSPORT!
HOLD THEM OFF, INMATE!
GET THEM OFF US WHILE WE HOTWIRE THIS JUNKER!
WAIT! WAIT!
WHAT ABOUT US?
TAKE ME WITH YOU!
GET BACK! ALL OF YOU!
THERE'S SCARCE ROOM ON THE SHIP AS IT IS.

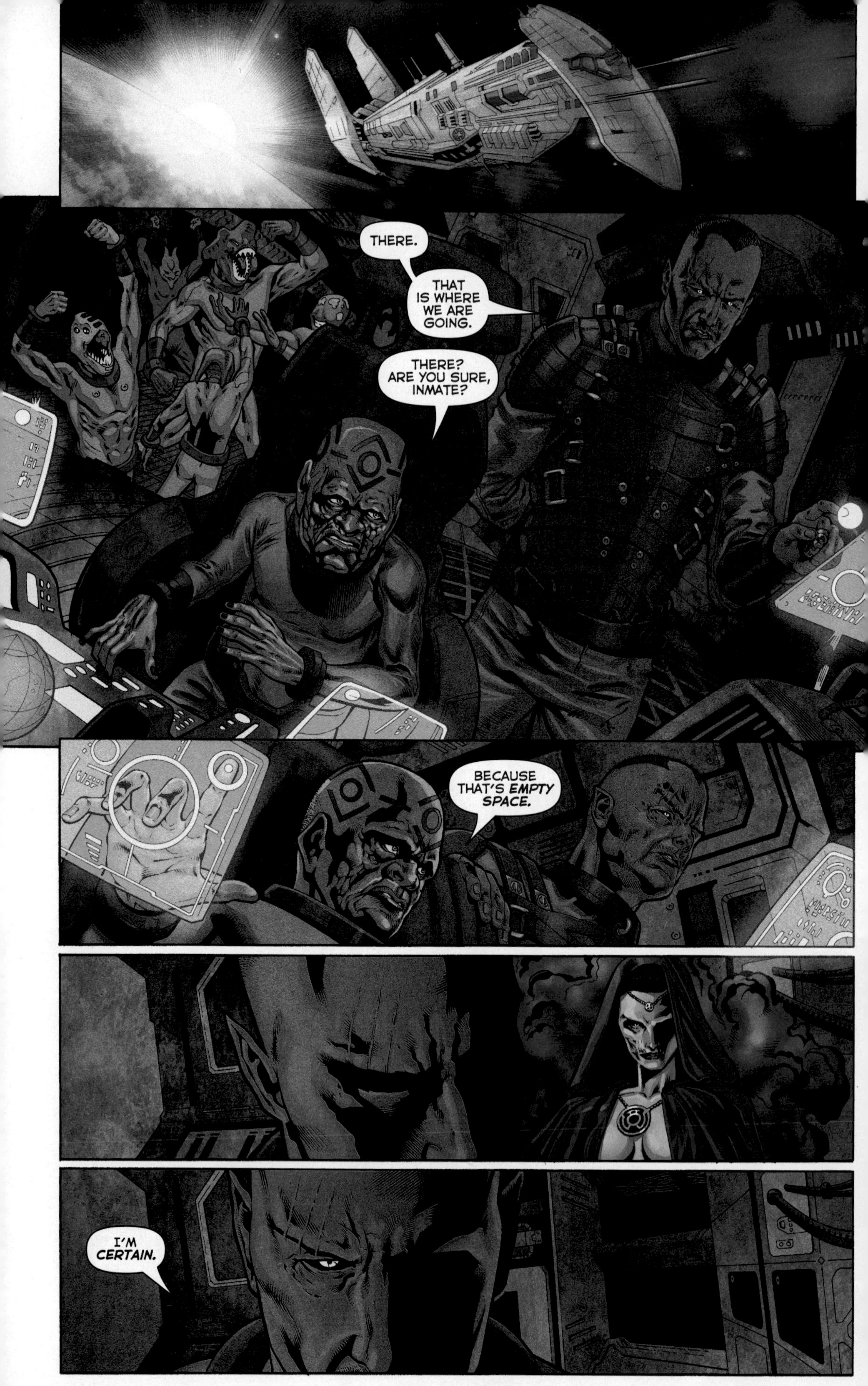
THERE.
THAT IS WHERE WE ARE GOING.
THERE? ARE YOU SURE, INMATE?
BECAUSE THAT'S *EMPTY SPACE.*
I'M *CERTAIN.*

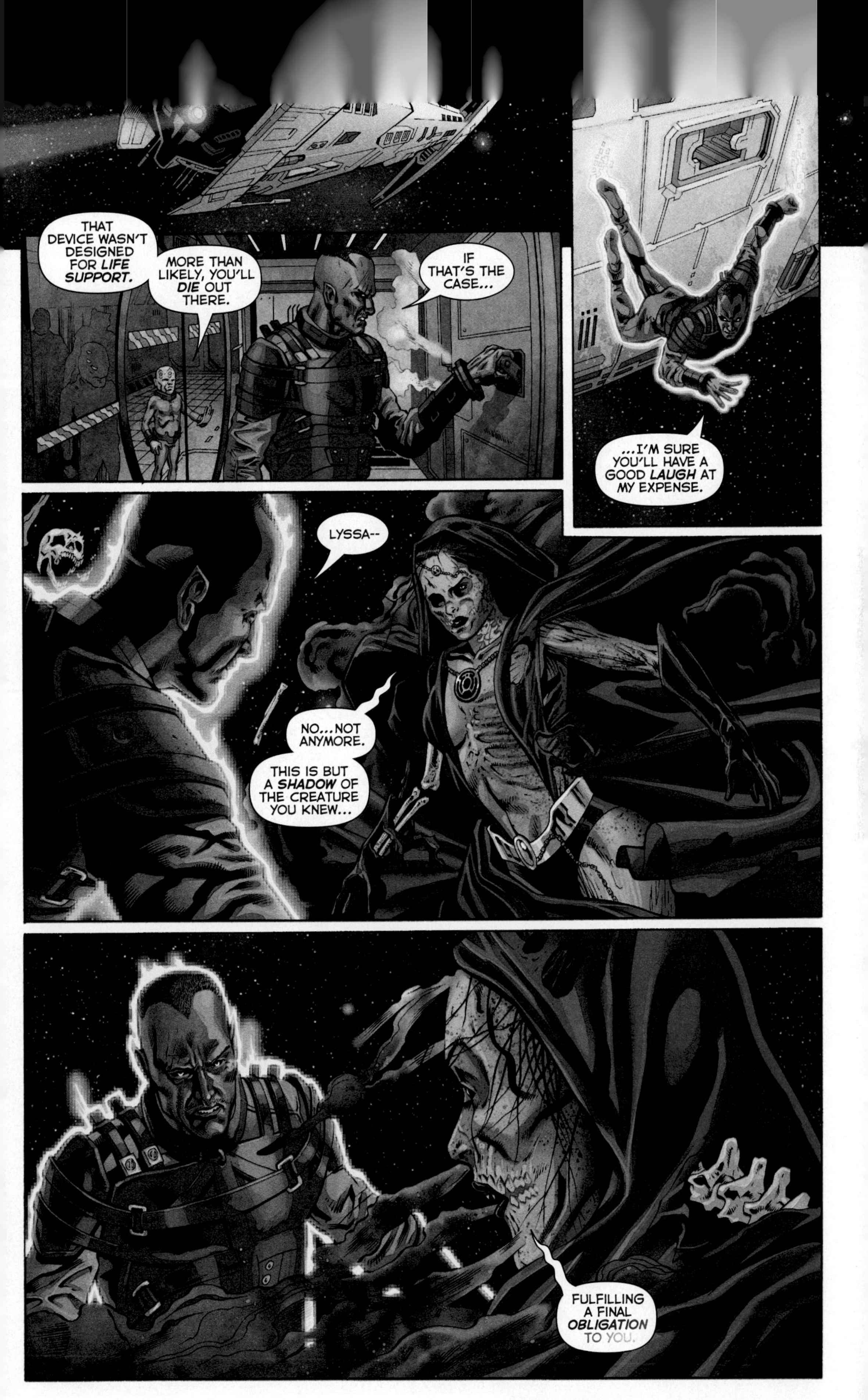
THAT DEVICE WASN'T DESIGNED FOR LIFE SUPPORT.
MORE THAN LIKELY, YOU'LL DIE OUT THERE.
IF THAT'S THE CASE...
...I'M SURE YOU'LL HAVE A GOOD LAUGH AT MY EXPENSE.
LYSSA--
NO...NOT ANYMORE.
THIS IS BUT A SHADOW OF THE CREATURE YOU KNEW...
FULFILLING A FINAL OBLIGATION TO YOU.

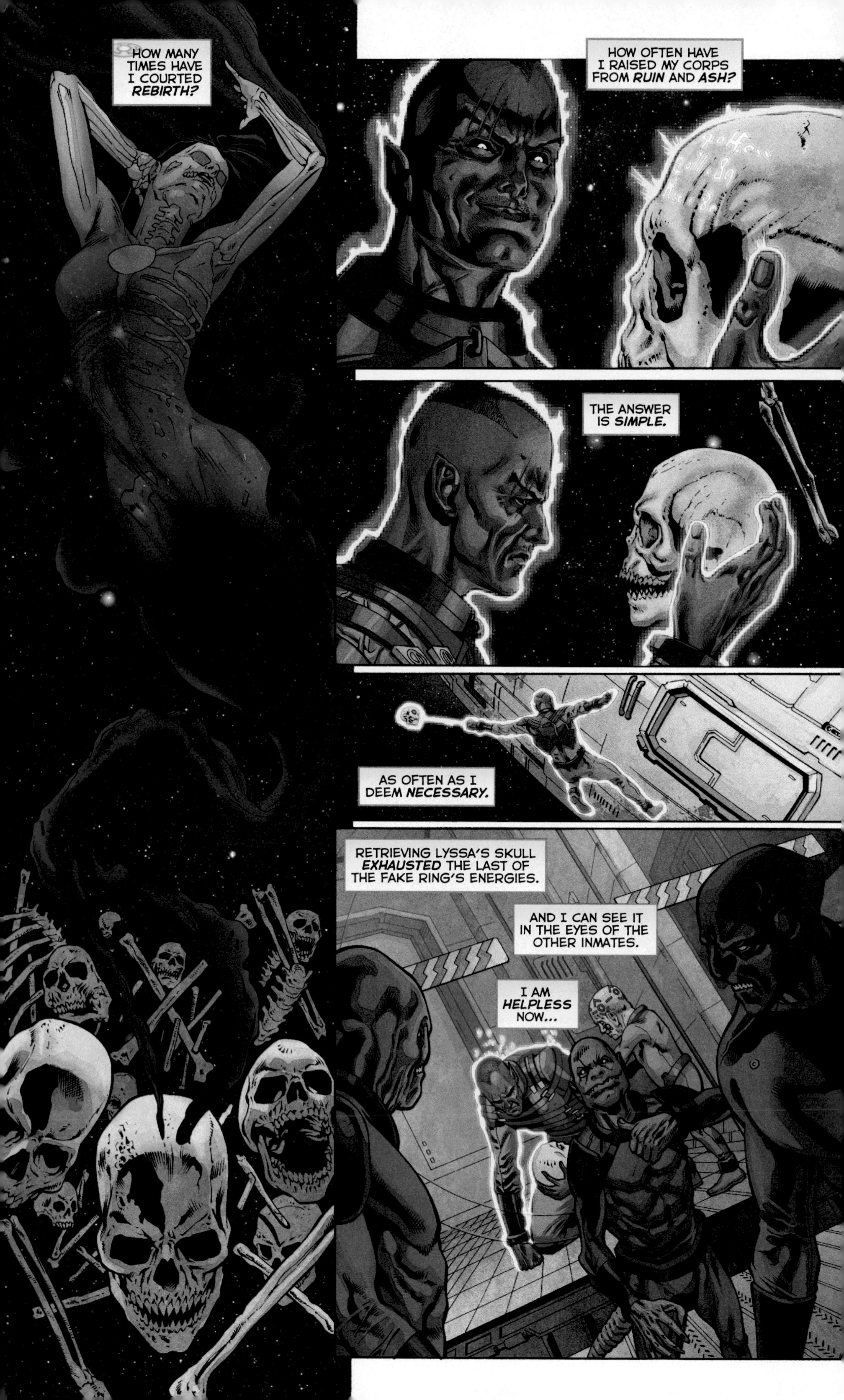
HOW MANY TIMES HAVE I COURTED REBIRTH?
HOW OFTEN HAVE I RAISED MY CORPS FROM RUIN AND ASH?
THE ANSWER IS SIMPLE.
AS OFTEN AS I DEEM NECESSARY.
RETRIEVING LYSSA'S SKULL EXHAUSTED THE LAST OF THE FAKE RING'S ENERGIES.
AND I CAN SEE IT IN THE EYES OF THE OTHER INMATES.
I AM HELPLESS NOW...

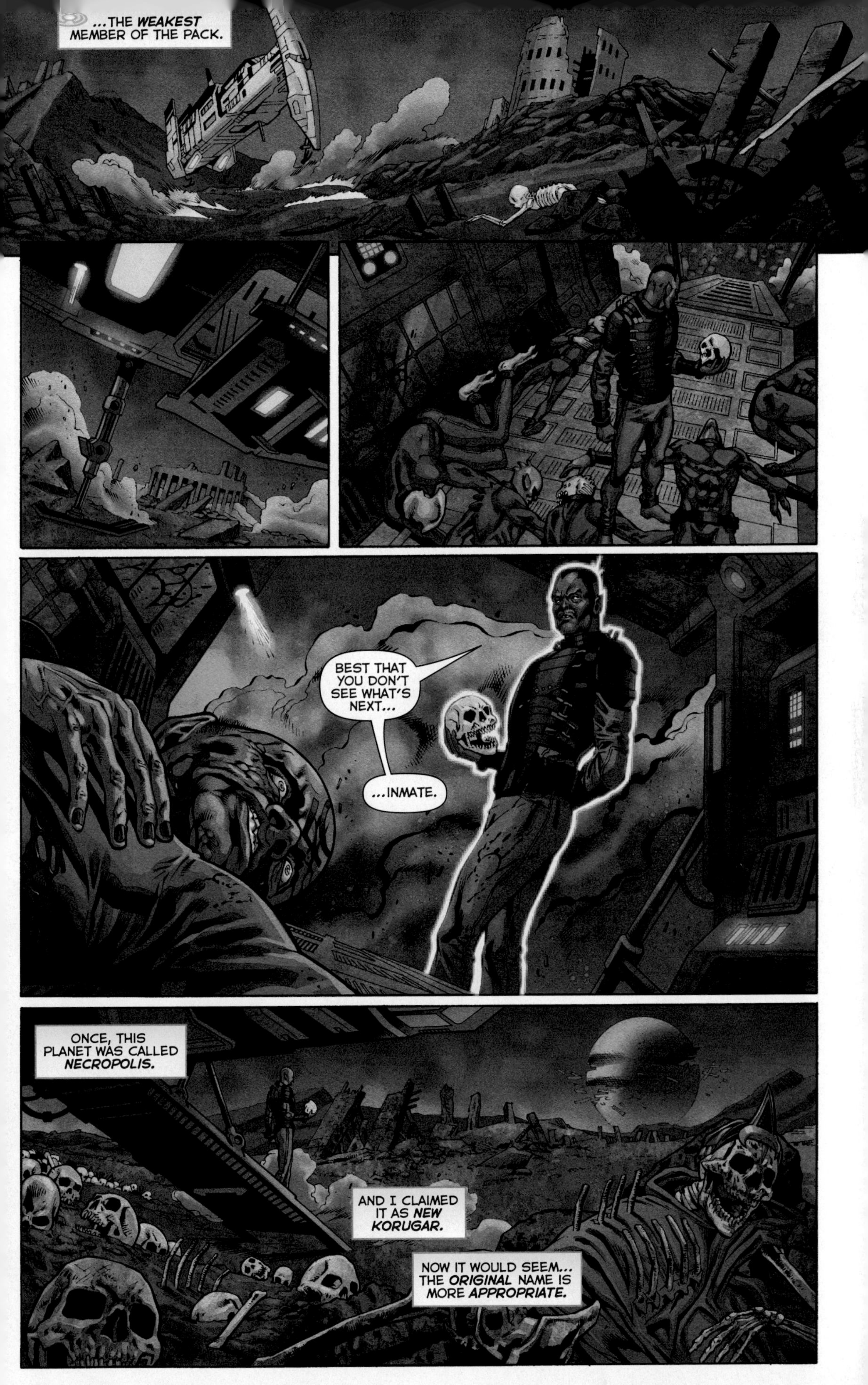
...THE WEAKEST MEMBER OF THE PACK.
BEST THAT YOU DON'T SEE WHAT'S NEXT...
...INMATE.
ONCE, THIS PLANET WAS CALLED NECROPOLIS.
AND I CLAIMED IT AS NEW KORUGAR.
NOW IT WOULD SEEM... THE ORIGINAL NAME IS MORE APPROPRIATE.

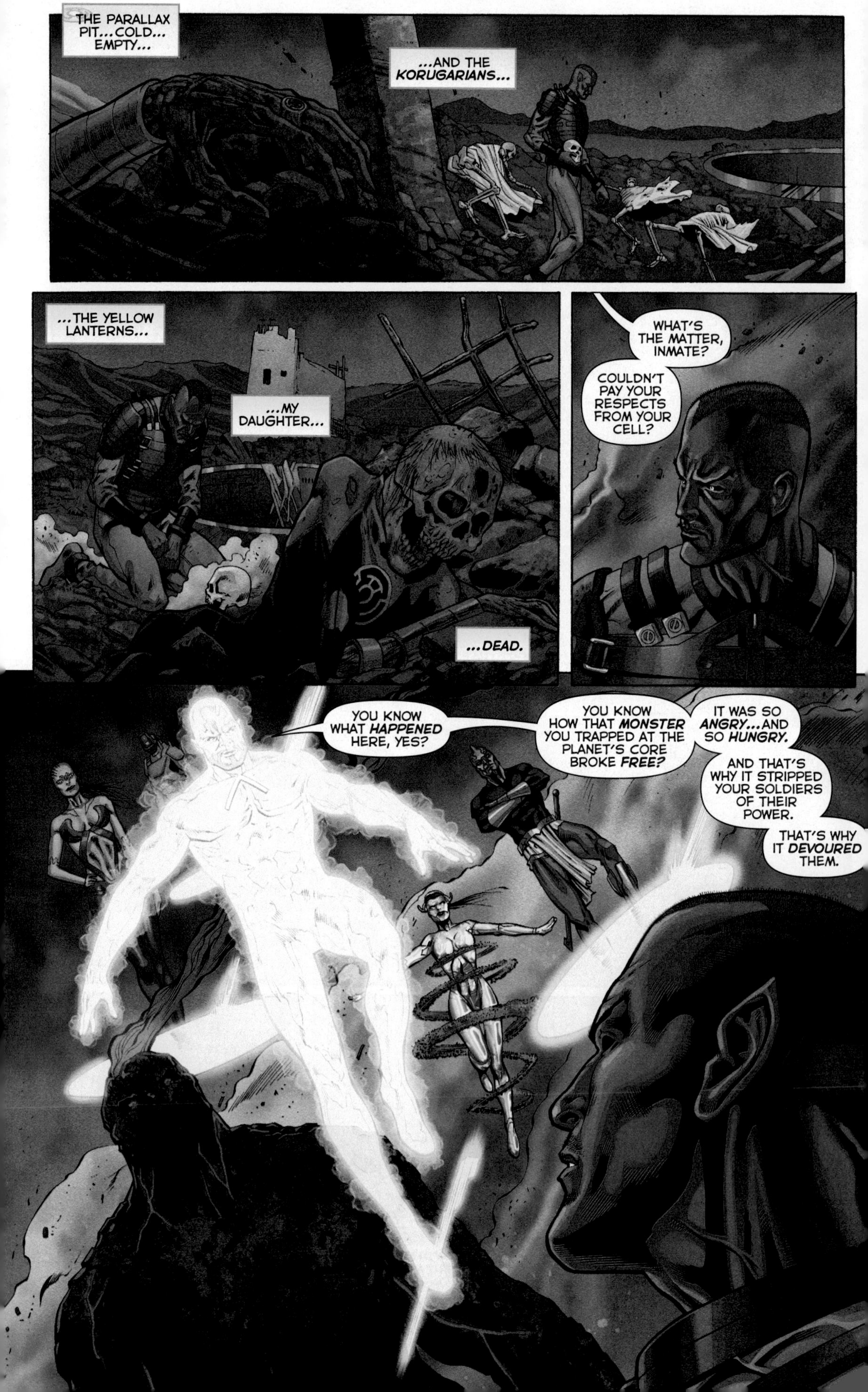
THE PARALLAX PIT...COLD... EMPTY...
...AND THE KORUGARIANS...
...THE YELLOW LANTERNS...
...MY DAUGHTER...
...DEAD.
WHAT'S THE MATTER, INMATE?
COULDN'T PAY YOUR RESPECTS FROM YOUR CELL?
YOU KNOW WHAT HAPPENED HERE, YES?
YOU KNOW HOW THAT MONSTER YOU TRAPPED AT THE PLANET'S CORE BROKE FREE?
IT WAS SO ANGRY...AND SO HUNGRY.
AND THAT'S WHY IT STRIPPED YOUR SOLDIERS OF THEIR POWER.
THAT'S WHY IT DEVOURED THEM.

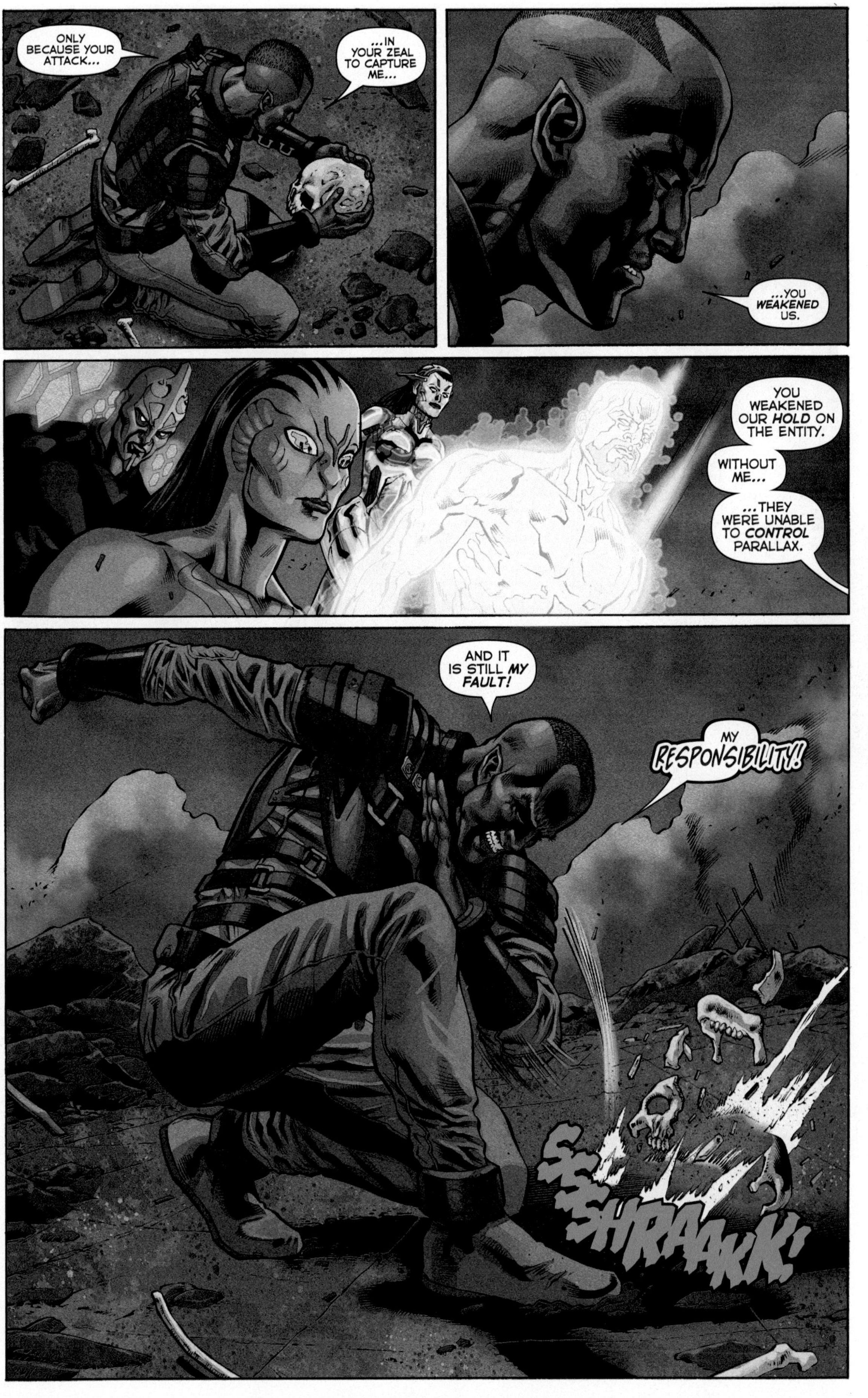
ONLY BECAUSE YOUR ATTACK...
...IN YOUR ZEAL TO CAPTURE ME...
...YOU WEAKENED US.
YOU WEAKENED OUR HOLD ON THE ENTITY.
WITHOUT ME...
...THEY WERE UNABLE TO CONTROL PARALLAX.
AND IT IS STILL MY FAULT!
MY RESPONSIBILITY!
SSSHRAAKK!

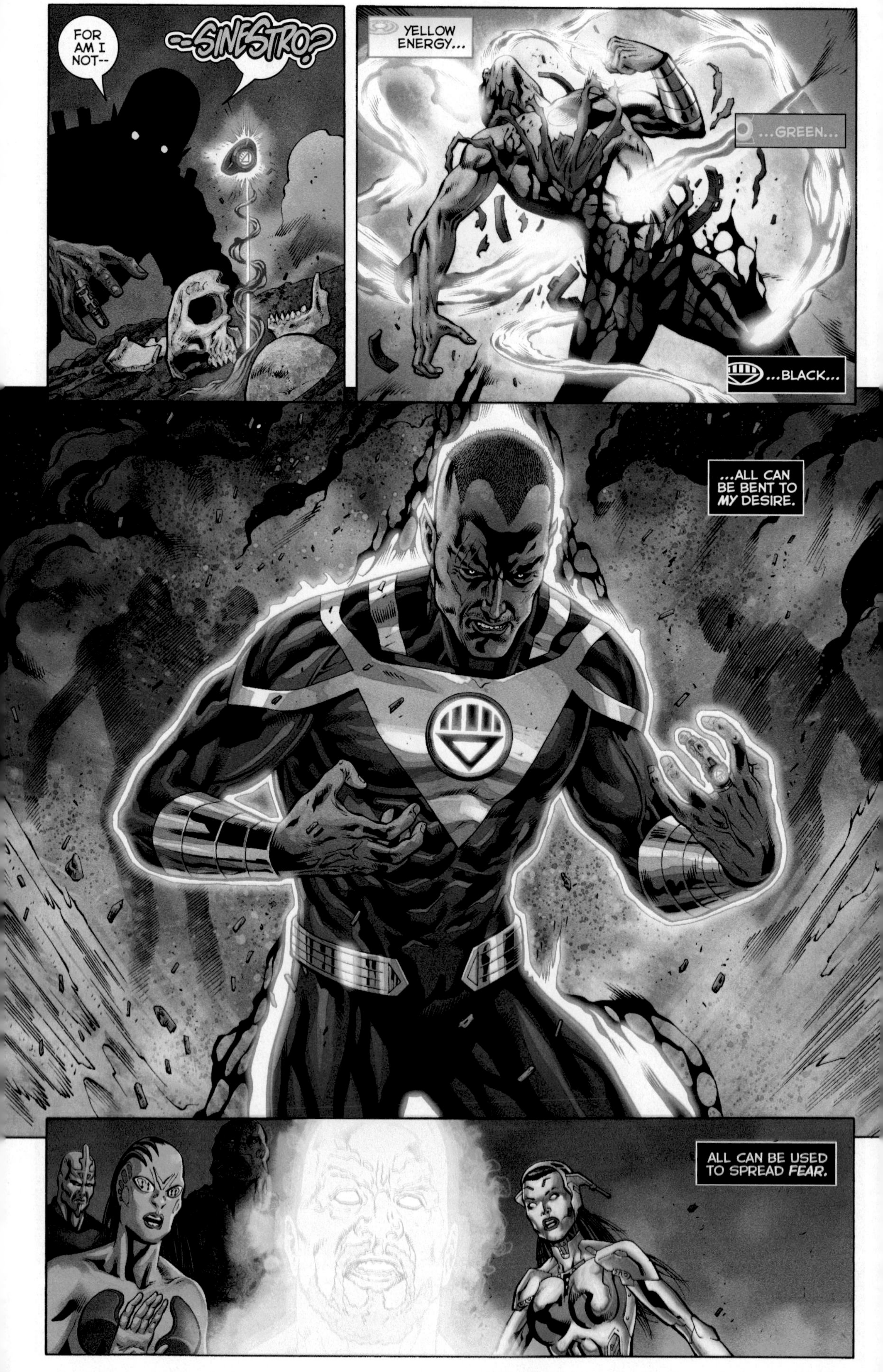
FOR AM I NOT--
--SINESTRO?
YELLOW ENERGY...
...GREEN...
...BLACK...
...ALL CAN BE BENT TO MY DESIRE.
ALL CAN BE USED TO SPREAD FEAR.

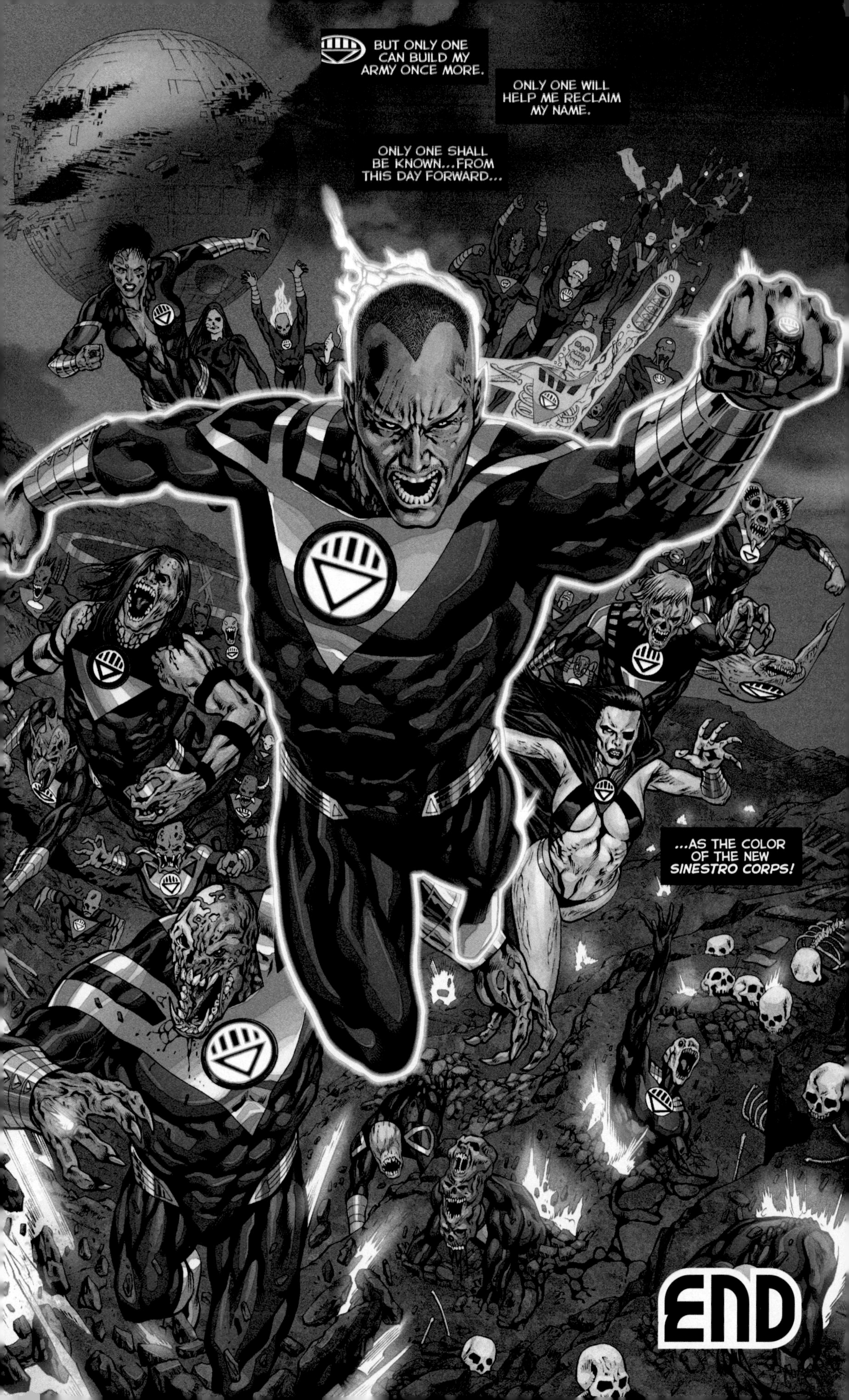

BUT ONLY ONE CAN BUILD MY ARMY ONCE MORE.
ONLY ONE WILL HELP ME RECLAIM MY NAME.
ONLY ONE SHALL BE KNOWN...FROM THIS DAY FORWARD...
...AS THE COLOR OF THE NEW SINESTRO CORPS!
END

SINESTRO: FUTURES END #1 "future" cover by Kevin Nowlan

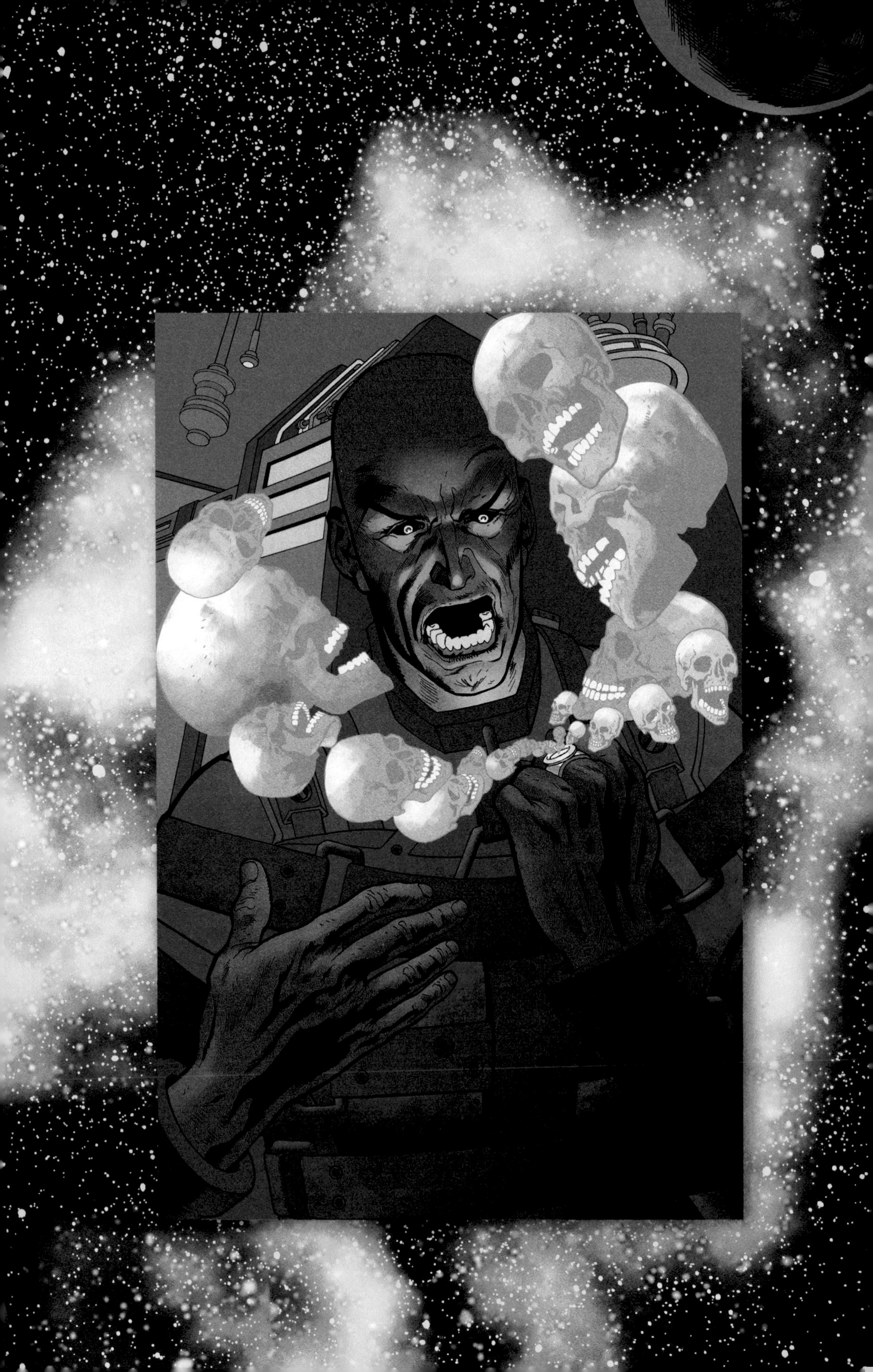

SINESTRO FUTURES END
SKETCHES BY IGOR LIMA

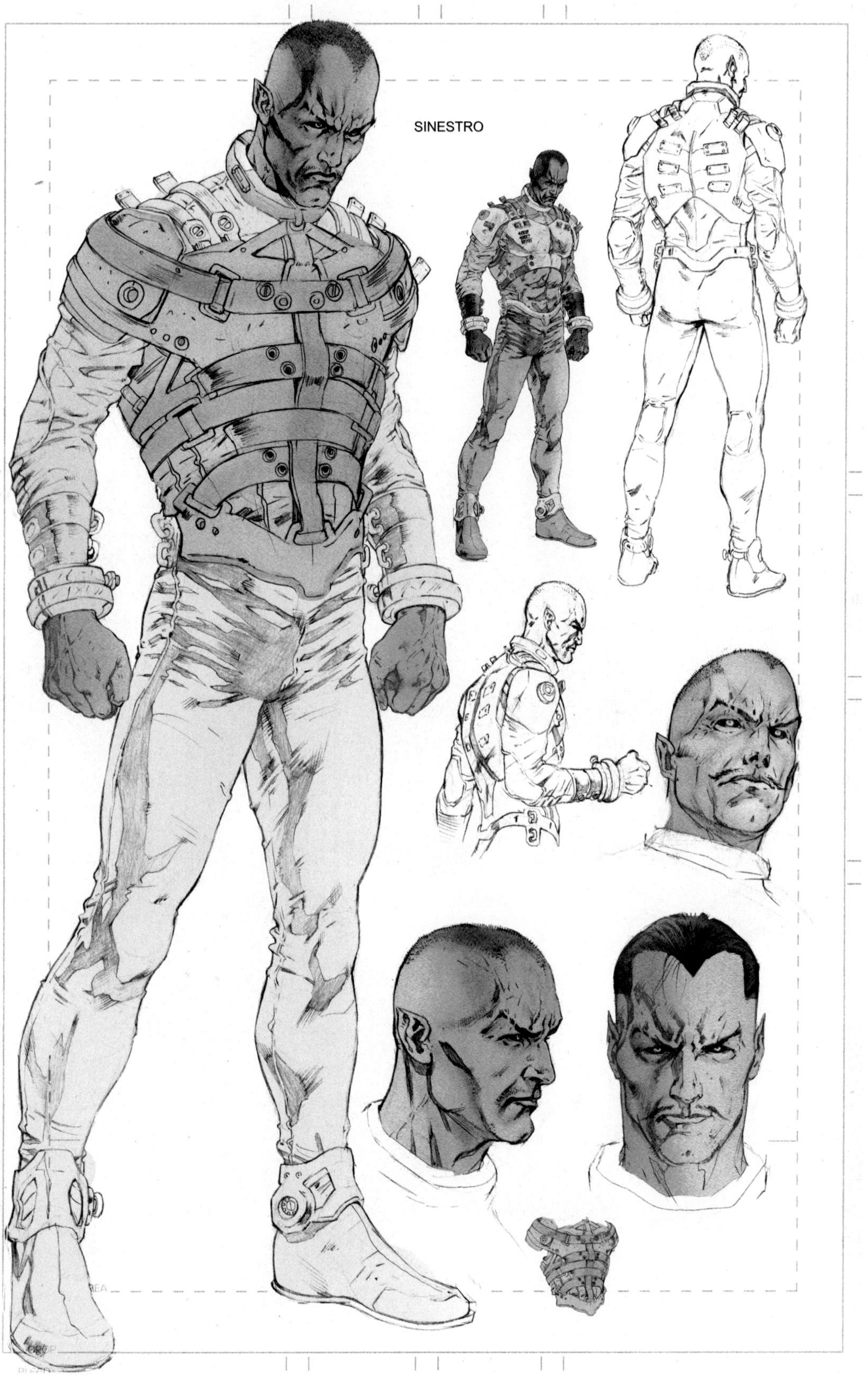
SINESTRO

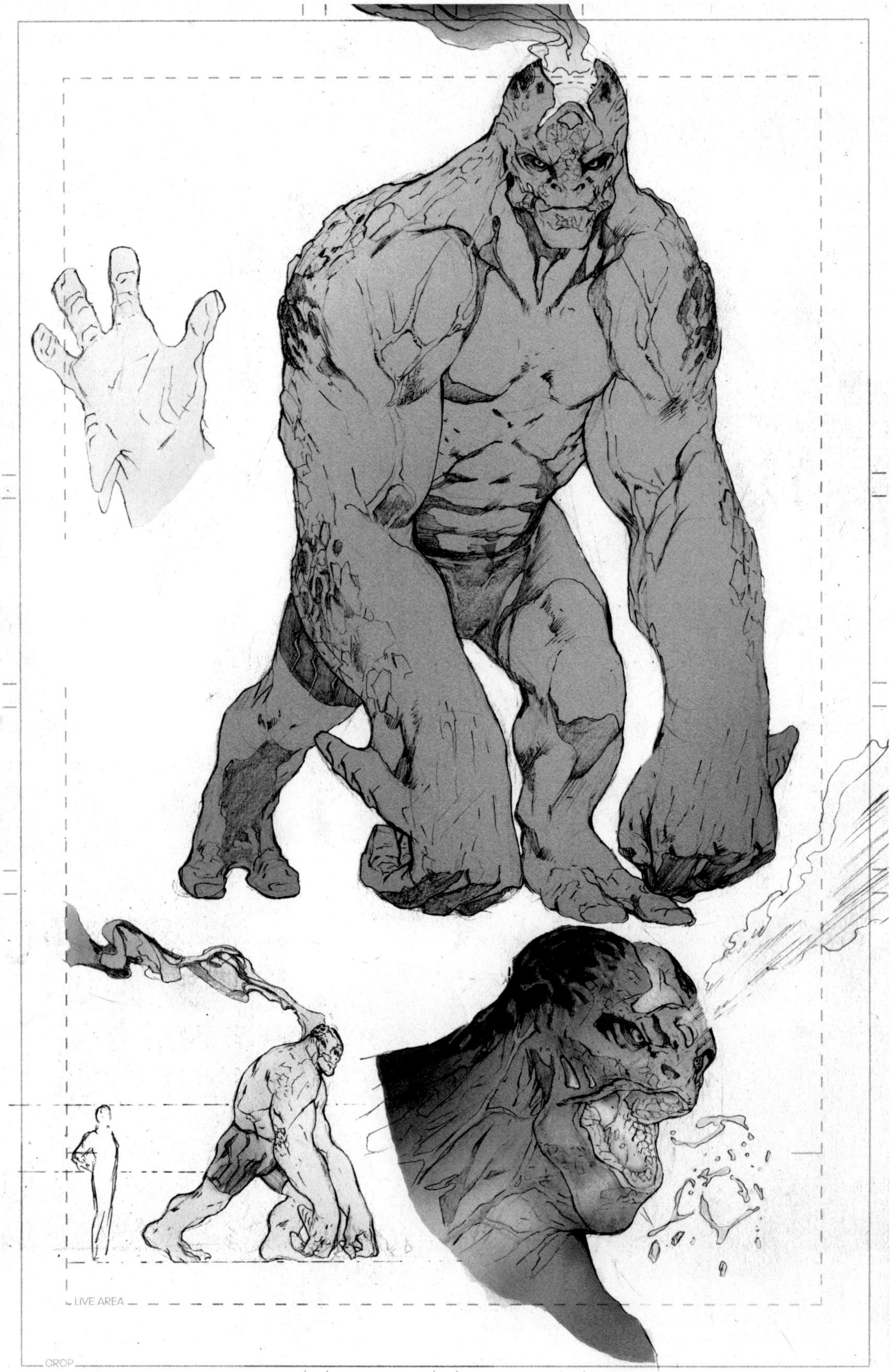
LIVE AREA
CROP

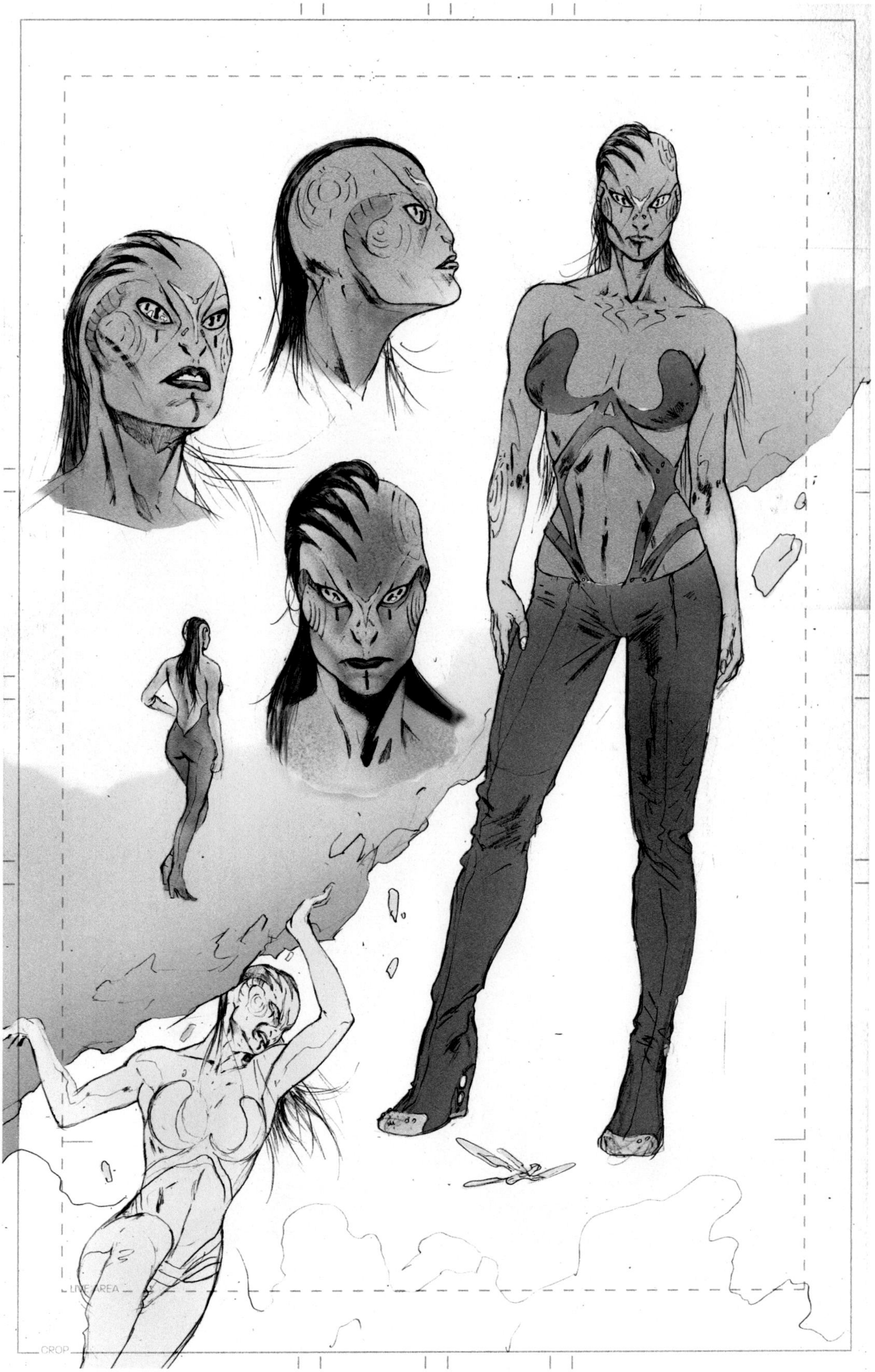
CROP

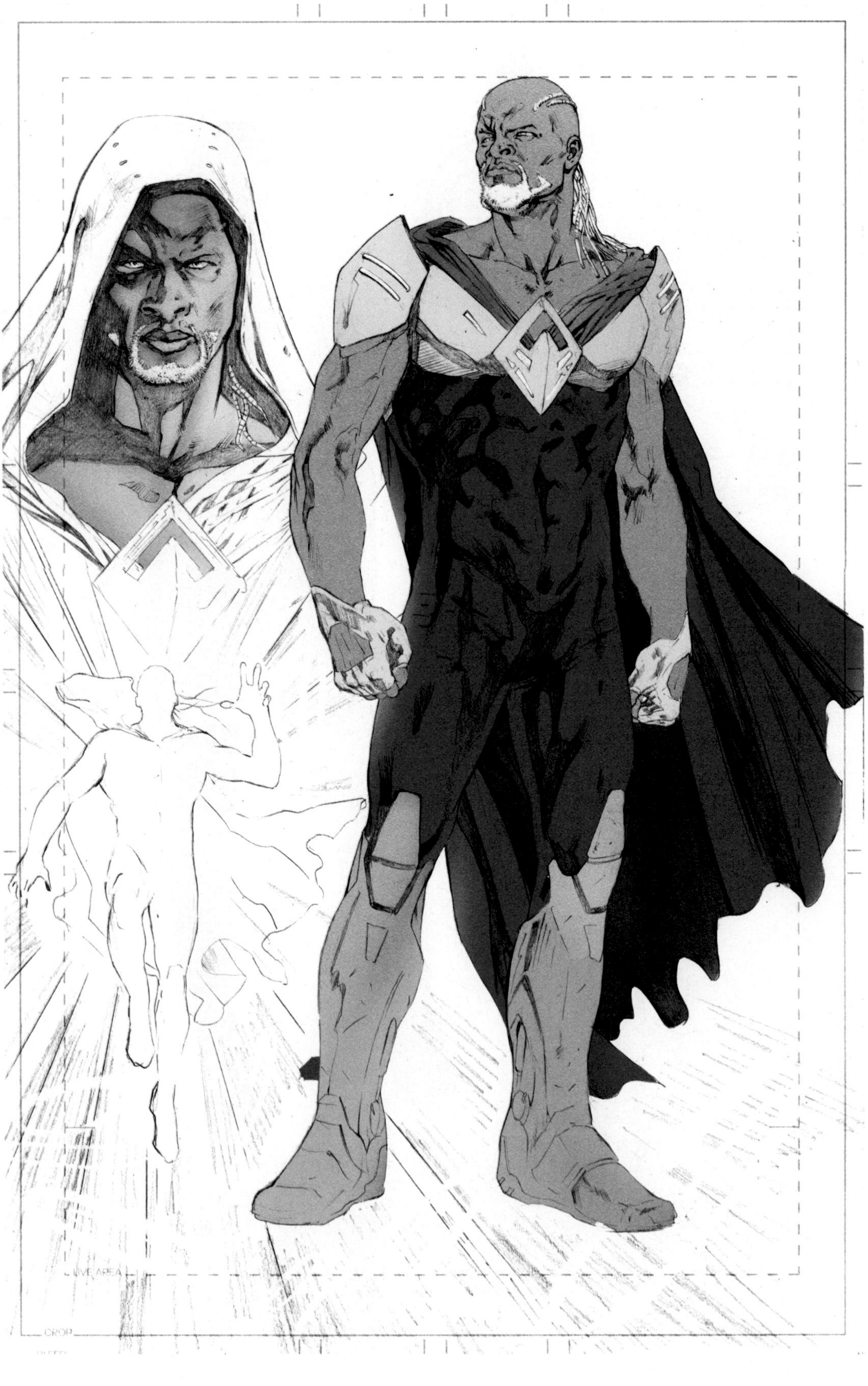
LIVE AREA
CROP

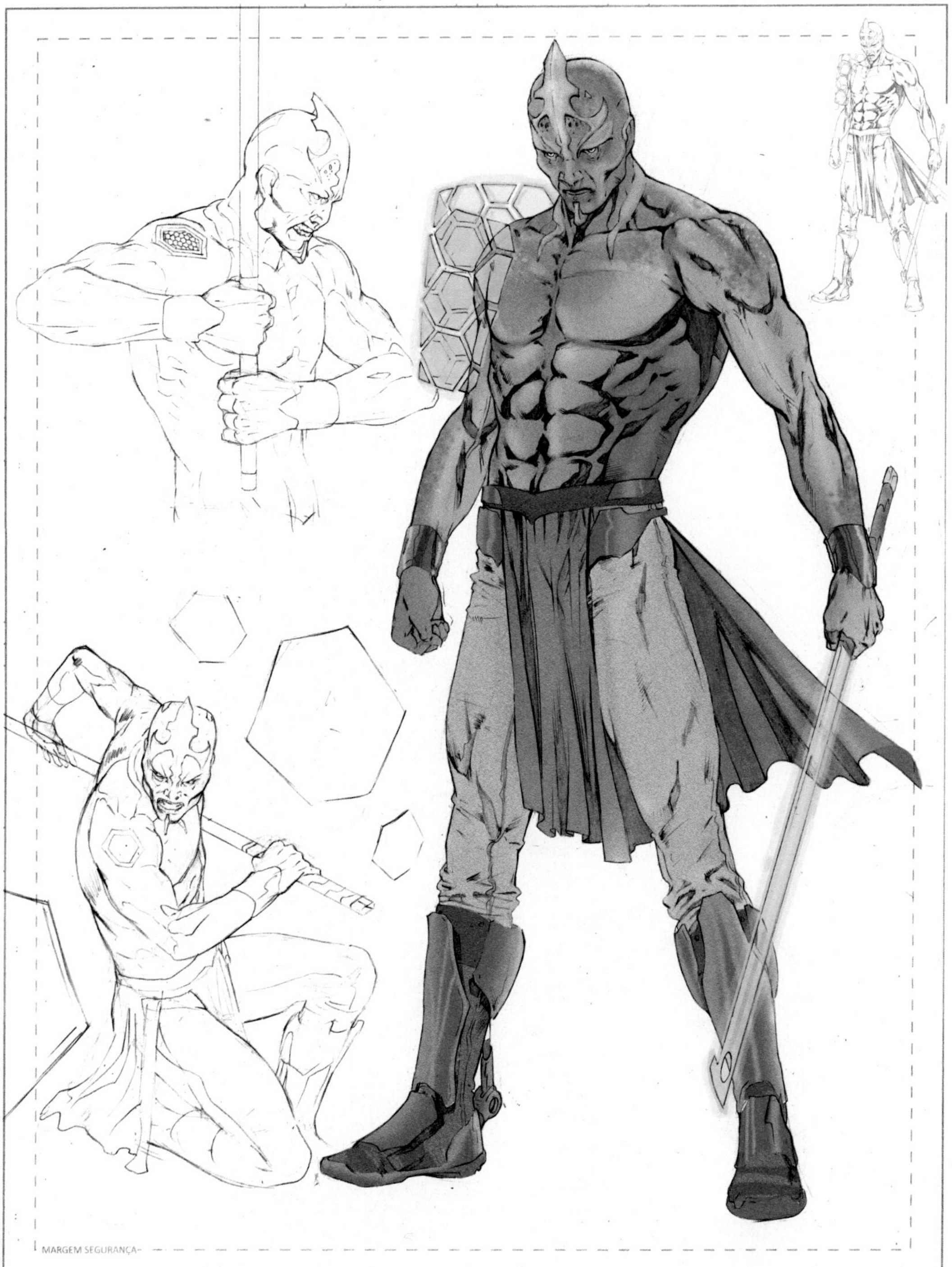
MARGEM SEGURANÇA

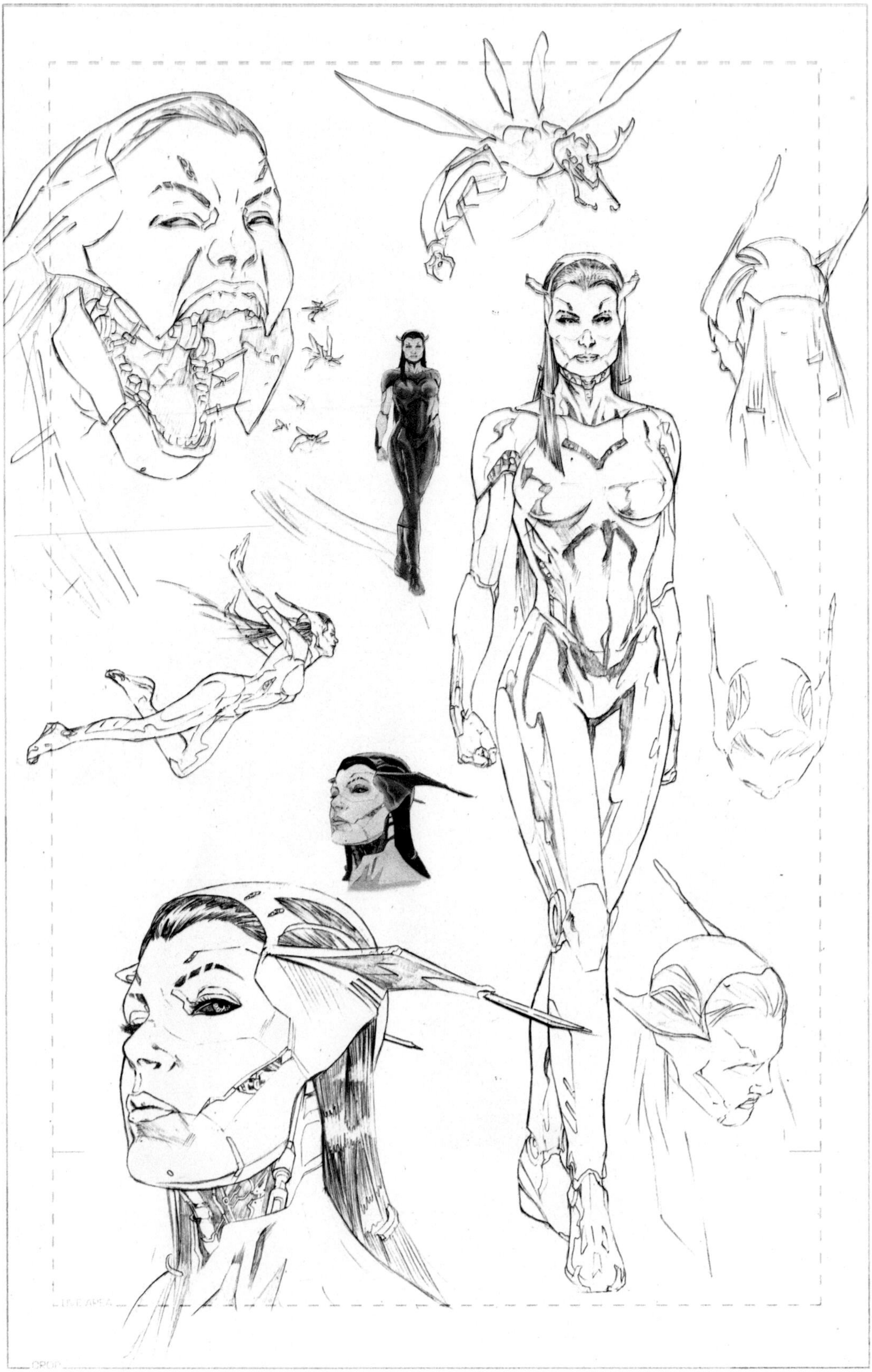